International Perspectives on the Design of Technology-Supported Learning Environments

International Perspectives on the Design of Technology-Supported Learning Environments

Edited by

STELLA VOSNIADOU
University of Athens

ERIK DE CORTE
University of Leuven

ROBERT GLASER
University of Pittsburgh

HEINZ MANDL
University of Munich

NEW YORK AND LONDON

First Published by
Lawrence Erlbaum Associates, Inc., Publishers
10 Industrial Avenue
Mahwah, New Jersey 07430

Transferred to Digital Printing 2009 by Routledge
270 Madison Ave, New York NY 10016
2 Park Square, Milton Park, Abingdon, Oxon, OX14 4RN

Library of Congress Cataloging-in-Publication Data

International perspectives on the design of technology-supported
  learning environments / edited by Stella Vosniadou . . . [et al.].
      p.   cm.
  Includes bibliographical references and indexes.
  ISBN 0-8058-1854-5 (cloth : alk. paper). — ISBN 0-8058-1853-7
(paper : alk. paper)
    1. Instructional systems—Design.   2. Computer-assisted
instruction.   3. Educational technology.   I. Vosniadou, Stella.
LB1028.38.I59   1996
371.3'078—dc20   95-47474
                                                         CIP

Publisher's Note
The publisher has gone to great lengths to ensure the quality
of this reprint but points out that some imperfections in the
original may be apparent.

Contents

Preface   ix

Introduction: Cognition and the Design of Environments
for Learning   1
Robert Glaser, Erika L. Ferguson, and Stella Vosniadou

PART I: REPRESENTATION

1. Learning Environments for Representational Growth
   and Cognitive Flexibility   13
   Stella Vosniadou

2. Externalizing Thinking Through Modeling: ESRC Tools
   for Exploratory Learning Research Program   25
   Joan Bliss

3. The Use of Multiple, Linked Representations to Facilitate
   Science Understanding   41
   *Robert B. Kozma, Joel Russell, Tricia Jones, Nancy Marx,
   and Joan Davis*

4. Acquisition of Meaning for Arithmetic Structures With
   the Planner   61
   Baruch B. Schwarz, Mitchell J. Nathan, and Lauren B. Resnick

5. From Cognitive Modeling to the Design of Pedagogical Tools   81
Kurt Reusser

6. Activity, Social Interaction, and Reflective Abstraction: Learning Advanced Mathematical Concepts in a Computer Environment   105
Erno Lehtinen and Sisko Repo

7. Changing Views of Computer-Supported Learning Environments for the Acquisition of Knowledge and Thinking Skills   129
Erik De Corte

PART II: SOCIAL INTERACTION

8. Adaptation and Understanding: A Case for New Cultures of Schooling   149
Marlene Scardamalia and Carl Bereiter

9. Distributing Cognition Over Humans and Machines   165
Pierre Dillenbourg

10. Interactivity in Cooperative Problem Solving With Computers   185
Gellof Kanselaar and Gijsbert Erkens

11. Conceptual Change Among Adolescents Using Computer Networks and Peer Collaboration in Studying International Political Issues   203
Judith Torney-Purta

PART III: MEANINGFUL CONTEXTS AND MULTIPLE PERSPECTIVES

12. MOST Environments for Accelerating Literacy Development   223
John D. Bransford et al.

13. Anchoring Science Instruction in Multimedia Learning Environments   257
Susan R. Goldman et al.

14. Multimedia Environments for Enhancing Learning in Mathematics   285
Cognition and Technology Group at Vanderbilt

15. Learning to Apply: From "School Garden Instruction" to Technology-Based Learning Environments 307
Heinz Mandl, Hans Gruber, and Alexander Renkl

16. Mapping Models of Cognitive Development to Design Principles of Learning Environments 323
Patrick Mendelsohn

PART IV: PRINCIPLES OF SYSTEM DESIGN

17. Design Issues for Learning Environments 347
Allan Collins

18. Studying Novel Learning Environments as Patterns of Change 363
Gavriel Salomon

Author Index 379
Subject Index 389

Preface

The use of technology for the purposes of improving and enriching traditional instructional practices has received a great deal of attention in recent years. It is to be noted, however, that many of the published works on this topic refer primarily to U.S. efforts, with little attention being paid to work done in other countries. Additionally, more attempts are needed to explicitly examine the psychological and educational principles on which technology-supported learning environments are based. This volume covers these two areas. It presents examples of technology-supported learning environments in a variety of international contexts, along with a discussion of the psychological and educational principles used to design these environments.

The idea for this book originated at the conclusion of the NATO Advanced Study Institute on "The Psychological and Educational Foundations of Technology-Based Learning Environments" held in Crete, Greece in 1992. The proceedings of the Advanced Study Institute (ASI), consisting of short chapters describing the work of the majority of the participants, have been published by Springer-Verlag in a volume entitled *Technology-Based Learning Environments: Psychological and Educational Foundations.* The exchanges and discussions that took place during this meeting made it apparent that the ASI proceedings should be supplemented by additional coverage of the issues involved in the design and theory of technology-operated learning environments. Therefore, we decided to solicit more detailed and theoretically oriented chapters from an internationally representative number of ASI participants, as well as from other researchers in the field. This volume is the result of these efforts.

We express our thanks to the University of Athens, the Center for the Study of Reading at the University of Illinois in Urbana–Champaign, and the National

Research Center on Student Learning at the Learning Research and Development Center of the University of Pittsburgh, for supporting the preparation of this book. We also thank the Scientific Affairs Division of NATO for its support of the ASI, which indirectly led to the publication of this volume. We are indebted to Gail Carlson and Dolores Plowman for their expert secretarial help. Last but not least, we thank Hollis Heimbouch for her support of the project and her editorial advice.

Stella Vosniadou
Erik De Corte
Robert Glaser
Heinz Mandl

Introduction: Cognition and the Design of Environments for Learning

Robert Glaser
Erika L. Ferguson
Learning Research and Development Center, University of Pittsburgh

Stella Vosniadou
University of Athens, Greece, University of Illinois at Urbana-Champaign

In current developments for the design of instructional systems and environments for learning, two major streams of effort are influencing the cognitive principles on which learning theory and its applications are based. The first pertains to the advances in modern knowledge of human cognitive performance, which are providing a foundation for new descriptions of how learning occurs. The second is the work of scientists who are designing instructional settings; for many of those involved, this work is being carried out to improve education as well as instructional learning theory. Through the design of technology-enhanced educational environments, scientists come to better understand the theories and principles that are explicit or implicit in their efforts at development (Bruer, 1993).

In these efforts, epistemological changes in research on learning are taking place. There is less emphasis on building theory from laboratory tasks and more on authentic, ecologically valid human performance in educational and social contexts. Attention is being focused on the bidirectional relationship between basic and applied science. Thus, progress occurs not only by moving basic research findings to application, but also by designing applications that test research and theory and raise new questions for investigation (Glaser, 1994). As Miller (1986) said, deliverance in science generally comes in the form of a new application, a new theory, or both.

At the present time, useful applications are beginning to revitalize and redirect research in learning. Most of the chapters in this book represent studies of learning that are conducted in the context of specific instructional designs and educational applications. Each of the chapters in this volume describes applications that affect learning in a number of complex ways. Thus, we grouped the chapters according to the authors' main focus. The chapters reflect three major themes: (a) representation of information, (b) constructing knowledge through cooperative social interaction, and (c) learning in meaningful contexts and from multiple perspectives. We end with two chapters that focus on the principles and strategies that affect the design and evaluation of technology-enhanced learning environments.

REPRESENTATION

Learning involves the acquisition and use of complex systems of symbolic expressions represented in different media. Learning to use oral and written language; acquiring the number system; learning arithmetic, algebra, and calculus; and understanding graphs, tables, and formalisms in science all require the ability to manipulate, connect, and understand the meaning and interrelationships of different kinds of external representations that are central for participation in cultural activity. As mentioned by Kozma et al. (chap. 3, this volume), and previously by Vygotsky (1978), Gardner (1993), and Geertz (1973), "symbolic expression is the way people in a culture commerce in understanding; it is the *lingua franca* with which culture enacts itself and by which individuals understand the culture. It is the interface between knowledge in the world and knowledge in the head" (p. 42).

Understanding and becoming proficient in the use of complex representational systems is not easy. Students often fail to understand the relationships that exist between symbolic expressions and the situations to which they refer. When students do not have the opportunity to externalize their informal representations and compare them to those used by experts in a domain, they fail to understand the qualitative representations that underlie formalisms in science or mathematics. As a result, they attempt to learn the subject matter through superficial memorization.

The learning environments described in this section attempt to promote learning by facilitating students' thinking with qualitative representations and mental models, as experienced scientists and mathematicians do. Different kinds of representations are linked to each other, and internal representations are externalized so that students can become aware of them.

In chapter 1, Vosniadou argues that we need to consider the implications of cognitive-developmental research, which shows that learning—and particularly learning and understanding science—requires the reorganization of prior knowledge, the revision of deeply held presuppositions and beliefs, and the creation of new representations. To do all that, we need learning environments that pay more attention to the constructive and creative aspects of human cognition—environments that encourage metaconceptual awareness, representational growth, and cognitive flexibility.

Vosniadou goes on to describe an intelligent microworld and problem-solving environment—the computer visualization learning environment (CVLE). In CVLE, students collaborate on the solution of meaningful and interesting problems in astronomy. They solve these problems by constructing models that use a set of available primitives derived from students' graphical representations of phenomena, such as the day-night cycle, the seasons, and so on. Once assembled, these computer visualizations of students' models can be run so that the students can see their consequences and test their explanatory adequacy.

In chapter 2, Bliss describes some of the work of the Tools for Exploratory Learning Programme, directed by the London Mental Models Group. This program has developed computer tools that allow students to either represent aspects of their own ideas about a domain (expressive mode), or to explore and interact with models based on the ideas of others (exploratory mode) when reasoning in topics such as traffic congestion, the process of keeping fit, or commercial business operations. Bliss believes that both expressive and exploratory modes are important and indispensable to successful learning. By expressing their own representations of these situations, students become aware of their models and their limitations. By exploring the models of others, students become experienced in using modeling tools, and they understand that they must make their assumptions about relevant causal mechanisms explicit for the models of the systems to operate as they predict.

In chapter 3, Kozma, Russell, Jones, Marx, and Davis argue that, in learning science, students often fail to accurately interpret symbolic representations such as graphs and equations. Students tend to link symbolic representations with literal, surface aspects of the situation they represent. This occurs because novices lack experts' necessary knowledge and qualitative representations when they interpret the same symbolic expressions.

To help novices in a domain understand symbolic expressions accurately, Kozma et al. propose a learning environment that links graphs and symbolic representations to the qualitative representations formed by experts, as well as literal aspects of the situation to which they refer. The educational application that Kozma et al. describe is a computer program for teaching chemistry that links dynamic representations of a chemical reaction on a screen. Chemical equations and graphs of chemical changes are presented simultaneously with animations of the reaction at the molecular level. This facilitates understanding of abstract concepts by integrating them with a visual representation of a normally invisible process.

The remaining chapters in Part I describe applications developed specifically to facilitate the integration of appropriate mathematical procedures with representations of story-problem situations. Problems presented as text require students to reason about the problem situation, determine relevant information, and form an accurate qualitative mental representation before applying the appropriate quantitative algorithm. Story problems are difficult because they require students to apply a situational understanding of mathematics problems, as well as to perform overlearned numerical procedures.

In chapter 4, Schwarz, Nathan, and Resnick discuss a simulation program (the Planner) that provides a real-world context for children learning to solve simple arithmetic story problems. The program takes advantage of children's understanding of relations in the real world and helps them map these onto the language of mathematics. This is achieved by having children manipulate objects that function both as descriptors of situations and as formal entities. In other words, objects are used as visual analogies for abstract arithmetic relations. For instance, students combine trains of different lengths while learning the "combine" relation. Working with these representations helps children understand the correspondence between abstract symbolic expressions and real-world situations.

In chapter 5, Reusser describes a graphical format, called *solution trees,* for the representation of complex mathematical story problems. The program presents a tree-structure representation that helps students: (a) recognize relevant and irrelevant information in the problem text, (b) identify subproblems, and (c) apply appropriate mathematical strategies to their qualitative representation of the problem. Reusser, like Schwarz et al., describes a representational format that allows students to relate the surface structures of a story problem to their implied mathematical deep structure.

In chapter 6, Lehtinen and Repo discuss the construction of an appropriate representation in the learning process. Their work focuses on different kinds of representational tools for learning advanced mathematical concepts. Some of these tools allow students to express their informal understanding of a mathematical problem, and others model the understanding of experts. Using these representational tools, students can gradually understand the general structural principles common to different situations. Lehtinen and Repo also discuss the results of an experiment in which a computer-based algebra program is used to help 11th-grade students understand concepts in differential calculus. In this environment, students view multiple, dynamic representations of mathematical functions. They input data from experiments they have performed, and they observe changes in depicted graphical functions. This occurs in a social situation where students can discuss the problems and learn from each others' contributions.

In chapter 7, De Corte discusses the fact that sophisticated, experimental computer systems are being developed to perform a large number of instructional functions. These systems integrate coaching strategies, such as scaffolding, with strategies for learning, such as metacognitive skills. They can provide opportunities for students to control their own learning, thus promoting active learner involvement. They can facilitate cooperative learning in collaborative classroom situations by serving as interactive communication devices. These learning environments also include some of the salient features of exploratory microworlds and simulation programs, such as facilitating representation and viewing problems from multiple perspectives. De Corte describes a learning environment that teaches Logo programming in a content intended to encourage such general strategies as problem decomposition and problem monitoring.

SOCIAL INTERACTION

Renewed interest in the psychological views of Vygotsky has brought the issue of social interaction and cooperative learning to the center of education reform. Vygotsky believes that signs or symbols are not invented by individuals as a result of pure logic, but originate in social interaction and then become intrapersonal. "Every function in the child's cultural development appears twice: first on the social level, and later, on the individual level; first, between people (interpsychological), and then inside the child (intrapsychological). This applies equally to voluntary attention, to logical memory and to the formation of concepts. All the higher functions originate as actual relations between human individuals" (Vygotsky, 1978, p. 57).

Adapting this approach to cognition, instructional theorists have used technology to facilitate social interaction and cooperative learning in the classroom. An example of such an effort is the computer-supported intentional learning environment (CSILE), developed by Scardamalia and Bereiter. In chapter 8, Scardamalia and Bereiter argue that, in many traditional classrooms, the pursuit of understanding is in fact inhibited; what is adaptive is *not* to try to understand. This is the case because school tasks are often arbitrary, oversimplified, and not meaningful to the learner. There is limited time for reflection, and there is an emphasis on the reproduction of facts, spelling lists, or endless classifications that are easily converted into test items. To make *understanding* a central goal in school, Scardamalia and Bereiter believe it is important to shift away from an individual orientation to a group orientation, where students work together on common problems, where the problems students try to solve are problems of understanding, and where explanation seeking is the main activity in the classroom. CSILE is a computerized discourse community in which social interaction and learning are facilitated by allowing students to cooperate in building a communal knowledge bank. Students learn by asking questions of themselves and others, and by accessing the communal knowledge base. They solve problems that are of interest to them, regulate their own learning, and develop the ability to explain phenomena.

In chapter 9, Dillenbourg considers situations in which the computer acts as an agent in a pseudosocial interaction with a human learner and plays the role of a coach or co-learner. In the type of system he describes, the computer serves as a collaborative problem-solving partner, and provides students with tools for problem solving. Dillenbourg uses the metaphor *socially distributed cognition* to describe the relationship between a human and a computer involved in shared problem solving. He examines the role that concepts such as *scaffolding, active student participation,* and *internalization of knowledge* play when learning takes place in a socially distributed cognitive system. He also discusses how these concepts can be translated into design features, focusing on three different learning environments.

In chapter 10, Kanselaar and Erkens describe their attempts to develop an intelligent cooperative system (ICS) that works with a student to solve puzzle problems. By engaging in appropriate dialogue and feedback, the student and computer can solve puzzles under conditions where neither partner has all the information necessary for the problem, nor knows what information the partner has. The interface displays a visual record of the steps in the problem-solving process, making thinking overt. Kanselaar and Erkens discuss some characteristics of students' behavior during interaction with a computer partner that should be considered by designers. For instance, the nature of students' dialogues showed that the way in which students tended to interact with the computer partner could influence the problem-solving process.

In chapter 11, Torney-Purta discusses a computer-based discourse community where students cooperate to simulate the complex, interactive problem solving involved in international diplomacy. Through a computer-conferencing network, teams of students work on questions that real diplomats face, such as "What would you do if you were the finance minister of a developing country and could not pay your interest debt to a developed country?" As a group, students construct the knowledge content and skills necessary to communicate in this domain.

MEANINGFUL CONTEXTS AND MULTIPLE PERSPECTIVES

The chapters in this part discuss technology-enhanced learning environments that emphasize meaningful, holistic learning tasks and encourage viewing problems from multiple perspectives. When learning is situated in real-world contexts, knowledge structures become more memorable and problem-solving skills become linked to situations in which they are used. Solving the same problem from different perspectives promotes cognitive flexibility; as a result, transfer to new situations is improved, which is an important goal of successful instruction.

Three chapters describe the work of the Cognition and Technology Group at Vanderbilt (CTGV), which has developed multimedia learning environments for instruction. Their approach, called *anchored instruction,* situates learning in real-world problem-solving contexts.

In chapter 12, Bransford and his colleagues describe a technology-enhanced learning environment that facilitates acquisition of the skills and strategies needed for basic literacy. The multimedia environments discussed in this work supply rich visual support for text comprehension and opportunities for interpreting texts in meaningful contexts.

The Goldman et al. program of instruction for science education, described in chapter 13, provides learners with multiple opportunities to solve problems that are relevant to the same context. The program promotes learning concepts from various perspectives, and helps students integrate information from hands-on experimentation in the classroom with information in a video. The stories are motivating and provide a model of what real scientists do.

In chapter 14, the Vanderbilt group shows how children are motivated through video scenarios to reason about complex mathematical problems and to recognize the utility of mathematical procedures. Groups of students learn to (a) represent problems, (b) formulate subgoals, (c) devise and test solution plans, (d) identify relevant data, and (e) evaluate problem solutions.

In chapter 15, Mandl, Gruber, and Renkl describe instructional applications for learning economics and medicine. The applications situate instruction in authentic contexts, which allow students to actively control instruction and to participate in a social-learning context where they interact with the perspectives of others. The authors point out how closely the principles of modern instructional approaches—such as constructivist theory, anchored instruction, and cognitive apprenticeship—resemble those prevalent in the German *Reformpädagogik* movement of the early 1900s.

In chapter 16, Mendelsohn describes a complex interactive microworld that can be adapted to different learning styles. This computer-learning environment teaches experimental psychology through a computer coach that provides scaffolding, adjusts its teaching style, and monitors learning goals in ways that reflect the instructional implications of different theories of learning. It also allows students to choose their own difficulty levels and problem sequence, and to access expert knowledge through an integrated hypertext system. Mendelsohn illustrates how the design of the environment varies such features as the amount of feedback given to learners in accordance with the theoretical principles of Skinner, Bloom, Vygotsky, Piaget, and Papert.

PRINCIPLES OF SYSTEM DESIGN

The two chapters in the last part of this volume approach the issues involved in the design and evaluation of technology-supported learning environments in a more direct manner. In chapter 17, Collins takes a cost-benefit analysis approach to the design of learning environments. He describes some of the cost-benefit trade-offs of different learning goals, learning contexts, learning sequences, and teaching methods. For example, one learning goal might be to design an environment that emphasizes thoughtfulness rather than memorization. The benefit would be that thoughtfulness produces greater depth of understanding and more flexible knowledge. However, this reduces the possibility of the automaticity of knowledge that comes about with extensive practice. A major issue that Collins believes must be considered is the authenticity of knowledge to be learned (i.e., how useful it is for students' lives and how well students are able to apply the knowledge). He suggests that designers consider the effects of their design decisions on students' learning and motivation within a constructivist framework, as opposed to viewing the learning environment as a knowledge-delivery system.

Technological advances, such as the ones in this book, engender new approaches to learning and instruction not previously possible, and can foster restructuring of the entire instructional setting. For this reason, in chapter 18, Salomon suggests that a new methodological framework is needed to evaluate the success of educational technologies—one that can use the entire learning environment as the unit of analysis, instead of attempting to isolate the effects of separate factors.

CONCLUSION

At this time in the development of learning theory relevant to instruction, applications are an important part of the theoretical frontier. Although many of the behavioral regularities that scientists discover are placed in the repository of scientific reports awaiting future applications, commerce across an application frontier goes in both directions (Newell, 1990). When applications are successful, the theory that spawned them becomes more memorable, and the applications contribute to new developments in both practice and theory. The chapters in this book attest to the importance of this relationship.

As technology begins to transform classrooms and learning environments in many countries, we must continue to discuss the principles on which they are based toward dual objectives: revising the accumulated knowledge gained from research, and making informed improvements to education.

ACKNOWLEDGMENT

Work on this chapter was facilitated by the resources of the National Research Center on Student Learning (NRCSL) of the Learning Research and Development Center (LRDC) at the University of Pittsburgh.

REFERENCES

Bruer, J. (1993). *Schools for thought.* Cambridge, MA: MIT Press.
Gardner, H. (1993). *Frames of mind.* New York: Basic Books.
Geertz, C. (1973). *Interpretation of cultures.* New York: Basic Books.
Glaser, R. (1994). Learning theory and instruction. In G. d'Ydewalle, P. Eelen, & P. Bertelson (Eds.), *International perspectives on psychological science, Vol. 2: The state of the art* (pp. 341–357). Hove, England: Lawrence Erlbaum Associates.

Miller, G. A. (1986). Dismembering cognition. In S. H. Hails & B. F. Green, Jr. (Eds.), *One hundred years of psychological research in America: C. Stanley Hall and the Johns Hopkins tradition* (pp. 277–298). Baltimore, MD: Johns Hopkins University Press.

Newell, A. (1990). *Unified theories of cognition.* Cambridge, MA: Harvard University Press.

Vygotsky, L. (1978). *Mind in society.* Cambridge, MA: Harvard University Press.

I
REPRESENTATION

1 Learning Environments for Representational Growth and Cognitive Flexibility

Stella Vosniadou
University of Athens, Greece
University of Illinois at Urbana–Champaign

Substantial changes have occurred in the conceptualization of learning in recent years, changes that have important implications for the construction of technology-supported learning environments. One of these changes is reflected in the analysis of knowledge as an activity that takes place among individuals in specific contexts, rather than as a substance contained in the mind of individuals independent of context (e.g., Brown, Collins, & Duguid, 1989; Cognition and Technology Group at Vanderbilt, 1990; Resnick, Levine, & Teasley, 1991). This approach, known as *situated* or *anchored* points out that learning cannot be easily separated from the "act of knowing" and that "what is learned" in an integral part of "how it is learned and used." Situated approaches to cognition emphasize the need to construct learning environments that engage students in meaningful and purposeful activities.

Another related change centers around the analysis of learning as a developmental process that occurs first in the social, interpersonal domain, and only then becomes intrapersonal. Following the writings of Vygotsky (1978), a number of researchers agree that learning is not something that individuals invent but is an activity that has its roots in participation in sociocultural interaction (e.g., Lave, 1988; Saxe, 1990). The implication of this view is that it is important to design learning environments that facilitate social interaction and cooperative learning in the classroom.

A third area where changes have taken place, but which have not affected the design of learning environments so far, has to do with the conceptualization of learning as an activity that requires substantial reorganization of existing conceptual structures. Recent experimental evidence clearly shows that by the time children go to school they have acquired a great deal of information about their physical and social environments. Although this early competence creates the

13

necessary foundations for further learning, it also acts as a constraint on the knowledge acquisition process. In many cases, but particularly in the case of learning science, learning cannot be achieved by simply adding more information to existing conceptual structures. It may require the reorganization of the knowledge base, the revision of basic beliefs and presuppositions, the creation of new qualitative representations, and the mastery of new representational systems.

The view that learning may require substantial changes in individual cognition is consistent with a dialectical analysis of the relationship between individuals and the culture in which they participate (e.g., Vygotsky, 1978). Although situated approaches to cognition have focused on the effect that culture has on individual cognition, the relationship between individuals and the culture in which they participate is more one of mutual interactions and influences.

Even if we accept that the beginnings of mental life should be traced to the individual participating in certain forms of organized activity (Bakhurst & Padden, 1991), the existence of individual cognition creates the preconditions for the reflective understanding of culture and the possibilities for changing it. As humans, we are capable of creating representations of our experiences which we can manipulate and change. Changes in these representations can result in changes in the physical reality of culture itself. Let us not forget that scientific discovery has proceeded through the radical restructuring of our representations of the physical world to the development of a technology that has totally reshaped Western culture and produced a different physical reality and different cultural tools and artifacts for most of us (Vosniadou, 1991).

The culture in which we now live has produced theories and explanations of phenomena that may not always be consistent with the layman's interpretation of everyday experience. Part of the purpose of schooling is to help students undergo the kinds of conceptual changes that are necessary so that their representations of experience and their explanations of phenomena come closer to what is currently accepted science. This must be done in a way that facilitates the development of the cognitive flexibility and creativity needed to move our culture to further scientific discoveries in the years to come.

The focus of the chapter is on learning and teaching in the physical sciences. It is argued that, in the physical sciences, learning is difficult because the qualitative representations implicit in many science concepts are not consistent with the representations invited by everyday experience, and thus, require the reinterpretation of fundamental assumptions about the way the physical world operates. This difficulty is accentuated by the fact that the same linguistic terms are used to express the layman's as well as the scientist's conceptual organization of the physical world.

It is argued that we need to seriously consider the instructional implications of cognitive science research which shows that substantial conceptual reorganization needs to take place in the process of learning science, and to design learning environments that support it. Finally, a computer visualization learning environment (CVLE) that uses technology to facilitate cognitive flexibility and representational growth in the area of astronomy is described.

THE PROCESS OF LEARNING SCIENCE

One of the most important findings of cognitive science research during the last years is the realization that experts organize and represent knowledge in memory in ways different than novices (Chi, Glaser, & Farr, 1988). Expert physicists seem to represent problems in physics in terms of the currently accepted scientific concepts and laws, whereas novices include surface features of the problem situation in their reasoning. For example, a novice has a representation of the concept of *incline plane* that is based primarily on surface features, such as angle of incline, length, and height. On the contrary, experts organize their representations of the incline plane around Newton's laws and the conservation of energy law (Chi, Glaser & Rees, 1982).

More recently, developmental studies have provided additional information about the way knowledge is acquired and the mechanisms with which novices become experts. These studies have shown that the knowledge acquisition process starts early in infancy, and that it is based on interpretations of everyday experience (see Baillargeon, 1990; Spelke, 1991). Developmental research on how children acquire knowledge about the physical world, has suggested that children interpret their everyday experiences to construct what I have called a *naive framework theory of physics* (Vosniadou, 1994a). This framework theory forms the foundation on which further knowledge about the physical world is organized, but also constrains and restricts the understanding of scientific information in important ways.[1]

For example, research in the area of mechanics has shown that young children construct an initial concept of force according to which force is a property of objects that feel heavy. This "internal" force appears to represent the potential these objects have to react to other objects with which they come in contact. It is also central in explaining the motion of inanimate objects. In the ontology of the young child, the natural state of inanimate objects is that of rest, while the motion of inanimate objects is a phenomenon that needs to be explained, usually in terms of a causal agent. This causal agent is the force of another object (Ioannides & Vosniadou, 1991).

This initial concept of *force* is obviously different from the way the linguistic term *force* is currently interpreted by the scientific community. In Newtonian physics, force is not an internal property of objects, but a process that explains changes in the kinetic state of physical objects. In the framework of the accepted

---

[1]The term *theory* is used to denote a relational, explanatory structure, not an explicit, well-formed theory that is subject to conscious awareness and hypothesis testing. It is *not* assumed that children have metaconceptual awareness of the presuppositions and beliefs that comprise what we refer to as a *framework theory.*

view, *motion* is a natural state that does not need to be explained. What needs to be explained is changes in kinetic state.

The process of understanding the meaning implicit in the scientific concept of force is usually a slow and gradual affair, likely to give rise to misconceptions. Research in science education has documented misconceptions in practically every area of the physical sciences. Most adults in our society who are not expert scientists do not have a clear understanding of even some of the most commonly used concepts in the physical sciences, such as *heat* and *temperature* (see Tiberghien, 1994; Wiser & Carey, 1983).

These findings pose the following question: Why is it so difficult to understand concepts in science, and how can we construct learning environments that facilitate the development of the qualitatively different representations required in the learning of science in particular, but also of learning in general?

SOURCES OF DIFFICULTY IN THE UNDERSTANDING OF SCIENCE CONCEPTS

The Reinterpretation of Deeply Entrenched Presuppositions and Beliefs

Developmental research in a number of areas in the physical sciences has shown that children's interpretations of scientific information is often constrained by a few deeply entrenched presuppositions about the way the physical world operates. For example, studies of children's representations of the earth show that elementary-school children have a great deal of difficulty creating an exact representation of the spherical shape of the earth and the regions of the earth where people live (Vosniadou & Brewer, 1992).

Many children believe that the earth is shaped like a flat rectangle or a disc, is supported by the ground below, and covered by the sky above its "top." Other children think of the earth as a hollow sphere with people living on flat ground deep inside it, or as a flattened sphere with people living on its flat "top" and "bottom." Finally, some children form the interesting model of a dual earth according to which there are two earths: a flat one on which people live, and a spherical one that is a planet up in the sky. These representations of the earth are not rare. In fact, only 23 of the 60 children (20 first graders, 20 third graders, and 20 fifth graders) that participated in this study had formed the accepted model of the spherical earth. This finding has been confirmed by a series of cross-cultural studies that investigated the concept of the *earth* in children from India, Greece, and Samoa (see Vosniadou, 1994b, for a discussion of the cross-cultural findings).

In previous work, we have explained children's difficulty in understanding the spherical model of the earth on the grounds that this model violates certain fundamental presuppositions about the physical world, such as the presupposition that space is organized in terms of "up" and "down" with respect to a flat ground, and that unsupported objects fall in a "downward" direction—what we call the *up/down gravity presupposition* (see Vosniadou & Brewer, 1992).

It appears that children start by thinking of the earth as a physical object that has all the characteristics of physical objects in general (i.e., it is solid, stable, stationary, and needing support, in the larger context of a physical world where unsupported objects fall "down"). When they are exposed to the information that the earth is a sphere, they find it difficult to understand because it violates their presuppositions about physical objects. Their "misconceptions" regarding the earth's spherical shape of the earth are in fact synthetic models, attempts to reconcile the accepted view with these entrenched presuppositions without giving them up, or by changing them only partially. For example, the synthetic model of the dual earth provides a good resolution of the conflict between the flat and spherical earth without giving up the presuppositions of the framework theory. In this model, the information regarding the earth's spherical shape is interpreted to refer to another earth-a planet that is up in the sky-and not to the flat, supported earth on which we live.

Our studies of the process of conceptual change in other areas of physics, such as thermal physics and mechanics, confirm the previously mentioned view (see Ioannides & Vosniadou, 1991; Vosniadou & Kempner, 1993). For example, we see that the successive mental models of force obtained in our studies of elementary and high school students in Greece can also be explained as students' attempts to reconcile the information they receive from the culture with certain basic presuppositions and beliefs about the nature of the physical world. As with the concept of the earth, the process of conceptual change appears to proceed through the gradual revision of these presuppositions and beliefs. For example, students gradually differentiate the concept of *weight* from the concept of *force* and replace the notion of an *internal force* with the notion of *gravity*. However, the presuppositions that force is a property of objects and that the motion of physical objects requires an explanation continues to remain in place in the conceptual system of high school students, despite that these students have been exposed to systematic instruction in Newtonian mechanics.

Mental Representations Act as Second Order Constraints in the Process of Acquiring Knowledge About the Physical World

In addition to deeply entrenched presuppositions, the specific mental representations students form when they try to understand new information seem to exert their own, unique influence on the knowledge acquisition process. I have used the construct of the *mental model* to describe individuals' representations of the physical world. This construct has been used differently by different researchers (e.g., Gentner & Stevens, 1983; Johnson-Laird, 1983). It is used here to refer to an analog representation which can be manipulated mentally to provide causal explanations of phenomena. It is assumed that most mental models are created on the spot to deal with the demands of specific situations.

The mental models that individuals generate (or sometimes retrieve from memory) during cognitive functioning can constrain the knowledge acquisition process in ways similar to presuppositions as was described earlier. For example, in our studies of students' explanations of the day/night cycle (Vosniadou & Brewer, 1994), we have found that these explanations are constrained by students' mental models of the earth. Thus, students with rectangle, disc, or dual earth models did not provide explanations of the day/night cycle in terms of the axis rotation of the earth, or even explanations according to which the sun "goes down to the other side of the earth." These explanations are obviously inconsistent with the mental model of a flat, stationary, earth rooted on the ground.

Mental models of the earth appear to also influence the way students interpret the information regarding the earth's axis rotation. For example, students who form the model of the earth as a sphere prefer an interpretation of the earth's axis rotation according to which the earth turns in an up/down fashion, rather than an east/west fashion. It appears that these students operate on the basis of a mental representation according to which the sun is located above the "top" of the earth—a representation that is consistent with our everyday experiences. Given such a representation of the earth and sun, children must assume that the direction of the earth's rotation is an up/down one if they are to produce an empirically adequate explanation of the day/night cycle (i.e., an explanation according to which the people located at the "top" part of the earth, facing the sun, will be away from the sun when it is night).

These examples demonstrate that when new information is provided, students try to interpret it in the context of their already existing representations. Because these representations seem to be the point where new information enters the cognitive system, they should be taken into consideration in the design of instruction.

The Sequence in Which the Concepts that Belong to a Given Subject-Matter Area Are Acquired

The concepts that belong to a subject-matter area have a relational structure that influences their order of acquisition. For example, in the subject-matter area of astronomy, students understand the spherical shape of the earth only after they have acquired an elementary notion of gravity. Explanations of the day/night cycle on the basis of the earth's axis rotation are not provided before students understand that the earth is a rotating sphere and that the moon revolves around the earth. Similarly, a scientific explanation of the seasons only occurs in students who have formed the mental model of a heliocentric solar system; know the relative sizes of the earth, the sun and the moon; and understand the scientific explanation of the day/night cycle.

At present such findings are not taken into consideration in the design of science curricula. A detailed investigation of the astronomy units in four leading science series in the United States, as well as an examination of the national curricula for teaching astronomy to elementary school children in Greece shows that many concepts are introduced in a sequence that does not provide students with all the information necessary for understanding them.

For example, the kind of instruction elementary school students typically receive regarding the shape of the earth involves a simple statement that the earth is "round like a ball" or sphere, sometimes accompanied by a class demonstration of a rotating globe. In this type of instruction, instructors do not stop to explain to students how it is possible for the earth to be spherical when it appears to be flat, or how it is possible for people to live on the "sides" and "bottom" of this sphere without falling "down." I have not found a single reference to the notion of *gravity* associated with astronomy instruction in the elementary-school grades. This is because gravity instruction is considered to belong to the subject-matter area of mechanics and not of astronomy. It is obvious that this type of instruction does not address students' entrenched presuppositions, and therefore does not provide the information they need in order to construct an appropriate representation of the earth as a sphere.

IMPLICATIONS FOR THE DESIGN
OF LEARNING ENVIRONMENTS

Michael Jacobson, Chip Bruce, and I have been trying to draw the implications of cognitive science research to design a computer learning environment in astronomy. The result of this effort is an intelligent microworld and problem-solving environment—the computer visualization learning environment (CVLE). The CVLE is intended to be one part of a larger collaborative learning environment where students work in groups and engage in a great deal of communication. This environment is meant to combine computer activities with hands-on science experiments and observations, visits to the library, and the planetarium. It can be used with very young children to create a situation where complex scientific problems can be approached in a meaningful way.

In the CVLE students are asked to solve problems that spring directly from their everyday experience, (i.e., problems related to the day/night cycle, the seasons, the phases of the moon, and so on). This is done in a way that is particularly interesting to children. For example, they fly to different parts of the globe and are asked to make predictions regarding the time of the day or the season of the year and to explain why. Or, they travel in space and are asked different questions regarding the locations, sizes, and movements of the various planets.

In addition to providing an environment where students can collaborate in the solution of meaningful problems the CVLE is designed to promote cognitive flexibility and representational growth. Some of the ways this is done are described below:

Amount and Sequence of Information to be Taught

The finding that the understanding of science concepts and explanations is a difficult and time consuming affair that is likely to give rise to misconceptions, calls for a reconsideration of current decisions regarding the breadth of coverage of the curriculum in science education.

First, it may be more profitable to design instruction that focuses on the deep exploration and understanding of a few, key concepts, rather than cover a great deal of material in a superficial way. The latter strategy is likely to lead students to logical incoherence and misconceptions. It also encourages the casual memorization of facts, and does not develop the analytic skills necessary for conceptual change and the development of new representations.

Second, if the concepts that comprise a subject-matter area have a relational structure that influences their order of acquisition then the design of curricula needs to be based on the results of detailed empirical investigations that provide information about the way students acquire information in a given subject-matter area.

In the computer learning environment we are in the process of designing, students focus on the exploration of only a few key phenomena in astronomy, phenomena that we know children find difficult to understand. Children are provided with all the information they need in order to understand the scientific explanations of these phenomena. Particular attention is paid so that new information is presented in a way that takes into consideration both the relative complexity of the concepts that comprise the domain and their psychological order of acquisition. This is possible because the learning environment is based on the results of existing cognitive science research which provides information about how children actually acquire these concepts when they are exposed to instruction.

Facilitating Metaconceptual Awareness

Although children seem to be good interpreters of their everyday experiences, they are not aware of the explanatory frameworks they have constructed and even more so of the entrenched presuppositions that constrain their explanations. They do not seem to know that their explanations of physical phenomena are hypotheses that can be subject to experimentation and falsification. Lack of metaconceptual awareness of this sort prevents children from questioning their prior knowledge and encourages the assimilation of new information to existing conceptual structures. This type of assimilatory activity forms the basis for the creation of synthetic models and misconceptions, and lies at the root of the surface inconsistency so commonly observed in students' reasoning.

To help students increase their metaconceptual awareness, it is important to create learning environments that allow them to express their representations of phenomena and compare them to those of others. Such activities may be time-consuming, but they are important for ensuring that students become aware of exactly what they know and what they need to learn.

The CVLE attempts to facilitate metaconceptual awareness by having students solve the CVLE problems by constructing models using a set of available primitives (primitive objects, such as the earth, sun, moon, planets, as well as primitive forces and relations). These primitives are psychologically real because they have been derived directly from prior research on students' own graphical representations (Vosniadou & Brewer, 1992, 1994a). Once assembled these computer visualizations of the students' mental models are runnable. In this way, the students can become aware of the mental representations they use to explain phenomena in astronomy and test their empirical adequacy.

Addressing Entrenched Presuppositions

The CVLE goes even further in its attempt to create metaconceptual awareness by making students face the implications of the entrenched presuppositions (presuppositions such as that *force, heat,* or *weight* are properties of objects, that space is organized in the directions of "up" and "down," that unsupported objects fall in a *downward* direction, and so on) that constrain their mental representations of the physical world.

In the CVLE students can become aware of the constraints these presuppositions pose on their thinking because the computer environment is programmed to run according to the principles of a naive theory of physics. For example, all physical objects operate on the basis of an up/down gravity presupposition (that is, they fall in a downward direction when not supported). This implies that in order to have people stay on the surface of the spherical earth, students must explicitly change the up/down gravity presupposition. The "buggy" runnability of the system helps students become aware of their prior knowledge and understand how it constrains their representations of the physical world.

Facilitating Representational Growth and Cognitive Flexibility

Entrenched presuppositions are difficult to change even when students become aware of them, because they are based on everyday experiences, they function adequately in the everyday world, and they are tied to years of confirmation. In addition, such presuppositions form coherent systems of explanation that lie at the root of our conceptual system. To motivate students to reexamine their presuppositions about the physical world, it is important to provide them with additional information, information that helps them enrich their everyday representations and see things from different points of view. This additional information can come in the form of systematic observations, hands-on experiments, and simulations.

If students' thinking about the physical world is in terms of models and experience-based representations, instruction that is model based may be more successful in moving students toward an understanding of the qualitative models that scientists use to support their quantitative reasoning. Computer learning environments, such as microworlds and simulations, have an advantage over traditional methods of instruction in providing model based instruction. Computer models can make abstract concepts concrete and manipulable, reveal their properties and constraints, relate them to the everyday situations they represent, and connect them to other representations of the same information. For example, in the CVLE students can understand the spherical shape of the earth better when they see how the earth looks from the point of view of someone on the earth, or from the point of view of someone in a spaceship orbiting the earth or looking at the earth from the moon.

Representational growth and cognitive flexibility is achieved when students become aware of their representations, understand how different representations are connected to each other, and are able to see things from different points of view.

SUMMARY

Research in cognitive science and cognitive development has made it possible to progressively move to new levels of thinking about educational environments that promote learning. In this chapter, I argued that we need to consider the instructional implications of the research results that learning involves not only the enrichment of existing conceptual structures, but also the substantial reorganization of prior knowledge, the revision of entrenched presuppositions and beliefs, and the creation of new representations. To do so, we need to design learning environments that take seriously the issue of metaconceptual awareness and representational growth. We need to pay more attention to the constructive and creative aspects of human cognition, to encourage reflection, the questioning of old ideas, and the creation of new representations. We need to create situations where students can express their own representations of situations, share them with others and revise them. We also need to create situations where students can explore the qualitative representations hidden behind science concepts and formalisms in science, so that they will understand the situations to which they refer and the reasons why it became necessary to develop them.

ACKNOWLEDGMENTS

The work on this chapter was facilitated by a grant from the University of Athens, Greece. I would like to thank my colleagues-William F. Brewer, Bertram Bruce, and Michael Jacobson—and students-Christos Ioannides and

Lianne Kempner—for their contributions to the research projects referred to in this chapter.

REFERENCES

Bakhurst, D., & Padden, C. (1991). The Meshcheryakov experiment: Soviet work on the education of blind-deaf children. *Learning and Instruction, 1*, 179–185.

Baillargeon, R. (1990, March). *The development of young infants intuition about support.* Paper presented at the seventh International Conference on Infant Studies, Montreal, Canada.

Brown, J. S., Collins, A., & Duguid, P. (1989). Situated cognition and the culture of learning, *Educational Researcher, 18*, 32–34.

Chi, M. T. H., Glaser, R., & Farr, M. J. (Eds.). (1988). *The nature of expertise.* Hillsdale, NJ: Lawrence Erlbaum Associates.

Chi, M. T. H., Glaser, R., & Rees, E. (1982). Expertise in problem solving. In R. Sternberg (Ed.), *Advances in the psychology of human intelligence, Volume 1.* Hillsdale, NJ: Lawrence Erlbaum Associates.

Cognition and Technology Group at Vanderbilt, (1990). Anchored instruction and its elationship to situated cognition. *Educational Researcher, 19*(6) 2–10.

Gentner, D., & Stevens, A. L. (Eds.). (1983). *Mental models.* Hillsdale, NJ: Lawrence Erlbaum Associates.

Ioannides, C., & Vosniadou, S. (1991, August). *The development of the concept of force in Greek children.* Paper presented at the biennial meeting of the European Society for Research on Learning and Instruction, Turku, Finland.

Johnson-Laird, P. N. (1983). *Mental models.* Cambridge, MA.: Harvard University Press.

Lave, J. (1988). *Cognition in practice: Mind, mathematics, and culture in everyday life.* Cambridge, England: Cambridge University Press.

Resnick, L. B., Levine, J. M., & Teasley, S. D. (Eds.). (1991). *Perspectives on socially shared cognition.* Washington, DC: American Psychological Association.

Saxe, G. B. (1990). *Culture and cognitive development: Studies in mathematical understanding.* Hillsdale, NJ: Lawrence Erlbaum Associates.

Spelke, S. E. (1991). Physical knowledge in infancy: Reflections on Piaget's theory. In S. Carey & R. Gelman (Eds.), *The epigenesis of mind: Essays on biology and cognition* (pp. 133–170). Hillsdale, NJ: Lawrence Erlbaum Associates.

Tiberghien, A. (1994). Analysing teaching-learning situations. *Learning and Instruction, 4*, 71–87.

Vosniadou, S, (1991). Are we ready for a psychology of learning and culture? *Learning and Instruction, 1*(3), 283–287.

Vosniadou, S. (1994a). Capturing and modeling the process of conceptual change. *Learning and Instruction, 4*, 45–69.

Vosniadou, S. (1994b). Universal and culture specific properties of children's mental models of the earth. In L. A. Hirschfield & S. A. Gelman (Eds.), *Mapping the mind* (pp. 421–430). New York: Cambridge University Press.

Vosniadou, S., & Brewer, W. F. (1992). Mental models of the earth: A study of conceptual change in childhood. *Cognitive Psychology, 24*, 535–585.

Vosniadou, S., & Brewer, W. F. (1994). Mental models of the day/night cycle. *Cognitive Science, 18*, 123–183.

Vosniadou, S., & Kempner, L (1993, April). *Mental models of heat.* Paper presented at the biennial meeting of the Society for Research in Child Development, New Orleans, LA.

Vygotsky, L. S. (1978). *Mind in society.* Cambridge, MA: Harvard University Press.

Wiser, M., & Carey, S. (1983). When heat and temperature were one. In D. Gentner & A. L. Stevens (Eds.), *Mental models* (pp. 267–297). Hillsdale, NJ: Lawrence Erlbaum Associates.

2 Externalizing Thinking Through Modeling: ESRC Tools for Exploratory Learning Research Program

Joan Bliss
University of London

This chapter describes some of the work of the Tools for Exploratory Learning Program, which was part of the Economic and Social Research Council (ESRC) National Initiative on Information Technology in Education (Bliss & Ogborn, 1989, 1992a, 1992b), and is an outcome of the work of the London Mental Models Group (see appendix a). The program looks at pupils' reasoning when they are modeling with computer tools.

Technology, particularly information technology, can play an important role in a modeling curriculum for pupils, Ogborn (1990) argued; "To make a model on the computer is to create a world but a world which evolves or changes in front of ones' eyes. It is an imaginary world which may or may not reflect something important about the real world" (p. 103). We would argue that modeling is a vital thinking process that needs to be encouraged within the teaching situation. When pupils have the opportunity to create models, such models may—by being simpler than the real world—help pupils gain insights into the real world, and also make connections or see similarities between apparently disparate phenomena. Models are used to explain the world; to predict what might happen; and to test alternative policies, actions, and ideas. Most important, models can run on a computer.

We approach the research in the following ways:

- analysis of the theoretical framework in terms of learning activities, types of reasoning, and research questions;
- description of the research design;
- specific focus on one of the major aspects of our work—semiquantitative reasoning;

- general description and discussion of the overall findings of the research; and
- implications for education.

THEORETICAL FRAMEWORK

Exploratory and Expressive Modes of Learning

Initially within the program, we made a distinction between exploratory and expressive tools: Exploratory tools were microworlds, simulations, and so on, whereas expressive ones were modeling systems, spread sheets, and shells of various kinds. However, such a distinction appeared too limited in terms of the tools and the pupils' activity using these tools. We now define two modes of learning activity: *exploratory* and *expressive*. The exploratory mode permits pupils to investigate the views of a teacher or an adult about a given domain—views that will often be quite different from their own spontaneous ideas. The expressive mode permits pupils to represent aspects of their own ideas about a domain, and in this way to reflect on and explore their own models. In the former mode, learners are interacting with models based on the assumptions and ideas of others; in the latter, they are modeling their own assumptions. These two modes of learning are conceived of as different, but complementary.

Software tools can be used in both exploratory and expressive modes. In exploratory mode, the use of tools containing domain models permits the pupil to examine the consequences of different models, some of which fit and others of which conflict with the pupils' own ideas. However, the role of conflict in influencing pupils to change their ideas is problematic. It is possible that exploratory work with a tool can provide the opportunity to "try out" and experiment with other ideas. It has been suggested that conflict is not helpful if it does not provide alternatives; that to learn from contradictions requires considerably more than simply being made aware of conflict (Bryant, 1982). It may be possible in this manner to examine the passage from adherence to one way of seeing the world to an "acceptance" or assimilation of an alternative view.

In the expressive mode, learners can examine their own knowledge of a domain by being encouraged to experiment with their own theorizing. For this purpose, it is crucial that the use of the tool is as transparent as possible, and that the manner in which ideas are expressed in it is easily accessible, thus permitting learners to recognize and explore their knowledge. It could be argued that it is only when learners have the chance to become aware of their own ideas about a problem, and to reflect on them, that there is any opportunity for progress. Such situations can provide important learning opportunities.

In summary, the exploratory mode can be seen as a way to ask the learner,

Can you understand how somebody else is thinking about the problem?, whereas the expressive mode is a way to ask, Can you understand your own thinking about the problem? We take it that both modes are indispensable to successful learning.

REASONING

Many studies of learning can be criticized for not allowing enough time for significant learning to occur. Learning of the kind discussed previously seems to require weeks or months, rather than hours. However, our research prevented us from studying children over such a long period of time. Therefore, it seemed more reasonable to limit the scope of the study to an investigation of the quality of children's reasoning with modeling tools, which can be seen as valuable in itself, rather than to claim to be a study investigating learning. We focused on three types of reasoning in task–tool situations: quantitative, qualitative, and semiquantitative.

Quantitative Reasoning

Quantitative reasoning can involve a variety of aspects, from recognizing simple numerical relationships, to working with sets of numbers and comparing sizes and magnitudes, to manipulating algebraic relationships. Our task–tool situations are limited to quantitative reasoning about variables linked by simple algebraic relationships ($+$, $\times$, $-$, $/$), providing means for constructing and manipulating algebraic relationships between variables.

Qualitative Reasoning

Qualitative reasoning involves making categorical distinctions and decisions. Thus, it may require considering a set of choices or decisions and taking into account their consequences, or, given a certain goal, formulating what is necessary to reach that goal. It may require noting and taking account of alternatives, weighing up evidence, or considering what follows if a certain condition is realized. In our qualitative task–tool combinations, the reasoning concerns problematic situations, the actions that are possible in each situation, and the further situations and associated actions to which these might lead.

Semiquantitative Reasoning

The distinction between quantitative and qualitative reasoning is not enough. Recent work in artificial intelligence (AI) and cognitive science (e.g., work on "naive physics") points to the importance of what is often called *qualitative,* but is actually semiquantitative, reasoning (i.e., reasoning in which the direction but not the size of effects of one part of a system on another is known).

Quantitative modeling is familiar in science and mathematics as well as in geography and economics. Qualitative modeling is also known and familiar because of its use in decision games, expert systems, models of grammar, etc., where it allows the expression of rules and structures. By contrast, semiquantitative modeling is new and important. It involves thinking about systems in terms of the rough-and-ready size of things and directions of effects only. Psychological research on causality (Piaget, 1974) provided evidence of children's semiquantitative reasoning. For example, children think that more force makes things go faster, but their reasoning does not necessarily extend to knowing by how much. Work on mental models (Gentner & Stephens, 1983) showed that adults—novices and experts—use semiquantitative reasoning when dealing with complex technological situations. For example, de Kleer and Brown (1983) made a case for this kind of reasoning as essential to envisioning the functioning of machines. But the same clearly applies to reasoning about economic systems, or to social questions about whether increased policing will decrease crime.

Guiding Research Questions

Two main questions guided the research design for this chapter: (a) Can reasoning with modeling tools containing representations (models) of a domain facilitate reasoning in that domain? (b) Are learners helped to reason about a domain by using modeling tools to represent and explore their own ideas about that domain?

RESEARCH DESIGN

The research program was not intended to be either tool- or task-driven. We chose one tool for use in each of the areas of reasoning: quantitative, semiquantitative, and qualitative. These tools were designed for use in both exploratory and expressive tasks. Hardware and software improve faster than research can deliver results. We chose to work with Apple Macintosh machines because we could then have tools using direct manipulation (i.e., pointing and clicking on icons to construct models). We believed that direct-manipulation tools would be easy to learn and understand. Thus, we chose to develop software ideas that might only be usable in schools at the end of the research. As it turns out, Macintosh machines are appearing in schools, and Windows has brought IBM machines up to a similar standard.

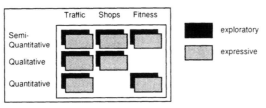

Research design

FIG. 2.1.   Schema representing research design.

TOPICS

We selected three cross-cirricular topics for common use with all three tools, and within which all three types of reasoning can be exhibited. Three such topics, chosen on the grounds of being familiar to children and meaningful to them in terms of a task, were: shops and making a profit, traffic and congestion, and staying healthy and diet. In each case, we needed parallel tasks—one for exploratory work and one for expressive—using the same tool for both. These decisions led to the design shown in Fig. 2.1, in which two cells are missing only for lack of time.

TASKS

In exploratory mode, all tasks ask pupils to work in a "what-if" framework. Several (three or more) points of view about what might happen in reality are put to them, and they are asked if they agree. Thus, the pupils think through a problem in terms of "what happens if you do this or that?", reflect on alternatives, make decisions, and use the tool to see the consequences of decisions. In practical terms, they first inspect a basic model of the situation and then manipulate variables in the model, or additional ones, according to the different points of view, running the model to test the idea. In expressive mode, pupils are encouraged, after having constructed their own model of keeping a shop in profit, reducing congestion in a town, or how to keep fit, to test it from several different points of view (e.g., "In your model, how can you keep profits up even if other things make matters worse?"). In expressive or exploratory modes, pupils are asked to give their views of either the model given or their own model through modifying the model or creating a new one.

PROCEDURE

The time spent with any one pupil is fairly extensive, being spread through a series of sessions, as detailed later. Pupils work on a one-to-one basis with the researcher, and any one pupil completes only one task in a given topic area. The schedule is similar in both expressive and exploratory modes and for all types of reasoning:

1. reasoning about a task without a computer (approximately 30–40 min)
2. introduction to the computer through a drawing task (approximately 30 min)
3. learning to use the tool (approximately 60 min)
4. carrying out a task on a given topic (approximately 60–90 min)

Sessions 1 and 2 are carried out at the same time, with Sessions 3 and 4 done separately but close to one another, and no more than a week apart from the first two sessions. Pupils carrying out expressive tasks are given informal work on the topic. Although most children will have some intuitive knowledge of these topics, we thought it important to provide at least a general-level awareness of the area in which they would construct a model.

SAMPLE

The pupils chosen were between the ages of 11–14, with the main focus on 12- to 13-year-olds. There were three main reasons for the choice of the sample: (a) some research with modeling has already been carried out with 16- to 18-year-olds; (b) with the introduction of General Certificate of Secondary Education (GCSE) in the United Kingdom, classes of 14- to 16-year-olds were not obtainable because the research might interrupt the curriculum and assessment program; and (c) we had particular interest in the 12- to 13-year-olds because evidence shows the beginnings of abstract ways of thinking at about this age. We planned eight pupils in each cell in the previous design, but limitation of time reduced this to five in each cell for the quantitative and qualitative tools. Pupils came from the London area: one middle and three comprehensive schools. They were selected by their teachers based on being near average ability, excluding the extremes and those with much previous computer experience.

SEMIQUANTITATIVE REASONING: RESEARCH FINDINGS

The focus of this section is the classroom research into children's reasoning while working with a semiquantitative tool because there is little or no research of this kind in the field.

Semiquantitative Tool and Tasks

No suitable practical semiquantitative tool existed when we began the research. One source of ideas was the notion of *causal loop diagrams,* which form part of the metaphor used in the system dynamics thinking behind STELLA (see e.g., Roberts, Anderson, Deal, Garet, & Shaffer, 1983). Another more general source was thinking in AI about qualitative reasoning about processes of causal change (e.g., de Kleer & Brown, 1983; Forbus, 1983; Kuipers, 1982).

A direct manipulation tool (IQON) was developed in SMALLTALK for making models, but in which no mathematics is needed to create the relationships between variables. IQON allows the user to represent a system in terms of interacting variables, specifying the relations between them. Variables are depicted as boxes, and the relations between them are depicted as arrows linking one box to another. A plus link says that one variable being high causes the one to which it is linked to slowly increase; if low, the effect is reversed. A minus link says the opposite. All variables have a middle, normal level at which they have no effect on others. Links can be made stronger or weaker (see Fig. 2.2).

Tasks were written to encourage semiquantitative reasoning by presenting points of view expressed on problems in semiquantitative terms. An example from our tasks is: "Member of the Local Environmental Group: 'Cars carrying one or two people take up too much space on the roads. So we want to increase public transport. That will reduce congestion by making more efficient use of the roads.'" The semiquantitative tasks were well understood by the majority of pupils, who would argue points of view with which they disagreed. They were surprised when a point of view they supported had consequences the opposite of what was intended when run on the computer. Pupils worked at tasks for up to an hour without their interest waning.

Expressive Mode: Building, Testing, and Modifying Models

All pupils attempted the task, creating a model. Nearly all were reasonably successful. In building models, there were some difficulties in understanding

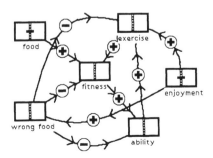

FIG. 2.2.   Thirteen-year-old Anthony's IQON model for fitness and health.

negative relationships. Most pupils can think of several relevant variables when building their model, most containing between four and six variables. Pupils can think of ways in which variables affect one another, with no model containing any variable not linked to some other. Three quarters of the models averaged one or more linkages for every variable. Some pupils' thinking went beyond simple effects of one thing on another, with about half of the models showing considerable interdependence and variables affecting one another in multiple ways or with feedback. Variables were often first imagined as objects, events, actions, or properties. But in reasoning about them, pupils would often convert them to amounts (e.g., *cars* became *number of cars*). Evidence of pupils thinking in terms of models and modeling came from: testing a model, modifying a model to improve results, formally manipulating a model, reflecting on a model, and identifying modeling strategies. When testing a model, pupils used a number of approaches: manipulating variables, comparing results with reality, and formulating and testing hypotheses. The majority of pupils could manipulate models to make simple tests (e.g., increasing profits in their shop mode). On a more complex test, just over half carried out the test or made some sensible attempt, whereas the others were puzzled by accidental results of their manipulations or had difficulty knowing which manipulations to make. Two thirds of the pupils building models either modified their original model or built a new one. Most modified or made new models that were more complex than the original ones.

Exploratory Mode: Exploring and Modifying Models

On the exploratory tasks, pupils needed to understand systems of relationships including complex feedback. The simplest model contained one positive (destabilizing) feedback loop; other models contained several interacting feedback loops, both positive and negative. The fitness model is an example of the models with which pupils worked (see Fig. 2.3). This system is composed of three feedback loops. All three go through the variable *excess food over need*. There is one stabilizing, negative feedback loop from *excess food over need*, through

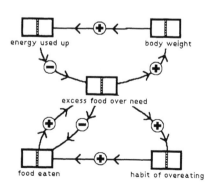

FIG. 2.3. Fitness model presented to pupils in exploratory work.

body weight, and *energy used up* back to *excess food over need* (in the upper half of the system). There is a positive destabilizing loop from *excess food over need,* through *habit of overeating,* and *food eaten* back to *excess food over need* (in the bottom half of the system). Within the positive loop, there is a small negative stabilizing loop (*excess food over need/food eaten*).

The majority of pupils appropriately chose and manipulated the variables relevant to achieving a goal. Pupils had some difficulties with the tool; for example, they often neglected indirect effects of a variable on other variables. Reasoning with feedback loops showed how far pupils saw a model as an interconnected system and reasoned about it as a system. Overall, the majority of pupils took some account of feedback loops. There was much variety in the use or nonuse of feedback loops in reasoning. Any pupil might use any strategy both to cope with and avoid reasoning about feedback. Tasks differed in how pupils managed to deal with feedback. On the shop model with one feedback loop, about half avoided thinking about the whole loop, considering only the effect of the part that suited their argument. On other more complex models, only a minority avoided considering feedback at all, and only a minority coped with it in most of their thinking. About half paid some attention to feedback, but not consistently.

When invited to express their own ideas on the exploratory task, only one pupil created a new model. All others accepted the main features of the model given, although over half made modifications, adding links and/or variables. Modifications added extra components to a model, and pupils never attempted to simplify a model further. Hence, although models were larger than the original, they were less interdependent because of extra independent variables.

Reasoning: In Exploratory or Expressive Modes

Noncausal reasoning dominated pupils' commentaries when following a model running, and such commentaries are screen-bound (i.e., tied to the computer screen). Pupils used causal reasoning when explaining why models produce results, often moving to noncausal reasoning when faced with unanticipated results.

In the expressive mode, when pupils reasoned with their own models, those with complex models used sophisticated reasoning. Pupils with simpler models used sophisticated reasoning if the model was interlinked, but models with just one variable influenced by others tended to limit reasoning to simple causal connections. Some pupils could not cope with the complexity of their own models—where effects were not limited to simple connections, but affected the whole system—because results were unexpected and difficult to reason about.

In the exploratory mode, when pupils reasoned about models, the majority used causal reasoning, with half of these achieving complex interconnected patterns of reasoning, and less than half mixing causal and other reasoning. A minority of pupils reasoned mainly noncausally, attending only to how the model on the screen was behaving. Causal reasoning and reasoning about the model as a connected system containing feedback were related. Pupils who produced sophisticated causal reasoning mainly coped with feedback loops, seeing the system as a whole. Pupils who reasoned mainly noncausally, looking just at how the model behaved, also generally avoided thinking about feedback loops. About half reasoned causally, sometimes dealing with feedback loops and sometimes avoiding them.

Examples of Pupils' Work

In the expressive mode, while carrying out tests with her shop model, Nesta put her model (Fig. 2.4) into an unexpected oscillation by decreasing the independent variable (*helpful staff*) and the dependent variable (*prices*). She tried to make sense of this situation with the following casual argument: "I've put the prices down a tiny bit, and this (decreasing *helpful staff*) a tiny bit past (down) so there's less *helpful staff* so they (the *customers*) would come because of the prices but maybe not because of the staff (it is understood that customers affect profits)." Not content with this explanation, she went on: "I suppose sometimes the customers would come and sometimes they wouldn't because it's not anything special, like they could go somewhere else that's cheaper. That's why it keeps going up and down—sometimes they might come and sometimes they might not." Here, faced with a difficulty, the pupil uses her own knowledge of shops and shopping, not represented in the model to explain the unexpected result.

Another pupil, Burgess, built a first model but, when carrying out tests, realized that he had not adequately represented the situation in his model. (In Fig. 2.5 the negative links *traffic lights* to *congestion* and *car parks* to *cars* were not included in original model.) Burgess then modified his model and argued about it. The amount of cars on the road and the amount of cars in the car parks are affected, but get changed by the other things that go on.

Also in the expressive mode, Anthony, whose model was used as an example of IQON (Fig. 2.2), carried out seven trials with it. However, these trials did not enlighten him to any great extent about the behavior of the model because of his difficulty in thinking about how to carry out trials systematically. On the second

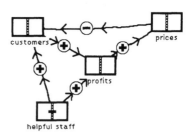

FIG. 2.4.   Nesta's shop model.

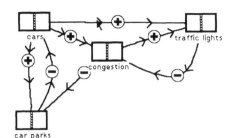

FIG. 2.5. Burgess' second model.

trial, he commented: "It's really hard because they all affect each other—*ability* went right down, *exercise* went right down, *enjoyment* stayed the same, *wrong foods* stayed the same, and *food* stayed the same. So the real key ones are *exercise* and *ability*. That has really helped me. Now I know *exercise* and *ability* are the key ones. I'm slowly getting there." He also later remarked: "This would work on a slightly simpler model."

On the exploratory tasks, we look at one pupil's attempt to explain some of the feedback loops in the fitness model shown in Fig. 2.2. Henrietta was preoccupied with the feedback loop between *food eaten* and *excess food over need*. She argued (as shown in Fig. 2.6):

(addition of variable effort to diet into food eaten)
The *excess food* (1) is going up, so is the *body weight* (2), the *energy used up* is going up because of *body weight*. (3) The *excess food* is going down, which means that the *food eaten* should go down but it doesn't (4) (She then looks at graph of *food eaten*). It (*food eaten*) didn't go down at all, well it went down a little and then back (5), it's because of the habit of overeating, which would make *food eaten* go up (6), and the *excess food over need* would go up (7) so it (*food eaten*) wouldn't really go down because it's a negative loop (8).

But she did not go on to explain what she meant by a *negative loop*.

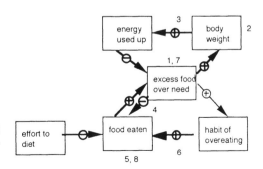

FIG. 2.6. Henrietta's attempt to understand a negative feedback loop.

GENERAL DISCUSSION OF OVERALL RESEARCH
AND CONCLUSION

Although we have only discussed in detail the results of the semiquantitative task–tool situations, we now situate these in relation to the overall results of the whole program.

Models Constructed or Explored

Some pupils can build rather complex semiquantitative models, although a similar number restrict themselves to simple models. Some pupils can move toward seeing such models as interconnected systems. With qualitative models, half or more of the pupils could conceive of such a kind of model as a connected system of alternative choices and consequences. However, some saw it simply as a set of narratives. All pupils in quantitative expressive tasks could build some model with the help of the tool, although many of them were limited or unsatisfactory in some respects. Models built were task-dependent, with pupils' prior knowledge being important. Many pupils saw a quantitative model as generating one answer. Some tested constraints on results using extreme cases.

Generally, pupils can engage in modeling tasks of reasonable complexity. Some have just the beginnings of the idea of a model and are ready to be taught more. They can explore models provided for them and can construct models of their own. All pupils could construct a model, even if limited, in all expressive tasks with all tools.

Reasoning

Given suitable IQON models to explore, some 11- to 14-year-old pupils produced quite sophisticated causal reasoning about complex systems. Those who produced sophisticated causal reasoning could also begin thinking about the nature of complex feedback systems. Pupils also focused on an IQON model just as itself, without interpretation, treating it as a phenomenon. Some attempted to understand the model in terms of its structure. Given suitable tasks, 11- to 14-year-old pupils contributed ideas about the relation of IQON models to reality. This reasoning may import reality to explain the model.

With qualitative reasoning, pupils needed to express both consequences and prior conditions. A good proportion of pupils considered a sequence of situations and actions as arising from localized choices that would have led to a different sequence. They also compared sequences in terms of themes they had in common. Fewer saw the whole qualitative model as an organized structure of alternatives. Much qualitative thinking initiates in narrative, and it is not trivial for 11- to 14-year-old pupils to move toward simplifying and dissecting a narrative into parts composed of discrete alternative situations and actions. With quantitative reasoning, several pupils had problems handling large negative and decimal numbers with compound quantities such as speeds, rates of flow, densities, and ratios. Some dealt with these by regarding them as "situated quantities" associated with concrete situations. This strategy can lead to intensive quantities being regarded, like extensive quantities, as additive. Quantitative variables were often treated as alterable constants.

Strategies for quantitative problem solving included forward reasoning, global planning, and trial and error. Forward reasoning tended to produce limited, but correct, models or results. Global planning, which was not common, tended to produce broadly conceived, but incorrect, models. Trial and error, frequent in exploratory tasks, often productively used the power of the computer to reach a result with little effort.

Overall, 11- to 14-year-old pupils engaged in quite complex reasoning about relationships and cause and effect in systems of practical interest and concern. They thought most naturally in terms of objects and events, not variables. Pupils have much to learn about the relationship of models to reality. The stimulus of using a modeling system can provoke ideas that can be built on, especially where pupils have made their own models. They had difficulty with the necessary simplification or idealization involved in any model. Semiquantitative reasoning is a natural form of expression for these pupils. With it, they managed to reason about quite complex phenomena. It was used in all types of task.

Exploratory and Expressive Activities

When pupils explored IQON models, the models were appreciably more complex than ones the pupils constructed. Complex IQON models encouraged a number of pupils to develop their reasoning. When expressing their own ideas in IQON, pupils saw their models as fallible, and thus were readier to consider redesigning the model than when exploring models given to them. When pupils in semiquantitative expressive tasks improved their models, they made more interesting changes than did pupils in exploratory tasks beginning to engage in modeling.

In qualitative tasks, pupils' experiences of expressive and exploratory modes with the qualitative tool were rather different. In expressing a model, they had to simplify and dissect rich and complex narratives into a structure of alternatives. In the exploratory mode, they had to synthesize existing sets of choices and consequences into wholes, so as to compare and evaluate them. In quantitative tasks, pupils profitably explored much more complex quantitative problems than when model-unaided. Quantitative expressive model building can be difficult because there is a lot to go wrong, and partial results may not be helpful. The difficulties of quantitative tasks often lead pupils to think only locally, thus not seeing a model as a whole.

In summary, pupils can understand more complex models given to them to explore than they can themselves make. Pupils who are given a model to explore may be reluctant to change it much, but can criticize it. Having made a model of their own, they are often willing to change or reconstruct it.

Relation to Reality

The majority of pupils broadly used reference to the real world, and to their own knowledge and experience, in a reasonable and appropriate manner. One advantage of having tasks based on everyday knowledge was that it permitted and valued the use of pupils' ordinary knowledge and experience. The more pupils wished to explain and interpret models, the more they tended to seek reasons in the real world. This was not without problems. Sometimes pupils would suggest a real-world event, not in any way represented in the model, as a reason for an effect of the model.

Topics

Personal knowledge of the fitness topic, which was large and well assimilated, found easy expression with the semiquantitative tool, but hindered use of the quantitative tool, making it difficult for pupils to take a quantitative model seriously. Where knowledge seemed to be less well articulated (traffic), the tools captured and exposed through the models the simplicity of the knowledge structure. Where knowledge of the topic was fairly extensive but not too well understood (shops), attempts to express complex but undigested ideas revealed pupils' difficulties in fully understanding the tool.

General Implications

We believe that the tasks we produced have potential value as benchmarks to indicate what 11- to 14-year-old pupils can be expected to do. Semiquantitative thinking should be given a greater and better recognized role in teaching. IQON models should be used to teach about formal structures (e.g., how feedback can lead to stability, oscillation, or runaway). They could provide useful opportunities to discuss the relation between models and reality, and about control of variables. The possibilities for computational tools to be used to teach about models as formal entities, whose behavior follows from their structure, deserve investigation. In planning semiquantitative modeling activities, opportunities for exploration and expression should be provided. In qualitative modeling, exploring a model and making one's own are valid, but different, activities; both need to be applied. For quantitative modeling, one must expect expressive work to be much simpler than that which can be achieved in exploratory work, but nevertheless useful.

Implications: Tools

In retrospect, the decision to develop an entirely new tool, IQON, for a novel way of doing modeling appears to have been justified. Young pupils of average ability did constructive and interesting work with this tool. Where they had great difficulty in constructing any complex quantitative models, they could manage complexity in IQON. IQON also provided opportunities for the pupils to learn more about some fundamental aspects of modeling. They still need to distinguish variables from objects and events. They have yet to grasp how feedback works in a system. They still find it hard to think of a system as a whole. We appear to have introduced IQON at an age where much useful work with it is possible, leading later to more intensively mathematical kinds of model.

Good-quality quantitative tools exist in quantity for students 16 years and older. However, there is a lack of good tools accessible to younger children for dealing with realistic problems. Younger pupils need a modeling tool that starts from their understanding of the world in terms of objects and events. Qualitative tools seem easy to conceive and develop, but are in fact difficult. Narrative tools are not hard to use, but narrative does not model. There is a need to experiment further with logic-based tools.

Implications: Tasks

The kinds of tasks we developed seem to be useful exemplars of curriculum or teaching materials using computational modeling tools. They readily provoke discussion and argument, even in the researcher–child relationship, and might be useful for work in pairs or groups. They are not useful if one is concerned about teaching a range of correct models. They are useful if one is concerned about teaching what modeling is, the relation of models to reality, and how a model or modeling system looks at the world in its own special way. They are useful if one wants children to produce, discuss, try out, and criticize ideas.

Finally, with the right tools, children of 11 or 12 years can make their own models, and our data suggest that if they do so they will understand better that a model is simplified, fallible, and can be changed or may need to be remade altogether. In this way, they may be helped to see what exploring a model is all about, through the experience of expressing it themselves.

REFERENCES

Bliss, J., & Ogborn, J. (1989). Tools for exploratory learning. *Journal for Computer Assisted Learning, 5*, 37–50.

Bliss, J., & Ogborn, J. (1992a). Reasoning supported by computational tools. *Computers in Education, 18*(1–3), 1–9.

Bliss, J., & Ogborn, J. (1992b). Tools for exploratory learning end of award report. ESRC

Bryant, P. (1982). The role of conflict and agreement between intellectual strategies in children's ideas about measurement. *British Journal of Psychology, 73*, 243–251.

de Kleer, J., & Brown, J. S. (1983). Assumptions and ambiguities in mechanistic mental models. In D. Gentner, & A. Stevens (Eds.), *Mental models* (pp. 155–190). Hillsdale, NJ: Lawrence Erlbaum Associates.

de Kleer, J., & Brown, J. S. (1985). A qualitative physics based on confluences. In J. R. Hobbs, & R. C. Moore (Eds.), *Formal theories of the commonsense world* (pp. 109–184). Norwood, NJ: Ablex.

Forbus, K. D. (1983). Qualitative reasoning about space and motion. In D. Gentner, & A. Stevens (Eds.), *Mental models* (pp. 53–72). Hillsdale, NJ: Lawrence Erlbaum Associates.

Gentner, D., & Stevens, A. L. (Eds.). (1983). *Mental models*. Hillsdale, NJ: Lawrence Erlbaum Associates.

Kuipers, B. (1982). *Commonsense reasoning about causality: Deriving behaviour from structure.* Unpublished manuscript, Tufts University, Medford, MA.

Ogborn, J. (1990). A future for modeling in science education. *Journal of Computer-Assisted Learning, 6*(1), 103–112.

Piaget, J. (1974). *Les Explications Causales* [Understanding Causality]. Paris: Presses Universitaires de France.

Roberts, N., Anderson, D., Deal, R., Garet, M., & Shaffer, W. (1983). *Introduction to computer simulation.* Reading, MA: Addison-Wesley.

APPENDIX A: THE LONDON MENTAL MODELS GROUP

The research proposal was put forward by the London Mental Models Group, which was established by Dr. Joan Bliss in spring 1986 at King's College London. It is a multidisciplinary group involving staff in science and mathematics education, cognitive psychology, linguistics, educational computing, expert systems, and artificial intelligence. It is also multiinstitutional, drawing members from four institutions: King's College London, Institute of Education, Imperial College, and Kingston Polytechnic. Its major interest is in modeling cognition; another important interest has been in the nature of explanation. It meets twice termly on a regular basis, and runs seminars and training for its members. For the Tools for Exploratory Learning Program, there are two co-directors: Joan Bliss at King's College and Jon Ogborn at the Institute of Education, who are also part of a management team with Derek Brough, Imperial College, Jonathan Briggs, Kingston Polytechnic, and Harvey Mellar, Institute of Education. The team also includes Rob Miller, Caroline Nash, Dick Boohan, Tim Brosnan, and Babis Sakonidis.

3 The Use of Multiple, Linked Representations to Facilitate Science Understanding

Robert B. Kozma
SRI International

Joel Russell
Oakland University

Tricia Jones
Nancy Marx
Joan Davis
University of Michigan

Since the 1960s, the information-processing approach to cognitive psychology has characterized thinking in terms of internal mental structures, or representations, and the operations that are performed on these structures (Newell & Simon, 1972). An important component of this approach has been research on expertise (Chi, Feltovich, & Glaser, 1989; Glaser & Chi, 1988; Larkin, McDermott, Simon & Simon, 1980). This research has provided us with detailed descriptions of the mental structures and processes that characterize how experts understand a domain (e.g., physics, chemistry, etc.), and how this understanding differs from that of novices.

More recently, research and theory in cognitive science have expanded these notions beyond internal characteristics of the individual to include the social, physical, and technological worlds within which experts operate (Greeno, 1989; Norman, 1990; Pea, 1993; Perkins, 1993; Resnick, 1987). Problem solving, thinking, and understanding are characterized as interactions between person and environment. These processes can be viewed from two frames of reference: psychological and sociocultural.

The psychological view emphasizes knowledge as a personal construction, in which understanding influences and is influenced by an individual's interaction with people and artifacts in the environment. An example of this is the physicist in Larkin's (1983) study who was given a written description of a problem situation in mechanics. He began his work by drawing a diagram, in which some symbolic elements represented the objects and spatial arrangements mentioned in the problem statement and others (i.e., force vectors) corresponded to conceptual entities (i.e., Newtonian force) that were evoked from memory. The physicist reasoned with this representation, moving back and forth between the components of the constructed diagram and the requirements of the solution held in memory. When conflicts between the representation and potential solution could not be resolved, he abandoned the diagram and created one that represented an alternative and ultimately successful solution. Finally, he used a mathematical equation that corresponded to the solution to produce the appropriate numerical answer.

The sociocultural view emphasizes knowledge as a social construction, in which understanding is negotiated collectively by people in interaction with each other and with cultural artifacts in the environment. This view is characterized by the activities of researchers in a genetics laboratory studied by Amman and Knorr-Cetina (1990). Scientists in the laboratory gathered around recently exposed X-ray films of DNA or RNA fragments. As they examined the film, they pointed, made verbal references to marks on the film, drew inferences, raised objections, asked questions, returned to the film, provided replies, and so on until a conclusion—not necessarily consensus—was reached. This socially constructed sense of "what was seen" was reproduced when the data were transformed into evidence that appeared in scientific papers or oral presentations. That is, in preparing these data for publication, the visual images that accompanied the text were edited, enhanced, and annotated in ways that reflected the meaning constructed by these scientists' interactions.

These binocular, psychological, and sociocultural perspectives converge on the same phenomena: symbolic expressions—the production and interpretation of verbal discourse, diagrams, pictures, charts, tables, and so on. These external representations are composed of organized markings or utterances that sometimes refer to objects and events in the social and physical world, sometimes refer to conceptual entities and cognitive operations in the minds of individuals, and sometimes refer to other symbolic expressions (Greeno, 1989). Symbolic expression is the way people in a culture commerce in understanding; it is the *linqua franca* with which a culture enacts itself (Geertz, 1973) and by which individuals understand the culture (Gardner, 1993; Vygotsky, 1978). It is the interface between knowledge in the world and knowledge in the head.

In this chapter, we examine the role that various symbolic representations play in understanding science—specifically chemistry and chemical equilibrium. We look at how expertise in a domain (or lack thereof) influences the understanding of symbolic expressions. We consider how designed symbolic environments—specifically one using multiple, linked representations—can facilitate novices' learning. We describe a software environment that instantiates this approach, and we analyze formative evaluation data that support the hypothesized mechanisms of learning.

REPRESENTATIONS AND EXPERTISE

The understanding of symbolic expressions depends on characteristics of both the expression and the users. Expertise is a crucial variable. On the one hand, those who are experts in a domain use their rich knowledge base to supplement information in the environment. On the other hand, novices have an incomplete and often inaccurate understanding of the domain, and this influences what they "see" in symbolic expressions.

For example, in the Larkin (1983) experiment, when novices are confronted with a problem statement, they build a mental representation, as do experts. However, whereas experts see "forces" in such problems, novices see only objects, such as the "blocks," "pulleys," and so on. The mental representations that novices construct with the problem statement are compared primarily or exclusively of these familiar, visible objects and events. Novices operate on these representations in ways that correspond to events or operations in the real world; they envision "pushing" and "pulling" the carts and blocks. But because these mental models do not have the conceptual entities contained in the representations of experts, they are insufficient to determine a solution.

On occasion, novices may resort to the use of formal symbolic representations, as do experts. Most often, this is an equation selected by mapping surface features of the problem statement onto example problems in the textbook (Chi & Bassok, 1988). But again, for novices these symbolic expressions do not correspond to an understanding of the constructs and principles of the domain, as they do for experts. Rather, students map the results of mathematical operations back onto the algebraic expressions. In effect, they engage in a form of symbolic puzzle solving.

The effects of expertise on the understanding of artifacts and symbols encountered in the environment can be illustrated in the domain of chemistry. Let us examine a hypothetical interaction that might occur between chemists and an object that they encounter in the real world of the chemistry laboratory: a vessel of unknown reddish-brown gas. Chemists may view this object and build a mental model of a "gaseous system" of indeterminate composition, consisting of one or more substances. They might infer that if the vessel contained more than one substance, they could be continually reacting at certain rates, determined in part by the temperature and pressure of the system and in part by properties of the substances. They could infer that at a stable temperature and pressure, these substances would be at "equilibrium," reacting at equal and opposite rates such that the adjusted ratio of their partial pressures is a constant.

If they heated the system and observed a color change, they might conclude that, indeed, the system is composed of more than one substance, and these undergo a shift in equilibrium due to the change in temperature. They might further state that whereas the original temperature and pressure were more favorable to one of the substances, the new temperature and pressure are more favorable to the other.

Let us say that, in addition, our chemists are supplied with the following symbolic expressions related to our gaseous system:

$$2NO_2(g) \rightleftharpoons N_2O_4(g) \qquad \Delta H° = -58 \text{ kJ}$$

They would now know that the system is composed of "nitrogen dioxide" and "dinitrogen tetroxide" in "equilibrium," and that this is an "exothermic reaction." They probably know that nitrogen dioxide is frequently found in the air around major cities as a result of the reaction of oxygen and the nitric oxide produced by automobile engines, that it is a principle component of photochemical smog, and that it accounts for the brownish color in the vessel.

However, students have little stored information, and the information that is stored may be inaccurate relative to that of chemists, or it may not be stored in a way that is evoked by certain situations or symbolic expressions. For example, in observing the vessel described previously, students may only form an internal representation of "a gas." Their representations of the phenomenon may not include the possible existence of more than one substance. A change of color over time may only mean that "something is happening." They might think that one property of the solitary substance is that it turns color when heated. If students' internal representations contain more than one substance, they may react in response to heat or some other change, but stop reacting when a new temperature is reached. These mental representations may not exhibit the dynamic characteristics of the chemists' "equilibrium system." Some of these statements correspond to the results of our initial research on students' understanding of chemical equilibrium (Kozma, Russell, Johnston, & Dershimer, 1990).

If students are given the symbolic expression noted earlier, they might say that it is a "chemical reaction" of "$2NO_2$" and "N_2O_4." They may not know the chemical names of these compounds or their properties. They may not know that one is the "dimer" of the other. Despite this, they might know that the "$\rightleftharpoons$" symbol means the system is in equilibrium, and they might be able to manipulate this equation to correctly predict the direction of "shift" in the equilibrium if the system were heated. In our initial study (Kozma et al., 1990), a significant number of students used these symbols "correctly," yet many held the misconception that the reaction stops at equilibrium.

REPRESENTATIONS AND LEARNING

Without the additional information that is contained in the minds of experts, the internal representation constructed by novices must rely heavily on and be severely constrained by the information that is contained in the world or in symbolic expressions. Novice understanding of physical phenomena is frequently based on the "literal," or surface, features of the situation. For example, it may be that because the color stops changing in the previous reaction, students conclude that the reaction stops at equilibrium.

Also, the literal features of symbolic expressions, as used by experts, frequently fail to convey to novices the information that experts have in their heads. The literal features of symbol systems frequently have only an arbitrary relationship to their field of reference (Goodman, 1976). For example, there is nothing literally dynamic about the symbol used to indicate equilibrium (i.e., "⇌") that would lead students to think that equilibrium is dynamic.

Literal features of information in the environment do not convey underlying structure, and expert symbolic expressions fail to provide literal information sufficient for understanding. This state leaves those charged with the education of novices in a profound dilemma: How can symbolic expressions (i.e., instructional materials) facilitate novices' learning when their understanding of such expressions draws heavily on an incomplete or inaccurate knowledge of the domain? Our response to this dilemma is an environment that uses multiple, linked representations. Some of the representations in this environment are designed with literal features that correspond to those in the real world, some are designed to correspond to the symbolic expressions used by experts, and some are designed to correspond to the conceptual entities and events in the minds of experts. These representations are referentially linked in such a way that, in traversing representations, novices elaborate on their initial understanding to include the conceptual entities and symbolic expressions used by experts.

For example, one symbolic expression of a chemical system at equilibrium might be an animation that uses literal objects (e.g., balls of different colors) that move around, collide, and change upon collision. These changes could continue in both directions at the same rate. The literal features of this symbolic representation would more closely represent the characteristics of an expert understanding of equilibrium than do the literal features of a chemical equation or a verbal description of the construct. To make this animated representation "chemical," it may need to be linked in some symbolic way to other representations of the chemical phenomena, such as real-world chemical reactions (or video presentations of them) and the conventional chemical-symbolic expressions used by experts.

The linking could be accomplished by any of a variety of symbolic conventions that would allow students to map literal features of one representation onto those of another. For example, the number and relative location of symbolic entities could be the same in both representations. The color of entities in one representation might be the same as those in another. The onset of an event in one representation could coincide with the onset of an event in another, and so on. This common information would serve two cognitive functions: It would increase the likelihood that redundant information be stored in memory, and it would provide a cognitively useful means for traversing the multiple representations. Students could use this common literal information to create identities across representations—that something in one representation is in some way "the same" as something in another representation.

Information in one representation would not, of course, be completely identical to that in another (otherwise the representations would not be different). Having used the common literal features to traverse representations, students then encounter information in the second representation that is in some way "different" from that in the first. The unique literal features of this representation express some aspect of the phenomenon in a way that was not or could not be expressed in the corresponding representation to which it is linked. Students can use this additional information to elaborate the internal representation formed from the first representation, and perhaps with this additional understanding they can return to the first representation to gain additional information.

Five hypotheses follow from this analysis:

1. A learner's understanding of a phenomenon will correspond to the literal features of a given representation.
2. The understanding formed with one representation will be elaborated by unique features of a second representation to the extent that these representations share literal features.
3. The shared literal features will be particularly memorable.
4. Students will be able to evoke and use their understanding in response to real-world situations to the extent that literal features in one or more of these representations correspond to those of real-world situations.
5. Students' understanding will be like that of experts to the extent that the literal features in one or more of the representations correspond to the understanding of experts.

THE 4M:CHEM ENVIRONMENT

We have developed a prototype environment called *MultiMedia and Mental Models*, or *4M:Chem*. In this section, we describe the system and show how it implements the multiple, linked representation approach to learning chemical equilibrium. In the subsequent section, we examine preliminary evidence that supports the effectiveness of this approach.

The environment currently includes four chemical systems: a physical equilibrium, a gas-phase equilibrium, a solution equilibrium, and a heterogeneous equilibrium. These are structured progressively so that students can move from a simple mental model of equilibrium to a more elaborate, complex understanding of the concept (White, 1993).

Development on the system continues, but we estimate that in its current form

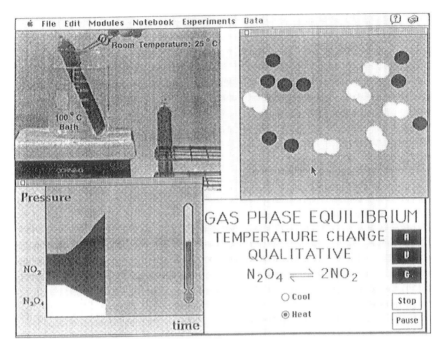

FIG. 3.1.   Screen display of *4M:Chem* showing multiple, linked representations (original in color).

it would take up to 8 hours in lecture and another 5–6 hours in laboratory sessions to thoroughly explore the completed portions. It is designed both for use with projection equipment in the lecture hall and individual work stations in classroom laboratories. In lecture, it is designed to make the class more interactive and engaging. In the classroom laboratory, it allows students, working individually or in small groups, to conduct structured, in-depth investigations of chemical phenomena.

The symbol systems or representations that we use include: chemical notation, video of the reactions, molecular-level animations, dynamic graphs, displays of absorption spectra, and tabular data (see Fig. 3.1 for a sample screen display). The software allows learners to act on a chemical system and see the results of these actions propagate across the multiple representations. Let us examine how the use of these representations, individually and together, might act to influence understanding.

Symbolic Elements and Events

There is an operational space we present on the screen called the *control window.* It contains one representation of the chemical system that students have selected from a menu of available systems; it is expressed in the standard notation of chemists:

$$N_2O_4(g) \rightleftharpoons 2NO_2(g)$$

The equation expresses a relationship between two symbolic entities. The entities and their relationship are, perhaps, yet to be understood by the students. The buttons present the students with two symbolic actions that can be performed on the system: "heat" or "cool." These symbolic elements and buttons are what we term the *literal features* of the representation.

The students can choose to see the results of their actions in the video (V), graph (G), or animation (A) windows. Let us say that a student decides to heat the chemical system and observe this in the video window.

Connecting to the Real World.   Information in the video window can be characterized in this way: It shows the chemical system, a beaker of water, and an energy source as they would appear in the real-world context of the chemistry laboratory. There is an operation performed on the system: It is put in boiling water. Over time, the system changes color. These are the literal features of this representation.

What mappings are possible so far? Students may make mappings within a symbolic expression. For example, in the control window, students may observe that, in the equation, there are two symbolic elements that have some kind of relationship: "$\rightleftharpoons$." They may make another connection between their symbolic action of clicking a button and the equation that is next to it, such that they are in some way acting on this expression.

Students may also make connections across representations within our environment. They may make the connection that the equation in the control window describes, in some way, the chemical system observed in the video window. They may connect the action they take in the control window with the observed phenomenon in the video window—that the system is being heated.

Other mapping may be made, for example, from the symbolic domain of the instructional system out in the real-world domain. That is, students may see in the video window objects that they encounter in the real world of the laboratory. This may allow them to infer that what happens in the video window corresponds to what would happen in the laboratory. There may also be mappings between the symbolic world and the conceptual domain of the student. That is, the chemical expressions in the control window and the objects they see in the video window may map onto their current mental models of the phenomenon.

Connecting to Graph Representations.   Graphs are important forms of symbolic expression for chemists, yet they are sometimes difficult for students to understand. For example, Mokros and Tinker (1987) found that middle-school students were confused by the graphs' literal features. The graphs these students drew of a bicyclist's speed uphill, downhill, and on level stretches corresponded to the hills and valleys, rather than the bicycle's speed. This problem has been successfully addressed by linking real-time graphic representations to the dynamic phenomena that they represent (Brasell, 1987).

We have incorporated this into our system. In our hypothetical episode, the students choose to "rerun" the experiment, this time observing it both in the video window and the graph window. In the graph window, there are two perpendicular lines labeled *pressure* and *time*. There is a key indicating that the brown area of the graph is "NO_2" and the white area is "N_2O_4." Also in the window is an iconic representation of a thermometer. Over time, the brown area increases at twice the rate that the white area decreases on the graph, and the red line moves up in the thermometer. After a while, the graph's lines level off, and the red line in the thermometer stops moving. These are the literal features.

The key in the graph window labels the chemical substances, and this allows the rather direct mapping to the equation in the control window and, through it, projections to the action in the control window and to objects and events in the video window. A direct connection might be made between the graph window and the video window based on the simultaneous onset of two events. That is, the areas in the graph window begin to increase and decrease when the vessel is put into the bath in the video window, and they continue to change for a while and then level off. The graphs level off at the same time that the color stops changing in the video window. With the additional information from these various sources, the inference may now be made that, indeed, there are two substances in the vessel: NO_2 and N_2O_4. They are both present in some amount at any given time; the relative amounts, or "pressures," of these two substances change while the vessel is in the bath and the color is changing. However, note that the information available so far does nothing to contradict the mental model that we found among some students in our study, which posits that the reaction stops at equilibrium (Kozma et al., 1990). Indeed, it is consonant with this model.

Connecting with Conceptual Entities and Mental Models.   What is missing so far is a representation that corresponds to the molecular-level mental models that chemists have of such systems. This requires the design of a representation that has literal features that more closely correspond to characteristics of expert knowledge structures. The animation is meant to provide a representation that bridges the gap between the novice mental model and the expert model.

The students run the experiment again, this time displaying the animation window as well. In the animation window, the students see two sorts of symbolic entities differing in color and composition (single brown balls and coupled white ones). Initially, there are more white balls than there are brown ones. All of them are moving and colliding with each other and the sides of the box, or container. When balls of different types hit each other, they sometimes change, or "react"; white one split into two single brown ones, and brown ones combine to form white pairs. As the vessel in the video window is put in the bath, the balls in the animation window speed up and hit each other and the sides of the container more often. Collisions more often result in the formation of brown balls than the other way around, hence there are more brown ones than white ones. Finally, when the color of the gas in the vessel stops changing in the video window, the overall numbers of brown and white balls remain constant in the animation window, even though they keep moving and reacting.

Mappings and Inferences

What new inferences can be made based on the literal features within and across representations? The students can now infer that there are two types of substances in the vessel (i.e., NO_2 and N_2O_4), that they are in some sense particulate, that the changes or reactions that take place in the system depend in some way on collisions between these types of particles, that the difference in relative amounts of these substances is reflected by the overall color of the system, that the relative amounts of these substances are dependent on the temperature of the system, and that the reactions continue even when the relative amounts stop changing. This is the phenomenon that experts call *chemical equilibrium.*

However, it is important to remember that the described mappings are only potential. Although the mappings are intended by our design, they may not be apparent to students; mappings within and across representations may not occur. The source of the failure may be perceptual or conceptual. For example, in looking at the video, individual students may not notice the flat object that the beaker of water sits on, or they may not know that this is a hot plate of the sort they encounter in their laboratory. Thus, they may fail to understand that the system is being heated, or they may fail to make a mapping from the video window to the real world. This failure may cascade through the referential web.

Mappings across representations, or from within the system to outside it, may need to be explicitly made or guided by accompanying instruction (Mayer & Anderson, 1992). That is, the students may need to be directed to notice that, as the system is heated and turns brown in the video window, the molecules speed up, collide, and form more brown molecules in the animation window. This explicit mapping across representations is provided and guided by a narrative track built into software, by a user's manual, or by the instructor in lecture. The advantage of a lecturer is that, in addition to providing an explicit mapping across representations, he or she can provide the verbal representation of an expert understanding of the domain, and he or she can do this in interaction with students' questions, predictions, and explanations.

Qualitative and Quantitative Representation

The previous description refers to what we call the *qualitative mode.* But in the *quantitative mode,* students begin to connect their qualitative representations to the more quantitative analyses and representations of chemists. In the quantitative mode, the experiment can be rerun with students specifying their action decisions as numeric amounts (e.g., increase the temperature from 25°C to 30°C, rather than just heat the system). The axes of the graphs are numerically labeled. Students take and record measurements. These data are passed to an integrated spreadsheet, where students can perform statistical analyses. Thus, students engage in a larger set of symbolic manipulations, which is more typical of the formal-symbolic behavior of expert chemists.

FORMATIVE EVALUATION

Although development on the project continues, we have done a preliminary examination of a completed portion of *4M:Chem* to test the linked, multiple representation model. We have studied the use of the software by faculty members in the lecture hall and its effect on student learning. We have also conducted a detailed examination of students' individual use of the system in our research laboratory to test the relationship between the process of student learning and the hypothesized mappings embedded in our design. The data provide initial support for our general approach and the cognitive mechanisms implied by it. They also identify some problems and suggest future directions for our research and development efforts.

Faculty Use

The system was used by two faculty members (not associated with the development project) in different sections of a general chemistry course. Both faculty members practiced using *4M:Chem* prior to their use of it in class. This included a session of approximately 1 hour, during which project staff demonstrated the function of the system, described the curricular objectives, illustrated how it could be used in lecture, and made it available for practice. One of the lecturers spent another 3 hours, during which she practiced using the software on her own and planned her use of it in class.

In both cases, the software was used during two 1-hour lectures on the topic of equilibrium. These were the only lectures given on this topic. The lectures used both qualitative and quantitative experiments in the unit on gas-phase equilibrium. During their lectures, both participating faculty members made heavy use of *4M:Chem* representations. The software was projected on a large screen in front of the class and actively used for nearly the entire lecture time. The instructors spent approximately 70% of their lecture time making direct reference to information presented by the software. The rest of the time was spent generating and referring to additional information presented on the chalkboard or overhead projector.

The lectures focused on three major points related to equilibrium: (a) that equilibrium is dynamic; (b) that Le Chatelier's Principle can be used to predict the results of stresses on the system, such as changes in temperature and pressure; and (c) that the equilibrium constant can be used to quantitatively express the relationship between the concentrations of reactants and products. The professors introduced each of these concepts with the video and the animation in the software, and then later elaborated on the concepts with chemical terminology, equations, and graphs.

For instance, one professor introduced the idea of dynamic equilibrium by pointing out that chemical reactions continue to occur at equilibrium, as shown by the animation. She later wrote the words *dynamic equilibrium* on the board, and wrote the equation of the reaction with double arrows—the standard chemical notation for a reaction that occurs in both directions. Before showing the graph in the software, she wrote equations on the board, elaborating on the connection between the number of molecules (the measure of quantity used in the animation) and the partial pressures (the measure used in the graph). The professor also explained the difference between macroscopic and microscopic views of a reaction, saying, "At the end [the graph] again levels off because it's now at equilibrium. . . . The macroscopic view is that things are static, but the microscopic view of it, the molecular view [pointing to the animation], is that things are still very much moving, which is precisely what the [term] dynamic equilibrium is trying to show."

One role played by our participating professors was to provide students with a verbal representation of chemical equilibrium. They also used verbal statements and direct references (i.e., pointing) to guide students' attention, and to link elements and events across representations in the software and to additional chemical terms and equations written on the board.

Gains in Learning

There were approximately 200 students in one section and 300 students in the other section. Of these 500 students, 295 attended both lectures and responded to both the brief pre- and posttests given during the sessions. There were no control or nontreatment comparison groups for this formative evaluation. The pre- and posttests consisted of five constructed-response questions (students were asked to give brief answers, draw diagrams, and compute answers) that were parallel across the tests. It should be noted, however, that the tests did not count toward their grade, which likely provided little incentive for students to respond thoroughly to the test.

The open-ended responses were coded for the occurrence of any one of 12 possible "correct" conceptual statements. The mean pretest score was 3.18 ($SD = 1.75$) correct statements. The mean posttest score was significantly greater at 5.50 ($SD = 2.49$, $t = 15.61$, $p < .0001$).

Of particular note were the responses on questions related to the nature of a system at equilibrium; there were three questions related to this concept. On the first question, students could have made up to five statements that accurately defined or described a chemical system at equilibrium (the system is dynamic, equal rates in opposite directions, constant concentrations, all species present, and a ratio of the concentrations gives the equilibrium constant). Table 3.1 shows that, for Question 1 on the pretest, only 33.9% of the students made an accurate, error-free statement ($M = .63, SD = .87$). On the posttest, 55.9% (165 students) made one or more accurate statements ($M = .84, SD = .87, t = 3.48, p < .0003$). Of these, 154, or 52.4% of all students, gave an accurate, error-free definition.

Particularly important was the decrease in "misconceptual" statements on the item asking students to describe chemical equilibrium. There were five possible misconceptual statements that students could have made. As a group, students made a mean of .50 ($SD = .60$) misconceptual statements on the pretest. As in our earlier research (Kozma et al., 1990), a large majority of these statements either asserted that concentrations of products and reactants are equal or balanced at equilibrium, or that the reaction comes to a stop at equilibrium. On the posttest, the mean was only .20 ($SD = .43$)—reduction of over 50% ($t = -7.58, p < .0001$).

The second question was in three parts (Q2A, Q2B, and Q2C in Table 3.1). The question provided students with an equation (of two gases reacting to make a third) and a diagram of two glass bulbs (each containing one of the gaseous reactants) that were connected by a closed stopcock. They were then given a second diagram of two empty globes with the stopcock open, and were asked to complete the diagram as it would be at equilibrium. Only 8.1% answered Ques-

TABLE 3.1
Pre- and Posttest Scores for Students Using 4M:Chem in Lecture

| | Equilibrium State (%) | | | | Equilibrium Constant(%) | Factors (%) | |
| | | | | | | Temperature | Pressure |
Test	Q1	Q2A	Q2B	Q2C	Q3	Q4	Q5
Pretest	33.9	8.1	9.5	13.2	12.9	13.2	.7
Posttest	52.4	38.4	40.7	47.1	44.4	33.9	4.7

Note. Q1 = Question 1, Q2A = Question 2A, Q2B = Question 2B, Q2C = Question 2C, Q3 = Question 3, Q4 = Question 4, Q5 = Question 5.

tion 2A correctly on the pretest; 84% of the students answered it incorrectly, and another 7.1% did not answer it. On the posttest, 38.4% diagrammed the correct situation. In Question 2B, students were asked to list the chemical reactions (if any) that would occur at equilibrium. Only 9.5% of the students showed both reactions occurring at equilibrium on the pretest. On the posttest, 40.7% listed both reactions. On Question 2C, students were asked if it were possible to have a bulb containing pure product, and to explain their answer. On the pretest, only 13.2% gave a correct answer and explanation. This increased to 47.1% on the posttest.

We also tested the students' ability to compute the equilibrium constant for a given reaction condition. On the pretest, only 12.9% of the students could calculate the equilibrium constant when given the equation and partial pressures (Q3 in Table 3.1). On the posttest, 44.4% gave the correct response, and another 10.8% gave the correct formula, but made a computational error.

Important to understanding equilibrium is the effect of certain forces on a system at equilibrium (changes in concentration, pressure, and temperature), which is called *Le Chatelier's Principle*. There were two questions related to this principle: one dealing with temperature and the other with pressure. On the pretest, 54.6% of the students correctly predicted the effect of a temperature change on the system, but only 13.2% accompanied their answers with a correct explanation (Q4 in Table 3.1). On the posttest, 78.3% gave the correct answer, and 33.9% accompanied it with a correct explanation. However, we were unsuccessful in helping students understand the effect of pressure on equilibrium. On the posttest, only 21% correctly predicted the effect of a pressure change, and only 4.7% accompanied this with a correct explanation.

In summary, college students come into chemistry courses with an incomplete or inaccurate understanding about characteristics of chemical systems at equilibrium, and about the influence of temperature and pressure on equilibrium. The use of *4M:Chem* in two lecture sections for two 1-hour presentations increased students' understanding of characteristics of systems at equilibrium and the effects of temperature on these systems. Still, the percentage of students that did not understand is surprisingly large. *4M:Chem* was not successful in improving students' understanding of the effect of pressure on equilibrium.

Validating the Mechanisms of Learning

In addition to evaluating the impact of *4M:Chem* on learning outcomes, we wanted to explicitly examine the hypothesized mechanisms by which the software influences the learning process. That is, we wanted to take a detailed look at the interactions between students' internal representations (as exhibited by think-aloud protocols) and the various symbolic representations in the system to see if students made the sorts of connections between features within and across *4M:Chem* representations described in the earlier section.

We selected five students from another section of the general chemistry course whose professor did not use *4M:Chem* in lectures. These students used the system individually in our experimental laboratory. Their exploration of the system was guided by a manual, much as it would be for a homework assignment or an exercise in a laboratory section of the course. The manual suggested manipulations to the chemical systems, and asked students to make predictions, observe results, and make comparisons across the different symbolic expressions that represented the same phenomenon. The manual did not tell the students the "right answer" or explain the results that they got; this was left for the student to do. Students were asked to think aloud during the session. They were given 2 hours to progress through the *4M:Chem* materials on gas-phase equilibrium. The sessions were recorded and later transcribed.

We examined the pre- and posttest scores for each student to identify the particular knowledge gained, and then we identified the corresponding portion of the protocol that seemed associated with the learning event. We were interested in how the students interacted with the system at this point, and, in particular, how they used the literal features of the representations singularly and in combination. This analysis provided initial support for our hypotheses in the learning of two concepts: the characteristics of the state of equilibrium, and the effect of temperature on equilibrium.

Several students improved their understanding of the state of equilibrium as a result of their use of the system. On the pretest, one of our subjects, who we call Mary (all names are fictitious), made three incorrect statements related to the nature of the equilibrium state. She exhibited both "static" and "balanced" misconceptions. But on the posttest, Mary acquired an understanding of equilibrium as a dynamic state, although she still saw it as balanced. Looking at her think-aloud protocols, it is clear that Mary's new understanding of equilibrium as a continuous process was directly affected by the use of the system, particularly the animations and their literal features:

> [The manual asks:] *In this animation are monomers combining to form dimers and dimers associating to form monomers?* Let's hit pause again, um . . . I don't see anything dissociating, I just see well, oh wait, yes I do . . . okay, so I guess that would mean if the monomers are combining, yeah, I could say they're combining with each other and they click together and they become dimers and dimers every once in a while will come apart and form monomers. (Writes: yes.)

On the pretest, Paul responded that, at equilibrium, "there is interaction among the molecules, bumping into each other, etc. but no new compound is formed." On the posttest, he showed both forward and reverse reactions continuing at equilibrium. The protocols suggest that Paul's learning is directly connected to the literal features of the animations:

> *Are dimerization and dissociation still occurring?* Dimerization beats me. It's that one more . . . omigosh . . . I'm watching, watching, watching, watching, shoot, watching out, watching out, watching out, now it looks like the two are turning

into. . . . Stop . . . go back to N_2O_4. Go. I'm watching these two right here and see the two turn into one right there, split up, keep looking for the . . . split up . . . the um looking for the white dimers to split up into NO_2 molecules. There it goes. Keep watching and see if it really splits I can see if it really split. I'm watching, I'm watching, I'm watching . . . try to figure out . . . God, stop . . . motion, try to pause it. Keep looking, trying to pause it, trying to get it to . . . (mumble) two red actually turning into one white. Two red there, two red . . . looking for a white to turn into two red . . . OK, now I can guess that I can say that the (mumble) rate of equilibrium is two . . . monomers going into . . . and then the two dimers (mumble) separating into the two monomers. . . .

Several students also came to understand the effect of temperature on equilibrium. This resulted from using several representations in coordination. While Sue watches the video, she notes: ". . . (mumble) mixture into hot water. The mixture is getting darker, reddish brown, so um . . . as the . . . um . . . mixture is heated, it becomes darker." She connects heating and color change in the video with the motion and shift in the number of molecules in the animation: ". . . mixture into the hot water and as he does so, he um, the molecules are moving a lot more rapidly and the NO_2 is becoming a lot more dominant . . . um (mumble) the um . . . N_2O_4 doesn't exist as much as um. . . ." Finally, she also connects heating in the video with the constant concentration at equilibrium, as expressed by the graph: "Heated . . . the concentration of NO_2 increases while the N_2O_4 decreases. Then it becomes constant because it's at equilibrium and it can't do anything else."

Similarly, Paul comes to understand the effect of temperature on equilibrium through the coordination of the various representations, connecting cooling in the video with its effect on molecular motion and pressure in the animation and pressure in the graph:

Stop and cool it and look at all this stuff, it's cool [video]. That means there should be more of the white dimers going all around [animation] and this should get small [graph, one line] and this right here [graph, second line] should get bigger and it reaches that negative degrees and it equilibriums [sic] and begins to condense so that means that the pressure of both of them's getting smaller . . . because it's maybe starting to go slower. It begins to condense . . . graph. . . .

Failures in Learning

We were also able to use the protocols to specify some dysfunctional relationships between the software and the learning process. This leads to speculations on the limitations of the multiple, linked representation model, and changes in the software system that may improve its effectiveness.

One problem with the multiple, linked representation approach is the excessive demands on the limited capacities of visual perception and attention. First of all, each representation is complex and has many literal features that change over time. Learning a specific aspect of the concept may require attention to a specific literal feature at a specific time; sometimes this does not occur. For example, in her examination of temperature effect, Sue looked at the animation and noticed the increased speed of the molecules and the shift in concentration. But she did not notice the continued reaction at equilibrium. This would require her to observe that, within the animation, there are collisions from time to time, and sometimes these result in reactions. At low temperatures, collisions occur infrequently and result in reactions even less often. Failure to notice their occurrence would be quite possible, and perhaps likely. Because of her attention failure, she continues to misunderstand the nature of the system once it reaches equilibrium.

The complexity of individual representations is compounded by the need to attend to two or more representations, and to simultaneously notice literal features in both. These problems suggest that our system makes significant demands on the visual system. Some of these demands could be off-loaded to the auditory system in ways that could complement and reinforce the visual representations. That is, we could create yet another representation—an auditory one—that would carry time-based information without creating competing demands on visual attention.

For example, we could sound a tone of a certain pitch (or an iconic sound, such as *oomph*) every time there is a collision in the animation that does not result in a reaction. A different pitch could be sounded when a reaction occurs. At equilibrium, the sounds symbolizing reactions would be perceivable, even at low temperatures when the incidence is relatively infrequent. This could be supplemented by a visual event (such as a flash) that would appear at the locations where reactions occur. This could attract visual attention to specific reactions, and their temporal coincidence with the occurrence of the sound symbol would reinforce the meaning of both.

An analysis of the protocols also made it clear why our laboratory students (and perhaps those in the lecture sections) did not learn the effect of pressure change on partial pressures of reagents at equilibrium. First of all, the target concept is inherently difficult to understand; whereas pressure is an experienced phenomenon (blowing up bicycle tires, etc.), partial pressure (the amount of the total pressure due to one reagent or the other) is not something experienced in everyday life. The experiment was also cognitively difficult; a complex series of inferences need to be learned and understood from the experiments. The chain of inferences is manageable for chemists, but it was very difficult for students. When a student failed to make an inference, the experiment no longer made sense, and many students indicated that they were "lost" before they completed the unit. The cognitive demands of the pressure unit were compounded by perceptual ones. The effect that pressure change has on equilibrium is indicated by a change in color—a change that is often quite subtle and difficult to detect even comparing it to a standard. In addition, color reproduction in video is sometimes not faithful, and refraction through the glassware can create several shades of color in the test tubes. Consequently, several students made inaccurate assessments of color during the experiment.

The pressure experiment needs to be redesigned to require fewer inferences, or to provide more support for those inferences that need to remain. But beyond the difficulties of this particular experiment, our data identified important limitations to this approach, relative to human cognitive and perceptual abilities. These limitations need to be honored during the design process. Specifically, representations must be as simple as possible while still containing essential literal features. This may sometimes require the sacrifice of detail that conveys information important for other purposes. This detail can be restored in subsequent units as learning progresses, and increased understanding can more adequately assimilate increasingly complex representations. Visual attention to specific literal features at specific times within and across representations can be supported by audiolinguistic and other auditory representations. Required inferences must be kept to a minimum, relative to student prior knowledge, and must be supported by the instructional materials.

SUMMARY

In this study, as in our earlier study (Kozma et al., 1990), we found that students came into their college chemistry courses with significant problems in their understanding of chemical equilibrium. There was a range of misconceptions related to the state of equilibrium, the effect that temperature and pressure have on equilibrium, and on the quantitative means of representing equilibrium. The use of multiple, linked representations helped students understand these concepts. *4M:Chem* was designed so that the symbolic elements, or "literal features," of one of the representations (a video of the experiment) corresponded to features of the real world of the chemistry laboratory, those of two other representations (chemical symbols and graphs) corresponded to symbolic expressions that chemists use to represent chemical systems, and the literal features of one of the representations (an animation) corresponded to the conceptual entities and mental processes in the minds of experts. These representations were linked by common literal-symbolic elements.

Our design hypothesis is that students act on a chemical system within our environment and use the literal features of a representation to gain an understanding of their actions' effects. The understanding derived from this representation will closely correspond to the symbolic objects and events designed into the representation—its literal features. Students use the common literal features of two representations to traverse from one to the other, and they extend their understanding to include unique features of the subsequent representation. Our intent is that the various representations are designed such that their conjunctive use results in an accurate, expertlike understanding of equilibrium that is evoked in response to real-world situations, and that is used to understand the symbolic expressions of experts.

A formative evaluation of *4M:Chem* in two lectures and in our experimental laboratory resulted in a significant gain in equilibrium understanding and a reduction in misconceptions. Observations of students using the software in the laboratory suggest that this learning was due to the use of the multiple, linked representations in the ways we had intended.

ACKNOWLEDGMENTS

Robert Kozma is the director of the Center for Technology in Learning, SRI International, Menlo Park, CA. Joe Russell is a professor of the Department of Chemistry, Oakland University, Rochester, MI. Tricia Jones, Nancy Marx, and Joan Davis were graduate students in the Instructional Technology Program, School of Education, University of Michigan, Ann Arbor, MI. This chapter was based on presentations made at the NATO Symposium on International Perspectives on the Psychological Foundations of Technology-Based Learning Environments, Crete, Greece, July 1992, and at the 5th EARLI Conference, Aix-en-Provence, September 1993. The project described in this chapter was performed pursuant to grants USE-9150617 and RED-9353614 from the National Science Foundation. The opinions expressed herein do not necessarily reflect the position or policy of the National Science Foundation or the Regents of The University of Michigan.

REFERENCES

Amman, K., & Knorr-Cetina, K. (1990). The fixation of (visual) evidence. In M. Lynch & S. Wolgar (Eds.), *Representation in scientific practice* (pp. 85–122). Cambridge, MA: MIT Press.

Brasell, H. (1987). The effect of real-time laboratory graphing on learning graphic representations of distance and velocity. *Journal of Research in Science Teaching, 24*(4), 385–395.

Chi, M., & Bassok, M. (1988). Learning from examples via self-explanations. In L. Resnick (Ed.), *Knowing, learning, and instruction: Essays in honor of Robert Glaser* (pp. 251–282). Hillsdale, NJ: Lawrence Erlbaum Associates.

Chi, M., Feltovich, P., & Glaser, R. (1981). Categorization and representation of physics problems by experts and novices. *Cognitive Science, 5,* 121–152.

Gardner, H. (1993). *Frames of mind* (2nd ed.). New York: Basic Books.

Geertz, C. (1973). *Interpretation of cultures.* New York: Basic Books.

Glaser, R., & Chi, M. (1988). Overview. In M. Chi, R. Glaser, & M. Farr (Eds.), *The nature of expertise* (pp. xv–xxviii). Hillsdale, NJ: Lawrence Erlbaum Associates.

Goodman, N. (1976). *Languages of art: An approach to a theory of symbol systems* (2nd ed.). Indianapolis, IN: Hackett.

Greeno, J. (1989). Situations, mental models, and generative knowledge. In D. Klahr & K. Kotovsky (Eds.), *Complex information processing* (pp. 285–318). Hillsdale, NJ: Lawrence Erlbaum Associates.

Kozma, R., Russell, J., Johnston, J., & Dershimer, C. (1990, April). *College students' understanding of chemical equilibrium.* A paper presented at the annual meeting of the American Educational Research Association, Boston, MA.

Larkin, J. (1983). The role of problem representation in physics. In D. Gentner & A. Stevens (Eds.), *Mental models* (pp. 75–98). Hillsdale, NJ: Lawrence Erlbaum Associates.

Larkin, J., McDermott, J., Simon, D., & Simon, H. (1980). Expert and novice performance in solving physics problems. *Science, 208,* 1335–1342.

Mayer, R., & Anderson, R. (1992). The instructive animation: Helping students build connections between words and pictures in multimedia learning. *Journal of Educational Psychology, 84,* 444–452.

Mokros, J., & Tinker, R. (1987). The impact of microcomputer-based labs on children's ability to interpret graphs. *Journal of Research in Science Teaching, 24*(4), 369–383.

Newell, A., & Simon, H. (1972). *Human problem solving.* Englewood Cliffs, NJ: Prentice-Hall.

Norman, D. (1990). Cognitive artifacts. In J. M. Carroll (Ed.), *Designing interaction: Psychology at the human-computer interface* (pp. 17–38). New York: Cambridge University Press.

Pea, R. (1993). Practices of distributed intelligence and designs for education. In G. Salomon (Ed.), *Distributed cognitions* (pp. 47–87). New York: Cambridge University Press.

Perkins, D. (1993). Person plus: A distributed view of thinking and learning. In G. Salomon (Ed.), *Distributed cognitions* (pp. 88–110). New York: Cambridge University Press.

Resnick, L. (1987). Learning in school and out. *Educational Researcher, 16*(9), 13–20.

Vygotsky, L. (1978). *Mind in society.* Cambridge, MA: Harvard University Press.

White, B. (1993). ThinkerTools: Causal models, conceptual change, and science education. *Cognition and Instruction, 10*(1), 1–100.

4 Acquisition of Meaning for Arithmetic Structures With the Planner

Baruch B. Schwarz
Mitchell J. Nathan
Lauren B. Resnick
Learning Research and Development Center,
University of Pittsburgh

UNDERSTANDING ARITHMETIC STRUCTURES

Different perspectives generate different conceptions of what it is to understand arithmetic. For this purpose, Ohlsson (1987) distinguished three aspects of arithmetic: theory, activity and language. The theory involves mathematical principles such as *closure, associativity,* or *laws of distribution.* Arithmetic in the activity sense enables the student to apply procedures to compute values of arithmetic functions. To understand arithmetic in the language sense is to understand its symbols and the expressions in which they appear. As in natural language, the study of the semantics of arithmetic symbols leads to the distinction between sense and reference. For instance, the operation of adding has several senses: *combine* expresses that two quantities are joined together, *change* means that a quantity is modified by adding to it a new quantity, and *increase* conveys that a certain quantity is bigger than another by a certain amount (see Carpenter, 1985). However, understanding the referential aspect of addition is being able to identify a referent for "a + b" when "a" and "b" are assigned to referents. Similarly, understanding the referential aspect of multiplication is being able to identify a referent for "a × b" (e.g., an area, or a space of possible couples [a, b]).

Understanding arithmetic means understanding all the aspects listed previously, that is, its theory, activities, and language (the semantics of both its multiple meanings and its referents). Ohlsson (1987) hypothesized that the acquisition of arithmetical understanding starts with the different meanings and referents of symbols and expressions, proceeds to an understanding of the computational procedures, and ends with an understanding of the number system and its prealgebraic properties (see also Nesher, 1989). Educators, developers, and researchers have recognized the importance of linking several representations or illustrations to provide informative feedback on the appropriateness of actions taken (see Kaput, 1987). However, research on the effectiveness of learning procedures or prealgebraic properties through illustrations has proved this method to be questionable sometimes (e.g., learning subtraction via Dienes blocks; Resnick & Omanson, 1987). As stated by Ohlsson, "the main task of an illustration for initial instruction in arithmetic is not to provide an isomorphic procedure to the arithmetical procedure, because (a) isomorphism is hard to achieve, (b) if the isomorphism is imperfect, there is no reason to expect transfer from the illustrative procedure to the target procedure, and (c) if the isomorphism is perfect, there is no reason to expect the illustrative procedure to be easier to learn" (p. 310). The main hypothesis proposed here is that the primary function of an illustration in teaching arithmetic is to help the young learner understand the language of mathematics by providing referential semantics. The first function of having referential semantics for a mathematical concept is, we believe, to give the learner something from which to abstract. Another function is to trigger the formation of correct representations (situation model and problem model[1]) for arithmetic and prealgebra word problems. The last function is checked in the present study. In the next section, we present an illustration that is intended to provide referential semantics for arithmetic. This chapter describes a comparative study to assess understanding word problems. Although several researchers linked performance at recall tests to understanding word problems (e.g., Cummins, Kintsch, Reusser, & Weimer, 1988; Mayer, 1982), the method was refined to include the use of clues in the recall test. Therefore, the conclusions drawn from this study are about the efficiency of the Planner, as well as the appropriateness in the use of cued recall tests to measure understanding for students using illustrations to learn mathematical concepts.

DESCRIPTION OF THE PLANNER

The Planner is based on a primitive computerized environment, TRAINWORLD (Peled & Resnick, 1988). This system was elaborated to enable students to plan and solve arithmetic word problems. Many researchers analyzed children's competence and cognitive development on such problems (see Carpenter, 1985; Carpenter & Moser, 1982; Vergnaud, 1983). These studies showed three meanings for *addition* alone: addition as an increment that changes quantities (referred

---

[1] A situation model is a special kind of mental model in which all the objects of the situation and relationships among them are represented. When a formal structure is created, it is called a problem model.

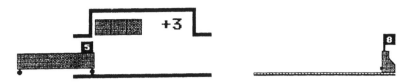

FIG. 4.1. Representing a *change* problem with the Planner.

to as *change* in the following), addition as a combination of two quantities (referred to here as *combine*), and addition as a means to compare between two quantities (referred to here as *compare*). The system developed was sensible to such meanings (for addition, and for other operations).

Description of the System's Objects

The environment consists of trains, tracks, and machines. The trains represent numbers, the tracks are used to designate goals in solving word problems, and the machines represent operations, that is, they correspond to the senses of the operations—(*change, join/separate, increase/compare,* etc.). TRAINWORLD displays these different senses of addition, subtraction, and multiplication. As an example, consider the following *change* problem: "Five children were playing a game together. Three more children joined them in the middle of the game. How many children participated in the game?"

This problem is represented by a 5 long train that is loaded with 3 units by a load machine. The final number of children is represented by an 8 track (see Fig. 4.1).

Similarly, *combine* problems are represented with *gluing* and *cutting* machines. The story problem is this: "Connie has 5 red marbles and 8 blue marbles. How many marbles does she have?" It is represented by means of a gluing machine that combines a 5 train and an 8 train. The result is represented by a 13 long train (see Fig. 4.2). *Compare* problems are represented by the *compare* machine. A representation of the story problem "Ruth has seven pencils; she has

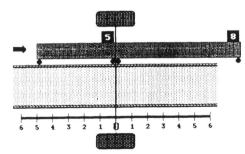

FIG. 4.2. Representing a *com-bine* problem with the Planner.

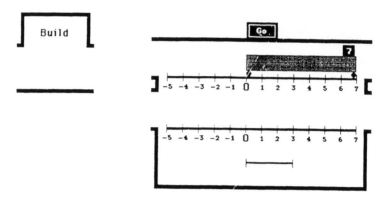

FIG. 4.3.   Representing a *compare* problem with the Planner.

three more pencils than Bob. How many pencils does Bob have?" is shown in
Fig. 4.3. First a *build* machine allows the user to create a train. Then a *compare*
machine is used with a 7 long train in it. The solver has to build a train that, when
compared with the 7 long train, will generate a 3 long segment.

Other machines were created to represent different senses of multiplication
and division. For example, a *stack* machine disposed trains in stacks, this machine expressing multiplication as "repeated additions." A *stretching* machine
stretched trains and exemplified multiplication as a scalar-unary operation. In
summary, the objects of the system exemplify different aspects of the basic
operations, and they can be used to represent word problems. The Planning
component helps to solve them.

The Planning Component

The goal of the Planner is to help the learner manipulate operators at a level of
control. Children solve tasks by choosing a sequence of operators. They do not
focus on carrying out procedures, but on the relations among operators. The
operator structures of problems are modeled, and the links between these operators and the semantic structures of word problems are made explicit. The Planner
permits children to build, save, test, and execute plans. There are three stages in
the construction of a plan. These stages are exemplified by representing and
solving the following problem: "Terry loves books. He wants to renew his
library. But some books no longer interest him and there are others he wants but
doesn't have. So he gives his little brother Al 13 books that are no longer good
for his age. Then he receives 7 new books from his father. He has now 19 books.
How many did Terry have before he changed his library?"

1. Selection of a set of machines: The child is presented with a strip representing all the machines in the system. The child uses a browser and

4 a

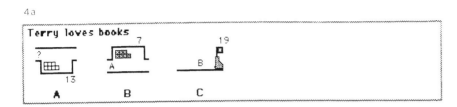

4 b

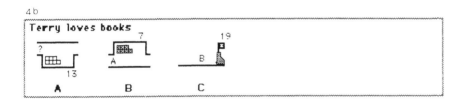

4 c

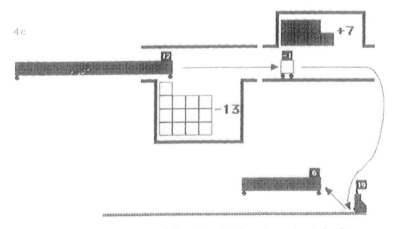

FIG. 4.4.   Modeling and Running the Terry loves books's plan.

chooses a set of machines that then appear, in sequence, in a "scratchpad." Each machine is labeled with a letter. At this point, no numerical values are indicated. The plan does not specify how much to add, subtract, and so on, or what size trains will be operated on. For *Terry loves books*, the correct set of machines is an unload machine, a load machine, and a track corresponding to the final number of books as shown in Fig. 4.4a.

2. Numerical instantiation of the machines: The child specifies numerical values for the operators by replacing the question marks on the machines with specific numbers or letters representing the output of another machine in the plan. Whenever users choose letters, they create a "chain." For *Terry loves books*, the instantiation of the machines should give the strip shown in Fig. 4.4b.

3. The execution of the plan: When the plan is finished (saved, named, and stored), the child can "run" it. Therefore, the plan behaves as a program: It can be run, stored and debugged as if it were a "real" computer program. For running the plan for *Terry loves books*, the solvers first have to specify the initial value (the initial number of books). If students choose "12" as the initial value (a classical mistake), the "running" will proceed as follows (see Fig. 4.4c): (a) a 12 train automatically enters a [-13] unload machine and is processed in a -1 train; (b) the -1 train enters a [+7] load machine and is processed in a 6 train; and (c) the 6 train enters the 19 track, but bounces off (with a "boing" sound because it does not "fit"). If the children want to try another train, they can remove the 6 train and run another train. In this case, the modifications can be driven by considerations such as "if I put 12, I don't tell the whole story, because I forget all the books Terry gave to his brother."

THE ASSUMPTIONS OF THE STUDY

The Planner has been built to embody the senses of arithmetic operations and to provide referents for them. That is, the Planner was built to provide a language for arithmetic. The assumption is that children properly trained to use the objects of the Planner to model and solve word problems would construct effective mental representations for word problems. The objects and relations of word problems are hypothesized to trigger the formation of corresponding objects in the Planner. In a previous study (Schwarz, Kohn, & Resnick, 1992), four students learned to use the Planner as a formal system: they solved problems with trains, tracks, and machines without being trained to use these objects for solving word problems. In this study, the emphasis was put on the embodiment of negative numbers. After the sessions with the Planner, the students were able to solve word problems about negatives, with referents such as *temperature, elevators,* or *time* (AD, BC). However, little is known about the nature of the mental structures formed by students working with a system such as the Planner. To understand how the match (objects of word problems ↔ objects of the Planner) is possible, we first review some research on discourse processing and word problem solving.

Research on discourse processing has teased out several levels of representations used by word problem solvers (Cummins et al., 1988; Kintsch & Greeno, 1985; Nathan, Kintsch, & Young, 1992; Reusser, 1988). These studies have shown that arithmetic word problem comprehension can be understood within the general theory of discourse processing of van Dijk and Kintsch (1983). When reading a problem, a *textbase* is formed to capture the meaning of the text. The reader also forms a representation for the actions in the text, termed the *situation model*. Nathan et al. distinguished between a representation of events in everyday terms (the *situation model*) and one that is constructed from formal relations in mind (the *problem model*). In other terms, the situation model allows the solver to make qualitative inferences from the text, whereas the problem model is the representational level at which students can apply formal calculation methods for finding the solution of the problem. The problem model is erroneous when it omits or violates certain aspects of the situation model. Nathan et al. constructed an environment, ANIMATE, in which the construction of the problem model was consistent with the situation model: Students built an "algebraic network" and "ran" a program representing a situation. If the situation was in conflict with the situation described by the word problem, students had to modify the network accordingly. The algebraic network neither displayed the underlying principle of the algebraic schema corresponding to a particular situation, nor an explanation for the choice of this schema. Our approach with the Planner is different: The objects of the system function both as formal entities and as descriptors of situations. This transparency to these two referents establishes a correspondence of the symbols to situations, and roots the formalisms in the spaces of permissible and expected events (Greeno, 1989).

We hypothesize that students trained to use the objects of the Planner to model word problems are able to form adequate situation models and problem models. We predict that their performance in such tasks will be superior to that of students manipulating symbols because any of the quantities and operations that the text induces can be referred to a configuration of trains and machines in the Planner. A good way to check the nature of the representations of word problems solvers is to ask them to recall stories they already solved. Following Kintsch (1986), we posit that once children have solved a problem, they tend to recall it by reconstructing the text from their problem model, rather than by reproducing the original textbase. Therefore, the recall task gives a measurement of the arithmetic structure that children derived from their formulation of the story problems. If, as we predict, experimental students' recall is high, it means one out of two alternatives: (a) they tap into their memory from macrostructure they formed summarizing the propositions they read in the text, or (b) they tap from their situation and/or problem model. By considering the information reproduced from the text, the information omitted and the information obtained by inference, we can decide about the nature of students' representations. In particular, because we predict that the experimental students will construct rich problem models, it is likely that they will recall the inferences done during the problem solving. Moreover, research using standard text demonstrates that likelihood of recall of a proposition is dependent on the position of that proposition in the textbase hierarchy, the *levels effect* (Kintsch, 1974): As a proposition becomes more subordinate, it is less likely to be recalled. A levels effect is produced from students who internalized the textbase (Weaver & Kintsch, 1987). Failure to see a levels effect in portions of the recall data for a story suggests that subjects are tapping into a memory structure that is different from the textbase. As stated by Weaver and Kintsch, such a deviation is due to a reconstructive recall. We hypothesize that students trained to use the objects of the Planner to model and solve word problems will not exhibit a levels effect in their recalls because they will reconstruct their problem and situation models.

In addition to this classic recall technique, another test was used to further check the nature of the representations that "Planner student" form when solving word problems. After the recall session, students were given pictorial cues in the form of objects of the Planner; and we examined how these cues improved the quality of the recall. We then studied the improvement in the recall caused by these cues: If the improvement is substantial, the conclusion will be that the objects of the system play an important role in triggering the formation of students' internal representations.

THE EXPERIMENT

Subjects

Fourth-grade students from two inner-city parochial schools participated in the study. The children were sorted into two groups of six in each school. Each group in each school was chosen according to similar ability in mathematical performance tests. All four groups completed a paper-and-pencil pretest, in which they were asked to solve word problems. The posttest was identical to the pre-test. The same experimental study with the Planner was undertaken with one group in each school. These two groups were called Groups A1 ($n = 6$) and A2 ($n = 6$), or Group A ($N = 12$) for all the experimental students together. Group A underwent a treatment with the Planner, during which students solved difficult word problems by manipulating objects of the Planner. The second group in the first school (Group B; $N = 6$) received a treatment similar to that of Group A— the manipulation of objects from the Planner being replaced by symbolic manipulations. The second group in the second school (Group C; $N = 6$) was the

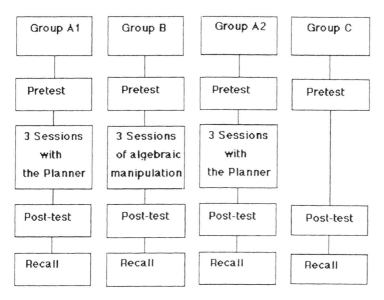

FIG. 4.5.   General description of the experiment.

control group. Five days after the posttest, all groups were asked to recall the word problems. An experimenter provided cues to complete recall. A chart showing the structure of the study is shown in Fig. 4.5.

Materials

The Pre- and the Posttests.   The pre- and the posttests both consisted of three story problems: one additive start-unknown problem[2] (*Terry loves books*); one multiplicative problem (*Mom is fair*); and one long additive, multiple-step problem (*Tom and Bob like to test their luck in lottery games*):

Mom is fair! Every week I get an A or B in math, I receive $3 from my Mom! After several weeks of doing a good job I bought a skateboard for $11 and I had $7 left. For how many weeks did I get A or B in math?

Tom and Bob like to test their luck in lottery games. Tom came with $5. He participated in three games. In the second game he lost $5, but in the third he won $12. Bob began with $8 and participated in only 2 games. He won $4 in the first

---

[2]In start-unknown problems, the unknown quantity appears first in the story. Simple start-unknown problems are of the form $x \pm a = b$. Such problems have been recognized as being difficult (Riley, Greeno, & Heller, 1983). *Terry loves books* is a two-step start-unknown problem that can be represented formally as "$x - 13 + 7 = 19$."

game and lost $2 in the second one. Then Tom had $3 more than Bob. How much did Tom win in the first game?

The treatment of Experimental Group A.   During all the treatment, an experimenter worked with pairs of students. In a 15-minute preliminary session, the experimenter presented all the objects (including trains and tracks) and showed how they function. Then, during three 45-minute sessions, the experimenter presented a set of twelve word problems (four per session). In the first session, the experimenter first showed how to tell stories with the machines (in fact, he modeled the stories). Then he used this set of trains and machines to solve the problem (running backward, chunking problems into subproblems). During Sessions 2 and 3, children were first presented a formulation of a word problem. They were asked to tell the problem with the objects of the system. Whenever the students used a number that was not given, the experimenter acknowledged them: "This number is not in the story." In that way, the experimenter forced the students to tell (to model) stories without solving them. After the students agreed on a set of machines, they were invited to find the solution with the plan on which they agreed. The solution was then run on the Planner. Students were finally invited to discuss and decide whether their plan was correct. They modified the plan if needed.

In summary, this experiment was almost deprived of instruction. During their treatment, students were given activities where they discovered, by themselves a "match" between a story problem and a "strip" from the Planner. The role of the experimenter was to ensure that technical problems linked to the functioning of the system would not hinder the students' actions. An example of activity around a word problem named "It is a secret" is exemplified in the following excerpt. It is one of the more complex tasks, done during Session 3 of the treatment. The protocol of this activity is reproduced next in its integrality. It exemplifies the phases that students working with the Planner need to undergo to model and solve a word problem. Students A and D, were invited by Experimenter Exp to model the story (Line 15), and then to solve it (Line 69). To follow the students' progression on the computer, a strip that represents the different phases of the modeling of the word problem by the two students is displayed in Figure 4.6.

```
 1    D:    I read it. It's a secret. Kathy and Sarah are two sisters. Many times,
 2          Sarah is jealous of Kathy, for, when it comes to get cookies, Sarah
 3          does not tell her sister how much she gets just to tease her. Once,
 4          Sarah and Kathy had both four cookies. Kathy received three and
 5          Sarah did not want to tell her how many cookies she got from her
 6          mother. Then Sarah gave three cookies to her little brother, Tommy
 7          and asked for more cookies from Dad who did not know that Mom
 8          already gave some to her. Dad gave her eleven cookies, and gave to
 9          Kathy eight cookies because Sarah told him she gave three to Tom-
10          my. It's not fair cried Kathy. Now Sarah has four cookies more than
```

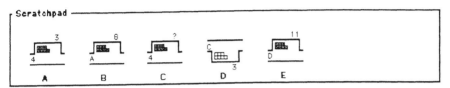

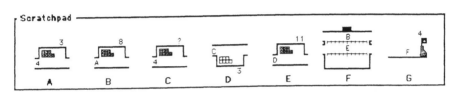

FIG. 4.6.   Solving a word problem with the Planner.

11		Kathy because Mom gave her many. How many cookies did Mom
12		give you, Sarah, asked Dad. I'll not tell, said Sarah with contempt.
13		It's a secret. How many cookies did Sarah get from her Mom? I don't
14		know [*one minute* pause].
15	Exp:	You want to try to, to tell the story with the computer? Okay?
16	D:	She has fifteen cookies and she has, (*mumble*) um, with Kate, Kathy
17		only gave cookies away. I counted fifteen. So far . . . [*D correctly*
18		*found that Kathy got fifteen cookies at the end.*] (*15 sec pause*). Well,
19		if, um, Sarah and Kathy both got four cookies, and then, Kathy
20		received three and Sarah did not, and Sarah did not tell her sister how
21		much she got. Then Sarah gave three cookies to her little brother
22		. . . So then, four cookies, and then, I don't know how much she
23		got, but if she didn't get any, and she still had three when she gave
24		three to her brother, then she had one left. But we have to find out
25		first, how many she got the second time.
26	Exp:	Ah you know what I'll do? I'll ask you to try to do together first the
27		story of Kathy, and then the story of Sarah. OK? [*The experimenter*
28		*intervenes to help A and D modeling the story by asking them to*
29		*model the stories of Kathy and Sarah separately*
30	A:	Kathy, we need a Build machine. OK Um Kathy had four cookies . . .
31	D:	I know, I know.
32	A:	(whispers to herself) . . . Gets, that's seven so far. [*A chooses a load*
33		*machine* and then she gave three to her brother.
34	D:	No. Because that's how many Kathy got the second time [*A mixed up*
35		*Kathy with Sarah and D corrected her* and this is how many she had

36		the first time.[*D adds a unload machine to the first load machine;*
37		*see Fig. 4.6 phase 1*]. That is to saythat she has four and she gets
38		three, yeah.
39	A:	*(whispers the story to herself)* I lost a number.
40	D:	And then she got eight cookies, this is Kathy. Now would we do
41		Sarah?
42	Exp:	Sarah, yeah, do Sarah just after that.
43	D:	Okay, Sarah has four cookies, and then . . . Oh, we don't know how
44		many she got . . . because she did not tell.
45	A:	So, Sarah gave three cookies to her little brother, Tommy (*10*
46		*seconds pause*).
47	D:	She had . . .
48	A:	She gave three to her little, cookies to her brother.
49	D:	No, she has, we have to find out how many she gave . . . so it's a
50		unload machine. Three [*D attaches a unload machine*]. She gives to
51		her brother, Tommy. And then, she has, um, Sarah, would then have
52		four more cookies than Carol.
53	A:	Ahh, you forgot, you forgot Dad gave her . . .
54	D:	Oh. Eleven more . . . [*A and D complete the strip appearing in the*
55		*second phase of Figure 4.6*
56	D:	And then we have to compare . . .
57	A:	And she has . . . we have to find out . . .
58	D:	E and B.
59	Exp:	To compare? what and what?
60	D:	The E and B, cause E is um, from one would be the answer, and B
61		would be from the other answer. [*In this excerpt D matches between*
62		*a sequence of events and relationships described in a text and objects*
63		*(machines) of the system.*
64	A:	Okay, we have to find out what the answers are first. Oh! why don't
65		you put two tracks for Kathy and Sarah?. . . .
66	D:	But it says how many cookies Sarah got . . . plus four. We compare
67		between how much Sarah has and how much Kathy has . . . [*A and*
68		*D complete correctly the strip representing the whole story*
69	Exp:	So, how much do you think we have to add there?
70	A:	We, you know that we have to add four on to, (*sighs*). To
71		. . . (*pause*). Twenty six?
72		[*Seemingly, A adds all the positives in the strip: 4 + 3 + 8 + 11.*]
73	D:	Can we run it?
74	A:	Return . . . Adding on how many cookies Kathy has.
75	D:	Why is she fighting? she has like fifteen cookies? (*laughs*)
76	Exp:	Okay, now we have to resume. Do you know how much to put there?
77	A:	Fifteen, because she has fifteen cookies and then . . .
78	D:	Yeah, 'cause she has four more that her, so we put fifteen.
79	Exp:	Okay. We'll see what happens. (*20 seconds pause*)
80	D:	How many cookies does she have? . . . I think she'll get mad.
81	A:	Twenty one?

82	D:	Why should he give her eleven, and not eight, just to be cruel to her?
83	Exp:	So we have here twenty seven.
84	D:	Can't blame that on Kathy. (*Computer boings*) Um its not four, no. I
85		will run it again. It's sure that we put the wrong number on the load
86		machine (*fifteen*)
87	A:	To compare, to have four, so how much do I have to put? . . .
88	D:	Um, eleven.
89	Exp:	It can be eleven
90	D:	Nine . . . teen
91	Exp:	It can be also nineteen. Okay, eleven or nineteen. What do you think
92		it will be?
93	Both:	Nineteen.
94	D:	We have the nineteen after the plus eleven. So before the plus eleven,
95		I have eight . . .
96	A:	. . . and in the load machine it will be eleven.
97	D:	Nineteen.
98	A:	And if we have eleven out of the load machine with the four train,
99		seven is there.
100	Exp:	Okay, so put 7 and resume the run (*the story is run while A and D*
101		*comment on each of the episodes of this story*).

The excerpt shows how A and D use the objects of the Planner at two different levels. First, during the "modeling" stage, the objects of the Planner refer to events and relationships of the word problem (e.g., Lines 40–53). At the end of the modeling stage, the same phenomenon occurs during the "running" stage (e.g., Lines 74 and 79–84). During the "computation" of the solution (e.g., Lines 94–95), the objects of the system are mathematical objects on which operations can be done. When A and D correct and check their solution, the objects of the Planner are mathematical and refer to objects of the word problem.

The Treatment of Group B.   Group B received the same set of twelve problems as Group A did during 3 sessions of 45 minutes long each. The only modification was that, instead of using the objects of the system, the students manipulated square pads. Some of the pads were blank; on the others, one of the eight characters displayed in Fig. 4.7a was inscribed. The children were provided numerals inscribed on round chips. The chips could be put inside some of the blank pads. Group B was first shown how to tell stories with the pads. For example, *Terry loves books* "can be told" by using the strip of pads shown in Figure 4.7b.

Similar to the experimental group, Group B negotiated the objects that could model the stories (the pads) with the experimenter. After the modeling stage, the students were asked to solve the problem while using their pads.

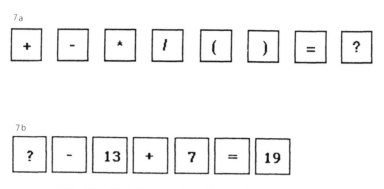

FIG. 4.7. Modeling word problems with square pads.

The Recall Session

Five days after the posttest, students of all groups were asked to recall the stories they solved in the pre- and posttests. The children were also supplied with a series of three progressive cues. The first cue was the title of the story, the second cue showed an ordered series of uninstantiated machines for Group A and a series of empty pads for Groups B and C (see Fig. 4.8), and the third cue was a full representation of the problem, i.e., an ordered series of instantiated machines or pads. The cues were presented until the students could remember the whole story. If the students failed to find the formulation after the third cue, the experimenter read the story. Then the student was asked to solve the problem.

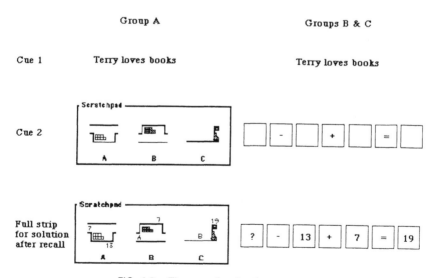

FIG. 4.8. The cues for the three groups.

When presented with Cue 2, the students could fill in values by asking the experimenter information included in the text. The experimenter could answer the question only when this information could be accessed directly in the text. A typical example is provided by J for *Terry loves books*. (*J is presented Cue 2.*)

J: Alright, how, how much did um, she give her brother?
Exp: Thirteen.
J: And how much did she, how did she get?
Exp: Seven.
J: This was . . . this will be B. . . .This will be A. And how many books did she end up with?
Exp: Nineteen.
J: Nineteen? So that'll go there.
[*At this point J completes the instantiation of Cue 2 and finds the solution of the problem.*]

In this excerpt, we can see that J was able to use an uninstantiated "strip" to reconstruct the whole story. It is interesting to notice that, when asked to reformulate *Terry loves books* after his reconstruction, J could recall the story almost verbatim, completing details such as "she wanted to renew his library" or "her father gave her new books." Such details were absent from the recall after Cues 1 and 2.

RESULTS

Figure 4.9a shows the average number of problems solved correctly by the three groups in the pretest, the posttest and after being given Cue 3. From this figure, it appears that: (a) Group A performs slightly better than Group B on the posttest and after the recall; (b) Groups A and B performed substantially better than the control group (Group C) on the posttest; and (c) performance for the control

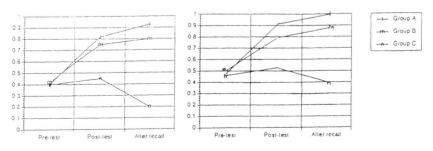

9a. Scores for the three problems   9b. Scores for the two first problems

FIG. 4.9.   Performance of the three groups on the pretest, the posttest, and recall session.

group dropped when Cue 3 was presented. These findings show the effectiveness of training to use the Planner objects to model and to solve word problems.

The performances of the three groups in the memory tasks brought much more insight to students' understanding of the word problems. To score subjects' recall of the three stories, we decomposed all the texts into idea units (for a similar method, see Mayer, 1982). For example, the *Terry loves books* story could be decomposed into the following segments:

a	Terry wants to renew his library
b(13)	Terry gives 13 books to his little brother
c(7)	Terry receives 7 new books from his father.
d(19)	Terry has now 19 books.
e(?)	How many books did Terry have at the beginning?

Note that the idea *Terry loves books* was not inserted because the title was given to the students as a first clue. Idea b(13) contains two bits of information: Terry gives books to his little brother, and the number of books he gives (thirteen) is thus instantiated. The first information is *relational*, whereas the second one is an *assignment*.

Using this partitioning of the story, it can be decomposed into nine idea units, four among them being assignments and five being relations. Overall, 39 idea units were found in the three stories, 18 among them being assignments. Each problem was analyzed into propositions. Children's protocols were also parsed into propositions and then compared to the propositions of the original problem. A "match" was recorded if a protocol proposition contained the same variables and relations as the original proposition, even if the specific numerical values did not match. In total, the three problems contained propositions. Figure 4.10a shows the percentage of correct propositions recalled by the three groups after each clue and performance for solving the problems. Figure 4.10b shows the percentage of correct relations recalled by the three groups.

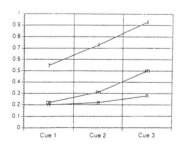

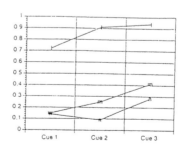

10a Percentage of correct propositions   10b Percentage of correct relations

FIG. 4.10.   Results for the memory task.

A list of qualitative conclusions about the understanding of algebraic structures is presented:

1. Group A remembered most of the propositions. Moreover, the experimental group remembered relations more often than assignments, although relations are generally poorly recalled by children. Many of the missing assignment propositions given Cue 1 were reconstructed by the students when they were given Cue 2 (see the typical excerpt of J shown previously). These results indicate that the experimental group correctly represent the structure of the problems. For Groups B and C, the recall was poor and the propositions recalled were generally assignments. Moreover, a detailed analysis of the percentage of correct intrusions (i.e., correct inferences that can be drawn from the word problems) show that Group A often recalled the numerical solutions of the problem and/or intermediate results leading to the solution.

2. Group C was not really trained to use representations for the solution of word problems. The ability of these students to remember propositions declined when presented with Cues 2 and 3, and sometimes those students could not even restate the correct propositions they had recalled with Cue 1. The fact that they were unable to find problem solutions is perhaps due, in part, to their preoccupation with the "boxes." They may have drawn attention away from executing other problem-solving processes, such as forming a meaningful, integrated representation of the problem situation and carrying out the arithmetic operations necessary for solution. This result is consistent with a finding of Lewis (1989).

In conclusion, the students exposed to the Planner were able to solve difficult story problems. More significant, they were able to remember the structure of such problems (i.e., their relational propositions). They could use cues related to the meaning of the operations embedded in the machines of the Planner to reconstruct the problems, and they could integrate the solution within such referential semantics.

CONCLUSIONS AND DISCUSSION

The results reported in this chapter show that students trained to model and solve word problems with the Planner performed slightly better than the other groups on a paper-and pencil test (the posttest). When considering the two first questions only (leaving out the multistep problem), the difference between the groups turned to be very sensible. This is a surprising result, having in mind that the treatment was short, and that all students were used to solving word problems with algebraic conventional methods close to the treatment of Group B. Moreover, the protocol showing how Students A and D could solve difficult multistep problems was typical in the sense that, during computer sessions, students were able to use the objects of the Planner as referring to objects and events of the word problems, as well as to mathematical entities (in contrast with Group B). So, even if no significant difference among groups was detected on the performance test, Group A knew to use representational tools (the objects of the Planner) to model and solve difficult word problems.

The results of Group A for the recall session seem to indicate that they tapped into correct situation models for each of the problems. On the contrary, Groups B and C tapped into the text base, and their recall was rather weak. Moreover, the fact that Group A recalled particularly well relations (even better than the other idea units) suggests that students' representations were probably perceptual or episodic. In addition, the cues given to Group A activated reconstructive memory and triggered the formation of complete situation and problem models. We interpret this ability to (re)construct such correct mental models for solving difficult word problems as a good indicator of understanding arithmetic word problems.

In conclusion, with appropriate epistemological analysis, we created a system that captured learners' informal knowledge about the physical world without all the real-world constraints. The Planner is a hypothetical world that contains recognizable, but "fictional," entities that behave according to well structured rules. The results of Group A indicate that students constructed rich representations encompassing the objects and events of the situations described in the word problems, as well as mathematical tools and entities. This approach has been used by White (1993), who constructed intermediate causal models for concepts in physics. These are readily mappable to a variety of real-world contexts because their objects and operators are generic and causal. She traced the development of students' mental models as they worked through a learning system about electrical circuits (see also Roschelle, 1992; Snir, Smith, & Grosslight, 1992).

The experiment was almost deprived of instruction. During their treatment, students were given activities where they discovered by themselves a "match" between a story problem and a "strip" from the Planner. The role of the experimenter was to monitor students' actions, and to ensure that technical problems linked to the functioning of the system would not hinder their actions. However, no overt guidance was provided. An interesting question with pedagogical outcomes is to investigate the role of direct instruction. What if the instructor would tutor the translation (objects and events of word problems→objects of the Planner) systematically? Or perhaps more promising, given a strip from the Planner, what if the instructor would control the invention of stories matching the "running" of the strip?

Although results obtained in this study are positive, it is necessary to replicate the experiment under different conditions. First, the number of subjects was too small in all the groups to obtain significant results. Second, the recall sessions were coded in terms of idea units. This method is not sensible enough to capture the structure of representations. A propositional approach—where all the nouns, predicates, and conjunctions are coded according to their level of subordination in the formulation of the problems—is much more instructive about what the students remembered from the problems. Such experiments will shed more light on the role of intermediate abstractions as bridges between formal entities and applications for the acquisition of concepts that cannot be learned informally.

REFERENCES

Carpenter, T. (1985). Learning to add and subtract: An exercise in problem solving. In E. Silver (Ed.), *Teaching and learning mathematical problem solving: Multiple research perspectives* (pp. 17–40). Philadelphia, PA: The Franklin Institute Press.

Carpenter, T., & Moser, J. M. (1982). The development of addition and subtraction problem solving skills. In T. Carpenter, J. M. Moser, & T. A. Romberg (Eds.), *Addition and subtraction: A cognitive perspective* (pp. 9–24). Hillsdale, NJ: Lawrence Erlbaum Associates.

Cummins, D., Kintsch, W., Reusser, K., & Weimer, R. (1988). The role of understanding in solving word problems. *Cognitive Psychology, 20,* 439–462.

Greeno, J. G. (1989). Situation models, mental models, and generative knowledge. In D. Klahr & K. Kotovsky (Eds.), *Complex information processing: The impact of Herbert Simon* (pp. 285–318). Hillsdale, NJ: Lawrence Erlbaum Associates.

Kaput, J. J. (1987). Towards a theory of symbol use in mathematics. In C. Janvier (Ed.), *Problems of representation in the teaching and learning of mathematics* (pp. 159–196). Hillsdale, NJ: Lawrence Erlbaum Associates.

Kintsch, W. (1974). *The representation of meaning in memory.* Hillsdale, NJ: Lawrence Erlbaum Associates.

Kintsch, W. (1986). Learning from text. *Cognition and Instruction. 3,* 87–108.

Lewis, A. M. (1989). Training students to represent arithmetic word problems. *Journal of Educational Psychology, 81,* 521–531.

Mayer, R. E. (1982). Memory for algebra story problems. *Journal of Education Psychology, 74,* 199–216.

Nathan, M. J., Kintsch, W., & Young, E. (1992). A theory of algebra word problem comprehension and its implications for the design of learning environments. *Cognition and Instruction, 9,* 329–389.

Nesher, P. (1989). Microworlds in mathematics education: A pedagogical realism. In L. B. Resnick (Ed.), *Knowing, learning, and instruction: Essays in honour of Robert Glaser* (pp. 187–215). Hillsdale, NJ: Lawrence Erlbaum Associates.

Ohlsson, S. (1987). Sense and reference in the design of interactive illustrations for rational numbers. In R. Lawler & M. Yazdani (Eds.), *Artificial intelligence and education* (Vol. 1, pp. 307–344). Norwood, NJ: Ablex.

Peled, I., & Resnick, L. B. (1988). Building semantic computer models for teaching number systems and word problems. *Proceedings of the 11th PME Conference, 2,* 184–190.

Resnick, L. B., & Omanson, S. F. (1987). Learning to understand arithmetic. In R. Glaser (Ed.), *Advances in instructional psychology* (Vol. 3, pp. 41–95). Hillsdale, NJ: Lawrence Erlbaum Associates.

Reusser, K. (1988). *From text to situation to equation: Cognitive simulation of understanding and solving mathematical word problems* (Res. Rep. No. 5). Switzerland: Universitaet Bern.

Riley, M. S., Greeno, J. G., & Heller, J. I. (1983). Development of children's problem solving abilities in arithmetic. In Ginsburgh (Ed.), *The development of mathematical thinking* (pp. 153–196). New York: Academic Press.

Roschelle, J. (1992). Learning by collaboration: Convergent conceptual change. *The Journal of the Learning Sciences, 2,* 235–276.

Schwarz, B., Kohn, A. S., & Resnick, L. B. (1992). Bootstrapping mental constructions: The case of negative numbers. In C. Frasson, G. Gauthier, & G. McCalla (Eds.), *Intelligent tutoring systems* (pp. 286–293). Montreal: Springer-Verlag.

Schwarz, B., Kohn, A. S., & Resnick, L. B. (1993). Positives about negatives. *The Journal of the Learning Sciences, 3,* 37–92.

Smith, C., Snir, J., & Grosslight, L. (1992). Using conceptual models to facilitate conceptual change: The case of weight density differentiation. *Cognition and Instruction., 9,* 221–283.

Turner, A. A. (1987). *The propositional analysis system. Version 1.0* (Tech. Rep. No. 872). Boulder, CO: Institute of Cognitive Science, University of Colorado.

van Dijk, T. A., & Kintsch, W. (1983). *Strategies of discourse comprehension.* New York: Academic Press.

Vergnaud, G. (1982). A classification of cognitive tasks and operations of thought involved in addition and subtraction. In T. P. Carpenter, J. M. Moser, & T. A. Romberg (Eds.), *Addition and Subtraction: A Cognitive Perspective.* Hillsdale, NJ: Lawrence Erlbaum Associates.

Weaver, C. A., & Kintsch, W. (1987). Reconstruction in recall of prose. *Text, 7.* 165–180

White, B. Y. (1993). Intermediate causal models: The missing links for successful science education? In Glaser (Ed.), *Advances in instructional psychology* (Vol. 4, pp. 177–252). Hillsdale, NJ: Lawrence Erlbaum Associates.

5 From Cognitive Modeling to the Design of Pedagogical Tools

Kurt Reusser
University of Zurich

DESIGNING TECHNOLOGY-BASED TOOLS FOR LEARNING AND INSTRUCTION: A DIDACTIC TASK

Since Comenius' (1659) *Orbis Pictus,* educators have debated how learning and teaching can be improved and facilitated by the design of instructional media, methods, and materials. For the last several decades, this debate has also encompassed the use of electronic media and technology. Research on computer-aided instruction goes back to the end of the 1950s, whereas the educational use of computers began in the 1970s. Inspired by Skinner's behaviorist conception of learning, which called for the successive approximation of carefully decomposed, sequentially presented, and reinforced tasks, a broad variety of instructional programs for computers and textbooks was developed. The pedagogical idea behind this early phase of computer-assisted, or programmed, instruction was to provide for an improved efficiency and individualization of learning. Each student should be able to acquire skills and domain knowledge at his or her own pace by practicing skills according to his or her abilities. However, because of both the minimal power of the hardware and the underlying theory of learning, which failed to foster conceptual learning and comprehension, most of the early programs (in fact, little more than electronic page-turning devices) did not meet the expectations of educators and the requirements of any demanding type of instruction.

Three decades after the cognitive revolution in psychology, and with the advent of powerful and inexpensive computers, computer-assisted instruction— or the more ambitious intelligent tutoring system (ITS)—has again become a central topic of research in the field of education. Behind the present efforts to make learning more efficient, motivating, and individually adaptive, there are widespread and, in part, romantically high expectations about the role and didactic power of computers in education and instruction. Computers seem to be conceived of as not merely tools, among other tools, for future teaching and learning, but, for example, as (a) intelligent and mind-empowering prosthetic devices, (b) amplifiers of human intelligence (allowing one to do more things faster and more accurately, (c) reorganizers of mental functioning (leading to a shift in the kinds of problem types and levels of difficulty that can be managed and in the types of methods used to solve problems), or (d) even instruments of cultural redefinition (Table 5.1). Computers are perceived as personal electronic teachers—as intelligent teaching systems associated with the vision of the computer as the "future dominant delivery system in education for almost all age levels and in most subject areas" (Bork, 1985, p. 1).

Because computer-supported instruction is a rather expensive way to teach, one should consider the purpose for which it will be used in education. Because of the elevated costs of building high-quality software, one has to think carefully about what things are worth doing with computers as well as what can be done best with them.

Thus, the design of any computer-based educational system should be based on two foundations: on content-specific research on learning and comprehension, and on a pedagogical model of the learner and the learning process. The latter must include an account of how computers are to be integrated into the classroom, as well as the use of technology-based pedagogical tools in general.

TABLE 5.1
Metaphors and Views Concerning the Role of Computers in Learning and Teaching

Computer Uses

- systems for automating education (Anderson, Boyle, Corbett, & Lewis, 1990)
- idea amplifiers; personal electronic teachers (Brown, 1984)
- cultural amplifiers; part of cultural tool kit; prosthetic devices (Bruner, 1986)
- reorganizers of mental functions; extracortical organizers of thought; a medium that helps transcend the limitations of the mind (Pea, 1985, 1987)
- instruments of cultural refefinition (Bruner, 1986; Pea, 1987)
- intelligent tutoring systems (Anderson, Boyle, Farrell, & Reisser, 1984; Ohlsson, 1986; Sleeman & Brown, 1982)
- intelligent learning environments (Brown, 1984)
- idea amplifiers; facilitators of learning (Brown, 1984)
- amplifiers of the mind (Bruner, 1986; Pea, 1987)
- mirrors of the mind (Brown, 1984)
- an electronic workbook; a tool for learning through reflection (Collins & Brown, 1988)
- a medium for experiential learning (Lepper & Gurtner, 1989; Papert, 1980)
- a foundation for new learning cultures (diSessa, 1989)
- cognitive tools (Lajoie & Derry, 1993; Pea, 1987)
- partners in cognition (Salomon, Perkins, & Globerson, 1991)

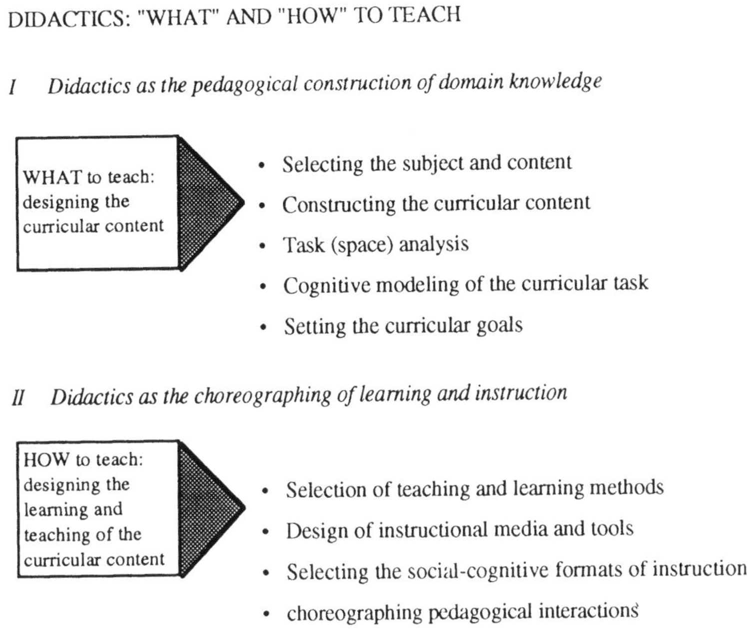

DIDACTICS: "WHAT" AND "HOW" TO TEACH

I   Didactics as the pedagogical construction of domain knowledge

WHAT to teach: designing the curricular content	• Selecting the subject and content
	• Constructing the curricular content
	• Task (space) analysis
	• Cognitive modeling of the curricular task
	• Setting the curricular goals

II   Didactics as the choreographing of learning and instruction

HOW to teach: designing the learning and teaching of the curricular content	• Selection of teaching and learning methods
	• Design of instructional media and tools
	• Selecting the social-cognitive formats of instruction
	• choreographing pedagogical interactions

FIG. 5.1.   The dual *bildung* theoretical task of didactics as pedagogical knowledge construction and choreography of learning and instruction.

In contrast to any type of opportunistic, technology-driven design, and in accordance with the concept of *didactics* as a design science (Simon, 1981; Wittmann, 1992), the design of computer-based teaching and learning environments should be considered a genuine didactic task. In the original sense of the classical theory of *Bildung* (Klafki, 1963; Weniger, 1952; Willmann, 1889/1957), the concept of *didactics* (Fig. 5.1) includes the questions of what to teach and how to teach. The former is concerned with selecting, analyzing, and modeling the curricular content and goal structure. The latter relates to decisions about pedagogical methods, presentation forms, and media use, as well as an understanding of patterns of sociocognitive interactions. It must be based on a philosophical and developmental view of the learner and the nature of learning processes.

Thus, at the heart of any pedagogical design is the didactic analysis (Klafki, 1958) of key concepts, structures, and representations; learning methods, skills, and strategies; as well as patterns of instruction related to a task or domain. As is often observed, insufficient attention to the sound cognitive-didactic decomposition of a curricular task can ruin costly and well-meant instructional efforts.

A THEORY OF MATHEMATICAL STORY-PROBLEM COMPREHENSION AND SOME INSTRUCTIONAL IMPLICATIONS

Mathematical text, word, or story problems (MSPs), which are used to assess students' application of mathematical knowledge and skills, consist of two interwoven semiotic worlds: a storylike description of a nonmathematical situation or event, and an implicit web of mathematical relations. Thus, cognitive-didactic analysis with respect to solving MSPs has to focus on the interplay among language processes, the understanding of a denoted situation, and mathematical problem solving, as well as on students' comprehension strategies, errors, and difficulties. Because any comprehension of an MSP is mediated by the way the problem is presented linguistically, and with respect to the situational context in which a mathematical structure is embedded, didactic task analysis must focus on the role of problem language and real-world knowledge (i.e., on the broad variety of presentational factors involved in problem posing and wording; Staub & Reusser, 1995).

Situation Problem Solver

Our theory of mathematical word- or story-problem comprehension (Reusser, 1985, 1990) integrates work of Piaget (1947) and Aebli (1980–1981) on the nature and development of mathematical thinking, of van Dijk and Kintsch (1983) on discourse processing, and of Kintsch and Greeno (1985) and Cummins, Kintsch, Reusser, and Weimer (1988) on arithmetic word problems. We have developed a production rule model that is based on a decompositional analysis of the tacit knowledge, the difficulties of the language and situation comprehension processes, and the skills involved in solving word problems. The computational model takes elementary word problems as natural language input (within some range of complexity) and simulates the processes of their understanding and solving by accessing linguistic and general world knowledge and applying various kinds of strategies. Tracing the comprehension, mathematization, and solution process as leading from text to situation to equation, several mutually constraining levels of mental representation (textual, situational, and mathematical) are generated by the situation problem solver (SPS; see Fig. 5.2):

1. a text base as a propositional representation of the task extracted from the textual input;
2. an episodic situation model as a goal- and task-specific, qualitative representation of the elaborated nonmathematical (problem) situation or event denoted by the story text;
3. a mathematical problem model capturing the inferred gist of the mathematical situation, that is, the elements and relations of the episodic situa-

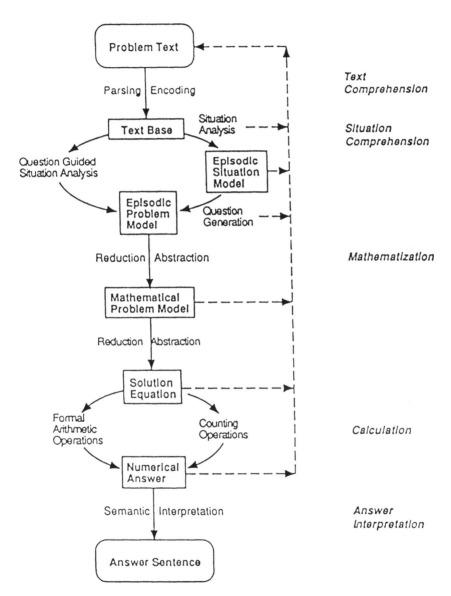

FIG. 5.2.   Types and levels of mental representations generated in the process model SPS during problem comprehension and mathematization.

tion model that are relevant from the point of view of a mathematical question to be answered; and

4. a formal equation as the densest form of the mathematical situation inherent in a word problem.

According to our process model of problem comprehension (for more details, see Reusser, 1989a, 1990), the crucial steps in successful problem comprehension are those that lead to the formation of an adequate qualitative and—derived from it—a semiquantitative situation model, or problem model. Successful comprehension processes consist of a sequence of inferential and elaborative steps that are elicited or induced by the wording of the problem and guided by an explicit problem question. The semiquantitative situation model in SPS is seen as a necessary bridge in meaningful problem comprehension, connecting to both the initial linguistic input (problem text) and the abstract expression of the inherent mathematical relations (symbolic equation formulae).

Faulty problem solving can be simulated in SPS by introducing deficient knowledge into the program, which leads to erroneous problem representations. Empirical evidence gathered so far (Reusser, 1989b; Staub & Reusser, 1995) supports the view of competent comprehension and solving of MSPs as rooted in the development of language comprehension strategies, rather than in the development of mathematical skills alone. Presentational factors (Staub & Reusser, 1995), that is, the linguistic and pragmatic forms employed by the authors of MSPs, have been repeatedly identified as a critical and diverse source of problem difficulty (cf. Cummins et al., 1988; De Corte, Verschaffel, & de Win, 1985; Stern, 1991; Stern & Lehrndorfer, 1992).

EDUCATIONAL IMPLICATIONS

What this implies for instruction with SPS is that mathematical word problems should be taught as problems of comprehension. This means that MSPs should be treated as a significant object of discourse and reasoning in mathematics education. With the goal of achieving basic mathematical literacy, it is not enough (but often the case in mathematics education) to teach students formal structures and isolated procedural skills. To do so is to develop decontexualized symbolic structures and proceduralized operational skills, both types of knowledge disassociated from deeper comprehension and situational referents and application. Following this line of argument, it is not enough to teach students to solve MSPs, for instance, by means of keyword-driven and structurally blind "direct-translation" rules (cf. the STUDENT program of Bobrow, 1964; Paige & Simon, 1966), that is, picking up and mapping syntactic cues into algebraic language (cf. Nesher & Teubal, 1975). In contrast, in instructing applied formats of mathematical problem solving (e.g., word problems), mathematics education should focus on the bridging of abstract, symbolic problem solving with concrete, situational reasoning. That is, formal, symbolic expressions that result from word problems should become transparent and situationally meaningful by rooting them in their corresponding events—in the real-world situations from which they are derived.

For the process of teaching, this requires formats and notations by which mathematical word problems can be overtly represented, inspected, reflected upon, and communicated in appropriate ways. Students need instruction on how to use representational systems and languages (and how to generate their own formats and notations) to express their situational and mathematical understanding of a problem in meaningful and cognitively efficient, often semiquantitative ways. Because the use of representational notations belongs to the tool kit of expertise in any domain, powerful (especially culturally shared and canonical) general notations and domain-specific representations—together with representation-building skills—need to be taught and conveyed to students as a significant part of achieving mathematical and scientific literacy (Mitman, Mergendoller, Marchman, & Packer, 1987).

Computers have the potential to serve as powerful representational tools (Reusser, 1993). Before turning to the description of a tutoring environment that was derived from our cognitive modeling work, our instructional design philosophy, including a set of principles, is outlined. Although these principles are consistent with the described cognitive simulation work, they are—as is discussed—only in part strictly derived from it.

FROM COGNITIVE MODELING TO THE DESIGN OF A TECHNOLOGY-BASED EPISTEMIC TOOL

The Romantic Dream of "Automating Education"

What are the pedagogical ideas associated with the high hopes—the "computer dream" (Lepper & Gurtner, 1989)—that accompany the new generation of instructional technology? I think they have multiple roots, with an emphasis on three topics. First, there is the perennial effort for more individualization and adaptivity in learning and instruction (an idea than can be traced back far in the history of education). A second motive is learning by doing, or learning from experience (an idea going back beyond Dewey and Piaget, to Rousseau and Pestalozzi): Computers should provide students with supportive contexts for discovery and experiential learning. A third idea that has been associated with educational technology, especially with environments such as *Logo* (Papert, 1980) or *Boxer* (diSessa, 1989), is an emphasis on cognitive skills, or the expectation that properly designed systems will contribute to the development of higher order learning and thinking skills. This issue relates to the 19th-century debate on *formale* versus *materiale Bildung* (formal vs. content-oriented education) in the German-speaking history of schooling (Lehmensick, 1926), and to the problem of formal discipline and training of mental faculties in Anglo-American tradition (Mann, 1979).

An ambitious type of computational system—with which high expectations about didactic power and value have been associated—is the intelligent tutoring system (ITS; Anderson, 1989; Mandl & Lesgold, 1988; Ohlsson, 1986; Sleeman & Brown, 1982). Such a system assumes that computers might eventually function as adaptive and self-sufficient substitutes for intelligent human teachers. The architecture of an ITS consists of four components (see Table 5.2): an expert or knowledge component (containing the model of a specific content or domain), a learner model associated with diagnostic capabilities (allowing inferences about what a student thinks and knows), a tutorial planning and teaching module, and an easily manipulable user interface. The first three components refer to the presumed threefold intelligence of an ITS, namely, task representation (modeling the content), student diagnostic (learner modeling), and didactic (teaching) intelligence. Obviously, it is not a trivial task to build a system whose goal is to provide learners with individually tailored feedback and adaptive instructional supports on the basis of a constantly retuned student model. Such a system

TABLE 5.2
Four Modules of an ITS Architecture

Module	Description
Expert domain-knowledge module	Explicit model of the domain • representation of the domain knowledge of experts:facts, concepts, strategies, skills, tasks • expert program that solves problems in the domain
Learner module	Cognitive simulation of the learner • fine-grained cognitive diagnosis and evaluation of the student's understanding: knowledge states and reasoning processes, bugs, misconceptions • Identification and dynamic representation of the emerging knowledge and skill of the student
Tutoring module	Orchestration of didactic interventions and control • modeling the teacher-student interaction • adaptive selection and presentation of task material • adaptive diagnostic feedback and tutorial help • tutoring activities: explanation, advice, remediation, testing
User-interface module	Ergonomy of interaction • communication/interaction between user and system • direct manipulation, graphics, natural language

implies no less than putting a fully competent (ideal) teacher inside a computer. Despite some notable success stories (cf. Anderson et al., 1990; Shute & Glaser, 1990), there are reasons to be skeptical about both the feasibility and the wisdom of intelligent systems based on full system control and deep student modeling.

Feasibility.   Based on cognitive modeling (including our own on mathematical word problems), and by taking into account the state of the art in knowledge engineering and cognitive psychology, we conclude that machine tutoring based on cognitive simulation of the student is still not possible across a full range of tasks and in open-ended domains. Fuzzy language and the enormous amount of qualitative world knowledge and situated-reasoning skills that are required form an insurmountable obstacle. Our psychological theories about learning, knowing, and comprehension are still inadequate to enable computer modeling of qualitatively rich and contextualized knowledge processes.

Should educators worry about this situation? Not too much, I think. First, evidence shows that human teaching is not based on fine-grained diagnostic behavior as much as the ITS philosophy presumes (i.e., expert teachers do not carry out extensive cognitive diagnosis; cf. McArthur, Stasz, & Zmuidzinas, 1990). Second, even if the ITS is not within the reach of today's knowledge technologies,[1] instructional systems—where a machine sensitively adapts its teaching on the basis of a fine-grained learner model—might still be seen as a long-term goal (Kintsch, 1989). Third, there are alternative and more robust ways to support and facilitate learning and problem solving through interaction with a computer.

Pedagogical Wisdom.   Furthermore, one can question a didactic approach to learning—with or without computers—that takes students by the neck and forces them down some predefined, presumably efficient solution path,[2] without allowing students to make errors or to get lost, and without encouraging planning, goal setting, diagnosis, and self-assessment. This skeptical view is consistent with remarks made by Scardamalia, Bereiter, McLean, Swallow, and Woodruff (1989), who called on the active and intelligent learner, not the computer system—which is merely seen as a facilitating tool—to perform the diagnosing, goal setting, and planning (see also De Corte, chap. 7, this volume).

Alternative and less directive (un)intelligent computer-based systems for learning and instruction can contribute to the ultimate goal of developing virtually autonomous learners and reflective problem solvers.[3] This does not require

---

[1]At best, today's cognitive modeling techniques provide educational researchers with a heuristic tool for further exploring the rich phenomenology of cognition and instruction (cf. Reusser, 1990).

[2]This seems to be the underlying pedagogy reflected by some principles of the ITS (cf. Anderson et al., 1984).

[3]For a discussion of unintelligent tutoring, compare Nathan, Kintsch, and Young (1992).

intelligent systems, but rather facilitative and flexible structures, that is, didactic supports that, instead of being located solely in the computer, reside in many brains and machines (Dillenbourg, chap. 9, this volume). The burden of providing intelligence should not be borne by a computer system. Instead, intelligence is distributed across the entire didactic setting and consists of the combined pedagogical and domain-related intelligence of teachers, learners, contexts, and technology-based tools.

The Myth of the Learner as a Radical Constructivist

Underlying the ideas of individualization, cognitive skill enhancement, and didactic adaptivity, which are driving current research on the development of educational technology, there is an even deeper motive or presupposition that is having an impact on the design of learning environments: the fuzzy issues of *constructivism*—often called *radical constructivism*—and *learner autonomy*, which are currently in vogue. Both concepts are infiltrating the psychopedagogical zeitgeist. Ultimately philosophical and epistemological in nature, these concepts have a long history in philosophy and education. Epistemological constructivism—referring back to the work of Piaget (1950) and his philosophical predecessor, Kant (1781/1965), who introduced the doctrine of constructivism —seems to have found its pedagogical complement in a set of instructional methods that appear under labels such as *inductive, experiential, self-directed,* or *discovery learning.* Pedagogical or didactic constructivism relates to the perennial history of progressive education since Rousseau's (1762/1951) *Emile,* although the relation seems to be conceptually vague and historically complex.

According to the doctrine of epistemological constructivism that is implied, for example, in Piaget's cognitive–developmental psychology, the ideal learner, including the child, is seen as a spontaneously active, volitional learner, as a discoverer and explorer, and as a virtually autonomous subject who shapes his or her mind and conception of the world as the result of intentional socio-cognitive activity.

Epistemological constructivism—considered from a cognitive instructional point of view—rests on the fundamental assumption that no learner can be forced by any teacher, tool, or material to an insight, to an understanding of a concept, or to become intrinsically involved in deeper learning. That is, the child's learning is always fundamentally constructive in the sense of his or her basic epistemic activity. According to Piaget, any developmental change, as well as any knowledge construction, is a matter of building relationships (*mettre en relation*), thus a genuine mental structure-building activity that every child always has to do on his or her own, and that nobody ever can do for the child.

Many educational researchers, however, go beyond the epistemological constructivism that is broadly accepted today. As proponents of what is labeled *radical constructivism,* they adopt a romantic and almost mythical view of the self-constructive nature of children's minds, as well as an idyllic and over-idealized view of the societal task of learning and enculturation in a mass schooling system. Opposing all forms of directly guiding instruction, radical constructivism, in some of its proposed didactic consequences, comes close to *radical progressive education,* which is historically documented by more dead ends and failures than success stories (cf. Oelkers, 1989).

Assuming that all children possess almost unlimited capabilities, and viewing the knowledge and skills they acquire as emergent properties of largely nondirective interactions between children and more knowledgeable others, radical constructivism—if mapped into the didactic practices of nondirected instruction —may run the risk of underestimating the essential role of direct and indirect guidance of good teachers and carefully designed cognitive tools.

The following remarks are based on less optimistic assumptions regarding the constructive nature of learning with regard to the societal task of enculturation. First, adopting a constructivist view of the psychopedagogical nature of learning and comprehension must not lead us to equate the process of schooling with inductive discovery learning or exploratory activities under the almost unrestricted control of the learner. Children will not construct or discover in a few hours what has taken our culture years or centuries to develop. Discovery learning, in any demanding sense, is very slow; it mainly explains how cultures develop and change. School learning in a mass society, however, must be accelerated, with the goal of continuing and preserving culture and cultural identity across the time course of generations.

At the same time, we would not wish to underestimate the importance of other constructivist assumptions. These include a high regard for independent learning and the essential role of teachers in this process: as adaptive structural and procedural role models, as domain experts and scaffolds for expert learning, and, more generally, as impulse givers and facilitators of learning. Thus, to provide various forms of direct and indirect structural and procedural assistance is at the heart of professional teaching. This activity is equivalent to the pedagogical design of learning environments, and is in accordance with the concept of didactics as a design science (Simon, 1981; Wittmann, 1992).

Cognitive Tools for Intentional Learners: Six Design Principles

In this section, six principles for didactically intelligent computer-based tools are briefly sketched (for further elaboration, see Reusser, 1993). The principles help make up for the lack of attention received by two issues in the past: didactic learning theory and cognitive-instructional task analysis of content.

1. Design-intelligent technologies as cognitive tools for thoughtful teachers and learners. In contrast to technology-driven systems, cognitive tools should be used as means to pedagogical (didactic) ends or goals.

2. Stimulate and facilitate students' efforts toward domain-knowledge construction, understanding, and skill acquisition by providing expert procedural and domain conceptual (structural) assistance. This means implementing the qualities of expert learners and domain-knowledge experts—the latter representing the structure of a discipline—as instructional tools. Modern computers—with their direct-manipulation graphics interfaces—are ideally suited to provide representational and procedural support for students.

3. Provide students with intelligible representational tools of thought and communication. To understand a concept or a domain structure is to represent and express it in appropriate ways. As Simon (1981) remarked, reviving the spirit of Wertheimer (1945): "Solving a problem simply means representing it so as to make the solution transparent" (p. 153). Efficient and cognitively plausible representation of content is a fundamental problem for every theory of knowing and instruction. Effective representational skills, formats, and notations that constrain and support qualitative, semiquantitative, and quantitative reasoning in all scientific disciplines are part of the indispensible tool kit required for thinking and problem solving. Therefore, to teach culturally shared representational forms, and generic and domain-specific representation-building skills, is a significant and critical goal of instruction.

4. Provide as much learner control as possible and as much control of the learner as needed—or provide learners with some guidance according to the principle of *variable control and minimal help* (Aebli, 1961/1987). In contrast to the principle of *immediate feedback* in Anderson's (1989) teacher-centered approach to intelligent tutoring[4], the minimal-help principle states that learner control should be optimized by letting the system intervene only if help is needed and/or requested by the student. By making a virtue of necessity, the principle also adapts to rather limited capacity of most systems for student diagnosing and modeling.

5. By their potential as extracortical mirrors of the mind (Pea, 1985), computers should allow students to express and communicate their mental models and to reflect on their own processes and products of learning. Computers have the unique potential to provide learners with a powerful medium for representing, visualizing, and reflecting on their own mental models, as well as their learning and thought processes, including those of learning partners in collaborative learning. The long-term use of computers as tools for reflection on one's learning in different domains and disciplines may eventually lead to the overall reflectivity that characterizes mature learners and problem solvers.

6. Extend computer-based instruction from individual to cooperative contexts of learning. A questionable feature of our schooling culture is that students are

---

[4]"An error comes close to being a necessary and sufficient condition for tutorial intervention" (Anderson, 1989, p. 343).

treated almost exclusively as solo leaners (Bruner, 1986). However, intelligence is not a property of the mind alone, but rather a quality distributed among all components—agents (brains), tools (machines), and practices—of a learning environment (see also Dillenbourg, chap. 9, this volume). Therefore, because it is unlikely that computers will become truly adaptive cognitive partners or sensitive coaches in the near future, they should be integrated into the didactic settings of classrooms.

HERON: A COGNITIVE TOOL FOR UNDERSTANDING AND SOLVING MATHEMATICAL STORY PROBLEMS

We developed a cognitive tool, called HERON (after the Greek mathematician who was among the early inventors of mathematical word problems), based on our cognitive modeling work and on the previous cognitive-instructional principles. HERON is a mouse-driven, graphics-based problem-solving tool for understanding and solving complex mathematical story problems. HERON helps students from Grades 3 through 9 identify, conceptualize, and express the relevant pieces of information in a problem, and supports the reified planning and construction of a mathematical problem model, including the derivation of an equation.

Solution Trees

The design of conceptually faithful and cognitively efficient representations as instruments of thought and communication (Kaput, 1989) is more than a prerequisite pedagogical task, and far more than just ad hoc and tricky didactic art work. The issue of domain-representational form(at)s and notations touches the fundamental epistemological and ontological (cf. Greeno, 1983) questions of what constitutes our psychological building blocks and forms of knowing and thinking (Aebli, 1980–1981), that is, our most effective and satisfying cognitive models and activities.

HERON uses a graphical format for problem representation and planning called *solution trees*—a conceptual tool developed by Aebli, Ruthemann, and Staub (1986) for use with paper and pencil and employed in their empirical work. A similar format was developed by Derry and Hawkes (1989).

Solution trees provide students with a constraining format for planning and generating their solutions and, at the same time, for expressing their understanding of the problem in situational and mathematical forms (cf. the previous design principles). They consist of dynamically linked entities that capture the dual situational and mathematical deep structure implied in a broad range of story problems. Solution trees function as flexible, transparent, and visually inspectable tools for semiquantitative reasoning that allow the simultaneous grasping of both the semantic and the mathematical deep structure denoted by a problem text. Thus, solution trees are a type of the cognitively efficient notational formats proposed in our framework for cognitive instructional representation (Reusser, 1993).

Solution trees allow the problem solver to view together the semantic and underlying mathematical structure denoted by a problem text. Their value from an instructional point of view is that they invite and force students to focus on and visualize the logicomathematical deep structure of a problem, using a constraining format that relates problem comprehension to both the surface structure of the episodic problem text and its implied quantitative structure.

Working With HERON: An Example

Currently, HERON tutors any word or story problem that can be expressed by a solution tree. There are two implementations of the HERON environment: one is written in Loops (Kämpfer, 1991) and runs on a Xerox 1186, and the other is used in classrooms and runs on DOS machines (Stüssi, 1991).

HERON is designed so that it takes third graders about 20 minutes to become familiar with a mouse-driven interface, giving students a great deal of control over how to work with the system. To demonstrate its functioning, we use an example.

The specific problem that we assume a student decides to solve is depicted in the upper right window in Fig. 5.3. After carefully reading the problem text, the student is asked by the system to set up and instantiate problem-specific situation units or elements represented visually as boxes with the three value entries: *situation concept, quantity,* and *dimension* (unit of measurement). The generation of the boxes for quantities given in the problem text is done by highlighting a number or number placeholder in the text with the mouse cursor.

When quantity information (e.g., *15*) is selected, the system creates a box with the selected number filled in. The student then fills in a unit of measurement (e.g., *days*) and a label for an adequate situation concept (e.g., *remaining time until birthday*) that interprets the quantity in terms of a qualitative situation model. Both the dimension and the situation-concept label are selected from menus that can be activated by the mouse (cf. the problem-specific, situation-concept menu in Fig. 5.3). After the box representing a situation element has been completed, the student can select and interpret a new piece of quantitative information.

After instantiating two or more situation elements, the student can generate the first relational element of his or her solution tree (Fig. 5.3 and 5.4). To instantiate a first triadic-relational schema, for example, with the purpose of computing the number of rows still to be knitted, the situation units (boxes) labeled *length of the scarf* and *number of rows knitted so far* are selected, moved to the upper left corner of the screen, and linked together by a menu-selected

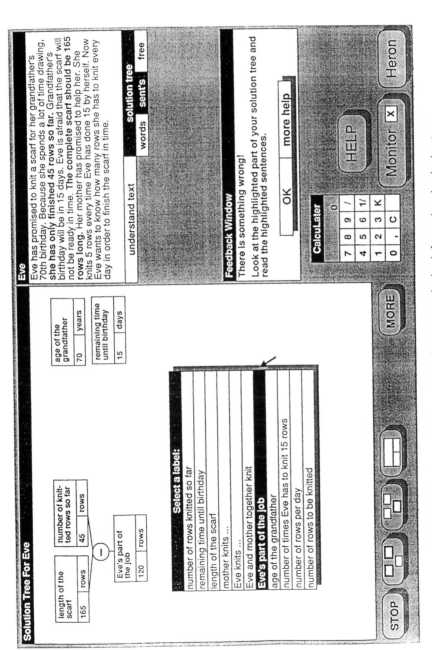

FIG. 5.3. Selecting and interpreting relevant quantitative information; beginning tree construction; current step: selecting an interpretive situational concept label and system feedback on a falsely selected label.

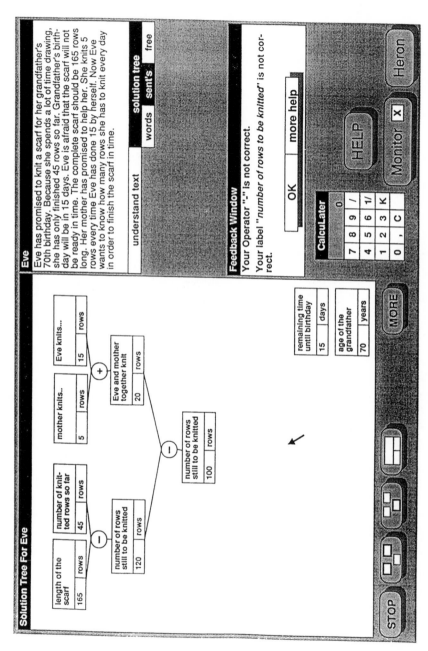

FIG. 5.4. Emerging solution tree; system feedback on an operation error.

empty-operator node. Hereby an empty box, representing an intermediary sub-goal unit, is generated by the system. Before the student can place the unit of measurement (*rows*) and label (*number of rows still to be knitted*), into the box, he or she has to select an appropriate mathematical operation from a menu that appears by clicking the mouse on the empty operator node. In our example, the student unfortunately has chosen the faulty situation concept *Eve's part of the job*, causing HERON to intervene with an error message and some (potentially gradual) advice on how to correct the erroneous label (feedback window in Fig. 5.3). Let us assume that the student (after this first message or after having received further—more constraining—advice from the system) has detected his or her error and changed the label to *number of rows still to be knitted*, thus, achieving his or her first subgoal.

Figures 5.4, 5.5, and 5.6 (Fig. 5.4 depicting an operation error made by the student and how the system responds to it) show, for any triadic relational schema being instantiated, how its resulting elements can be used to generate new schemata, that is, to achieve further subgoals by building on the emerging

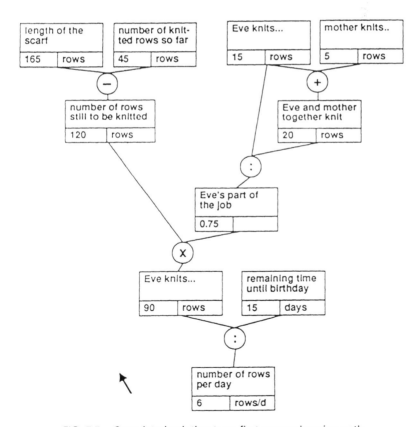

FIG. 5.5. Completed solution tree; first comprehension path.

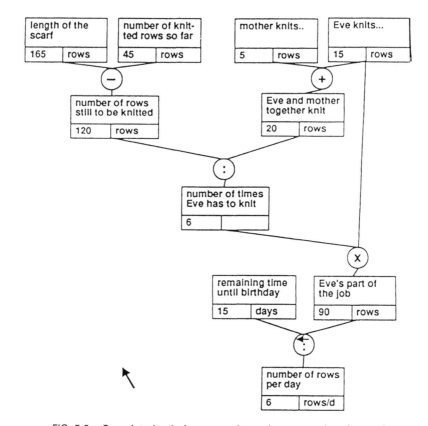

FIG. 5.6. Completed solution tree; alternative comprehension path.

solution-tree network. Solution trees can be constructed through a mixed forward and backward inferencing activity. In forward inferencing, the student's solution starts by constructing triads based on the quantities given in the problem statement; in backward inferencing, the student starts with the goal element, or with some inferred intermediary element, and works backward or upward to the given elements. The tree-constructing activity goes on until the student has completed a tree (Fig. 5.5 or 5.6) and decides that the problem is solved.

It is up to the student to choose which comprehension path to follow, that is, how to navigate through the problem space. Most problems allow more than one comprehension path. Figures 5.5 and 5.6 describe two alternative operative conceptualizations of the same problem.[5]

To generate equations from the solution tree, the student can push the right side of the mouse button on any numerical value in the tree. The system displays

---

[5]For an example of how a much more complex problem is solved, see Reusser (1993).

a partial equation or, if clicking on the numerical value in final result box, the solution equation of the problem.

Final Remarks

At any time while working on a problem, students can call for progressively constrained help for both deeper comprehension of the problem and construction of solution trees (design principle of *minimal help* or *variable control*). Help with text comprehension mainly consists of explanations of language patterns, paraphrasing of sentences, and hints for textual inferences. Construction help provides the student with increasingly detailed hints about what to do next, ultimately offering a next operative step.

To provide feedback, HERON does not try to model the students' thinking. Feedback is provided on the basis of a detailed analysis of the task space into which the observed construction activities of the students are mapped. HERON knows which situation elements can or must (not) be connected in a solution tree, and which labels and units of measurements are to be attached to quantified situation units. Thus, HERON monitors the students' construction activity and provides feedback on mathematical operation errors, situation-concept errors, unit-of-measurement errors, and errors regarding the inclusion or omission of (ir)relevant information in a solution tree.

Rather than being a solo instrument of learning, HERON is conceived of as a flute in an orchestra (Salomon, 1990), or in a carefully composed learning environment. So far, students mostly work in pairs. HERON records in a log file the activities performed on the screen. This allows students to replay their comprehension (solution) paths, which they can reflect on and discuss (cf. design principle 4). To evaluate the HERON system in a classroom setting, we compared pairs of fifth-grade students solving word problems with and without the system in an intervention study (H. Staub, Stebler, Reusser, & Pauli, 1994). So far, the results indicate that HERON was easily accepted by teachers and students, and that using the system was beneficial to the students in at least three ways: with respect to (a) an improvement in understanding and solving relatively complex story problems in a posttest, (b) the mindfulness of dialogue among the co-working students, and (c) the quality of cooperation in maintaining a mutually shared understanding of the problem (Pauli, 1994).

As with any educational technology, the design, use, and evaluation of an ITS requires a pedagogic-didactic philosophy of both what and how to tutor. That is, it must incorporate reflections about the child as a learner, a view of the pedagogical and cultural goals of schooling, a sound analysis of domain knowledge and tasks, as well as a psychopedagogical theory of development, learning, and instruction.

Like all educational technologies, computer-based learning environments should be considered as a means or an instrument to pedagogical ends or goals.

Computers, which are by their very nature multipurpose tools with many facets, will only become valuable cognitive-didactic tools for learners and teachers if they are designed for and used in the service of pedagogical goals.

ACKNOWLEDGMENTS

The work in this chapter was supported by a grant from the Swiss National Science Foundation (Contract 10–2052.86). I am grateful to the members of my research group (Xander Kämpfer, Fritz C. Staub, Rita Stebler, and Ruedi Stüssi), in which many of the ideas in this chapter were shaped. I am also very grateful to Eileen Kintsch for her invaluable comments on the final draft of this chapter.

REFERENCES

Aebli, H. (1980–1981). *Denken. Das Ordnen des Tuns* [Thinking]. (2 vols.). Stuttgart: Klett.

Aebli, H. (1987). *Zwölf Grundformen des Lehrens* [Twelve basic methods of teaching]. (3rd ed.). Stuttgart: Klett. (Original work published 1961)

Aebli, H., Ruthemann, U., & Staub, F. C. (1986). Sind Regeln des Problemlösens lehrbar? [Can rules of problem-solving be taught?]. *Zeitschrift für Pädagogik, 32,* 617–638.

Anderson, J. A. (1989, April). *Psychology and intelligent tutoring.* Paper presented at the fourth international conference on AI in Education, Amsterdam, Netherlands.

Anderson, J. A., Boyle, C. F., Farrell, R., & Reiser, B. (1984). Cognitive principles in the design of computer tutors. In *Proceedings of the sixth annual conference of the Cognitive Science Society* (pp. 1–9). Boulder: University of Colorado, Institute of Cognitive Science.

Anderson, J. R., Boyle, C. F., Corbett, A. T., & Lewis, M. W. (1990). Cognitive modeling and intelligent tutoring. In W. J. Clancey & E. Soloway (Eds.), *Artificial intelligence and learning environments* (pp. 7–49). Cambridge, MA: MIT Press.

Bobrow, D. G. (1964). *Natural language input for a computer problem solving system.* Unpublished doctoral dissertation, MIT, Cambridge, MA.

Bork, A. (1985). *Personal computers for education.* New York: Harper & Row.

Brown, J. S. (1984). *Idea amplifiers: New kinds of electronic learning environments.* Palo Alto, CA: Xerox Research Center.

Bruner, J. (1986). *Actual minds, possible worlds.* Cambridge, MA: Harvard University Press.

Collins, A., & Brown, J. S. (1988). The computer as a tool for learning through reflection. In H. Mandl & A. Lesgold (Eds.), *Learning issues for intelligent tutoring systems* (pp. 1–18). New York: Springer.

Comenius, J. A. (1659). *Orbis sensualium pictus.* London: J. Kirton.

Cummins, D., Kintsch, W., Reusser, K., & Weimer, R. (1988). The role of understanding in solving word problems. *Cognitive Psychology, 20,* 439–462.

De Corte, E., Verschaffel, L., & de Win, L. (1985). Influence of rewording problems on children's problem representations and solutions. *Journal of Educational Psychology, 77,* 460–470.

Derry, S. J., & Hawkes, L. W. (1989). *Error-driven cognitive apprenticeship: A feasible ITS approach.* Tallahassee: Florida State University Press.

diSessa, A. (1989). *Computational media as a foundation for new learning cultures* (Tech. Rep. No. G5). Berkeley: University of California Press.

Greeno, J. G. (1983). Conceptual entities. In D. Gentner & A. L. Stevens (Eds.), *Mental models* (pp. 227–252). Hillsdale, NJ: Lawrence Erlbaum Associates.

Kämpfer, A. (1991). *Prototypische Entwicklung eines adaptiven tutoriellen Systems zum Verstehen und Lösen mathematischer Textaufgeben* [Development of an adaptive ITS for understanding and solving mathematical word problems]. Unpublished master's thesis, University of Bern, Switzerland.

Kant, I. (1965). *The critique of pure reason* (N. Kemp, Trans.). New York: St. Martin's Press. (Original work published 1781)

Kaput, J. J. (1989). Linking representations in the symbol systems of algebra. In S. Wagner & C. Kieran (Eds.), *Research issues in the learning and teaching of algebra* (pp. 167–194). Reston, VI: The national Council of Teachers of Mathematics.

Kintsch, W., & Greeno, J. G. (1985). Understanding and solving word arithmetic problems. *Psychological Review, 92*, 109–129.

Kintsch, W. (1989, September). *A theory of discourse comprehension: Implications for a tutor for word algebra problems.* Paper presented in the third conference of the European Association for Research on Learning and Instruction EARLI, Madrid, Spain.

Klafki, W. (1958). Didaktische Analyse als Kern der Unterrichtsvorbereitung [Didactic analysis as core of teacher preparation]. *Die Deutsche Schule, 50*(10), 451–471.

Klafki, W. (1963). *Das pädagogische Problem des Elementaren und die Theorie der kategorialen Bildung* [The pedagogical problem of the basics in education]. Weinheim: Beltz.

Lajoie, S., & Derry, S. J. (Eds.). (1993). *Computers as cognitive tools.* Hillsdale, NJ: Lawrence Erlbaum Associates.

Lehmensick, E. (1926). *Die Theorie der formalen Bildung* [Theory of formal discipline]. Göttingen: Vandenhoeck & Ruprecht.

Lepper, M. R., & Gurtner, J.-L. (1989). Children and computers. *American Psychologist, 44*(2), 170–178.

Mandl, H., & Lesgold, A. (Eds.). (1988). *Learning issues for intelligent tutoring systems.* New York: Springer.

Mann, L. (1979). *On the trail of process.* New York: Grune & Stratton.

McArthur, D., Stasz, C., & Zmuidzinas, M. (1990). Tutoring techniques in algebra. *Cognition and Instruction, 7*, 161–195.

Mitman, A., Mergendoller, J., Marchman, V., & Packer, M. (1987). Instruction addressing the components of scientific literacy and its relation to students outcomes. *American Educational Research Journal, 23*, 611–633.

Nathan, M., Kintsch, W., & Young, E. (1992). A theory of algebra word problem comprehension and its implications for the design of learning environments. *Cognition and Instruction, 9*(4), 329–389.

Nesher, P., & Teubal, E. (1975). Verbal cues as interfering factors in verbal problem solving. *Educational Studies in Mathematics, 6*, 41–51.

Ohlsson, S. (1986). Some principles of intelligent tutoring. *Instructional Science, 14*, 293–326.

Oelkers, J. (1989). *Reformpädagogik* [Reform pedagogy]. München: Juventa.

Paige, J. M., & Simon, H. A. (1966). Cognitive processes in solving algebra word problems. In B. Kleinmuntz (Ed.), *Problem solving* (pp. 51–119). New York: Wiley.

Papert, S. (1980). *Mindstorms, Children, computers and powerful ideas.* New York: Basic Books.

Pauli, C. (1994). Mathematische Textaufgaben lösen mit HERON. Eine Analyse von Schüler dialogen in einer kooperativen Lernsituation mit und ohne Unterstützung duich ein tutorielles system [Solving mathematical word problems with HERON. An analysis of dialogues of student pairs cooperatively solving word problems with and without the use of a tutorial system]. Unpublished master's thesis, University of Zurich, Switzerland.

Pea, R. D. (1985). Beyond amplification: Using the computer to reorganize mental functioning. *Educational Psychohlogist, 20*, 167–182.

Pea, R. D. (1987). Cognitive technologies for mathematics education. In A. H. Schoenfeld (Ed.), *Cognitive science and mathematics education* (pp. 89–122). Hillsdale, NJ: Lawrence Erlbaum Associates.

Piaget, J. (1947). *La psychologie de l'intelligence* [Psychology of intelligence]. Paris: Colin.

Piaget, J. (1950). *Introduction à l'épistémologie génétique* [Introduction to genetic epistemology]. Paris: Presses Universitaires de France.

Reusser, K. (1985). *From text to situation to equation* (Tech. Rep. No. 143). Boulder: University of Colorado Press.

Reusser, K. (1989a). *Vom Text zur Situation zur Gleichung. Kognitive Simulation von Sprachverständnis und Mathematisierung beim Lösen von mathematischen Textaufgaben* [From text to situation to equation. Cognitive simulation of language comprehension and mathematization in solving mathematical word problems]. Unpublished habilitation thesis, University of Bern, Switzerland.

Reusser, K. (1989b, September). *Textual and situational factors in mathematical word problems.* Paper presented at the third conference of the European Association for Research on Learning and Instruction EARLI, Madrid, Spain.

Reusser, K. (1990). From text to situation to equation: Cognitive simulation of understanding and solving mathematical word problems. In H. Mandl, E. De Corte, N. Bennett, & H. F. Friedrich (Eds.), *Learning and instruction in an international context* (Vol. 2, pp. 477–498). New York: Pergamon.

Reusser, K. (1993). tutoring systems and pedagogical theory. In S. Lajoie & S. Derry (Eds.), *Computers as cognitive tools* (pp. 143–177). Hillsdale, NJ: Lawrence Erlbaum Associates.

Rousseau, J. J., (1951). *Emile ou de l'éducation* [On education]. Paris: Garnier. (Original work published 1762)

Salomon, G. (1990). Studying the flute and the orchestra. *International Journal of Educational Research, 14*(6), 521–532.

Salomon, G., Perkins, D. N., & Globerson, T. (1991). Partners in cognition: Extending human intelligence with intelligent technologies. *Educational Researcher, 20*(3), 2–9.

Scardamalia, M., Bereiter, C., McLean, R. S., Swallow, J., & Woodruff, E. (1989). Computer-supported intentional learning environments. *Journal of Educational Computing Research, 5,* 51–68.

Shute, V., & Glaser, R. (1990). A large scale evaluation of an intelligent discovery world: Smithtown. *Interactive Learning Environments, 1,* 59–77.

Simon, H. A. (1981). *The sciences of the artificial.* Cambridge, MA: MIT Press.

Sleeman, D., & Brown, J. S. (1982). *Intelligent tutoring systems.* New York: Academic Press.

Staub, F. C., & Reusser, K. (1995). The role of presentational structures in understanding and solving mathematical word problems. In C. A. Weaver, S. Mannes, & C. R. Fletcher (Eds.), *Discourse comprehension. Essays in honor of Walter Kintsch* (pp. 285–305). Hillsdale, NJ: Lawrence Erlbaum Associates.

Staub, F. C., Stebler, R., Reusser, K., & Pauli, C. (1994, April). *Improving understanding and solving of math story problems through collaborative use of a computer tool (HERON).* Paper presented at the annual meeting of the American Educational Research Association AERA, New Orleans.

Stern, E. (1991, April). *The role of language in solving word problems.* Paper presented at the annual meeting of the American Educational Research Association AERA, Chicago, IL.

Stern, E., & Lehrndorfer, A. (1992). The role of situational context in solving word problems. *Cognitive Development, 7,* 259–268.

Stüssi, R. (1991). *WATGRAF. Ein tutorielles System zum Lösen von handlungsbezogenen Sachaufgaben* [A tutorial system for solving mathematical word problems]. Unpublished master's thesis, University of Bern, Switzerland.

van Dijk, T., & Kintsch, W. (1983). *Strategies of discourse comprehension*. New York: Academic Press.

Weniger, E. (1952). *Didaktik als Bildungslehre* [Didactics as theory of bildung]. Weinheim: Beltz.

Wertheimer, M. (1945). *Productive thinking*. New York: Harper & Row.

Willmann, O. (1957). *Didaktik als Bildungslehre* [Didactics as theory of bildung]. Freiburg: Herder. (Original work published 1889)

Wittmann, E. C. (1992). Mathematikdidaktik als "design science" [Didactics of mathematics as design science]. *Journal Mathematikdidaktik, 13*(1), 55–70.

6 and Reflective Abstraction: Learning Advanced Mathematical Concepts in a Computer Environment

Erno Lehtinen
Sisko Repo
University of Joensuu, Finland

THEORETICAL AND EMPIRICAL BACKGROUND

The aim of this chapter is to investigate the construction of advanced mathematical concepts in a computer-based learning environment. The chapter deals especially with how a computer-based environment can facilitate individual and social activities that are related to the construction of abstract mathematical concepts. Although the aim of this chapter is to discuss the problems related to the learning of advanced mathematical content (the concept of *the derivative*), our hypothesis is that the basic problems regarding the quality of the mathematical construction process are not very different than those involved in other, less advanced mathematical topics. Thus, a general discussion of the main problems of the construction of mathematical concepts in typical school situations is justified.

Numerous investigations on errors in mathematical procedures have been made in recent years. In particular, insights from cognitive science and the production system approach have been useful for examining the typical errors that students make in mathematics. This detailed cognitive analysis of the systematic errors (bugs) in students' calculation procedures gives us the possibility to develop more adequate instructional strategies intended to help students develop procedural rules (Maurer, 1987; VanLehn, 1982, 1983). This approach, which concentrates on the errors in algorithmic procedures, involves some limitations, however, if we consider mathematics education. The serious problems that can be involved in students' automated and faultless mathematical procedures have been described by researchers over several decades (see Dreyfus, 1991; Schoenfeld, 1985; Selden, Mason, & Selden, 1989; Wertheimer, 1959). Besides the systematic process errors (bugs), many other, more general problems of mathematics learning, such as lack of understanding (Greeno, 1987), inadequate beliefs and metacognitions (Schoenfeld, 1985, 1987), and insufficient or erroneous strategies (Wenger, 1987), have been highlighted in recent research.

In one of our earlier studies (Lehtinen & Savimäki, 1993), our sample consisted of high-achieving lower secondary-school students (13- to 14-year-olds). This study was concerned with two areas of the mathematics curriculum: mathematical problems that were taught during primary school (1–3 years earlier), and the concept of *the equation*. Immediately after the mathematics test was administered, the students were interviewed individually. Although the students were able to correctly solve the problems, the results showed that they had a rather weak understanding of the mathematical basis of the algorithmic techniques they had used. We also found evidence for several misconceptions. For example, some students had solved hundreds of problems where they had canceled fractions, but they still believed that the value of the fraction changes if one divides or multiplies the numerator and denominator by the same number. This result shows that even frequent repetition of an algorithmic procedure can be insufficient to correct misconceptions or to increase understanding of mathematical concepts. We followed the same high-achieving students' mathematical thinking during the 8-week period in which they studied equations in the seventh grade. The students rapidly learned to use algorithmic procedures to correctly solve the unknown from an equation. However, the results of the individual interviews show that many of the students had an inadequate understanding of the equation concept. This included a poorly elaborated concept of *equality*, "mystical" beliefs about the unknown, and insufficient understanding of the construction of equations. Because of their inadequate concept of equality, many of the high-achieving students had no mathematical arguments for the algorithmic techniques they used when they solved complex equations. (For more detailed information, see Lehtinen & Savimäki, 1993.) Observations of students' goals indicate that task-oriented efforts to deeply understand the concepts to be learned and problems to be solved are only typical of a small percentage of top-achieving students. Many high-achieving students are oriented to fulfill the extrinsic demands of the school (conventional school-related task orientation; see Olkinuora, Lehtinen, & Salonen, 1988). They develop skilled strategies for learning the algorithmic procedures they need in the standard school examinations, without having any coherent understanding of the mathematical concepts.

The conclusions of our study concerning the quality of mathematical thinking in high achievers are similar to those of Davis (1988) and Selden et al. (1989). Often mathematics instruction—from elementary school through college courses—teaches what might be called *rituals*. Teachers typically accept correctly performed rituals as indicating mastery of the subject matter. As Dreyfus (1991) put it,

> what most students learn in their mathematics courses is, to carry out a large number of standardized procedures, cast in precisely defined formalisms, for ob-

taining answers to clearly defined classes of exercise questions . . . they have been taught the products of the activity of scores of mathematicians in their final form, but they have not gained insight into the processes that have led mathematicians to create these products. (p. 28)

Although a deeper understanding of mathematical concepts is stressed in the general aims of the mathematics curriculum, there are some systematic features in the characteristics of mathematical knowledge and in the conventional methods of mathematics teaching that make superficial learning so typical. In current teaching practice, considerable emphasis is placed on learning algorithms. Various types of problems are taken up and solved, usually by means of a given algorithmic procedure. An essential aim of mathematics teaching is to develop students' mastery of procedures. This aim is, indeed, a necessary condition for the attainment of the other aims as long as computing is done by hand, but it often leads to premature automatization of algorithms based on erroneous or insufficient conceptual understanding (Davis, 1988; Dreyfus, 1991; Hiebert & Lefevre, 1986; Lehtinen & Savimäki, 1993; Schoenfeld, 1989; Wertheimer, 1959). In other words, the connections between procedural and conceptual knowledge have not been satisfactorily established. Consequently, the pupils have no understanding of where and how the mathematics they have learned can be used outside the mathematics lessons (see Resnick, 1987).

REFLECTIVE ABSTRACTION: A FRAMEWORK FOR ANALYZING AND FACILITATING THE CONSTRUCTION PROCESS

From a constructivist point of view, typical mathematics teaching gives the student few opportunities and little support for the construction of a deep understanding. Generally, we can argue that the construction of conceptual structures of mathematics is based on the concrete activities undertaken by the student, as well as on communication with the cultural environment, especially with the teacher and other students (Aebli, 1987; Ernest, 1991). In traditional teaching, the student's activity is mostly oriented toward mechanical repetition of algorithmic procedures. Social interaction in the classroom is also normally oriented toward concrete problems in performing the algorithmic procedures. In situations where the teacher is dealing with more abstract mathematical concepts, there is seldom any reciprocal communication between the teacher and the students (see Lehtinen, Ketola, & Vuontela, 1995).

In the traditional mathematics classroom, the student's construction process is typically based on a generalization process that we call *empirical* or *horizontal generalization* (see Dubinsky, 1991; Karmiloff-Smith & Inhelder, 1974–1975; Piaget, 1978). Generalizations are not based on the construction of an abstract theoretical model, but on the similarities of the surface properties across problems. With the help of "horizontal generalization," students can solve typical textbook problems, but are not able to construct an adequate conceptual understanding because their mental models are limited to the level of concrete mathematical knowledge (entities). If our aim is to cover the deeper and more abstract levels of mathematical knowledge, another kind of construction process is needed. According to Piaget, we can call this other type of construction process *reflective abstraction*. This term refers to a process in which the student tries to construct abstract structures and operations by reflecting on his or her own activities and the arguments used in social interaction (Piaget, 1976, 1978).

Dubinsky (1991, p. 102) proposed a method called *genetic decomposition* as a basis for planning instruction that supports the process of reflective abstraction during learning of advanced mathematical concepts. The aim of genetic decomposition of a concept is to find the crucial construction steps necessary for developing an adequate understanding of the particular mathematical concept. These steps are dependent on the specific features of the concept in question, and they can be described in terms of subfunctions of reflective abstraction. The subfunctions of reflective abstraction have been summarized by Dubinsky (1991, p. 101):

a) Interiorization refers to translating a succession of material actions into a system of interiorized operations (Beth & Piaget, 1966, p. 206)
b) Co-ordination of two or more processes to construct a new one
c) Encapsulation of dynamic processes into an object that means that ". . . actions or operations become thematized objects of thought or assimilation" (Piaget, 1985, p. 49)
d) Generalization means that a subject learns to apply an existing schema to a wider collection of phenomena.

To design instruction that moves students along the cognitive steps, we have to develop a sequence of activities and create situations that will induce students to make the specific reflective abstractions that are called for. In this study, we have tried to systematically analyze the prerequisites for effective reflective abstractions in general and those belonging to the development of the derivative concept in particular. The prerequisites we focus on here are: (a) critical activities, (b) multiple representations, and (c) challenging and facilitating social interaction.

Critical Activities: Starting Point for Reflective Abstraction

In his book *Success and Understanding*, Piaget (1978) described "precociously successful actions" that the subject later conceptualizes and internalizes. In traditional mathematics education, the activities that students are typically involved in are related to algorithmic practicing. Although repeated exercise (and cumulative success) with mechanical tasks can certainly lead to rapid automatization of algorithmic skills, it is not the kind of activity that optimally supports construction of mathematics understanding in students (Dubinsky, 1991; VanLehn, 1980). Theoretically, we have assumed that, to be helpful for reflective abstraction, the basic activities should fulfill the following requirements. (a) The activities should be of optimal difficulty, that is, they must be demanding enough so that all the students experience the tasks as challenging, but not so difficult that students cannot adequately deal with them with the help of their previous knowledge. (b) To allow time for the construction process, the duration of critical activities must be long enough. A complex long-term task, instead of numerous simple examples, is assumed to create the necessary conditions for higher order construction (Achtenhagen, 1992). (c) The critical activities should be related to the concept to be learned in a way that activates the relevant prior knowledge of the student and gives opportunities for interiorization, coordination, encapsulation, and generalization (Dubinsky, 1991). It is our assumption that a computer environment can render activities that are optimal for reflective abstraction, but would be difficult to fulfill in a natural environment (Collins & Brown, 1988; Dubinsky & Tall, 1991; Wenger, 1987). To create optimal possibilities for the student to develop mathematical understanding, the learning environment should offer concrete support in the form of distributed expertise (Brown et al., 1993). This means that students should participate in complex problem-solving activity even before they are familiar with the subskills and special knowledge that are needed for the complete fulfillment of the task. This is possible if the learning environment facilitates students' activities by offering them intelligent tools (e.g., computer programs) that are able to solve subproblems or display necessary information.

One of the aims of this study is to develop a technology-rich environment appropriate for activities that support the construction of advanced mathematical concepts. In the present tradition of constructivism, free spontaneous exploration and discovery have been stressed. However, this "romantic" interpretation of constructivism (see the Piaget criticism by Aebli, 1987; Reusser, 1991) does not offer an appropriate theoretical basis for designing a learning environment for advanced concepts. The development of advanced mathematical concepts has taken hundreds of years of intentional effort by mathematicians. It would be naive to think that students would be able to construct these concepts spontaneously with the help of random activities (Ernest, 1991). Systematic guidance by the teacher is needed, but not necessarily in the form of direct transmission of knowledge. In classrooms organized according to the ideas of constructivism, the role of the teacher is problematic (Brown et al., 1993). In this study, we have tried to develop constructivism-based models for indirect instructional interventions that teachers could apply in secondary-school mathematics classes. According to this framework, we can argue that a sequence of adequate activities is essential for successful construction. Students are not able to discover this sequence spontaneously, but the sequence of activities must be planned by an expert (teacher) who is able to carry through the genetic decomposition of the mathematical concepts to be learned. Although the basic idea is that the students are carrying out the activities themselves, more or less continuous guidance by the teacher is also needed. Like the computer environment, the teacher can also offer support for the students' activities in the form of distributed expertise. This means that the teacher can carry out some subprocesses that are involved in the meaningful manipulation of a larger task, but are still unfamiliar to the students.

Multiple Representations: Content of Mental Activities

Appropriate representations are important elements in any learning and construction process, but the problem of relevant external representations is highlighted when advanced and abstract mathematical concepts are the content of learning. It can be assumed that, in concrete and simple learning tasks, students are able to spontaneously construct a variety of relevant representations, but, in the domain of advanced mathematics, these representations are not self-evidently available. In traditional teaching, the relationship between representations and concepts is not usually explicitly considered. In fact, teachers and students typically believe that the concrete external representations are the concepts as such (cf. the differences between novices and experts reported by Chi, Glaser, & Rees, 1982).

Typically, the representations used by teachers are closely related to the algorithmic procedures based on the concepts and operations in question. When students are not encouraged to pay attention to the abstract concepts and operations "behind" the concrete algorithmic routines, it is obvious that they try to learn the subject matter by imitation and memorization of the mechanical procedures and symbolic expressions. "But imitation and memorization do not lead to cognitive constructions and the result is that the students' desire to learn through growth is suppressed. He or she has turned off mathematics" (Dubinsky, 1991, p. 120). This "turning off" involves both motivational and cognitive changes in the students' learning process.

Our hypothesis is that it is the use of multiple representations and the continuous movement between different representational formats that encourage students toward reflective abstraction, especially when they are learning abstract concepts in advanced mathematics. By using different representations, students can become aware of the existence of more general structural principles common to the different external representations. They become able to disengage themselves from naive beliefs as to what mathematics is about (Schoenfeld, 1985).

One aim of our study is to facilitate, with the help of a technology-rich environment, students' construction process by giving them a variety of representational tools. These tools should help students externalize their idiosyncratic and informal hypotheses, and to compare these hypotheses with scientific concepts and culturally shared definitions (cf. Collins & Brown, 1988; Reusser, 1988, 1991). We have assumed that, in the case of learning advanced mathematical concepts, it is not enough to have representational tools available. Expert modeling of the use of these tools in the particular domain is also needed. This is another way in which the teacher can facilitate the construction process of the students by indirect intervention.

Stimulating and Facilitating Reflective Abstraction by Social Interaction and Teacher Intervention

Although we have a planned sequence of activities, an appropriate environment for them, and a rich variety of representational tools, it is still doubtful whether students really commit themselves to the challenging process of reflective abstraction. Instructional models based on peer cooperation have been stressed in recent research on learning and instruction. There has also been an increasing movement toward the use of small groups for mathematics instruction (Artzt & Armour-Thomas, 1992; Davidson, 1990; Good, Mulryan, & McCaslin, 1992; Johnson & Johnson, 1990; Slavin, 1990). However, the theoretical arguments and empirical evidence supporting the benefits of cooperative learning arrangements is rather contradictory (e.g., Good et al., 1992; Mulryan, 1992). A cooperative small group does not automatically improve the construction of higher order cognitive skills and complex knowledge structures. It is obvious that the mathematical symbol language of advanced mathematics is not a sufficient tool for teaching–learning interaction—whether it takes place between teacher and student or between students. To increase possibilities for mutual understanding, interaction tools are needed that are adequately related both to the new mathematical concepts to be learned and to the previous experience and knowledge of the students. Flexible methods should be available to help students externalize their preliminary ideas and make their thinking processes transparent to others. On the one hand, the tools available in an activity environment should allow students to follow one another's thinking processes even in situations where verbal expressions are not possible. On the other hand, the environment and the working methods should encourage students toward internal and mutual reflection.

In our model, the teacher participates in the social interaction during lessons in four ways:

1. The teacher models the expertlike task interpretation, problem solving, and conceptual construction. On the basis of the results in another learning environment (Lehtinen, Enkenberg, & Järvelä, 1992), we have assumed that the teacher's modeling is adequate only if it is closely related to current problem situations experienced by the students.

2. The teacher scaffolds the students when they are carrying out the critical

activities by clarifying the tasks and giving technical advice. Although the scaffolding metaphors have proved to be useful, there are serious problems that should be considered. For some students, scaffolding given by the teacher systematically increases social dependence on and avoidance of autonomous learning (Vauras, Lehtinen, Kinnunen, & Salonen, 1992).

3. The teacher induces "pressure for accommodation and reflective abstraction" by analyzing the students' work and by demonstrating the consequences of students' erroneous or insufficient generalizations (misconceptions). However, it is obvious that some students tend to interpret the teacher's feedback as ego threatening. Among these students, the teacher's feedback sometimes does not guide toward reflection and accommodation, but instead increases the students' tendency toward ego-defensive orientation (Olkinuora & Salonen, 1992).

4. When opportunity allows, the teacher mediates the formal mathematical tradition to the classroom to facilitate students' construction process with effective conceptual systems, and to help them label—with culturally accepted symbols—the concepts and operations they are learning. From the constructivism point of view, the problem is that this kind of conceptual intervention can also disturb students' self-guided construction processes and tempt them to transfer the cognitive responsibility to the teacher.

To develop a learning environment to improve the construction of advanced mathematical concepts, we have elaborated a model that summarizes the previously described presuppositions of adequate reflective abstraction (Fig. 6.1). This theoretical model has been applied in an empirical experiment where the concepts of the derivative were taught in a computer-based learning environment. The aim of this experiment was to improve students' understanding of the derivative concept by developing cognitive and didactic tools that optimally stimulate new kinds of activities and social interaction among teacher and students. The intention was to construct a learning environment where students would carry out activities that would require them to externalize their abstract thinking processes, would inspire them to reflect on their own and their peers' thinking processes, and would enable teacher and students to discuss mathematical concepts and operations using a common language.

METHOD

Subjects

The experiment was carried out in an upper secondary school that had good technical equipment and a voluntary teacher for the experiment. The experimental subjects ($N = 17$) were 11th graders (16- to 17-year-olds) who were presently enrolled in the most advanced courses in mathematics. Initially there were four

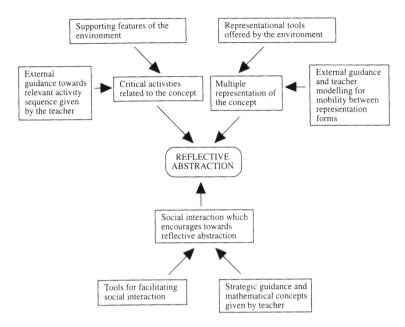

FIG. 6.1. Presuppositions of adequate reflective abstraction.

control classes form four different schools. All the schools (experimental and control) were located in a similar socioeconomic areas. The control students had selected the same courses in mathematics as the experiment subjects. Before teaching a unit on differential calculus, the experimental and control groups were given a pretest to ascertain the students' command of a number of basic features of the previous knowledge. On the basis of this paper-and-pencil pretest, the final control group ($N = 22$) was selected by matching the results with the experimental group.

Materials and Procedure

The experimental group was taught the concept of *the derivative* and applications of differential calculus with the aid of a computer algebra program, DERIVE, which is a symbolic algebra program originally developed for professional use in solving complex mathematical equations (Rich, Rich, & Stoutemyer, 1988). The program allows the user to construct, simplify, and solve equations numerically and symbolically. It can also solve the derivative of different functions. In addition, the program allows graphical presentations of functions, including the possibility to zoom in on selected parts of graphs. With the help of this feature, it is possible, for example, to demonstrate that the slope of the graph at a point is equal to the tangent of the graph at that point. The instruction of the experimental intervention (5 hours a week for 10 weeks) was structured so that, instead of concentrating on computational skills, concept formation was emphasized. The theoretical model for reflective abstraction, described previously, was applied as follows.

Critical Activities Related to the Derivative Concept.   A detailed plan of the sequence of the activities was designed by the researchers. The students started the experimental program by exploring the features of different functions with the help of the DERIVE program. The aim of this activity was to (a) activate students' previous knowledge about functions, (b) help students generalize and integrate fragmented ideas and beliefs about functions into the abstract and procedural mathematical concept of functions (Eisenberg, 1991; Moschkovich, Schoenfeld, & Arcavi, 1994), and (c) focus attention on the important features of function (e.g., acceleration, slope, and inflection points). The second aim was to encapsulate the procedural function concept so that the students could assimilate it into subsequent activities.

In the second main activity, the students explored evenly accelerated motion by letting a ball roll along an inclined plane. They measured the rolling time for different distances and formulated a table describing the relationship between the distance and time. These data were then analyzed with the help of DERIVE. The students first tried to find a function type and appropriate coefficient that would describe the relationship between observed variables. The next task was to count average speed for different distances. The mathematical concepts the students were supposed to construct during this activity were those involved in the differ- ence quotient. The next problem was to determine the speed of the ball at a given point of time. Students were encouraged to do experiments with the different tools in DERIVE to create methods of determining the momentary speed. This critical activity was aimed to help students integrate the concepts of *difference quotient, slope of the curve* (secant and tangent), and *the limit* to construct the spontaneous conception of the derivative.

During the following activities, students tried to find derivatives of some simple functions by using the various tools of DERIVE and algebraic symbol manipulation by hand. By reflecting on these procedures and results, they had to generalize the derivation rules for a variety of elementary functions. In a similar way, they constructed rules for complicated composite functions and general derivation rules.

Representational Tools Related to the Derivative Concept.   From the begin- ning of the program, students practiced analyzing mathematical concepts and operations from the point of view of different representation forms. It was as- sumed that the students' previous knowledge about functions included only one or two typical representations of functions (graphical, algebraic). On the basis of previous research, we assumed that few students have an adequate function concept that would make it possible for them to see the deeper relationships between the different concrete representations. Because of this, the DERIVE program was used to enable systematic manipulation of a function and its representations.

In the concept-formation stage, special attention was paid to the dynamic interpretation of the derivative as the instantaneous rate of change by the presentation of the derivative in numerical, graphical, and algebraic modes (Fig. 6.2). The students used DERIVE to observe and interpret the different modes of representation and to discover the rules of differentiation (algorithmization). At the application stage, the students were allowed to perform all the routine computations and problems involving graphics using a computer algebra program. The students could freely choose which representational tool they used when they began solving each application problem. They then solved the same problems using an alternative form of representation.

Social Interaction and Teacher Interventions in the Learning Environment. In the experiment, the students were encouraged to work in pairs, and free interaction between pairs was allowed. There were more computers in the classroom than student pairs, and thus all students always had the possibility to work individually with a computer. Consequently, working in pairs was a free choice for them. One aim of the activity sequence's plan was to make the normally abstract steps of the construction of derivative concept as transparent as possible. It was assumed that concrete activities (e.g., investigation of the evenly accelerated motion) and the visible change between different external representation forms would allow an optimal environment for intensive peer interaction concerning the mathematical concepts. The idea of distributed cognition was also explicitly used. For instance, student pairs would try to find derivative for

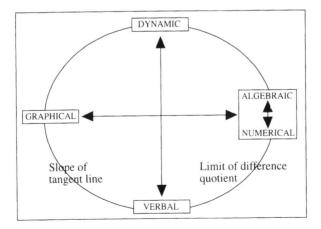

FIG. 6.2. External representations of derivate.

different concrete functions. When each pair had solved its own problem, a general rule abstracted from the results of the pairs was constructed in joint discussion in the class. According to the instructional plan, the teacher cooperated with the pairs in a flexible way at all times. The idea was to provide complementary explanations for the written instructions for each activity, and to help students use the computer program (modeling and scaffolding). In some phases, the teacher's task was to summarize and evaluate the experiences of students' activities, and to give the "standard" names and descriptions for the constructed concepts and operations that are used in the tradition of mathematics.

Pretest

The pretest was composed of a paper-and-pencil group test and an individual interview. The paper-and-pencil test lasted $1\frac{1}{2}$ hours. Students had to solve 20 tasks dealing with the *function* concept presented in graphical, numerical, and symbolic modes. The test also addressed the concept of *limit,* and the nature of the naive conception the students had of the concept of *derivatives*. Experimental ($n = 17$) and final control groups ($n = 22$) took part in a individual pretest interview. In the interview, the students were confronted with questions pertaining to the function and limit concepts, and they were asked to justify their solutions to the written pretest problems. The results of the paper-and-pencil tests and interviews were combined in nine variables, each describing a qualitatively different aspect of students' previous knowledge: (a) mastery of the expressions connected to functions, (b) comprehension of the concepts describing the course of functions, (c) ability to construct the limits of functions and inverse functions, (d) spontaneous conceptions of derivative concept, (e) verbal interpretation of the concepts needed in the construction of derivative concept, (f) algebraic mastery of the concepts needed in the construction of derivative concept, (g) numeric comprehension of the concepts needed in the construction of derivative concept, (h) ability to use the previous concepts in application situations, and (i) ability to move between multiple representation forms.

Posttest and Delayed Posttest

Immediately upon completion of the experimental intervention, the posttest was administered to both groups of students. The mathematical paper-and-pencil posttest tasks and the interviews were meant to provide an understanding of the students' mental models pertaining to the concept of derivatives and their computational or algorithmic skills. The paper-and-pencil test contained tasks dealing with the different qualitative aspects of the derivative concept and the computational and algorithmic skills by means of a written test. All the students were interviewed individually after the paper-and-pencil posttest. The students were again asked to justify their solutions to the written posttest tasks. In addition, they had to explain their conception of derivative, and they were asked to interpret and determine the values of derivative in different representational forms. The following detailed variables describing the qualitative features of the derivative were constructed by combining the results of the paper-and-pencil test and the interview: (a) introductory ideas of the derivative, (b) verbal definition of the derivative, (c) ability to determine the derivative, (d) interpretation of the values of the derivative, (e) algorithmic application of the derivative, (f) comprehension of the algebraic definition of the derivative, (g) understanding the graphical interpretation of the derivative, (h) dynamic interpretation of the derivative, (i) ability to shift between different representations of the derivative, (j) understanding the derivative as a function, and (k) reversibility of the derivation operation.

Six months later, a delayed posttest was administered to investigate the stability of the students' cognitive structures related to the concept of derivatives and the permanence of the algorithmic solution skills. The same paper-and-pencil test, containing 27 tasks, was used, as in the immediate posttest. In the immediate and delayed posttests, 18 tasks dealt with the different qualitative aspects of the derivative concept. Two sum variables were constructed from these items: *immediate conceptual understanding* and *long-lasting conceptual understanding*. Similar sum variables, *immediate algorithmic skills* and *long-lasting algorithmic skills,* were constructed from nine tasks measuring the computational and algorithmic skills by means of a standard-type school test.

To analyze the level of abstraction of the learned mathematical operation, students were, in an interview situation, given a task that required the ability to transfer their conception of derivative into a more abstract domain. As a transfer task, the students were asked to construct the concept of the *second derivative* (derivative of the derivative) and to interpret the function's features on the basis of the second derivative's values (the concept of second derivative was not taught during the experiment). On the basis of the answers to questions dealing with the different aspects of the second derivative, a sum variable *abstraction of the derivative concept* was constructed.

Process Observations

The lessons of the experimental intervention were videotaped. There was one video camera in the classroom. Sometimes the camera followed the activities going on in the whole classroom, and sometimes it focused for longer periods on individual working pairs. The aim of the first analysis of the video films was to control, in general, how well the planned program was implemented in the real classroom situation. For more detailed analysis, the fragments of the video films were selected; in this way it was possible to follow a meaningful working episode of a particular pair. Because of the limitations of the videotapes (only a random selection of working episodes of individual student pairs; only a few episodes were technically so good that it was possible to follow simultaneously the events on the computer screen and the discussion of the students and teacher), no quantitative classifications were made to describe the whole process. Rather, a selection of interaction episodes was analyzed as examples of the types of interaction episodes possible in the learning environment used in this experiment. In analyzing videotape data, one can use coding instruments that are method-driven, theory-driven, or problem-driven (Schoenfeld, 1992). In this research, we used a method that combined theory- and problem-driven coding. According to the theoretical framework and the aims of the study, we focused our attention on three aspects of interaction:

1. The quality and conceptual level of discussion between the students:
   *   appearance of utterances referring to the algorithmic procedures
   *   appearance of utterances referring to the abstract mathematical concepts
   *   appearance of utterances referring to the metacognitive processes and comprehension strategies
   *   appearance of a cognitive conflict between the students
   *   appearance of explicit concluding utterances referring to shared understanding

2. The quality and conceptual level of the reciprocal discussion between teacher and student:
   *   appearance of utterances referring to the algorithmic procedures
   *   appearance of utterances referring to the abstract mathematical concepts
   *   appearance of utterances referring to the metacognitive processes and comprehension strategies
   *   who started the discussion, teacher–student

3. The types of content-related nonverbal communication between students.

The videotapes were analyzed by the researcher, and no formal methods of reliability or validity estimation were used.

RESULTS

How the Activities of the Experimental Program Were Fulfilled

The videotaped lessons (50 hours) were analyzed to evaluate the functioning of the experimental program. Although the students worked with the DERIVE program for 50 hours, most of them did not learn enough about the program to use it autonomously. Besides the rather detailed written instructions given by the researchers, the continuous scaffoldings given by the teacher were also necessary for most of the students, especially at the beginning of the program.

On the basis of behavioral observations, it was possible to assume that most of the students were not able to connect the first fulfilled activities with the construction of a new mathematical concept, but they remained for a time isolated and the students were not involved with the tasks. At the beginning of the program, many students were not able to carry out the activities autonomously, but needed continuous support from the teacher. It is our interpretation that this problem was more motivational than cognitive. The tasks were not too demanding cognitively, but the students were slightly confused and could not see the meaning of the activities that were different from the typical routines of the mathematics classroom. However, the situation soon changed, and the students became much more autonomous. The episodes indicated that students' meaningful use of verbal utterances, referring to the derivative concepts during practical problem-solving processes, became more frequent toward the end of the experiment.

An essential principle in the experimental instruction was the continuous changeover from one representation form to another. This idea seemed to be useful to the students who were observed during their use of multiple representations. For example, a student pair was comparing the numerical changes of the value of derivative at different points with the features of the corresponding graph, and they seemed to discover the relationship themselves. In another situation, a student pair solved the derivative function for an original function algebraically, and controlled the result by comparing the graphs of the original and the derivative function. Only a few students, who had successfully used algorithmic strategies in earlier mathematics classes, expressed negative attitudes toward the continuous use of multiple representations. We get the impression that they believed that comparison between different representation forms was a waste of time, and that they wanted to concentrate on algebraic and algorithmic training without the DERIVE program.

The Quality of Social Interaction During the Experimental Program

One aim of this study was to investigate the quality of teacher–student and student–student interactions during the experimental program (for a complete process analysis and qualitative description of the social interaction, see Repo & Lehtinen, 1993). The learning environment and instruction plan were aimed to support social interaction, which facilitates reflective abstraction in students. Concerning the learning of the *equation* concept, we found that, during normal mathematics lessons, there is almost no reciprocal discussion among teacher and students concerning the abstract mathematical concepts (Lehtinen et al., 1995). Because the students used the computer environment in pairs, one trivial result was that there was much more discussion between students than in traditional teacher-centered classrooms. However, an important observation concerned the quality of the discussions.

In the experimental class, there were frequently episodes in which students—when they realized they were in a puzzling situation—started to elaborate abstract concepts by reciprocal argumentation. For example, in one situation, students had to estimate the course of the function (also the derivative function was known) of a given point. One student pair first tried to solve the problem by placing the given values in the original function. However, the result was of no help in answering the question. Student A continued attempts to solve the problem according to the original plan, while Student B started to ask if they could somehow use the derivative function. Because Student A could not grasp the point, Student B was forced to articulate her ideas, which were not at all clear in the beginning: "Derivative function is different from the function (she was pointing at the original function) . . . but it is somehow related to it." Then they started to discuss the meaning of the derivative, but were not able, in the beginning, to understand the derivative as a function. After a long discussion, they finally concluded that the individual values of the derivative describe the slope of a function at different points, but the derivative also can be seen as a function that describes how the slopes are changing. Thus, it is possible to calculate the slope of the function at a given point by placing the given value in the derivative function.

Expressions indicating reflection and content-specific metacogniton were also observed in the experimental group. For example, a student pair was investigating the derivative of a function at a point in which there was a discontinuity point in the derivative function. In the graphical exploration, they found that there could be several tangents of the curve at that point. After minor tutoring by the teacher, they started to reflect their first finding and made conscious comparisons with their earlier knowledge about tangents. With the help of this metacognitive control, they realized it was necessary to reinterpret their previous results, and thus they were able to conclude that no tangent of the function exists at that point. Thus, there is a discontinuity point in the derivative function. This kind of discussion was infrequent at the beginning of the experiment; toward the end of the program, expressions indicating reciprocal reasoning of abstract concepts became more typical among student pairs. During the episodes, for example, students were talking about how to generalize the "universal" rule after they had solved the derivative of an individual function. They also had rather profound discussions on how to interpret the course of the function on the basis of the knowledge of derivative function. Only a few interaction episodes between teacher and student were oriented toward joint deliberation upon the concepts of the derivative. More typically, students asked technical advice from the teacher, and when the teacher was talking about mathematical concepts the students listened passively.

Although reflective verbal interaction was not as typical as we had assumed, we found another interesting phenomenon in the videotapes. During the interaction within pairs, students continuously referred to the procedures presented on the computer screen. It was obvious that in many situations, which were important for the construction of conceptual understanding, students were communicating intensively with the help of the computer. During long interaction episodes, there were almost no verbal utterances, or the utterances were only intended to call the partner's attention to some manipulation by the student or some results displayed on the screen. Turn-taking behavior was also typical in this communication. First one student performed some manipulation with the computer and then both students looked at the results. After a period of nonverbal communication (e.g., gestures and eye contact), the other took the keyboard and carried out the next manipulation. The computer-based learning environment made it possible for the students to overcome the problem that was induced by their lack of an adequate language for talking about abstract mathematical ideas and operations. The teacher of the experimental class also gradually accepted this nonverbal communication through computer mediation. Toward the end of the program, she was no longer using that much verbal explanation, but preferred demonstrations on the computer screen. This was not part of the instructional plan, but an unconscious change in the teaching strategy.

Development of Conceptual Understanding

According to the pretest's results, there were no significant differences between experimental and control groups in the level of previous knowledge adequate for learning differential calculus. The results of the posttest, based on the variables describing the different aspects of the comprehension of the derivative concept, indicate a clear difference between the experimental and control groups (Table 6.1). Although there were significant differences in all variables, the most noticeable differences were in the variables describing the more abstract understanding of the derivative concept. The most important result was that all the students of the experimental group had constructed an understanding of the derivative as a function. The differences in standard algebraic definition and determination were not very strong, but the experimental group had a much more dynamic and flexible conception of the derivative than the control group.

The Stability of Conceptual Understanding and Algorithmic Skills

The stability of the effect was investigated with the help of the paper-and-pencil test, which was administered as part of the posttest immediately after the experiment and as the delayed posttest 6 months later. In the posttest (Table 6.2), there was no difference in the algorithmic achievement (sum variable of the algorithmic items) between the experimental and control groups, but there was a significant difference in the sum variable that describes the level of conceptual understanding of the derivative. Students in the experimental group had a much

TABLE 6.1
The Level of Comprehension of Different Qualitative Aspects of Derivative Concepts in the
Experimental and Control Groups

Comprehended Aspect of Derivative	Experimental Group		Control Group			
	M	SD	M	SD	t test	p
Introductory ideas	3.08	1.66	1.65	1.89	2.4	.01
Verbal definition	3.93	1.49	1.68	1.59	4.51	.001
Ability to determine	6.84	2.11	3.42	2.42	4.63	.001
Interpretation of the values	5.61	1.95	2.61	2.35	4.23	.001
Algorithmic application	6.41	0.71	5.74	1.03	2.29	.05
Algebraic definition	2.65	1.80	1.68	1.31	1.94	.05
Graphical interpretation	7.77	2.22	3.83	2.88	4.67	.001
Dynamic interpretation	3.78	1.62	1.80	1.72	3.66	.001
Shift between representations	4.40	1.90	2.00	2.10	3.70	.001
Derivative as a function	1.00	0.00	0.27	0.46	6.56	.001
Reversibility of the operation	0.91	0.26	0.39	0.49	4.01	.001

higher level of conceptual understanding than the students in the control group ($t = 4.43$, $p < .001$).

In the delayed posttest (Table 6.3), there were significant differences between the groups on both variables. The experimental group scored higher on both measurements. The difference in conceptual understanding was about the same after 6 months as it was in the immediate posttest ($t = 2.42$, $p < .05$). The results indicate that students in the experimental group had maintained their ability to

TABLE 6.2
Conceptual Understanding and Algorithmic Skills in Posttest

Group	Conceptual Understanding		Algorithmic Skills	
	Mean	SD	Mean	SD
Experimental ($N = 17$)	24.29	7.95	5.65	1.79
Control ($N = 22$)	12.96	8.06	5.13	1.44

TABLE 6.3
Conceptual Understanding and Algorithmic Skills in Delayed Posttest

Group	Conceptual Understanding		Algorithmic Skills	
	Mean	SD	Mean	SD
Experimental (N = 17)	21.28	7.08	5.06	1.85
Control (N = 22)	15.22	8.75	3.88	2.07

carry out algorithmic-solving processes better than the control students ($t =$ 1.94, $p < .05$).

Students' ability to independently generalize and transfer the learned concepts and operations onto a more abstract and complex level is an important indicator of reflective abstraction. In this study, we examined the abstraction level of the derivative conceptions of students by asking them to consider the second derivative and to interpret the relationship between the features of the function and its second derivative (derivative of the derivative). The second derivative was taught neither in the experimental nor in the control group. This examination took place in an individual interview situation, and the students' utterances were divided into three qualitatively different classes. The first group was composed of students who had no idea about the second derivative and its relationship to the function (*no abstraction*). The second group was composed of classified students who were able to imagine what the second derivative could mean, and had some relevant ideas about the interpretations that could be made about the features of the function on the basis of its second derivative (*partial abstraction*). The third

TABLE 6.4
Students' Ability to Abstract the Concept of the Derivative and to Construct Independently
the Concept of the Second Derivative

Group	No Abstraction		Partial Abstraction		Complete Abstraction	
	f	%	f	%	f	%
Experimental (N = 17)	6	35	4	24	7	41
Control (N = 22)	15	68	4	18	3	14

group consisted of students who were able to give a thorough explanation of the second derivative and its relations to the function (*complete abstraction*). The frequencies of experimental and control groups are shown in Table 6.4. There was a statistically significant difference between frequency distributions [$\chi^2(2) = 6.88, p < .05$]. The majority of the experimental students were able to construct a reasonable interpretation of the second derivative, whereas only a third of the control students achieved such an abstract level of understanding.

CONCLUSIONS

On the basis of empirical research on the quality of school learning, we can conclude that good school achievement in mathematics is not always a valid indicator of a high-level understanding of mathematical concepts and operations. It is a well-known finding that most students do not attain an adequate understanding of the concepts and operations of differential calculus, but develop isolated algorithmic skills for solving concrete tasks (Artigue, 1991). There is a strong tendency among students, as well as many teachers, to prefer rather superficial strategies that stress the rapid learning of algorithms without any emphasis on the larger mathematical knowledge structures and abstract concepts. This tendency is partly a consequence of the general culture of institutional schooling, and partly of the characteristics of the mathematical subject matter. The fundamental part of mathematical knowledge (abstract concepts and operations) cannot be demonstrated or described directly with the help of a common language or traditional didactic tools. To improve the quality of learning of advanced mathematics, we need an adequate theoretical model to describe the presuppositions for the adequate construction of abstract cognitive structures. In this study, we elaborated on the Piagetian theory of reflective abstraction; we also tried to design some outlines for an "ideal" learning environment for abstract mathematical concepts. On the basis of these ideas, we designed a concrete computer-based learning environment and a plan of activities that could be implemented in that environment. In this program, the computer was considered a cognitive, didactic, and social tool that helps students (and the teacher) externalize abstract thinking procedures. The use of different external representations were intended to inspire students toward reflection and social interaction.

Although the groups of students in the experimental design were small, this study gives some preliminary evidence that the strategic use of a computer algebra program, according to a designed activity plan, can promote essential development in the social interaction among students and also, to some extent, between teacher and students. In particular, the ability to carry out complex algorithmic procedures in a few seconds, and the flexible means of changing between different representation forms, seemed to be helpful for this kind of cooperative reflection. During the computer manipulations, it was possible to externalize the hypothesis and abstract thinking process for joint reflection. However, this interaction was not based primarily on verbal utterances, but on the nonverbal interaction mediated by the computer. This kind of communication was obviously helpful for the construction of abstract and complex concepts of mathematical knowledge. However, it is still an open question whether we need even better methods for students to improve their verbal articulation during construction processes. In our experiment, the students could not optimally benefit from the preorganized conceptual structures of the mathematical tradition mediated by the teacher.

A broadly shared observation among mathematics teachers and researchers of mathematics learning is that the shift from more elementary mathematics to differential calculus is especially hard for many students, including those with rather high previous achievement in mathematics. Many students do not learn to understand the concepts of *limit* or *derivative,* but they learn to cope with the demands of school tests with the help of well-learned mechanical and algorithmic skills (e.g., Tall, 1991). The transition from the classical mathematics to differential calculus has also been problematic in the history of mathematics (Maula & Kasanen, 1989). There are reasons to assume that the problems with understanding calculus are partly due to the need to combine, from an ontological point of view, different knowledge with the previous mathematical knowledge (see Chi, 1992). Our results concerning learning in the traditional classroom also show that, despite high-level algorithmic achievement, only a few students developed an adequate understanding of the derivative concept. An important result of this study is that the average level of conceptual understanding can be improved noticeably by involving students in a sequence of critical activities and by changing the quality of their social interaction. The results, indicating that the majority of experimental students were able to independently carry out an abstraction process of learned concepts onto new levels, are promising. Thus, it seems that it is possible for this kind of thinking, which is typical for mathematicians, to be learned as early as secondary school. On the basis of process observations, we can conclude that, for most of the students, the construction process leading to adequate understanding takes a long time. It is obvious that, during the long periods without any external progress, the students were confronting a confusing problem situation that resulted from tying to combine the ontologically different knowledge they were learning with previous mathematical knowledge. It seems to us that the learning environment—including the exploratory activities, the computer as a representational tool, and the intensive social interaction—offered better possibilities for coping with this epistemic discontinuity than traditional classroom teaching.

The results also support the need to emphasize deep conceptual understanding for learning practical calculation skills. Students who achieved high-level conceptual understanding also showed greater permanence in their algorithmic procedures. On this basis, it can be assumed that the longer time needed for deeper understanding of the mathematical concepts can be compensated for by the decreasing need for repeated practice of algorithmic procedures.

ACKNOWLEDGMENTS

Preparation of this chapter was sponsored by the Academy of Finland and University of Joensuu. We would like to thank Erik De Corte, Robert Glaser, Erika Ferguson, and Sharon Lesgold for help with preparing the manuscript.

REFERENCES

Achtenhagen, F. (1992, April). *Economic theory in a simulation of complex economic systems.* Paper presented at the 1992 AERA annual meeting, San Francisco, CA.

Aebli, H. (1987). Mental development: Construction in a cultural context. In B. Inhelder, D. Caprona, & A. Cornu-Wells (Eds.), *Piaget today* (pp. 217–232). Hove, England: Lawrence Erlbaum Associates.

Artigue, M. (1991). Analysis. In D. Tall (Ed.), *Advanced mathematical thinking* (pp. 167–198). Dortrecht, Netherlands: Kluwer.

Artzt, A. F., & Armour-Thomas, E. (1992). Development of a cognitive-metacognitive framework for protocol analysis of mathematical problem solving in small groups. *Cognition and Instruction, 9,* 137–175.

Beth, E. W., & Piaget, J. (1966). *Mathematical epistemology and psychology.* Dordrecht, Netherlands: Reidel.

Brown, A. L., Ash, D., Rutherford, M., Nakagawa, K., Gordon, A., & Campione, C. (1993). Distributed expertise in the classroom (pp. 188–228). In G. Salomon (Ed.), *Distributed cognitions.* New York: Cambridge University Press.

Chi, M. (1992). Conceptual change within and across ontological categories: Examples from learning and discovery in science. In R. Giere (Ed.), *Cognitive models of science: Minnesota studies in the philosophy of science* (pp. 129–186). Minneapolis, MN: University of Minnesota Press.

Chi, M., Glaser, R., & Rees, E. (1982). Expertise in problem solving. In R. Sternberg (Ed.), *Advances in the psychology of human intelligence* (Vol. 1, pp. 7–75). Hillsdale, NJ: Lawrence Erlbaum Associates.

Collins, A., & Brown, J. S. (1988). Computer as a tool for learning through reflection. In H. Mandl & A. Lesgold (Eds.), *Learning issues for intelligent tutoring systems* (pp. 1–18). New York: Springer-Verlag.

Davidson, N. (1990). *Cooperative learning in mathematics.* New York: Addison-Wesley.

Davis, R. B. (1988). The interplay of algebra, geometry, and logic. *Journal of Mathematical Behavior, 7,* 9–28.

Dreyfus, T. (1991). Advanced mathematical thinking processes. In D. Tall (Ed.), *Advanced mathematical thinking* (pp. 25–41). Dordrecht, Netherlands: Kluwer.

Dubinsky, E. (1991). Reflective abstraction in advanced mathematical thinking. In D. Tall (Ed.), *Advanced mathematical thinking* (pp. 95–123). Dordrecht, Netherlands: Kluwer.

Dubinsky, E., & Tall, D. (1991). Advanced mathematical thinking and the computer. In D. Tall (Ed.), *Advanced mathematical thinking* (pp. 231–243). Dordrecht, Netherlands: Kluwer.

Eisenberg, T. (1991). Functions and associated learning difficulties. In D. Tall (Ed.), *Advanced mathematical thinking* (pp. 140–152). Dordrecht, Netherlands: Kluwer.

Ernest, P. (1991). *The philosophy of mathematics education.* London: The Falmer Press.

Good, T. L., Mulryan, C., & McCaslin, M. (1992). Grouping for instruction in mathematics: A call for programmatic research on small-group processes. In D. Grouws (Ed.), *Handbook of research on mathematics teaching and learning.* New York: Macmillan.

Greeno, J. (1987). Instructional representations based on research about understanding. In A. H. Schoenfeld (Ed.), *Cognitive science and mathematics education* (pp. 61–89). Hillsdale, NJ: Lawrence Erlbaum Associates.

Hiebert, J., & Lefevre, P. (1986). Conceptual and procedural knowledge in mathematics: An introductory analysis. In J. Hiebert (Ed.), *Conceptual and procedural knowledge: The case of mathematics* (pp. 1–27). Hillsdale, NJ: Lawrence Erlbaum Associates.

Johnson, D. W., & Johnson, R. T. (1990). Using cooperative learning in math. In N. Davidson (Ed.), *Cooperative learning in mathematics* (pp. 103–124). Menlo Park, CA: Addison-Wesley.

Karmiloff-Smith, A., & Inhelder, B. (1947–1975). If you want to get ahead, get a theory. *Cognition, 3,* 195–212.

Lehtinen, E., Enkenberg, J., & Jarvela, S. (1992). Constructing mental models of everyday automates. *International Journal of Psychology, 25,* 566.

Lehtinen, E., Ketola, T., & Vuontela, U.-M. (1995). *Teaching equation concept in lower secondary school: Process oriented approach.* Unpublished manuscript, Center for Learning Research, University of Turku, Finland.

Lehtinen, E., Olkinuora, E., & Salonen, P. (1986). The research project on interactive formation of learning difficulties. *Annales Universitatis Turkuensis, A, 171.* University of Turku, Finland.

Lehtinen, E., & Savimäki, A. (1993). *Success and understanding in mathematics among high achieving secondary school students.* Unpublished manuscript, Center for Learning Research, University of Turku, Finland.

Maula, E., & Kasanen, E. (1989). Chez Fermat A.D. 1937. *Philosophica, 43,* 127–162.

Maurer, S. B. (1987). New knowledge about errors and new views about learners: What they mean to educators and more educators would like to know. In A. H. Schoenfeld (Ed.), *Cognitive science and mathematics education* (pp. 165–187). Hillsdale, NJ: Lawrence Erlbaum Associates.

Moschkovich, J., Schoenfeld, A. H., & Arcavi, A. (1994). Aspects of understanding: On multiple perspectives and representations of linear relations and connections among them. In T. A. Romberg, E. Fennema, & T. P. Carpenter (Eds.), *Integrating research on the graphical representation of function.* Hillsdale, NJ: Lawrence Erlbaum Associates.

Mulryan, C. M. (1992). Student passivity during cooperative small groups in mathematics. *Journal of Educational Research, 85*(5), 261–273.

Olkinuora, E., Lehtinen, E., & Salonen, P. (1988). On the foundation of the systemic approach to learning difficulties. *Nordisk Pedagogik, 8,* 55–58.

Olkinuora, E., & Salonen, P. (1992). Adaptation, motivational orientation, and cognition in a subnormally performing child: A systemic perspective for training. In B. Wong (Ed.), *Contemporary intervention research in learning disabilities* (pp. 190–213). New York: Springer-Verlag.

Piaget, J. (1976). *The grasp of consciousness.* Cambridge, MA: Harvard University Press.

Piaget, J. (1978). *Success and understanding.* London: Routledge & Kegan Paul.

Piaget, J. (1985). *The equilibration of cognitive structures.* Cambridge, MA: Harvard University Press.

Repo, S., & Lehtinen, E. (1993). *Social interaction in experimental mathematics classroom.* Unpublished manuscript, Research and Development Center for Information Technology in Education, University of Joensuu, Finland.

Resnick, L. B. (1987). Learning in school and out. *Educational Researcher, 16*(9), 13–20.

Reusser, K. (1988). Problem solving beyond the logic of things: Contextual effects on understanding and solving word problems. *Instructional Science, 17,* 309–338.

Reusser, K. (1991, August). *Intelligent technologies and pedagogical theory: Computers as tools for thoughtful teaching and learning.* Paper presented at the fourth European Conference for Research on Learning and Instruction, Turku, Finland.

Rich, A., Rich, J., & Stoutenmyer, D. (1988). *Derive: A mathematical assistant for your personal computer.* Honolulu: Soft Warehouse.

Schoenfeld, A. (1987). Cognitive science and mathematics education: An overview. In A. Schoenfeld (Ed.), *Cognitive science and mathematics education* (pp. 1–31). Hillsdale, NJ: Lawrence Erlbaum Associates.

Schoenfeld, A. H. (1985). *Mathematical problem solving.* Orlando, FL: Academic Press.

Schoenfeld, A. H. (1989). Teaching mathematical thinking and problem solving. In L. B. Resnick & L. E. Klopfer (Eds.), *Towards the thinking curriculum: Current cognitive research* (pp. 1–18). Yearbook of the Association for Supervision and Curriculum Development. Alexandria, VA: Association for Supervision.

Schoenfeld, A. H. (1992). On paradigms and methods: What do you do when he ones you know don't do what you want them to? Issues in the analysis of data in the form of videotapes. *The Journal of the Learning Sciences, 2,* 179–214.

Selden, J., Mason, A., & Selden, A. (1989). Can average calculus students solve non-routine problems? *Journal of Mathematical Behavior, 8*(2), 45–50.

Slavin, R. E. (1990). Student team learning in mathematics. In N. Davidson (Ed.), *Cooperative learning in mathematics* (pp. 69–102). Menlo Park, CA: Addison-Wesley.

Tall, D. (Ed.). (1991). *Advanced mathematical thinking.* Dordrecht, Netherlands: Kluwer.

VanLehn, K. (1980). Bugs are not enough: Empirical studies of bugs, impasses, and repairs in procedural skills. *The Journal of Mathematical Behavior, 3,* 3–71.

VanLehn, K. (1982). Bugs are not enough: Empirical studies of bugs, impasses and repairs in procedural skills. *Journal of Mathematical Behavior, 3*(2), 3–71.

VanLehn, K. (1983). On the representation of procedures in repair theory. In H. P. Ginsburg (Ed.), *The development of mathematics thinking* (pp. 197–252). New York: Academic Press.

Vauras, M., Lehtinen, E., Kinnunen, R., & Salonen, P. (1992). Socio-emotional and cognitive processes in training learning disabled children. In B. Wong (Ed.), *Intervention research in learning disabilities: An international perspective* (pp. 163–189). New York: Springer-Verlag.

Wenger, R. H. (1987). Cognitive science and algebra learning. In A. H. Schoenfeld (Ed.), *Cognitive science and mathematics education* (pp. 217–251). Hillsdale, NJ: Lawrence Erlbaum Associates.

Wertheimer, M. (1959). *Productive thinking.* New York: Harper & Row.

7

Supported Learning Environments for the Acquisition of Knowledge and Thinking Skills

Erik De Corte
University of Leuven, Belgium

COMPUTERS IN EDUCATION: A BRIEF STATE OF THE ART

With the advent of the microcomputer in the early 1980s, high expectations rose with respect to its potential as a lever for the innovation and improvement of schooling. Today, over a decade later, it is obvious that the expectations ran too high, or at least that they have not been realized to a substantial degree. This holds true for the use of computers in schools on a worldwide scale, as is shown by the results of a survey on "Computers in Education" carried out in 19 educational systems by the International Association for Educational Achievement (IEA; Pelgrum & Plomp, 1991). Even for the United States, where the situation is certainly most advanced, an analysis of the IEA data by Becker (1991) revealed the following: the number of computers available in schools increased strongly between 1985 and 1989 (from an average of 4 to 17 in "K–6" elementary schools, and from 16 to 39 in high schools); nevertheless "only a small minority of teachers and students can be said to yet be major computer users—where a large portion of instruction, learning, or productive work in one class is being accomplished through the use of computers" (pp. 405–406).

With respect to mathematics education—a domain where one would maybe have expected the most obvious breakthrough of the computer—Kaput (1992) recently described the current state of affairs:

1. Notwithstanding the increase over the past years, only few and mostly obsolete computers are available in schools.

2. There is still a lack of software in sufficient quantity and of sufficient quality to warrant the investment necessary for large-scale computer use.

3. Computers are too difficult for the average teacher to use in the typical classroom on a sustained basis (because the available software is not sufficiently tied to and certainly not integrated in the school curriculum).

4. Preservice teacher training falls short in providing future teachers systematic, in-depth experience with computers.

5. Because of the preceding circumstances, teachers have low, if any at all, expectations concerning computer support for their teaching.

Additionally, one takes into account the traditional resistance of the school system to change, the spontaneous reluctance of many educational practitioners to the introduction of any technological device in schools, and the tendency of the school system to neutralize potential effects of innovations through absorption and adaptation to the existing situation, it is probably not surprising that computers have not affected education in a substantial way during the past decade. In this respect, it can be remarked that history (of educational technology) repeats itself, and that we do not learn too much from it. For example, in a historical overview of the classroom use of technology since 1920, Cuban (1986) quoted the following claims: "The central and dominant aim of education by radio is to bring the world to the classroom, to make universally available the services of the finest teachers, the inspiration of the greatest leaders" (Darrow, 1932, p. 79, quoted in Cuban, 1986, p. 19); "The time may come when a portable radio receiver will be as common in the classroom as is the blackboard. Radio instruction will be integrated into school life as an accepted educational medium" (Levenson, 1945, p. 457, quoted in Cuban, 1986, p. 19). These statements echo many similar ones heard in the 1980s with respect to the educational use of the computer.

MAJOR FAILURES OF CURRENT COMPUTER APPLICATIONS IN SCHOOLS

A major reason for the relative failure of educational computing, as well as the failure of previous "latest novelties" in the instructional technology arsenal, is that the medium has been introduced too much as an add on to an existing, unchanged classroom setting. In mathematics, for example, the majority of available software fits into the category of *drill-and-practice* programs, and aims mainly to exercise computational skills, replacing in this respect traditional worksheets (Kaput, 1992). In other words, computers are mainly used to reproduce and preserve the status quo. But this existing situation has been sharply criticized for a number of years. Consequently, major efforts are made to transform mathematical learning and teaching from the individual absorption and memorization of a fixed body of decontextualized and fragmented concepts and procedural skills, transmitted by the teacher, into the collaborative, teacher-mediated construction of meaningful and useful knowledge and problem-solving skills based on mathematical modeling of authentic, real-life situations and contexts (see De Corte, Greer, & Verschaffel, in press; National Council of Teachers of Mathematics, 1989).

The bulk of the available software in the domain of language (no less than in mathematics) focuses on drill and practice of rules from spelling and grammar, instead of supporting the more essential aspects of reading and writing—namely, comprehension and communication. Taking into account the present emphasis on higher order cognitive skills as educational objectives, as well as the prevailing conception of learning as an active and constructive process, it is obvious that this mere add-on strategy of computer use, focusing on drill and practice, cannot produce the improvements in educational outcomes that were originally naively anticipated. Indeed, the majority of the available educational software elicits only lower level mental processes in students, and is more oriented toward exercising than constructing new knowledge. Moreover, it does not exploit the specific potential of the computer, such as its tremendous capacity for data presentation and handling, and its interactive possibilities (see e.g., Makrakis, 1988).

An important implication derived from the preceding discussion is that computers, as well as other technological devices, do not elicit productive learning by themselves. This standpoint was taken to an extreme by Clark (1983, 1992; see also Clark & Sugrue, 1990), who claimed that media, including computers, are mere vehicles that deliver instruction, but they do not influence the psychological aspects of learning. The critical factors in producing learning effects are the method and the content of instruction, albeit the medium can influence the efficiency and cost of delivering instruction. Clark and Sugrue (1990) summarized this so-called "weak" media theory as follows: "the primary advantages of using new electronic media such as computers, television and video disks for teaching may be *economic* and not psychological, i.e., under some conditions they make learning faster and/or cheaper but no one medium contributes unique learning benefits that cannot be obtained from another medium" (p. 519).

Kozma (1991) contested this view, and can be considered as an adherent of what Clark and Sugrue called a "strong" media theory, according to which computers can have learning benefits and can produce unique cognitive skills. Based on an extensive review of the literature, Kozma argued that, in a good instructional design, media and method are narrowly integrated, and, consequently, that the learner constructs knowledge in interaction with medium and method.

Against the background of this ongoing dispute, which will hopefully elicit further research, a justifiable, provisional point of view is that the productive educational application of computers requires that they are embedded in powerful teaching–learning environments (i.e., instructional settings that elicit in students the acquisition processes required to attain worthwhile and desirable educational objectives). With respect to mathematics education, Kaput (1992) pleaded in the same spirit for "implementing technology toward reformed objectives" (p. 548).

Over the past two decades, research on learning and instruction has produced a knowledge base involving ideas and principles that should guide the design of such powerful instructional environments in general, and computer-supported learning environments in particular. For example, major orienting principles with respect to mathematics education are: (a) the constructivist view of learning, (b) the orientation toward understanding, problem-solving skills and the acquisition of a mathematical disposition as educational objectives, (c) the conception of mathematics as human activity, (d) the crucial role of student's prior—informal as well as formal—knowledge for future learning, (e) the importance of social interaction and collaboration in doing and learning mathematics, and (f) the need to embed mathematics learning into authentic and meaningful contexts (for further details, see De Corte et al., in press).

INTELLIGENT TUTORING SYSTEMS: AN APPROPRIATE SOLUTION?

Concurrent with, but independent from, the large-scale introduction of computers in schools, the cognitive-science community interested in learning and instruction has focused its research and developmental work on the design of intelligent tutoring systems (ITS; for an overview, see Goodyear, 1991; Sleeman & Brown, 1982; Wenger, 1987). It is interesting to ask whether the interdisciplinary research effort invested in the development of ITS has contributed to a solution of the major problems and difficulties relating to educational computing in schools, the more because a main incentive to design ITS derived from dissatisfaction with traditional computer-assisted instruction (CAI) that prevailed and still prevails in educational practice. In fact, instructional programs involving artificial intelligence (AI) were originally called "intelligent" computer-assisted instruction (ICAI).

According to Wenger (1987), the critical distinction between CAI and ICAI, or ITS, is that CAI are static, preprogrammed systems that embody the decisions of expert teachers based on their domain and pedagogical knowledge, whereas in ITS the knowledge itself is represented in such a way that it can be used by a computer-based system to make decisions about instructional interactions. In other words, CAI involves the expert decisions, whereas ITS contain the expertise itself. It is common to distinguish four components in an ITS: a model of the domain representing the expert knowledge of the subject matter, a student model representing the knowledge state of the learner at a given moment, a tutorial model involving pedagogical knowledge, and an interface with the student.

Research and development relating to ITS constitute an interdisciplinary crossroad involving contributions from AI, epistemology, cognitive science, psychology in general and educational psychology in particular, education, linguistics, anthropology, and human–computer interaction. As such, a lot of expertise is involved in this field, and one can expect that the construction of intelligent tutors has been guided by available inquiry-based knowledge, such as the findings of research on learning and instruction referred to earlier. Although this is largely the case, this domain is nevertheless filled with questions that appeal for further research.

For example, one robust finding from learning research is that the acquisition of new knowledge is strongly influenced by students' prior knowledge (see e.g., Dochy, 1992). Consequently, instruction in general, and computer-supported learning environments in particular, should explicitly link up to the learners' prior knowledge and skills. One can say that the ITS community has taken this message seriously. Indeed, as mentioned, a major component of an intelligent tutor is the so-called student model, which, as Wenger (1987) stated, "should include all the aspects of the student's behavior and knowledge that have repercussions for his performance and learning" (p. 16). However, the same author added immediately that building such a student model is a difficult task for computer-based systems. Moreover, it is neither obvious how far one should go in building a student model, nor how flexible and diagnostic a computer environment should be in view of providing the most appropriate guidance. For instance, Putnam (1987) explored the thoughts and actions of experienced teachers as they tutored individual children in whole-number addition. A goal of this study was to test the idea that a detailed model of a student's knowledge, including his or her misconceptions and defensive procedures, is a prerequisite to successful remediation. Putnam found no support for this so-called *diagnostic–remedial model*. Indeed, one of his major findings was that experienced teachers did not try to construct highly detailed models of a child's wrong procedure before attempting remedial instruction. Such a finding questions the level of analysis of prior knowledge that is most appropriate for instructional purposes.

Another, even more fundamental issue relates to the nature of the support and guidance that ITS should provide. As already referred to, learning is currently conceived of as an active and constructive process. Learners are not passive recipients of information, but actively construct their knowledge and skills through interaction with the environment and through reorganization of their own mental structures. Consequently, as argued by Scardamalia, Bereiter, McLean, Swallow, and Woodruff (1989), computer-supported learning environments should support the active and constructive acquisition processes in students, and, moreover, they must try to develop and enhance more active learning strategies in passive learners. One could question whether the existing ITS are in line with this basic conception of acquisition processes. Indeed, ITS that base their decisions about instructional interventions on a detailed diagnosis of a student's knowledge can easily lead to a preponderance of highly structured learning environments that do not provide sufficient opportunity for active learner involvement and participation. An illustration of such a directive system is Anderson's Geometry Tutor (Anderson, Boyle, & Reiser, 1985), one of the most frequently quoted examples of ITS. It is based on a nonconstructivist view of learning, and more specifically on a production rule-based S–R model. As remarked by Glaser and Bassok (1989; see also Glaser, 1994), it is reminiscent of Skinnerian shaping and successive approximation, and of the sequential, component skill reinforcement of programmed instruction. Although it may teach specific procedural skills efficiently, it does not help students develop and enhance their own learning potential. As argued by Kaput (1992), suggested attempts to make this tutor more flexible and educationally adjustable will not modify its underlying fixed epistemology: "the knowledge and the underlying authority of the tutor reside in the computer" (p. 545).

Taking this state of affairs into account, the following idea has gained more and more ground: Computer-supported environments should not involve the knowledge and intelligence to guide and structure learning processes, but rather should create situations and offer tools that simulate students to make maximum use of their own cognitive potential (Scardamalia et al., 1989). In this connection, Kintsch (1991) launched the idea of *unintelligent tutoring:* "A tutor should not provide the intelligence to guide learning, it should not do the planning and monitoring of the student's progress, because those are the very activities the students must perform themselves in order to learn. What a tutor should do is to provide temporary support for learners that allows them to perform at a level just beyond their current ability level" (p. 245). It is obvious that Vygotsky's (1978) notion of the *zone of proximal development* underlies this view about the optimum nature of the interventions to support constructive learning processes.

In line with this evolving conception of computer-supported learning (see also Brown, 1990), there is a clear shift toward supportive systems that are less structured and less directive, that are more focused on coaching than on tutoring, that involve student-controlled tools for the acquisition of knowledge, and that attempt to integrate both tools and coaching strategies in collaborative learning environments (see also Kaput, 1992). A number of successful environments that embody this shift have already been developed (see e.g., De Corte, Linn, Mandl, & Verschaffel, 1992a). The remaining part of this chapter describes a project that aims to construct a Logo-based system in line with the basic idea that derives from the preceding discussion—namely, embedding the computer in a powerful learning environment that elicits and mediates constructive learning processes in students.

LOGO: A LEVER FOR THE ACQUISITION OF THINKING SKILLS?

Logo originates from an AI approach to educational computing that is at right angles to the early stages of ITS, as was manifested during the second International Conference on Artificial Intelligence and Education, held at the University of Exeter in 1985 (see Lawler & Yazdani, 1987). Indeed, in contrast to the highly structured ITS, Papert (1980) advocated a self-discovery pedagogy: In the Logo environment, children will learn to program in the same spontaneous way as they learn to speak, and, moreover, this will be conducive to the acquisition of more general, transferable cognitive skills. Papert called this *learning without a curriculum*, and his standpoint approaches the radical version of the constructivist view of learning (Cobb, 1994).

One could say that the emerging conception of computer-supported learning and tutoring described at the end of the previous section represents a move in that direction. However, the proverbial swing of the pendulum in this case is not to the extreme; it is not a shift from the overly directive traditional ITS toward totally open learning environments. This may be due, at least indirectly, to the fact that the outcomes of a series of investigations about the effects of Logo programming on children's thinking and problem-solving skills, carried out in the first part of the past decade according to the Papert self-discovery approach, did not report any positive results supporting the so-called "cognitive-effects hypothesis" (De Corte & Verschaffel, 1989). Nevertheless, these investigations have not led to a rejection of this hypothesis. One reason for this is the poor quality of the Logo learning environments that were designed and implemented in those studies: Systematic and direct intervention was kept to a minimum, and it was, so to say, hoped that the acquisition of the programming skills would somehow "happen" to the pupils due to the unique characteristics of the Logo language (Leron, 1985). At present, this viewpoint has largely been abandoned, and most researchers now agree that Logo environments, although still supporting students' knowledge construction, should also involve systematic guidance and mediation aimed at the acquisition of problem-solving skills in programming and, eventually, their transfer to other contexts and situations.

In line with this point of view, more recent investigations have attempted to overcome the weaknesses of the earlier work. Interestingly, positive results were found both with respect to the mastery of thinking skills within the Logo environment, and with regard to the transfer of these skills to new content domains (see De Corte, Verschaffel, & Schrooten, 1992c). This was also the case in our own teaching experiment, in which a Logo environment was implemented in two sixth-grade classes for one school year (De Corte, Verschaffel, & Schrooten, 1992b). However, taken as a whole, those results strongly suggest that Logo is not a genuine vehicle for thinking, but that it can be a useful device for the acquisition of thinking skills if embedded in a powerful teaching–learning environment that is particularly aimed toward the mastery and transfer of these skills. However, Logo should not be interpreted as merely a context for the teaching of general skills; to the contrary, those skills should be acquired through the learning and teaching of domain-specific Logo programming skills.

With respect to the design of such powerful teaching–learning environments, the following issue is raised. Until now, most of the instructional support to students learning Logo was provided by the teacher, by written materials, and so on. But taking into account the new ideas concerning tutoring described previously, and the advances in information technology, one can ask whether it is possible and desirable to build (part of) the instructional support in the Logo software (see also Salomon, 1992; Scardamalia et al., 1989). We have attempted to construct and evaluate a new Logo system, aimed at fostering the acquisition of programming skills, that has such built-in support. Before describing its design, it is useful to outline the Logo teaching–learning environment developed in our previous work because it constitutes the basis of this computer-based system.

A LOGO TEACHING–LEARNING ENVIRONMENT

In a project on "Computers and Thinking," we developed, implemented, and evaluated a Logo teaching–learning environment that focuses on a subset of four thinking skills considered to be sensitive to programming experience and instrumental in acquiring competence in programming: two metacognitive skills (planning and debugging) and two heuristics (problem decomposition and construction of an external problem presentation). The crucial part of the Logo environment is the teaching of a Logo programming strategy, which consists of two main phases: a planning phase, carried out independently from the computer, and an integrated coding-and-testing phase at the machine (for a more detailed discussion, see De Corte et al., 1992b).

In the planning phase, a treelike diagram (see Fig. 7.1) is constructed, in which the complex drawing is subdivided into building blocks that are easy to program (e.g., rectangles and triangles). In this phase, planning as a metacognitive activity takes place and elicits the application of the two heuristics—namely, problem decomposition and construction of an external representation.

Once the planning is completed, the integrated coding-and-testing phase at the machine can begin. This activity, which involves debugging, is guided by two principles—namely, top–down programming and immediate testing and debugging. *Top–down programming* means that the children are taught to start with the most global procedure, called the *mother procedure*, consisting of the names of all the subsequent parts from the second level of the treelike diagram. Subsequently, each component of this procedure is specified until the lowest level of the treelike diagram is reached. The second principle consists of the immediate testing and debugging of each newly defined procedure after defining it. By calling the mother procedure, the result appears on the screen and can instantly be evaluated; furthermore, the error message ("There is no procedure named . . .") indicates which procedure has to be written next.

As said before, instruction of this programming strategy constituted the major component of the Logo course, which was taught in 2 sixth-grade classes one

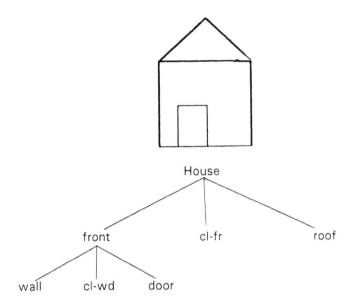

(cl-fr means : connecting link between front and roof)

FIG. 7.1.   Treelike diagram for the drawing of a house.

afternoon each week during a whole school year (approximately 60 hours). In line with our moderate or realistic (Cobb, 1994) constructivist view of the learning process, this instruction was characterized by a good balance of exploratory learning activities, on the one hand, and systematic teaching aimed at mastery of the domain-specific Logo concepts and programming skills, on the other hand. In this respect, our learning environment involved major aspects of cognitive apprenticeship (Collins, Brown, & Newman, 1989). The programming strategy was first demonstrated as a whole by a member of the research team, and the different steps were explained with a view toward helping students build a conceptual model of the processes required to carry out the task (modeling). Then each component of the strategy was treated and practiced separately; the teacher provided direct support whenever necessary (scaffolding). Finally, the children were given ample opportunity to practice the whole strategy in small groups of three pupils, working on progressively more difficult problems. In the beginning, the groups were guided intensively using hints, feedback, and support (coaching, scaffolding), but the interventions were gradually removed as children's mastery of the skills increased (fading).

The scores on a series of Logo mastery tests showed that the children were able to apply the intended general thinking skills within the Logo environment. These results justify that it is possible to successfully teach 12-year-olds a metacognitive strategy for programming, involving the systematic application of heuristic methods such as decomposing a problem into subgoals. In addition, we found that mastery of those cognitive skills within the domain of Logo programming was sufficient to achieve near transfer. Indeed, the multivariate analyses of the scores of the experimental and control groups on a series of five transfer tests showed that the Logo course yielded near-transfer effects for three out of the four thinking skills that were taught—namely, debugging, problem decomposition, and construction of an external representation (for a more detailed description of the instructional system, as well as the obtained achievement and transfer outcomes, see De Corte et al., 1992b, 1992c).

A LOGO-BASED TOOL KIT AND COMPUTER COACH

Based on our experience with and evaluation of the Logo teaching–learning environment outlined in the previous section, we began constructing a new Logo-based system with built-in instructional capability (e.g., scaffolding and coaching facilities to support children's learning of planning, programming, and debugging skills). A major reason for computerizing a part of the instruction derives from the observation that the teaching of thinking is time-consuming and effort-intensive. Therefore, it is worthwhile and interesting to explore the possible benefits of "shared instruction" between the teacher and the computer.

At the outset, it was decided that the new Logo environment should meet the following requirements:

1. The system should allow pupils to acquire the Logo turtle graphics in an easy and user-friendly way.
2. The system should especially support the acquisition of the programming strategy described earlier by offering pupils tools that scaffold planning and debugging activities.
3. A computer coach should provide part of the problem-solving instruction usually given by the teacher. The system should also be able to reduce the rigor of this coaching when pupils progress.
4. The whole environment should be user friendly for primary-school children. For instance, the system should be highly self-explanatory, a help facility with respect to the structure of the system should be available at any point, and the system should be menu- and mouse-driven.
5. Finally, some additional conditions were stated to make the system useful as a prototype (e.g., being easy to extend and modify, and allowing smooth conversions from Dutch to other natural languages, such as French and English).

These requirements have led to the development of a Logo-based computer system involving three levels: (a) The first level corresponds with the traditional Logo turtle graphics—the pupil can write Logo commands and programs for making drawings; (b) at the second level, two additional tools are available as scaffolds that stimulate and facilitate planning and debugging activities; and (c) at the third level, the pupils' activities are analyzed by a computer coach that gives comments and orienting help—this support is based on a comparison between the pupils' activities and the expert programming strategy described earlier. Two types of coaching, differing in terms of the rigor of the diagnosis and the subsequent messages, are being implemented. To give a more concrete idea of the system, short descriptions of the three levels follow (for a more detailed overview, see De Corte, Verschaffel, Schrooten, Olivié, & Vansina, 1993).

Level One: Logo Turtle Graphics

The first level is similar to the traditional Logo turtle graphics and consists of two parts: an *execution part* and an *editor*. In the execution part, the pupil can type Logo commands that are executed immediately. To write a procedure or a program, the pupil has to indicate in the menu that he or she wants to go to the editor. After finishing the program, the pupil again switches to the execution part. When a program is called by typing its name, the entire program is checked first. If it does not contain syntactical errors, it is executed. If not, the pupil receives an error message and has to go back to the editor to correct the bug in the program.

Level Two: Scaffolding Tools for Planning and Debugging

At this level, Logo is supplemented with two tools that support planning and debugging activities. However, use of these scaffolding tools is not compulsory. Taking into account the level of competency already acquired, the pupil can decide—possibly in consultation with the teacher—whether to utilize these tools.

The *planning tool* is a graphical editor that constructs and manipulates a graphic representation of a program's structure in a treelike diagram. This graphical editor has special boxes for the following Logo constructs: *procedures, procedures with parameters, iteration, recursion,* and *conditional statements* (see Fig. 7.2).

With the help of this tool, pupils can add, delete, replace, and rename parts of the treelike diagram. Being able to do this at the computer, instead of on a piece of paper, has several advantages. First, during the construction process at the machine, the arrangement of the treelike diagram as a whole stays clear and tidy.

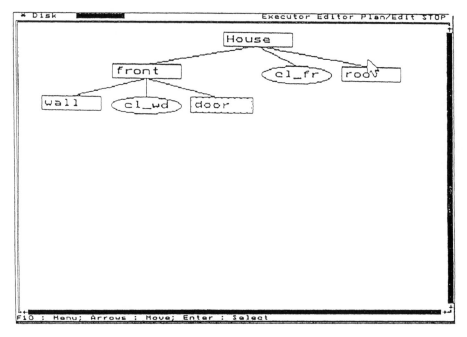

FIG. 7.2 Planning tool: Treelike diagram for writing a program that draws a house.

Experience has learned that pupils are often rather sloppy in constructing diagrams on paper, which makes it difficult to see the correct structure. Second, the plan and corresponding program can be saved together under a common name, which prevents the plan from getting lost. Third, the constructed treelike diagram is also available on the screen in the editor; this can stimulate pupils to use it as a reference point in coding the program. Finally, making the treelike diagram at the computer will allow the computer coach at Level Three to analyze and possibly criticize the construction of that diagram, as well as the process of transposing the treelike diagram in Logo code.

The *debugging tool* has been added because, in most Logo versions, it is difficult for pupils to trace a bug in their program: The code and corresponding drawing are not available at the same time, and the execution speed is too high to see where and how an error occurs. The debugging tool in our system enables pupils to view the code and the corresponding graphical output together on the screen; each command is highlighted as it is being executed (see Fig. 7.3). Moreover, the execution speed can be slowed down, and procedures can be carried out step by step; the name of the actual procedure and the actual values of its parameters can be asked for after each step.

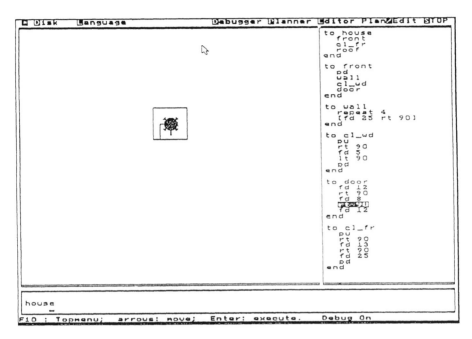

FIG. 7.3. Debugging tool showing the program code and the graphical output (the program line *rt 90* in the procedure *to door* is highlighted on the screen).

Level Three: Computer Coach

The main difference with Level Three is that a coach checks the pupils' activities in both the planning and coding-and-testing phases. In both phases, this coach, which is much less sophisticated than in traditional ITS, locates syntactic and semantic errors, as well as errors in the programming strategy.

Level Three contains two sublevels. At the first, or tolerant, sublevel, the coach only gives a warning when an error is made; pupils can ignore this warning. At the second, or rigorous, sublevel, pupils are not able to proceed if the error is not corrected, or if the prescribed step from the programming strategy is not followed.

In the planning phase, the coach checks syntactic and semantic aspects of the pupils' input during the construction of a treelike diagram. Examples of syntactic errors are: the name of a procedure starts with a numerical character instead of a letter, and the name of a procedure is a Logo primitive (e.g., *forward, penup*) or a reserved word (e.g., *if, end*). Examples of semantic errors are: a repeat or conditional construct that contains no statement, formal parameters that are defined but not used, or statements that are placed after the stop command. The coach also reacts when certain criteria for an expert tree diagram are not fulfilled: when a procedure has too many subprocedures at the same level, or when two identical procedures are defined twice.

In the editor, the coach reacts when the syntax of the programming code is not correct, and when the semantics of the code are not in accordance with the plan. Furthermore, the coach examines if pupils take into account the two principles underlying the coding-and-testing phase—namely, top–down programming and immediate testing and debugging. The principle of top–down programming means that pupils have to start with the coding of the mother procedure. This implies that the names of the parts, as well as their sequence, have to correspond to the second level of the treelike diagram. Moreover, the diagram has to be converted to code according to the depth-first method. The principle of immediate testing and debugging means that pupils are asked to run the program each time a new procedure is defined. This enables them to evaluate the screen effect, and, if necessary, to debug the program. The execution stops when an unknown procedure is encountered; thus, pupils know which procedure has to be defined next.

The preceding description clearly shows that this new Logo system has a lot of built-in support. But, as already mentioned, it is not intended as a stand-alone environment, but as a system that operates embedded in a teacher-mediated, collaborative context. Taking into account that the teaching of thinking is effortful and time-absorbing, shared instruction between a teacher and a computer can be beneficial. For instance, individualized or small-group activities guided by the computer during some stages of the teaching–learning process should allow a more efficient use of time, as well as an overall time gain. The teacher gets more opportunity to guide students' knowledge construction using cognitive apprenticeship methods such as modeling, explaining, coaching, and scaffolding; and learners get to articulate and reflect on their knowledge and problem-solving skills, as well as explore new problems, hypotheses, and solution methods (Collins, 1991; Collins et al., 1989). Depending on the intended goal, the present needs and difficulties of the learners, and the nature of the intervention, these methods can be used either individually, in small groups, or for the whole class. For example, modeling and explaining will often take the form of whole-class teaching, whereas scaffolding will frequently be used to support an individual learner facing an impasse; articulation and reflection in small groups is an appropriate setting for fostering metacognitive awareness.

CONCLUSIONS

Pelgrum and Plomp (1991) derived the following conclusion from data from the 1989 IEA "Computers in Education" survey, referred to in the beginning of this chapter: "the three most important reasons for not using computers, as well as the problems experienced as most serious in using computers, are the lack of teachers' knowledge and skills and the lack of hardware and software" (p. 103). Although this conclusion confirms three important facts observed in other studies (see e.g., Kaput's description of the state of the art, summarized in the beginning of this chapter), the issue arises as to what extent these are the real reasons of the relative failure of educational computing. This is especially important in view of the development of a strategy for improving the existing situation. For instance, introducing numerous sophisticated computers in schools would meet one of the three reasons, but it is doubtful whether it would help much.

This is not to deny the importance of a sufficient number of good machines in schools, and certainly not of the production of more high-quality software and the improvement of teachers' computer knowledge and experience. However, in remedying the facts, one should be especially concerned about elaborating on a strategy that guarantees the instructionally appropriate embedding of educational computing in powerful, collaborative learning environments on the one hand, and develops the expertise of the teachers to understand, build, and handle such computational environments, on the other. As contrasted with the traditional add-on strategy underlying the large majority of CAI and ITS, this requires a fundamentally different approach based on the empirically well-grounded outcomes of recent research on learning and instruction.

This does not necessarily mean that the application of drill-and-practice programs and intelligent tutors has to be excluded; if integrated in the curriculum of the school, they can be useful for specific purposes, such as remedial teaching in arithmetic. But the real contribution of educational computing to the improvement of schooling lies in the development of software tools and programs that elicit and support in learners—jointly with the teacher, peers, and other media—processes of knowledge and meaning construction. Although some progress has been made in that direction, as is shown in this volume (see also De Corte et al., 1992a; Harel & Papert, 1990), further elaboration and testing of principles for the design of powerful computer-supported learning environments is a challenging, joint task for researchers and practitioners interested in educational computing. One important issue that needs to be addressed in continued research relates to the appropriate degree of open-endedness of such learning environments.

REFERENCES

Anderson, J. R., Boyle, C. F., & Reiser, B. J. (1985). Intelligent tutoring systems. *Science, 228,* 456–462.

Becker, H. J. (1991). How computers are used in United States schools: Basic data from the 1989 I.E.A. computers in education survey. *Journal of Educational Computing Research, 7,* 385–406.

Brown, J. S. (1990). Toward a new epistemology for learning. In C. Frasson & J. Gauthiar (Eds.), *Intelligent tutoring systems: At the crossroads of artificial intelligence and education* (pp. 266–282). Norwood, NJ: Ablex.

Clark, R. (1983). Reconsidering research on learning from media. *Review of Educational Research, 53*, 445–459.

Clark, R. E. (1992). Facilitating domain-general problem solving: Computers, cognitive processes and instruction. In E. De Corte, M. C. Linn, H. Mandl, & L. Verschaffel (Eds.), *Computer-based learning environments and problem solving* (pp. 265–285). Berlin: Springer-Verlag.

Clark, R. E., & Sugrue, B. M. (1990). North American disputes about research on learning from media. *International Journal of Educational Research, 14*, 507–520.

Cobb, P. (1994). Constructivism and learning. In T. Husén & T. N. Postlethwaite (Eds.), *International encyclopedia of education* (2nd ed., pp. 1049–1052). Oxford, England: Pergamon.

Collins, A. (1991). Cognitive apprenticeship and instructional technology. In L. Idol & B. F. Jones (Eds.), *Educational values and cognitive instruction: Implications for reform* (pp. 121–138). Hillsdale, NJ: Lawrence Erlbaum Associates.

Collins, A., Brown, J. S., & Newman, S. E. (1989). Cognitive apprenticeship: Teaching the craft of reading, writing and mathematics. In L. B. Resnick (Ed.), *Knowing, learning and instruction. Essays in honour of Robert Glaser* (pp. 453–494). Hillsdale, NJ: Lawrence Erlbaum Associates.

Cuban, L. (1986). *Teachers and machines: The classroom use of technology since 1920.* New York: Teachers College Press.

Darrow, B. (1932). *Radio: The assistant teacher.* Columbus, OH: R. G. Adams.

De Corte, E., Greer, B., & Verschaffel, L. (in press). Learning and teaching mathematics. In D. Berliner & R. Calfee (Eds.), *Handbook of educational psychology.* New York: Macmillan.

De Corte, E., Linn, M. C., Mandl, H., & Verschaffel, L. (Eds.). (1992a). *Computer-based learning environments and problem solving.* Berlin: Springer-Verlag.

De Corte, E., & Verschaffel, L. (1989). Logo, a vehicle for thinking. In B. Greer & G. Mulhern (Eds.), *New directions in mathematics education* (pp. 63–81). London: Routledge & Kegan Paul.

De Corte, E., Verschaffel, L., & Schrooten, H. (1992b). Cognitive effects of learning to program in Logo: A one-year study with sixth graders. In E. De Corte, M. C. Linn, H. Mandl, & L. Verschaffel (Eds.), *Computer-based learning environments and problem solving* (pp. 207–228). Berlin: Springer-Verlag.

De Corte, E., Verschaffel, L., & Schrooten, H. (1992c). Kognitive Effekte Computergestutzten Lernens: Zum Stand der Forschung [Cognitive effects of computer-supported learning: A state-of-the-art]. *Unterrichtswissenschaft: Zeitschrift für Lernforschung, 20,* 12–33.

De Corte, E., Verschaffel, L., Schrooten, H., Olivié, H., & Vansina, A. (1993). A Logo-based tool-kit and computer coach to support the development of general thinking skills. In T. M. Duffy, J. Lowyck, & D. H. Jonassen (Eds.), *Designing environments for constructive learning* (pp. 109–124). Berlin: Springer-Verlag.

Dochy, F. J. R. C. (1992). *Assessment of prior knowledge as a determinant for future learning.* Utrecht, The Netherlands: Lemma.

Glaser, R. (1994). Learning theory and instruction. In G. d'Ydewalle, P. Eelen, & P. Bertelson (Eds.), *International perspectives on psychological sciences: Vol. 2. The state of the art* (pp. 341–357). Hove, England: Lawrence Erlbaum Associates.

Glaser, R., & Bassok, M. (1989). Learning theory and the study of instruction. *Annual Review of Psychology, 40,* 631–666.

Goodyear, P. (1991). *Teaching knowledge and intelligent tutoring.* Norwood, NJ: Ablex.

Harel, I., & Papert, S. (1990). Software design as a learning environment. *Interactive Learning Environments, 1,* 1–32.

Kaput, J. J. (1992). Technology and mathematics education. In D. A. Grouws (Ed.), *Handbook of research on mathematics teaching and learning* (pp. 515–556). New York: Macmillan.

Kintsch, W. (1991). A theory of discourse comprehension: Implications for a tutor for word algebra problems. In M. Carretero, M. Pope, R. J. Simons, & J. I. Pozo (Eds.), *Learning and instruction: European research in an international context* (Vol. 3, pp. 235–253). Oxford, England: Pergamon.

Kozma, R. B. (1991). Learning with media. *Review of Educational Research, 61,* 179–211.

Lawler, R. W., & Yazdani, M. (1987). *Artificial intelligence and education: Vol. 1. Learning environments and tutoring systems.* Norwood, NJ: Ablex.

Leron, U. (1985). Logo today: Vision and reality. *The Computer Teacher, 2,* 26–32.

Levenson, W. (1945). *Teaching through radio.* New York: Farrar and Rinehart.

Makrakis, V. (1988). *Computers in school education: The cases of Sweden and Greece.* Stockholm, Sweden: Institute of International Education, University of Stockholm.

National Council of Teachers of Mathematics. (1989). *Curriculum and evaluation standards for school mathematics.* Reston, VA: Author.

Papert, S. (1980). *Mindstorms. Children, computers, and powerful ideas.* New York: Basic Books.

Pelgrum, W. J., & Plomp, T. (1991). *The use of computers in education worldwide. Results from the IEA "Computers in Education" survey in 19 educational systems.* Oxford, England: Pergamon.

Putnam, R. T. (1987). Structuring and adjusting content for students: A study of live and simulated tutoring of addition. *American Educational Research Journal, 24,* 13–48.

Salomon, G. (1992). Effects with and of computers and the study of computer-based learning environments. In E. De Corte, M. C. Linn, H. Mandl, & Verschaffel, L. (Eds.), *Computer-based learning environments and problem solving* (pp. 249–263). Berlin: Springer-Verlag.

Scardamalia, M., Bereiter, C., McLean, R. S., Swallow, J., & Woodruff, E. (1989). Computer-supported intentional learning environments. *Journal of Educational Computing Research, 5,* 51–68.

Sleeman, D., & Brown, J. S. (Eds.). (1982). *Intelligent tutoring systems.* London: Academic Press.

Vygotsky, L. S. (1978). *Mind in society. The development of higher psychological processes.* Cambridge, MA: Harvard University Press.

Wenger, E. (1987). *Artificial intelligence and tutoring systems. Computational and cognitive approaches to the communication of knowledge.* Los Altos, CA: Kaufmann.

II SOCIAL INTERACTION

8 Adaptation and Understanding: A Case for New Cultures of Schooling

Marlene Scardamalia
Carl Bereiter
Centre for Applied Cognitive Science, Ontario Institute for Studies in Education

The effort to understand and explain phenomena can have considerable adaptive value, as Schank (1986) has shown. When events do not conform to our expectations, trying to explain them may provide a basis for more accurate predictions in the future. It is often suggested that an urge to understand is innate in humans. This may be true, but the statement needs qualification. In the first place, human beings are much more inclined to explain unusual phenomena than to explain usual ones. This is consistent with Schank's view that failed expectations, rather than some general explanatory urge, lie behind efforts at understanding, with van Lehn's (1990) account of explanation as impasse-driven, and with Berzonsky's (1971) demonstration that students are better at explaining malfunctions than normal functions. A second qualification is essential if we are to consider understanding within an adaptationist framework: Under some conditions, it is adaptive not to seek understanding. This fact takes on great importance in the context of schooling. School is a place where the pursuit of understanding is supposedly given a high priority, but it is also a social institution with conditions of its own to which students adapt, and it is therefore important to examine whether these conditions favor adaptation through or without understanding.

A great deal of cognitive instructional research suggests that students are not investing much effort in understanding what they are exposed to in school. Salient examples are research indicating: (a) lack of comprehension monitoring (August, Flavell, & Clift, 1984; Garner, 1980, 1987; Markman, 1979, 1981; Scardamalia & Bereiter, 1984); (b) use of the "copy–delete" strategy in summarization—evaluating propositions one by one, rather than identifying superordinate propositions (Brown & Day, 1983; Brown, Day, & Jones, 1983); (c) use of the "knowledge-telling" strategy in writing, which involves telling what

149

one knows under minimal topical and structural constraints (Bereiter & Scardamalia, 1987; Scardamalia & Bereiter, 1987); (d) prevalence of scientific misconceptions that are resistant to instruction (C. Anderson & E. L. Smith, 1984; Shayer & Wylam, 1981; C. Smith, Snir, & Grosslight, 1992; Vosniadou & Brewer, 1987); (e) poor comprehension of mathematical word problems and giving of implausible answers (Holt, 1964; Littlefield & Rieser, 1993; Schoenfeld & Herrmann, 1982); and (f) superficiality and competitiveness observed in student discussions (Eichinger, Anderson, Palincsar, & David, 1991).

Although these kinds of behavior are often regraded as maladaptive, an alternative view, persuasively argued by Holt (1964) in *How Children Fail*, is that such behaviors are in fact intelligent responses to school conditions in which it is adaptive *not* to invest effort in understanding. If this alternative is correct, then efforts to teach understanding-oriented strategies are likely to have limited success unless school conditions are changed to make them more adaptive. That is the view that underlies our approach to designing a computer-based environment for schools—CSILE (computer-supported intentional learning environments).

In this chapter, we examine a number of ways in which school conditions may make it adaptive not to seek understanding. Then we discuss school conditions that should shift the adaptive bias back in favor of understanding. Finally, we describe how CSILE's design is intended to support these more favorable school conditions.

Classroom discourse has many features that distinguish it from discourse aimed at understanding. Most class talk can be characterized as *recitation* (Doyle, 1986). When discussions are aimed at understanding, they are generally led by the teacher. Transcripts of classroom discussion indicate that such discussions typically consist of a string of three-step units, each unit being made up of the following conversational moves: teacher initiates, student responds, and teacher evaluates (Heap, 1985). Socratic dialogue is put forward as a model for classroom discourse, but here, too, the teacher gives the discussion such direction as it has, and thus is likely to be the only one whose goals have substantive influence on the outcome. The students' own goals may influence how successful the discussion is, but mainly through extent of cooperation.

WHEN IT IS ADAPTIVE *NOT* TO SEEK UNDERSTANDING

There is an old saying in the U.S. Army that there are three ways to do everything: the right way, the wrong way, and the army way. This is part of a lesson often explicitly stated to recruits—that they should not try to understand why they are supposed to do this or that because usually there is no explanation or, if there is, it is not worth knowing. It is better just to do as you are told and thereby stay out of trouble.

Similar advice might be, but usually is not, given to students entering school. Classroom work, even when it is meaningful in its underlying intent, is often characterized by arbitrariness in the standards and procedures that most immediately confront the student. Submitting outlines in advance of essay writing, writing papers of specified length, turning assignments in on specified dates, or having time allocations for schoolwork might all represent reasonable expectations, but they are nonetheless arbitrary. Likewise, students would have little chance of abstracting significant principles from arbitrary procedures involving arithmetic algorithms; spelling lists; outlines in advance of writing; and the need to eliminate double negatives, *and* and *but* as first words in sentences, and prepositions as last words in sentences. But perhaps the most damaging kinds of arbitrariness involve classification and lists—six causes of the French Revolution, five steps in problem solving, four examples of symbiosis, and so on. Textbooks and student assignments are filled with such lists and classifications, which take on undue importance because of the ease with which they can be converted into test items. Even when classifications have underlying significance, as in the case of plant and animal phyla, the value or meaning of the classification is often neglected in favor of merely teaching it as fact (Bereiter, 1992). Arbitrariness also leads to the use of mnemonics, rather than reasoning— the real aid to recall under such conditions.

Although there is a great deal of arbitrariness in school life, afflicting teachers and students alike, it is only one of a number of factors that can undermine the urge to understand. Other conditions of school life that we place in this category include: product orientation, incomprehensible texts and explanations, limited time for reflection coupled with competitive knowledge display, emphasis on reproducing authoritative statements of facts combined with disadvantages of producing interpretive accounts, overload, discontinuity of much of schoolwork with prior knowledge, and busywork.

Product Orientation

American industries are being criticized for their bias toward quantity versus quality production (Dobyns & Crawford-Mason, 1991). American schools may be similarly criticized for their emphasis on getting out a product. Accordingly, students cannot be blamed if they adapt in the way that adult workers adapt—by finding ways to meet production requirements with a minimum of time and effort. Although school tasks may vary considerably, and are sometimes selected by the students, they almost always center on a product (e.g., a completed workbook page, a piece of writing, a written problem solution, etc.), rather than on understanding. Stated differently, typical school environments do not directly confront students with needs for understanding, critical examination of beliefs, and the like. What they are confronted with are essentially endless series of tasks to be done within severe time constraints. It is also fairly common in schools to reward early task completion, with opportunities to do other things that are more enjoyable, such as free reading or playing a computer game. Under conditions of this sort, an adaptive organism will develop strategies that minimize time to complete tasks, and the most likely way to do this is by trimming away activities that do not directly yield the deliverable product.

Unintelligibility

School texts have been rendered unintelligible by various forms of simplification. These forms include eliminating connectives to obtain desired results with the application of readability formulas (Davison, 1984), and using simplified drawings and representational devices that stand in the way of understanding (Engestrom, 1991). Similarly, many texts offer explanations so attenuated that only knowledgeable readers might infer their deeper meaning (Armbruster, 1984; Armbruster & Anderson, 1981; Beck, McKeown, & Gromoll, 1989). Although we previously noted that there is considerable evidence that students fail to pick up discrepancies in texts, this may be, in part, an adaptation to the presence in school texts of allusions that students are not expected to understand, but that are put there to avoid criticism from subject-matter experts.

Lack of Opportunity for Reflection

Studies have indicated that the average time a teacher waits for response to a question is a few seconds (Rowe, 1986). Thus, students who can respond without taking time to think are favored. More generally, school processes that require outgoing, confident, speedy processing favor economical, rather than reflective, strategies. From this standpoint, we might rethink the copy–delete and knowledge-telling strategies mentioned earlier. Their virtue is that they are highly economical. Because they are single-pass strategies, it is possible to avoid going back over text, reconsidering decisions, or carrying out complex searches. They are perfect for time-constrained processing of information. Furthermore, the information-processing load is small compared with that of more sophisticated ways of processing text (Bereiter & Scardamalia, 1984; Scardamalia, 1981). Viewed from this perspective, they represent highly adaptive responses to school.

Emphasis on Reproduction of Information

Schools are frequently criticized for encouraging rote reproduction of information (in assignments, recitations, and tests) rather than understanding, placing undue emphasis on reproducing authoritative statements of facts, and discouraging interpretation. Comprehension tests are notorious for their emphasis on recall rather than understanding. But beyond the realm of multiple-choice and comprehension tests, there are classroom questioning routines that encourage students to reproduce authoritative statements of facts, rather than risk wrong answers through the use of paraphrased and interpretive accounts of material. For example, one study showed that students judged rightly that they would do better on exams if they copied notes verbatim from lectures, rather than trying to put material in their own words (Fillion & Mendelsohn, 1979).

Overload

School curricula typically require students to take up a different major topic of study every 2–6 weeks. Texts are frequently jammed with facts and lists so that the number of items to be committed to memory exceeds what can be learned with understanding. As a result, students attempt to learn through use of mnemonics and other cramming devices, which have little long-term value.

Remoteness From Experienced Reality

Curriculum materials and teachers' explanations frequently miss the mark. They provide little continuity between scientific accounts, which make sense to already sophisticated adults, and accounts that start with students' naive interpretations and build on them. As a result, the literature is replete with accounts of gaps between what is taught, what is understood, and everyday experiences (C. Anderson & Smith, 1984; Engestrom, 1991; Larkin, McDermott, Simon, & Simon, 1980; Nussbaum & Novak, 1976). In the extreme case, schooling may seem so unrelated to the world that students experience that they decide one set of beliefs is true in school and another set is true in the actual world (Vosniadou & Brewer, 1987).

Busywork

Like life in the army, where meaningless tasks are contrived for the sole purpose of keeping soldiers busy and under control, schooling often involves a great deal of busywork—filling in workbook pages, playing repetitive educational games, writing out answers to questions at the ends of chapters, writing letters to imaginary recipients, and so on. Many writers have criticized the use of workbooks— the classroom's most pronounced form of busywork. As studies suggest, workbooks are designed to minimize students' questions, and in so doing favor routinized and unthinking approaches to the content they present. Their deadening effect on school content and contribution to wastage of school time have made them the focus of critical reviews (L. Anderson, 1984). These same criticisms apply in varying degrees to other school activities, such as work in activity centers and research that involves little more than copying material from encyclopedias. Such activities are seen as a necessary part of the school culture because keeping students busy frees time for teachers to attend to individual needs and to conduct small-group sessions. But such time is bought at the expense of keeping the majority of students engaged in activities that discourage efforts at understanding. In rethinking the culture of schools, we must rethink the whole 1-to-30, teacher–learner paradigm that makes busywork so difficult to eliminate.

Powerlessness and Low Probability of Success

Conditions where there is no anticipation of success are also candidates for conserving the mental effort that might otherwise go into understanding. Literature on management suggests that, although managers would seemingly be the ones to experience the most stress due to the level of responsibility they bear, those who exert little control over situations experience more stress (Marmot, 1986; Marmot et al., 1991). Expending effort when one has little control or chance for success may simply increase frustration. A more adaptive approach would reserve efforts for spheres of activity where one has more control over outcomes.

REDESIGNING CLASSROOMS TO MAKE UNDERSTANDING ADAPTIVE

Although the conditions discussed in the preceding section have not generally been thought of in terms of their effects on understanding, most of them have been recognized as undesirable. For generations, there have been reform efforts aimed at remedying these conditions, and thereby making schooling a more reasonable process. Given the limited success of these efforts, we must ask whether the way to turn schools into institutions that encourage understanding is to focus on the elimination of negative attributes.

There is ample evidence that some students—ones we have termed *intentional learners* (Bereiter & Scardamalia, 1989)—are inclined to pursue understanding even in unsupportive circumstances. Restructuring environments to motivate understanding will also vary in its effects on different students. Piecemeal redesign of school practices might produce incremental changes in students' motivation to pursue understanding, but a more fundamental change would require a reorientation of the purposes of schooling so that understanding becomes central, not an incidental goal pursued according to students' personal inclinations.

We suggest that real school reform should not focus so much on making schooling conducive to understanding, but on making understanding the focus of schooling. That is what we have been trying to do in developing CSILE as an overall approach to education. Making understanding the focus of schooling sounds so obvious and reasonable that it is difficult to realize what a radical change this means for the design of education.

We believe, the greatest change will come from restructuring classroom discourse to give priority to progressive inquiry, with advancement of collective knowledge highly valued (Scardamalia, Bereiter, & Lamon, 1994). By comparison, conventional schooling places undue emphasis on individual initiative and time- and space-limited discourses. Individual students all work on the same task, with no distribution of responsibilities or building on each others' inputs. When ideas are recorded, they are retained in individual files, and there is little continuity from one activity to another. Thus, many contributions to understanding go unrecognized, with no corpus of material to represent a groups' advances, to return to for analysis and refinement, or to provide a basis for engaging others working on common problems beyond the school walls.

In the present context, CSILE is best viewed as a discourse medium. As explained in more detail elsewhere (Scardamalia & Bereiter 1992, 1993), CSILE runs on networked computers—usually eight to a classroom. It provides a single, communal database into which students may enter various kinds of text and graphic notes. They can retrieve notes by others, comment on them (with authors being notified of comments), link notes to one another, or create group discussion notes (which are illustrated later). CSILE-mediated discourse can be carried on in any or all academic areas, limited only by the availability of machine time.

CSILE is being used at all levels from grade 1 to university, although its most widespread use is at the upper-elementary and middle-school levels. It has been used in a variety of curricular areas, including social studies, art, history, science, geography, literature, and mathematics. However, limitations of machine time (each student typically gets 30 minutes a day on a computer) have generally meant that, at any given time, only one unit or subject is being worked on via CSILE.

There are no set patterns for CSILE use. Teachers work CSILE into the curriculum in a variety of ways. (Different models of use are compared in Bereiter & Scardamalia, 1992; Lamon, Lee, & Scardamalia, 1993.) In some cases, a unit will follow a sequence of activities. For instance, it might begin with a videotape, followed by whole-class discussion; then students individually enter questions and study plans as CSILE notes; then they do individual reading, entering what they learn as notes, which others may comment on; whole-class discussions or readings intervene; finally, selected text and graphic notes may be printed out and displayed on a bulletin board. In other cases, students work in small groups and plan their own work, with only general guidance from the teacher. Information brought into CSILE notes by students may come from a variety of sources: books, experimental observations, interviews, and electronic media.

How CSILE is intended to restructure classroom discourse can best be understood by comparing it to two other forms of discourse: ordinary classroom discussion and electronic mail. In ordinary classroom discourse, the teacher is pivotal. Even in relatively open discussion, students typically address the teacher. In a more controlled discussion, as previously noted, the teacher typically initiates and ends each discourse segment, with a student supplying the intervening step, which usually consists of a response to a question. In contrast to this central role, the teacher in CSILE discourse functions mainly as a participant in discourse, and is not obligated to respond to whatever is said. (However, the teacher usually sets the broad topic and general nature of what is to be accomplished in the curricular unit, forming the basis of a discourse.) Electronic mail is gaining interest in many schools because it also removes the teacher from the center, allowing students to communicate directly with each other and, increasingly, with people elsewhere. One of the difficulties we have had in getting the idea of CSILE across to teachers is that they tend to think of it as a variety of electronic mail, and then find it not very well suited to that purpose. Although CSILE is designed for communication within and across classrooms, and outward to other places, it differs fundamentally from electronic mail in that it is not a person-to-person medium. Notes entered into the communal database are not notes to anyone; rather, they are contributions to some collective knowledge-building effort. The only way to communicate directly with anyone is by writing a comment on their note, and this comment becomes a part of the community database, available for comment by others. Thus, instead of addressing the teacher, as in conventional class discussions, or addressing other individuals, as in electronic mail, students using CSILE are encouraged to address issues, problems, arguments, and the like.

Thus, in CSILE's communal database, collective knowledge—as contrasted with school exercises, activities, or private interests—is the center of attention. Specialized note-writing environments are designed to engage students in conjecture, theory building, explication of confusions, and analysis, rather than regurgitation of information. Our goal is to ensure that discourses are open and decentralized, replicating for school students much of the progressive inquiry supported by publication in scholarly journals (see Scardamalia & Bereiter, 1994). The teacher's own knowledge does not curtail what is to be learned or investigated. The teacher can contribute to the discourse, but there are other sources of information as well. The teacher remains the leader, but his or her role shifts form standing outside the learning process and guiding it to participating actively in the learning process and leading by virtue of being a more expert learner. Students are expected to formulate their own problems of understanding and to pursue them in a progressive manner, formulating new higher level problems as they go. We are continually modifying and adding functionality to CSILE to encourage such knowledge-building activity.

When students are at work on knowledge problems in CSILE, questions that push against the limits of current knowledge assume a natural importance. In the

TABLE 8.1
Example of CSILE Discussion Note

P:	How does a cell function? (AR)
MT:	I think a cell functions by oxygen coming into the cell and the cell then can do its work by breathing. (AR)
MT:	I agree with your theory but when the cell functions I don't think it is breathing, I think that the oxygen you're breathing in is doing it. (JD)
MT:	I think a cell functions by the "things" inside itself. (organelles) (AK)
INTO:	How does the oxygen get into the cell, if the cell really does breath oxygen? (AR)
MT:	I don't think that cells breath oxygen, I just think that the cells need oxygen to do their work. But if the cells do breath oxygen, I think there is some kind of a tube in the cell that helps the cell get the oxygen it needs. (AK)
NI:	I found out that the cell takes food and oxygen in through the membrane. This happens regularly. The cell then changes the food and oxygen into energy. It uses the energy to do its work. (AR)
INTU:	How do the food and oxygen get to the cell's membrane? (AR)
MT:	I think there are very small tubes that lead to each cell and the food and oxygen go down those tubes and into the cell through the cell's membrane. (AR)
MT:	I disagree with your theory, Andrea. I think that the oxygen and food go into the cell automatically as a daily process. (AK)
INTU:	What does the oxygen do when it gets to the cell? (AK)
MT:	This is what I think the oxygen does when it gets to the cell. I think that the oxygen goes into the cell through the membrane and then it goes to the nucleus where it is turned into energy. (AR)

Note. Topic is biology. Keywords are biology and cell function.
Key: P = Problem; MT = My Theory; INTU = I Need To Understand; NI = New Information. Letters in brackets are initials of students authoring the contributions.

words of one middle-school student, "I am discovering gold (knowledge) that has never been discovered before for me. A new understanding. . . ." In Table 8.1, we present an example of students engaged in an extended text–graphic discourse, with commentary aimed at understanding.[1] Students set out ideas with the expectation that these will be improved in the course of working on them, and with the appreciation that their ideas are ill-formed, so a wide variety of ideas can advance their understanding, not just those that violate expectations. Accordingly, they generate hypotheses (MT—My Theory), note constraints and related problems, and actively seek information that will help them improve their theories (INTU—I Need To Understand).

In another series of discussion notes in the CSILE database, students could be seen "unlayering" problems, iteratively applying a how-does-it-work? schema in search for underlying causes. The group begins by identifying the problem: Why do you have to change the denominator to add fractions? In the course of trying to understand that problem, they discover a related problem: Why do you have to change the denominator when you add fractions but not when you multi-

---

[1]This episode is based on work conducted by Jim Hewitt and Jim Webb in a CSILE-supported Grade 5–6 class.

ply them? In their attempt to solve this problem, they discovered yet another problem: Why do fractions get smaller when you multiply them? Note that, without any intervening activity that violates their assumptions and without help from more knowledgeable others, they think through problems enough to note insufficiencies in their own explanations. They literally identify additional problems to be understood and set out to understand them. It is through their own inventions—noting that what they understand does not provide sufficient explanation—that they make advances.

Although this behavior seems to be inconsistent with Schank's view that explaining is a response to "failed expectations" and with "impasse-driven" views of learning in general, there is an important difference in situation that should be noted. The situations that Schank and others consider are usually those in which people are engaged in a practical activity and encounter some unexpected obstacle or turn of events. In effect, people take time out from the main activity to seek understanding, which will enable them to proceed more successfully with the main activity. But in a CSILE classroom, explanation seeking is the main activity. The problems that students are trying to solve are problems of understanding. Surprises and impasses may occur. For instance, a new fact may come to light that invalidates a current explanation, or students may realize that something else must be understood before the main knowledge problem can be solved. In these cases, learning will occur just as impasse-driven learning views would predict, hence there is no basic contradiction. But it is important to realize that understanding can be a goal pursued in its own right, as well as a response to surprise or failure. Pursuing understanding is, after all, what many impasse-driven learning theorists do for a living.

Our efforts with CSILE do not speak to the question of whether explanation seeking is a natural, innately motivated activity. We believe the culture of schools needs to be changed before we can determine if schools or children's psychological makeup is at issue when we give evidence of nonpursuit of understanding. Schools typically do not afford the luxury of progressive refinement of problems driven by the goal of understanding for its own sake. There is too much curriculum to get through; information is pumped at students too fast for them to have a chance to wonder about things. However, the findings presented next suggest that in CSILE cultures, where understanding is highly valued and conditions are conducive to it, students show greater evidence of pursuing understanding than typical school experience would lead one to expect.

FINDINGS SUGGESTIVE OF CSILE'S ROLE IN THE DEVELOPMENT OF UNDERSTANDING

The strategy we have used to address issues particular to the role of understanding is to present students with material that is, by age-adjusted standards (readability levels, problem-solving difficulty), more demanding than typically dealt with successfully at their age. For this purpose, a "difficult texts" assessment device was designed that required grade 5 and 6 students to read difficult scientific texts and solve transfer problems based on them (Lamon, Chan, Scardamalia, Burtis, & Brett, 1993; Scardamalia et al., 1992). As predicted, CSILE students provide more sophisticated solutions to transfer problems, and they recall more of the original text as well. In like manner, grade 5 and 6 CSILE and non-CSILE students were required to convey their understanding of difficult concepts (e.g., *continental drift*) through use of graphics (via pencil and paper, rather than computer, to eliminate a possible computer advantage for CSILE students). CSILE students' graphics demonstrate greater conceptual understanding as evidenced in their more thorough explanations involving indications of movement, underlying processes, before–after perspectives, and so forth (Gobert-Wickham, Coleman, Scardamalia, & Bereiter, 1993).

On another measure, we looked for depth of explanations in students' written reports. Students wrote essays on what they had learned after a unit of study. Learning for CSILE students is more frequently judged toward the high end of the scale (elaborated description of the topic area as a system), whereas the work of control students is more frequently judged toward the low end (isolated bits of information). Also, CSILE and non-CSILE students keep writing, mathematics, and science portfolios, and write comments on their own selections and the selection of a peer. To a significantly greater extent than control students, students using CSILE are able to provide detailed accounts of gains in understanding resulting from their engagement in the work represented in their portfolios (Lamon, Abeygunawardena, Cohen, Lee, & Wasson, 1992).

Finally, we would expect CSILE students to have beliefs about learning that reflect mature views of understanding. For example, we would expect them to appreciate that understanding requires self-directed effort, that good marks are not a perfect reflection of learning, that uncertainty and unanswered questions can be signs of progress, and so forth. In line with such expectations, CSILE students—to a significantly greater degree than their control counterparts—show mature views of learning (for a more detailed analysis of these results, see Lamon et al., 1993).

In summary, CSILE students consistently outperform control students in ways that suggest more understanding.[2] Further, the longer students spend working with CSILE, the better the results. For example, students who spend 2 years in CSILE classrooms show significantly greater achievement than their first-year counterparts, and there is another increment in the third year (on measures of the sort presented previously). CSILE results are also distinct, to our knowledge, in

---

[2]Significant results favoring CSILE students have been found on other measures, including standardized achievement tests (see Scardamalia et al., 1992), but we do not review those here.

that there is equal engagement by students at low and high ends of the ability spectrum, and by females and males (in the sense of numbers of notes contributed to the database; Scardamalia & Bereiter, 1994).

CONCLUSION

We have been impressed with how our own thinking has changed as we have become increasingly sensitive to an adaptationist perspective. From this perspective, students' minimalist strategies are not consciously aimed at beating the system. These students are doing what adaptive organisms always do—behaving in ways that are locally optimal given the environment (cf. J. Anderson, 1990). We argue that efforts at school restructuring should focus on altering classroom conditions that make minimalist strategies adaptive. Toward this end, we analyze conditions of schooling that inhibit efforts at understanding, and we contrast these with conditions that encourage students to pursue understanding by their own initiative. The latter analysis is based on our experience in developing and implementing a computer-based system (CSILE) for information sharing and knowledge advancement. In an effort to determine whether students in CSILE-based classrooms benefit from environments that place understanding center-front, the CSILE team has conducted a series of investigations. These require demonstration of greater understanding in students' approach to and comprehension of difficult texts, in their ability to explain difficult concepts through use of graphics, in their writings and selections of material aimed at demonstrations of learning, and finally in their understanding of the active role they must play if they are to take charge of their own understanding. Positive results from these evaluations provide a basis for confidence in the possibility of creating school environments that give understanding a central role.

ACKNOWLEDGMENTS

The authors wish to acknowledge the generous support of the James S. McDonnell Foundation through its Program in Cognitive Studies for Educational Practice. We are indebted to the students and teachers at Huron Street Public School who contributed their time and talents to this project, and to the entire CSILE team, without whose contributions the work reported here would not have been possible.

REFERENCES

Anderson, C. W., & Smith, E. L. (1984). Children's preconceptions and content-area textbooks. In G. G. Duffy, L. R. Roehler, & J. Mason (Eds.), *Comprehension instructions: Perspectives and suggestions* (pp. 187–201). New York: Longman.

Anderson, J. R. (1990). *The adaptive character of thought.* Hillsdale, NJ: Lawrence Erlbaum Associates.

Anderson, L. (1984). The environment of instruction: The function of seatwork in a commercially developed curriculum. In G. G. Duffy, L. R. Roehler, & J. Mason (Eds.), *Comprehension instructions: Perspectives and suggestions* (pp. 93–103). New York: Longman.

Armbruster, B. B. (1984). The problem of "inconsiderate text." In G. G. Duffy, L. R. Roehler, & J. Mason (Eds.), *Comprehension instructions: Perspectives and suggestions* (pp. 202–217). New York: Longman.

Armbruster, B. B., & Anderson, T. H. (1981). *Content-area textbooks* (Reading Education Rep. No. 23). Champaign, IL: University of Illinois, Center for the Study of Reading.

August, D. I., Flavell, J. H., & Clift, R. (1984). Comparison of comprehension monitoring of skilled and less skilled readers. *Reading Research Quarterly, 20,* 39–53.

Beck, I. L., McKeown, M. G., & Gromoll, E. W. (1989). Learning from social studies texts. *Cognition and Instruction, 6,* 99–158.

Bereiter, C., & Scardamalia, M. (1989). Intentional learning as a goal of instruction. In L. B. Resnick (Eds.), *Knowing, learning, and instruction: Essays in honor of Robert Glaser* (pp. 361–392). Hillsdale, NJ: Lawrence Erlbaum Associates.

Bereiter, C. (1992). Referent-centered and problem-centered knowledge: Elements of an educational epistemology. *Interchange, 23*(4), 337–362.

Bereiter, C., & Scardamalia, M. (1984). Information-processing demand of text composition. In H. Mandl, N. Stein, & T. Trabasso (Eds.), *Learning and comprehension of text* (pp. 407–428). Hillsdale, NJ: Lawrence Erlbaum Associates.

Bereiter, C., & Scardamalia, M. (1987). *The psychology of written composition.* Hillsdale, NJ: Lawrence Erlbaum Associates.

Bereiter, C., & Scardamalia, M. (1992). Two models of classroom learning using a communal database. In S. Dijkstra (Ed.), *Instructional models in computer-based learning environments* (pp. 229–241). Berlin: Springer-Verlag.

Berzonsky, M. D. (1971). The role of familiarity in children's explanations of physical causality. *Child Development, 42*(2), 705–715.

Brown, A. L., & Day, J. D. (1983). Macrorules for summarizing text. *Journal of Verbal Behavior, 22,* 1–14.

Brown, A. L., Day, J. D., & Jones, R. S. (1983). The development of plans for summarizing texts. *Child Development, 54,* 968–979.

Davison, A. (1984). Readability formulas and comprehension. In G. G. Duffy, L. R. Roehler, & J. Mason (Eds.), *Comprehension instructions: Perspectives and suggestions* (pp. 128–143). New York: Longman.

Dobyns, L., & Crawford-Mason, C. (1991). *Quality or else.* Boston: Houghton Mifflin.

Doyle, W. (1986). Classroom organization and management. In M. C. Wittrock (Ed.), *Handbook of research on teaching* (pp. 392–431). New York: Macmillan.

Eichinger, D. C., Anderson, C. W., Palinscar, A. S., & David, Y. M. (1991, April). *An illustration of the roles of content knowledge, scientific argument, and social norms in collaborative problem solving.* Paper presented at the annual meeting of the American Educational Research Association, Chicago, IL.

Engestrom, Y. (1991). *Nonscolae sed vitae discimus*: Toward overcoming the encapsulation of school learning. *Learning and Instruction, 1,* 243–259.

Fillion, B., & Mendelsohn, D. (1979). *A pilot investigation into the effects of writing on learning.* Unpublished report, Ontario Institute for Studies in Education, Toronto.

Garner, R. (1980). Monitoring of understanding: An investigation of good and poor readers' awareness of induced miscomprehension of text. *Journal of Reading Behavior, 12,* 55–63.

Garner, R. (1987). *Metacognition and reading comprehension.* Norwood, NJ: Ablex.

Gobert-Wickham, J., Coleman, E. B. Scardamalia, M., & Bereiter, C. (1993, April). *Fostering the development of children's graphical representation and causal/dynamic models through CSILE.*

Paper presented at the annual meeting of the American Educational Research Association, Atlanta, GA.

Heap, J. L. (1985). Discourse in the production of classroom knowledge: Reading lessons. *Curriculum Inquiry, 15*(3), 245–280.

Holt, J. (1964). *How children fail.* New York: Pitman.

Lamon, M., Abeygunawardena, H., Cohen, A., Lee, E., & Wasson, B. (1992, April). *Students' reflections on learning: A portfolio study.* Paper presented at the American Educational Research Symposium, Peer Collaboration for Reflective Thinking, San Francisco, CA.

Lamon, M., Chan, C., Scardamalia, M., Burtis, J., & Brett, C. (1993, April). *Beliefs about learning and constructive processes in reading: Effects of a computer supported intentional learning environment.* Paper presented at the annual meeting of the American Educational Research Association, Atlanta, GA.

Lamon, M., Lee, E., & Scardamalia, M. (1993). *Cognitive technologies and peer collaboration.* Unpublished report, Ontario Institute for Studies in Education, Toronto.

Larkin, J., McDermott, J., Simon, D. P., & Simon, H. A. (1980). Expert and novice performance in solving physics problems. *Science, 208,* 1335–1342.

Littlefield, J., & Rieser, J. J. (1993). Semantic features of similarity and children's strategies for identifying relevant information in mathematical story problems. *Cognition and Instruction, 11,* 133–188.

Markman, E. M. (1979). Realizing that you don't understand: Elementary school children's awareness of inconsistencies. *Child Development, 50,* 643–655.

Markman, E. M. (1981). Comprehension monitoring. In W. P. Dixon (Ed.), *Children's oral communication skills* (pp. 61–84). New York: Academic Press.

Marmot, M. G. (1986). Social inequalities in mortality: The social environment. In R. G. Wilkenson (Ed.), *Class and health: Research and longitudinal data* (pp. 21–33). London: Tavistock.

Marmot, M. G., Smith, G. D., Stansfeld, S., Patel, C., North, F., Head, J., White, I., Brunner, E., & Feeney, A. (1991). Health inequalities among British civil servants: The Whitehall II study. *Lancet, 337*(8754), 1387–1393.

Nussbaum, J., & Novak, J. D. (1976). An assessment of children's conceptions of the earth using structured interviews. *Science Education, 60,* 535–550.

Rowe, M. B. (1986). Wait time: Slowing down may be speeding up! *Journal of Teacher Education, 37,* 43–50.

Scardamalia, M. (1981). How children cope with the cognitive demands of writing. In C. H. Frederiksen & J. F. Dominic (Eds.), *Writing: The nature, development and teaching of written communication* (Vol. 2, pp. 81–103). Hillsdale, NJ: Lawrence Erlbaum Associates.

Scardamalia, M., & Bereiter, C. (1984). Development of strategies in text processing. In H. Mandl, N. Stein, & T. Trabasso (Eds.), *Learning and comprehension of text* (pp. 407–428). Hillsdale, NJ: Lawrence Erlbaum Associates.

Scardamalia, M., & Bereiter, C. (1987). Knowledge telling and knowledge transforming in written composition. In S. Rosenberg (Ed.), *Advances in applied psycholinguistics: Vol. 2. Reading, writing, and language learning* (pp. 142–175). Cambridge, England: Cambridge University Press.

Scardamalia, M., & Bereiter, C. (1992). An architecture for collaborative knowledge-building. In E. De Corte, M. Linn, H. Mandl, & L. Verschaffel (Eds.), *Computer-based learning environments and problem solving* (Vol. 84, pp. 41–66). Berlin: Springer-Verlag.

Scardamalia, M., & Bereiter, C. (1993). Technologies for knowledge-building discourse. *CACM Special Issue: Technology in Education, 36*(5), 37–41.

Scardamalia, M., & Bereiter, C. (1994). Computer support for knowledge-building communities. *Journal of the Learning Sciences, 3,* 265–283.

Scardamalia, M., Bereiter, C., Brett, C., Burtis, P. J., Calhoun, C., & Smith, L. N. (1992). Educational applications of a networked communal database. *Interactive Learning Environments, 2*(1), 45–71.

Scardamalia, M., Bereiter, C., & Lamon, M. (1994). CSILE: Trying to bring students into world 3. In K. McGilley (Eds.), *Classroom lessons: Integrating cognitive theory and classroom practice* (pp. 201–228). Cambridge, MA: MIT Press.

Schank, R. C. (1986). *Explanation patterns: Understanding mechanically and creatively.* Hillsdale, NJ: Lawrence Erlbaum Associates.

Schoenfeld, A. H., & Herrmann, D. J. (1982). Problem perception and knowledge structure in expert and novice mathematical problem solvers. *Journal of Experimental Psychology: Learning, Memory and Cognition, 8,* 484–494.

Shayer, M., & Wylam, H. (1981). The development of the concepts of heat and temperature in 10–13-year-olds. *Journal of Research in Science Teaching, 18*(5), 419–435.

Smith, C., Snir, J., & Grosslight, L. (1992). Using conceptual models to facilitate conceptual change: The case of weight-density differentiation. *Cognition and Instruction, 9,* 221–283.

van Lehn, K. (1990). *Mind bugs: The origins of procedural misconceptions.* Cambridge, MA: MIT Press.

Vosniadou, S., & Brewer, W. F. (1987). Theories of knowledge restructuring in development. *Review of Educational Research, 57,* 51–67.

9 Distributing Cognition Over Humans and Machines

Pierre Dillenbourg[1]
University of Geneva, Switzerland

THE SOCIOCULTURAL APPROACH

The sociocultural approach to human cognition has recently gained influence in the field of educational technology. This emergence can be explained by the renewed interest in America for Vygotsky's theories since the translation of his book (Vygotsky, 1978) and by the attacks against the individualistic view of cognition that dominated cognitive science (Lave, 1988). Moreover, the actual use of computers in classrooms leads scientists to pay more attention to social factors: teachers often have to put two or more students in front of each computer because schools generally have more students than computers! This situation was originally viewed as a restriction to the potential of computer-assisted instruction, since it was contradictory to the principle of individualization. Today, it is perceived as a promising way of using computers (Blaye, Light, Joiner, & Sheldon, 1991).

The sociocultural approach postulates that, when an individual participates in a social system, the culture of this social system and the tools used for communication, especially the language, shape the individual's cognition, and constitute a source of learning and development. The social influence on individual cognition can be analyzed at various levels: participation in a dyadic interaction (hereafter inter-psychological plane), participation in a 'community of practice' (e.g. colleagues) (Lave, 1991), and participation in increasingly larger social circles until the whole society and its inherited culture is included (Wertsch, 1991). In the

---

[1]Address for correspondance: TECFA, PFSE, Université de Genève, Route de Drize, 9, 1227 Carouge. Switzerland. E-mail: pdillen@divsun.unige.ch

dyadic interaction, one also discriminates between studies of collaboration between peers (i.e., subjects with even skills) and studies of apprenticeship (where one partner is much more skilled than the other). Within the socio-cultural perspective, one can examine interactive learning environments from different angles:

The User–User Interaction as a Social Process, Mediated by the System

When two human users (two learners or a learner and a coach) interact through the network or in front of the same terminal, the system influences their interaction. How should we design systems that facilitate human interaction and improve learning? Which system features could, for instance, help the co-learners to solve their conflicts? This viewpoint has been adopted in 'computer-supported collaborative learning'. It is receiving a great deal of attention because of the increasing market demand for 'groupware' (Norman, 1991).

The User–Designer Relation as a Social Process Mediated by the System

When a user interacts with a system (e.g., a spreadsheet), his reasoning is influenced by the tools available in this system. These tools embody the designer's culture. How should we design tools in such a way that users progressively 'think in terms of these tools' (Salomon, 1988) and thereby internalize the designers' culture? This viewpoint relates to the concept of *semiotic mediation* proposed by Wertsch (1991) to extend Vygotsky's framework beyond the inter-psychological plane.

The User–System Interaction as a Social Process

When the learner interacts with a computerized agent performing (from the designer's viewpoint) a social role (a tutor, a coach, a co-learner, . . .), does this interaction have a potential for internalization similar to human-human conversations (Forrester, 1991; Salomon, 1990)? If the answer is yes, how should we design these agents to support learning?

This chapter concentrates on the third viewpoint: the design of computerized agents which are engaged with the learner in a 'pseudo-social' relationship. One could object that the discrimination between the second and third view, i.e. the extent to which a program is considered as a tool (second view) or as an agent (third view) is purely metaphorical. Of course, it is. The *tool* and *agent* labels are images. Agents are supposed to take initiatives while tools are only reactive, but initiatives can be interpreted as sophisticated responses to previous learner behaviours. Actually, it is the user who determines whether he feels involved or not in a social relation with the machine: " . . . the personification of a machine is reinforced by the way in which its inner workings are a mystery, and its behaviour at times surprises us" (Suchman, 1987, p. 16). This issue is even more complex since many Intelligent Learning Environments (ILEs) include both tools and agents. For instance, PEOPLE POWER (Dillenbourg, 1992a) includes both a microworld and a computerized co-learner. However, the first experiments with this ILE seem to indicate that learners are able to discriminate when the machine plays one role or the other.

The main impact of the socio-cultural approach on ILEs is the concept of an *apprenticeship system*. The AI literature refers to two kinds of apprenticeship systems: expert systems which apply machine learning techniques to integrate the user's solutions (Mitchell, Mabadevan, & Stienberg, 1990) and learning environments in which it is the human user who is supposed to learn (Newman, 1989). We refer here to the latter. For Collins, Brown and Newman (1989), apprenticeship is the most widespread educational method outside school: in schools, skills are abstracted from their uses in the world, while in apprenticeship, skills are practised for the joint accomplishment of tasks, in their natural context. They use the concept of *cognitive apprenticeship* to emphasize two differences from traditional apprenticeship: (a) the goal of cognitive apprenticeship is to transmit cognitive and metacognitive skills (while apprenticeship has traditionally been more concerned with concrete objects and behaviors), and (b) the goal of cognitive apprenticeship is that the learners progressively 'decontextualize' knowledge and hence become able to transfer it to other contexts.

THE METAPHOR: SOCIALLY DISTRIBUTED COGNITION

This chapter is concerned with the relation between the socio-cultural approach and learning environments. We review several concepts belonging to the socio-cultural vocabulary and translate them in terms of the features found in learning environments. These concepts are considered one by one for the sake of exposition but they actually form a whole. To help the reader to unify the various connections we establish, we propose the following metaphor (hereafter referred to as the SDC metaphor): View a human-computer pair (or any other pair) involved in shared problem solving as a single cognitive system

Since the boom in object-oriented languages, many designers think of the ILE as a multi-agent system. Similarly, some researchers think of a human subject as a society of agents (Minsky, 1987). The proposed metaphor unifies these two views and goes one step further. It suggests that two separate societies (the human and the machine), when they interact towards the joint accomplishment of some task, constitute a society of agents.

Two notions are implicit in this metaphor. First, a cognitive system is defined with respect to a particular task: it is an abstract entity that encloses the cognitive processes to be activated for solving this particular task. The same task may be solved by several cognitive systems, but the composition of a cognitive system is independent of the number of people who solve the task. The second implicit notion is that agents (or processes) can be considered independently from their implementation (i.e. their location in a human or a machine): a process that is performed by a subject at the beginning of a session can be performed later on by his partner. Studies of collaborative problem solving have shown that peers spontaneously distribute roles and that this role distribution changes frequently (Miyake, 1986; O'Malley, 1987; Blaye et al., 1991). We use the term *device* to refer indifferently to the person or the system that performs some process.

The following sections attempt to clarify how this model relates to the socio-cultural framework at one end, and at the other end, what it means in terms of implementation.

LEARNING ENVIRONMENTS

In the remainder of this chapter, we will refer frequently to three systems we have designed: PEOPLE POWER (Dillenbourg, 1992a; Dillenbourg and Self, 1992), MEMOLAB (Mendelsohn, this volume) and ETOILE (Dillenbourg, Hilario, Mendelsohn, Schneider and Borcic, 1993). We briefly describe these systems now in order to make later references shorter. Some features of these systems make sense within the socio-cultural perspective, even though these systems were not designed specifically to address socio-cultural issues.

PEOPLE POWER

PEOPLE POWER is a learning environment in which the human learner interacts with an artificial learning companion, hereafter referred to as the 'co-learner'. Its pedagogical goal is that the human learner discovers the mechanisms by which an electoral system is more or less proportional. The system includes four components (see Fig. 9.1): (1) a microworld in which the learner can design an electoral experiment (i.e. choose parties, candidates, laws, etc.), run the elections and analyze the results; (2) an interface by which the human learner (and conceptually the co-learner) plays with the microworld; (3) the co-learner, named Jerry Mander, and (4) an interface that allows the human and the computerized learners to communicate with each other.

The learners play a game in which the goal is to gain seats for one's own party. Both learners play for the same party. They engage in a dialogue to agree on a geographical organization of wards into constituencies. The co-learner has some naive knowledge to reason about elections. This knowledge is a set of rules (or arguments). For instance, a rule says "If a party gets more votes, then it will get

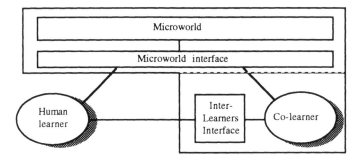

FIG. 9.1. Components of human–computer collaborative learning system.

more seats". This rule is naive but not basically wrong, it is only true in some circumstances. The co-learner learns how to apply this rule when it reasons about the way to gain seats for its party.

We tested PEOPLE POWER under two paradigms: with two artificial learners and with a human learner and an artificial learner (Dillenbourg & Self, 1992). The human/artificial experiments were informal and restricted to five subjects. Learners appreciated the possibility of interacting with the co-learner. Some expressed the feeling of actually collaborating with a partner, though this partner did not exhibit completely human behavior. We later report some observations that are related to the SDC metaphor.

MEMOLAB/ETOILE

The goal of MEMOLAB is for psychology students to acquire the basic skills in the methodology of experimentation. The learner builds an experiment on human memory. A typical experiment involves two groups of subjects each encoding a list of words. The two lists are different and these differences have an impact on the recall performance. An experiment is described by assembling events on a workbench. Then, the system simulates the experiment (by applying case-based reasoning techniques on data found in the literature). The learner can visualize the simulation results and perform an analysis of variance.

This artificial lab constitutes an instance of a microworld. Most learners need some external guidance to benefit from such a microworld. We added computational agents (coach, tutors and experts) to provide this guidance. But we also explored another way of helping the learner: by structuring the world. MEM-OLAB is actually a sequence of microworlds. The relationship between the objects and operators of two successive microworlds parallels the relationship between developmental stages in the neo-piagetian theory of Case (Mendelsohn, this volume). At the computational level, the relationship between successive worlds is encompassed in the interface: the language used in a microworld to describe the learner's work is used as the command language for the next micro-world. This relationship, referred to as a *language shift*, is discussed on p. 176.

A goal of this research project was to generalize the solutions developed for MEMOLAB and to come out with a toolbox for creating ILEs. We achieved domain independence by defining teaching styles as a set of rules which activate and monitor the interaction between an expert and the learner. The technical solutions chosen for obtaining a fine-grained interaction between the expert and the learner are described on pages 172 to 174. This toolbox is called ETOILE (Experimental Toolbox for Interactive Learning Environments).

FROM CONCEPTS TO SYSTEMS

In this section, we review several key concepts from the socio-cultural approach and attempt to translate them in terms of ILE design. We therefore use the proposed metaphor: view two interactive problem solvers as a single society of agents.

Zone of Proximal Development, Scaffolding and Fading

We start our review of socio-cultural concepts with Vygotsky's (1978) concept of *zone of proximal development* (ZPD). The ZPD is the difference between the child's capacity to solve a problem alone and his ability to solve it under adult guidance or in collaboration with a more capable peer. Although it was originally proposed for the assessment of intelligence, it nowadays inspires a great deal of instructional organisation (Wertsch, 1991). *Scaffolding* is the process of providing the learner with the help and guidance necessary to solve problems that are just beyond what he could manage independently (i.e. within his ZPD). The level of support should progressively decrease (fading) until the learner is able to solve the problem alone.

The process of scaffolding has been studied by Rogoff (1990, 1991) through various experiments in which children solved a spatial planning task with adults. She measured the performance of children in a post-test performed without adult help. She established a relationship between the type of adult-child interactions and the post-test results. Children scored better in the post-test in the cases where the problem solving strategy was made explicit by the adult. These results are slightly biased by the fact that the proposed task (planning) is typically a task in which metaknowledge plays the central role. Nevertheless, on the same task, Rogoff observed that children who worked with an adult performed better than those who worked with a more skilled peer. Similarly, she found that efficient adults involved the child in an explicit decision process, while skilled peers tended to dominate decision making.

In terms of the SDC metaphor, scaffolding can be translated as activating agents that the learner does not or cannot activate. Fading is interpreted as a quantitative variation of the distribution of resources: the number of agents activated by the machine decreases and the number of agents activated by the learner increases. In ETOILE for instance, a teaching style determines the quantitative distribution of steps among the expert and the learner (and its evolution over time). However, Rogoff's experiments show it is not relevant to count the number of agents activated by each partner, unless we take into consideration the hierarchical links between agents. Some agents are more important than others because they play a strategic role: when solving equations, the agent 'isolate X' will trigger several subordinated agents such as 'divide Y by X'. This implies that the agents society must be structured in several control layers. The issue of making control explicit has been a key issue for several years in the field of ILEs (Clancey, 1987). In other words, fading and scaffolding describe a variation in learner control, but this variation does not concern a quantitative ratio of agents activated by each participant. It refers to the qualitative relationship between the agents activated on each side.

Tuning the machine contribution to the joint accomplishment of a task may affect the learner's interest in collaboration. What one can expect from a partner partially determines one's motivation to collaborate with him. The experiments conducted with PEOPLE POWER showed interesting phenomena of this kind. Initially, the subjects who collaborated with the machine did not always accept that the computer was ignorant. Two subjects even interrupted their session to tell us that the program was buggy. They were surprised to see a computer suggesting something silly (though we announced that this would be the case). Later on, subjects appeared to lose their motivation to collaborate if the co-learner was not improving its suggestions quickly enough. Our machine-machine experiments showed that the co-learner performance depended on the amount of interactions among learners. In PEOPLE POWER, the cost of interaction with the co-learner was very high. The subjects reduced the number of interactions and hence the co-learner learned slowly. All dialogue patterns elaborated by the co-learner during these one-hour sessions were much more rudimentary that the patterns built with another artificial learner (where there was no communication bottle-neck). These patterns depend on the quantity and variety of interactions. They determine the level of elaboration of Jerry's arguments and hence the correctness of its suggestions. Jerry continued to provide the learners with suggestions that were not very good, and decreased the subjects' interest in its suggestions. In terms of the SDC model, these observations imply that the agents implemented on the computer should guarantee some minimal level of competence for the whole distributed system, at any stage of scaffolding/fading. This *minimal* level is the level below which the learner loses his interest in interacting with the machine.

PARTICIPATION AND APPROPRIATION

A core idea in the sociocultural approach is the notion of *participation:* "the skills a student will acquire in an instructional interaction are those required by the student's role in the joint cognitive process." (Bereiter & Scardamalia, 1989, p. 383). The challenge is to understand why participation in joint problem solving may sometimes change the understanding of a problem. Rogoff (1991) explains it by a process of appropriation. *Appropriation* is the socially oriented version of Piaget's biologically-originated concept of assimilation (Newman, Griffin & Cole, 1989). Appropriation is mutual: each partner gives meaning to the other's actions according to his own conceptual framework. Appropriation constitutes a form of feed-back: if two persons, A and B, interact, when A performs the first action and B the next one, B's action indicates to A how his first action is interpreted by B. In other words, B's action is information on how A's action makes sense within B's conceptualization of the problem. Fox (1987) reported that humans modify the meaning of their action retrospectively, according to the actions of others that follow it. This form of feed-back requires that problem solvers are opportunistic, i.e. able to escape from an established plan in order to integrate their partner's contribution into their own solution path.

The difference between this kind of feed-back and the behaviourist kind of feed-back is that the partner may have no didactic intention. In MEMOLAB, the expert's actions are purely egocentric, the expert wants to solve the task. These actions may constitute some kind of feed-back for the learner, but the expert does not teach. This different conception of feed-back gives more importance to collaboration than to diagnosis (Newman, 1989). We can illustrate the difference between diagnosis-based feedback and collaboration-oriented feed-back by the difference between a *mal-rule* and a repair rule. A mal-rule is something like 'if the problem state has these features, then do something wrong' or, more concretely, 'If you want to go from Paris to Brussels, fly West'. A mal-rule sets a hypothesis concerning the cognitive cause of an error. This concept has been frequently used in student modelling. In MEMOLAB, we used the concept of a repair rule to support certain types of expert-learner interactions. The format of a repair rule is" If the problem state is wrong then correct it this way, or more concretely 'If you fly from Paris to Brussels and see London, then turn to the East.' As any ordinary rule, a repair rule generates some expert's action. Note that we use this term independently from Brown's and Van Lehn's use of it (Brown & Van Lehn, 1980).

The specificity of an interactive expert system is that interaction may lead the expert outside its normal solution path. A genuine expert rule-base generates an optimal solution path. If this expert collaborates with a human learner, it may encounter problem states that do not belong to this optimal path, but which are still correct. The expert therefore has sub-optimal rules that are considered after the optimal rules have been evaluated (rules have a priority parameter). Repair rules are concerned with a third situation, when the interaction leads the expert to an incorrect problem state that would belong neither to the optimal nor to the sub-optimal solution path.

One must be careful with regard to the benefits expected from interactions which look collaborative but where partners execute processes independently from each other. "The presence of a partner may be irrelevant, unless the partners truly share their thinking processes in problem solving." (Rogoff, 1991, p. 361). The SDC metaphor provides us with a framework within which we implemented a 'shared thinking process', that is, we distributed sub-processes over partners. Sharing processes implies a high level of *granularity and opportunism*. Granularity refers to the size of agents. The limit for granularity is defined by a pedagogical criterion: learners must be able to talk about what an agent does. Opportunism means that each agent integrates in his reasoning any new element brought by its partner.

How to obtain a high level of granularity and opportunism? Technical solutions are emerging in 'distributed artificial intelligence' (Durfee, Lesser, & Corkill, 1989) for collaboration between computational agents. Regarding collaboration between a human and a machine, we learned from our observations made with subjects using PEOPLE POWER. As we designed it, the object of discussion was the set of arguments that constituted Jerry's naive knowledge. Actually, we observed that the main activity of learners was to look at the table showing the data for each party in each ward. Reasoning about the effect of moving a ward was more than simply manipulating arguments or rules, it was mentally moving a column of a table and re-computing the sums to check whether this new ordering led to the gain of a seat. The interaction with the co-learner would have been more relevant if it had been about moving columns. The interface should, for instance, provide facilities to move columns and recompute sums by constituencies. Hence, in MEMOLAB, we have chosen a solution based on what can be the most easily shared between a person and a machine: the interface. Let us imagine two production systems that use a common set of facts. They share the same representation of the problem. Any fact produced by one of them is added to this common set of facts. Hence, at the next cycle of the inference engine, this new fact may trigger a rule in either of the two rule-bases. Now, let us replace one computerized expert by a human learner. The principle may still apply provided we use an external problem representation instead of the internal one. The common set of facts is the problem representation as displayed on the interface (see Fig. 9.2).

All the conditions of the machine's rules refer only to objects displayed on the screen.[2] The actions performed by the rules modify the problem representation. In short, the shared representation is visible by both partners and can be modified

---

[2]Technically, we use an object-oriented inference engine. Any rule variable is defined with respect to a class. This variable can only be instantiated by the instances of its attached class. Objects of class X that are displayed on the screen are actually defined as instances of a subclass of X, the class Displayed-X.

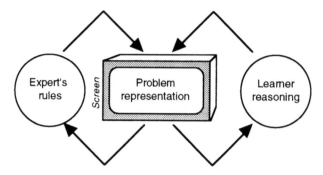

FIG. 9.2.   Opportunism in human–machine collaboration in MEMOLAB.

by both partners. We do not claim that they share the same 'internal' representation. Sharing an external representation does not imply at all that both partners build the same internal representation. The shared concrete representation simply facilitates the discussion of the differences between the internal representations and hence improves the co-ordination of actions.

INTERNALIZATION

The mechanism underlying the appropriation process is the process of *internalization,* a central concept in Vygotsky's framework: "Every function in the child's development appears twice: first, on the social level, and later on the individual level; first, between people (inter-psychological) and then inside the child (intra-psychological)" (Vygotsky, 1978). Internalization refers to the genetic link between the social (or inter-psychological) and the inner (or intra-psychological) planes. Social speech is used for interacting with humans, inner speech is used to talk to ourselves, to reflect, to think. Inner speech has a function of self-regulation.

The SDC model is based on the relationship between social speech and inner speech: if an individual and a group are both modelled as a society of agents, inner speech and social speech are two instances of communication among agents. Inner speech is communication among agents implemented on the same device (intra-device communication), social speech occurs between agents belonging to different devices (inter-device communication). These levels of speech are two instances of the class 'communication among agents'. There is however a difference: communication between agents from different devices is external, it is observable. Patterns of inter-device communication can hence be induced and applied to intra-device communication. These ideas can be summarized as follow:

1. An individual is a society of agents that communicate. A pair is also a society, variably partitioned into devices.

2. The device border determines two levels of communication: agent-agent communication and device-device communication. Inter-agent and inter-device communications are isomorphic.

3. Inter-device communication is observable by each device. Therefore, inter-device communication patterns generate intra-device communication patterns.

The three postulates of the SDC model have been implemented for designing Jerry Mander, the computerized co-learner in PEOPLE POWER. Jerry talks with the human learner (or another artificial learner) about the relation between the features of an electoral system and the results of elections. During this dialogue, Jerry stores relations between arguments. A network of arguments constitutes what we called a *communication pattern*. Let us assume Jerry claims that Ward-5 should be moved from Southshire to Northshire, because this would increase the score of his party in Northshire. His partner may raise the objection that the party would lose votes in Southshire. Jerry will then create a refutation link between the first argument and its counter-argument. Similarly, dialogue patterns include continue-links between arguments that have been verbalized consecutively in a successful argumentation. Jerry Mander reuses these dialogue patterns when it reasons alone. For instance, when it considers another move, Jerry Mander retrieves the counter-argument connected by a refutation-link and checks whether this counter-argument is valid in the new context. If it is, it refutes itself.[3] Using a refutation-link between arguments (stored as rules) corresponds to a mechanism of specialization (adding a condition), while the use of continue-links corresponds to a form of chunking.

To implement the isomorphism between inner speech and social speech (second axiom of the SDC model), we used the following trick: Jerry Mander uses the same procedure for talking with his partner and talking with itself. It uses a single procedure 'dialogue' which accepts two entries, a 'proposer' and a 'refuter'. The procedure call 'dialogue learner-X learner-Y' gives a real dialogue while the call 'dialogue learner-X learner-X' corresponds to individual reasoning (monologue). The implementation is actually a bit more complex. Each link is associated with a description of the context in which the connected arguments have been verbalized and has a numeric weight. This numeric weight evolves according to the partner's agreement ('social sensitivity') and to the electoral results ('environmental sensitivity'). A complete description of the learning mechanisms and their performance can be found in Dillenbourg and Self (1992).

Private Speech and Reification

Between inner speech and social speech, psychologists discriminate an intermediate level termed *egocentric speech* by Piaget and *private speech* by

---

[3]It backtracks in the process of proving that its proposition will lead to a seat gain.

Vygotsky. These concepts are not completely synonymous (Zivin, 1979). The most familiar examples of private or egocentric speech are the conversations conducted aloud by children who play alone. We might also refer to the verbal productions of people using computers on their own. Egocentric or private speech still has a rather social form (it is verbalized, it has some syntax, . . .), but it has lost its social function (it is produced in the absence of any other person). For Piaget, it corresponds to some kind of uncontrolled production, while for Vygotsky, it has a self-regulating function (Zivin, 1979). The interest in this intermediate level is that psychologists may extrapolate differences between social and private speech to speculate on the features of inner speech.

There is an interesting similarity between private speech and the idea of *reification*, a technique used in ILEs to support reflection. Reflection, i.e. the process of becoming aware of one's own knowledge and reasoning, is receiving growing attention from ILE designers (Collins & Brown, 1988). Systems that attempt to promote reflection often present some trace of the learner's activities and of the environment's responses. Systems such as ALGEBRALAND (Collins & Brown, 1988) or the GEOMETRY TUTOR (Anderson, Boyle, & Yost, 1985) facilitate the learner's reflection by displaying the learner's solution path as a tree structure. This representation shows that solving an equation or proving a theorem are not straightforward processes, but require numerous attempts and frequent backtracking. Such a representation reifies, makes concrete, some abstract features of the learner's cognition. It is not neutral, but results from an interpretation by the machine of the learner's action. Through this interpretation, the learner can understand how his action makes sense within the system conception of the domain (see page 172 on appropriation).

This graphical representation of behaviour has the ambiguous status of private speech. In systems such as ALGEBRALAND, TAPS (Derry, 1990) or HERON (Reusser, Kampfer, Sprenger, Staub, Stebler and Stussi, 1990), this graphical representation serves both as a way of communicating with the system and as a tool for self-regulation. One can argue whether Vygotsky's theories on (verbal) speech are compatible with graphical languages used in modern interfaces. For Salomon (1988), "all tools that we consider as prototypical and as intuitively appealing candidates for internalization have also a distinctive spatial form."

Language Shift

Wertsch (1985) reports an interesting study which investigates the role of languages in internalization. This study zooms in the inter-psychological plane, observing mothers helping their children (2 1/2 and 3 1/2 years old) to construct a puzzle in accordance with a model (the same puzzle already built). Wertsch contrasted the language used by mothers to refer to puzzle pieces according to the child's age: mothers of younger children designate directly the piece by pointing to it or by its color (e.g. "a green piece"), while mothers of older children refer to pieces with respect to the problem-solving strategy (e.g. "one colour that's not the same"). For Wertsch, the cognitive processes required to participate in a strategy-oriented dialogue are virtually equivalent to the cognitive processes necessary to apply this strategy without the mother. This study confirms Rogoff's view that participation changes understanding. It weakens the dichotomous distinction between the social and internal planes, since changes inside the social plane may be more important than the social-internal transition.

We suggested that a mechanism of shifting between two language levels, as observed by Wertsch, could be applied to the design of ILEs (Dillenbourg, 1992b). Let us decompose the difference between a novice and an expert into several levels of skills. When learners solve problems at level X, they interact with the system through some command language CLx. The system, as the mothers in Wertsch's observations, has a second language available, called the description language (DL). The description language reifies the implicit problem solving strategy by displaying a trace of the learner's activities. The system uses this description language in feed-back in order to associate the two descriptions of the same solution, one expressed in the command language and the second in the description language. The language shift occurs when the system moves up in the hierarchy of expertise levels. After a move to the next level (X+1), learners receive a new command language which includes the concepts that were introduced by the description language at level X. This language shift can be expressed by the equation $CL_{x+1} = DL_x$. After the language shift, learners are compelled to use explicitly the operators or strategies that where previously implicit (but reified in the description language). We illustrate this principle with two instances:

Let us imagine a courseware for learning to solve equations. At the first level, the learner would manually perform algebraic manipulations (CL_1). Sequences of transformations would be redisplayed as higher order operators, such as 'move X to LHS' (DL_1). After the language shift, the learner would transform equations by applying directly these operators ($CL_2 = DL_1$).

This principle has been applied to the definition of the microworlds in MEMOLAB (Mendelsohn, this volume). MEMOLAB includes three successive microworlds or levels, with increasingly powerful command languages (and increasingly complex problems to solve). At level 1, a psychological experiment is built by assembling chronological sequences of concrete events. At level 2, the learner does not describe each concrete event anymore but builds the treatment to be applied to each group of subjects. At level 3, the learner directly defines the experimental plan, i.e. the logical structure of the experiment. At levels 1 and 2, when an experiment design has been completed, the experiment is 'redisplayed' with the formalism used at the next level.

Social Grounding

In PEOPLE POWER, the internalization mechanism has been implemented as the simple storage of dialogue patterns. It is clear however that internalization is not a simple recording process, but a transformation process. There exist interesting similarities between the transformations which occur during internalization and those which occur during social grounding, although these processes been studied independently from each other. Social grounding is the mechanism by which two participants in a discussion try to elaborate the mutual belief that their partner has understood what they meant to a criterion sufficient for the current purpose (Clark & Brennan, 1991).

For Vygotsky, inner speech has a functional similarity with social speech but loses its structural similarity. For Luria (1969), "inner speech necessarily ceases to be detailed and grammatical" (p. 143). The difference between social and inner speech is due to the fact that "inner speech is just the ultimate point in the continuum of communicative conditions judged by the degree of 'intimacy' between the addresser and addressee" (Kozulin, 1990, p. 178). The main transformation observed as a result of the intimacy between the addresser and addressee is a process of abbreviation (Kozulin, 1990; Wertsch, 1979, 1991). Interestingly, Krauss and Fussell (1991) found the same abbreviation phenomena in social grounding. They report several experiments in which subjects have to establish expressions to refer to 'nonsense figures' and to use these references later on, in various conditions. Subjects first refer to a particular picture by saying

"Looks like a Martini glass with legs on each side."
"Martini glass with the legs"
"Martinin glass-shaped things"
"Martini glass"
"Martini"

Krauss and Fussell show that the decrease in expression length is a function of the feed-back given by the listener. Another interesting experiment compares expressions built by the subjects for themselves or for peers. They observe that personal messages were less than half as long as social messages. Why does abbreviation occur both during internalization and during social grounding? The explanation may be that internalization and social grounding are two phenomena during which the addresser acquires information about the addressee's understanding of his messages.

The work on grounding is very important for designers of ILEs, it is even at the heart of recent debates in artificial intelligence. The symbol grounding crisis (Harnad, 1990) launched intensive research to design situated robots (Maes, 1990), that is, robots which can physically ground their symbols in the environment, through actors and sensors. Less attention has been paid to the possibility of social grounding, i.e. grounding the system symbols in the user's experience. Any communication is ambiguous, it works because humans constantly detect and repair communication breakdowns, but computers have far fewer resources than humans for detecting and repairing communication failures (Suchman, 1987). Previous sections placed great expectations on the cognitive benefits of using graphical languages, but how do we guarantee that learners correctly interpret these symbols? Wenger (1987) defined the *epistemic fidelity* of a representation as the degree of consistency between the physical representation of some phenomena and the expert's mental representation of this phenomena. Roschelle (1990) attempted to apply this principle to the design of the Envisioning Machine (EM), a direct-manipulation graphical simulation of the concepts of *velocity* and *acceleration*. He successively designed several representations for the same set of physical phenomena (particle movements). The first EM design focused on epistemic fidelity. However, because mapping physical and mental representations is an inherently ambiguous interpretation process, the users did not read representations as experts did. Representations do not hold some trivial meaning but, inversely, can be used to support social grounding. Roschelle (1992) observed that learners use the computer to test under increasingly tighter constraints the degree to which their interpretation of physical phenomena were shared. Roschelle refers to this property of representations as *symbolic mediation.*

Two implications can be derived. The first has been quoted before: collaboration should be concerned with what is happening on the screen (not some hidden knowledge), since the screen is the main reference to establish shared meanings. The second implication is that dialogue should be more about understanding than about agreement. In PEOPLE POWER, our dialogue patterns were rudimentary, including only agreement or disagreement. This indicates a Piagetian bias. Doise and Mugny (1984) have extended the notion of conflict between a subject's beliefs and the world events to include conflict between opposite beliefs held by different subjects. This socio-cognitive conflict is more likely to be perceived and solved because of the social pressure to maintain partnership. However, Blaye (1988) found very little evidence of real conflict in pairs. The concept of conflict is not operationally defined. Where is the frontier between a divergence of focus (Miyake, 1986), some disagreement (Blaye, 1988) and an open conflict? There is no clear answer to that question. Actually, disagreement in itself seems to be less important than the fact that it generates communication between peer members (Blaye, 1988; Gilly, 1989). Bearison et al. (1986, quoted by Blaye, 1988) reported that non-verbal disagreement (manifested for instance by moving the object positioned by the partner) was not predictive of post-test score increase. Blaye (1988) suggests that "oppositions give rise to verbalizations that regulate the partner's activities and may possibly contribute to the internalization, by the producer, of an adequate regulation mode."[4] (p. 398). The notion of conflict results from a bipolarisation of the continuum which goes from a total

---

[4]My translation.

absence of understanding to fully shared understanding. Collaboration among agents should not be simplified to agreement or disagreement. It should be considered a complex social grounding process. Of course, artificial intelligence handles dialogue moves such as "continue" or "refute" more easily than it encodes meanings. Intermediate solutions could be to extend richer sets of dialogue moves able to generate sub-dialogues aiming to elaborate, disambiguate or repair communication (Baker, 1992). The person-machine interface must have some 'noise tolerance', some space where the meaning of concepts can be negotiated.

Some recent experiments with MEMOLAB (Dillenbourg et al., 1993) revealed mechanisms of human-machine grounding: the learner perceives how the machine understands him (i.e. he makes a diagnosis of the machine diagnosis) and reacts in order to correct eventual misdiagnosis. However, in the current implementation of MEMOLAB, rule variables unambiguously refer to screen objects. To support social grounding, the instantiation of rule variables by displayed objects should not be a completely internal process, but the result of some interaction with the learner.

SYNTHESIS

Let us integrate these various connections between theories and systems within the SDC model. The learner and the system form a single cognitive system. This system is a society of agents, characterized by high granularity (agents have narrow skills). All agents are implemented on the machine and on the learner. Implementing a computerized agent-X 'on the learner' means designing an interface function by which the learner may perform the same operation as agent-X. The total number of activated agents remains constant, in such a way that, from the beginning, the learner and the computer jointly achieve meaningful and motivating tasks. The machine agents are activated to complement the agents activated by the learner (scaffolding). An agent activated by the learner is deactivated by the machine (fading). Some agents encompass and make explicit the problem solving strategy.

The agents interact about what is on the screen. The behaviour of the computerized agents is determined by what is on the screen. The interface is the permanent updated representation of the problem which serves as the basis for activating computerized agents. Agents use the interface as a reference to establish mutual understanding (social grounding). The communication among agents is not didactic in itself, it serves the accomplishment of the task, but it may indirectly fulfil a didactic function (appropriation).

The forms of communication among agents are inspired by the reasoning processes the learner should acquire: the system-learner interactions are the source of the learner's future self-regulation mechanisms. To support this internalization, reified graphics serve both for reflection and communication with machine agents.

More generally, we argue that metaphors are useful for designers. Designers often complain about the lack of formal models of learning and teaching (with a few notable exceptions), which would generate clear design specifications. We do not believe that the design of a learning environment will ever be a deductive process. Design is a creative process during which one attempts to make sense of learning activities or system features within a theoretical framework.

ACKNOWLEDGEMENTS

Thanks to P. Brna, S. Bull, M. Gattis and to the editors for their comments of this chapter.

REFERENCES

Anderson, J. R., Boyle, C. F., & Yost, G. (1985). The Geometry Tutor. Proceedings of the Ninth International Joint Conference on Artificial Intelligence (Vol. I, 1–7). Los Angeles. August 18–23.

Baker, M. (1992). *The collaborative construction of explanations.* Paper presented to "Deuxièmes Journées Explication du PRC-GDR-IA du CNRS", Sophia-Antipolis, June 17–19 1992.

Bereiter, C., & Scardamalia, M. (1989). Intentional learning as a goal of instruction. In L.B. Resnick (Ed.), *Cognition and Instruction: Issues and Agendas* (361–392). Hillsdale, N.J.: Lawrence Erlbaum Associates.

Blaye, A. (1988). *Confrontation socio-cognitive et resolution de problèmes.* Doctoral dissertation, Centre de Recherche en Psychologie Cognitive, Université de Provence, 13261 Aix-en-Provence, France.

Blaye, A., Light, P., Joiner, R., & Sheldon, S. (1991). Collaboration as a facilitator of planning and problem solving on a computer based task. *British Journal of Psychology*, 9, 471–483.

Brown, J. S., & Van Lehn, K. (1980). Repair theory: a generative theory of "bugs" in procedural skills. *Cognitive Science*, 4, 379–426.

Case, R. (1985). *Intellectual Developpement: from Birth to Adulthood.* New York: Academic Press.

Clancey, W. J. (1987). *Knowledge-based tutoring: the Guidon Program.* Cambridge, Massachusetts: MIT Press.

Clark, H. H., & Brennan S. E. (1991). Grounding in Communication. In L. Resnick, J. Levine & S. Teasley (Eds.), *Perspectives on Socially Shared Cognition* (127–149). Hyattsville, MD: American Psychological Association.

Collins, A., & Brown, J. S. (1988). The Computer as a Tool for Learning through Reflection. In H. Mandl & A. Lesgold (Eds), *Learning Issues for Intelligent Tutoring Systems* (1–18). New York: Springer Verlag.

Collins, A., Brown J. S., & Newman, S. (1989). Cognitive apprenticeship: teaching the craft of reading, writing and mathematics. In L.B. Resnick (Ed.), *Cognition and Instruction: Issues and Agendas* (453–494). Hillsdale, N.J.: Lawrence Erlbaum Associates.

Derry, S. J. (1990). *Flexible Cognitive Tools for Problem Solving Instruction.* Paper presented at the AERA symposium, Computers as Cognitive Tools, April. Boston, MA.

Dillenbourg, P. (1992a). *Human-Computer Collaborative Learning*. Doctoral dissertation. Department of Computing. University of Lancaster, Lancaster LA14YR, UK.

Dillenbourg, P. (1992b). The Language Shift: a mechanism for triggering metacognitive activities. In P. Winne & M.Jones. *Adaptive Learning Environments.: foundations and frontiers.* Springer-Verlag. Hamburg

Dillenbourg, P., Hilario, M., Mendelsohn, P., Schneider, D., & Borcic, B. (1993). The Memolab Project. Research Report. TECFA Document. TECFA, University of Geneva.

Dillenbourg, P., & Self, J. A. (1992). A computational approach to socially distributed cognition. *European Journal of Psychology of Education.*, 3 (4), 353-372.

Doise, W., & Mugny, G. (1984). *The social development of the intellect.* Oxford: Pergamon Press.

Durfee, E. H., Lesser, V. R., & Corkill, D. D. (1989). Cooperative Distributed Problem Solving. In A. Barr, P.R. Cohen & E.A. Feigenbaum (Eds.),*The Handbook of Artificial Intelligence*, (Vol. IV, 83-127). Reading, Massachusetts: Addison-Wesley.

Forrester, M. A. (1991). A conceptual framework for investigating learning in conversations. *Computers in Education*, 17 (1), 61-72.

Fox, B. (1987). Interactional reconstruction in real-time language processing. *Cognitive Science*, 11 (3), 365-387.

Gilly, M. (1989). The psychosocial mechanisms of cognitive constructions, experimental research and teaching perspectives. *International Journal of Educational Research*, 13, 6, 607-621.

Kozulin, A. (1990). *Vygotsky's psychology.* A biography of ideas. Harvester, Hertfordshire.

Krauss, R. M., & Fussell, S. R. (1991). Constructing shared communicative environments. In L. Resnick, J. Levine & S. Teasley (Eds.), *Perspectives on Socially Shared Cognition* (172-202). Hyattsville, MD: American Psychological Association.

Lave J. (1988). Cognition in Practice. Cambridge: Cambridge University Press

Lave J. (1991). Situating learning in communities of practice. In L. Resnick, J. Levine & S. Teasley (Eds.), *Perspectives on Socially Shared Cognition* (63-84). Hyattsville, MD: American Psychological Association.

Luria, A. R. (1969). Speech development and the formation of social processes. In M. Cole & I. Maltzman (Eds.), *A handbook of contemporary Soviet psychology.* New York: Basic Books.

Maes, P. (1990). Situated agents can have goals. *Robotics and Autonomous Systems*, 6, 49-70.

Minsky, M. (1987). *The society of mind.* London: William Heinemann Ltd.

Mitchell, T. M., Mabadevan, S. M., & Stienberg, L. I. (1990). LEAP: A learning apprentice for VLSI design. In Y. Kodratoff & R.S. Michalski (Eds). *Machine Learning.* (Vol. III, 271-301). Palo Alto, CA: Morgan Kaufmann.

Miyake, N. (1986). Constructive Interaction and the Iterative Process of Understanding. *Cognitive Science*, 10, 151-177.

Newman, D. (1989). Is a student model necessary? Apprenticeship as a model for ITS. *Proceedings of the 4th AI & Education Conference* (177-184), May 24-26. Amsterdam, The Netherlands: IOS.

Newman, D., Griffin P., & Cole, M. (1989). *The construction zone: working for cognitive change in school.* Cambridge University Press: Cambridge.

Norman, D. A. (1991). Collaborative computing: collaboration first, computing second. *Communications of the ACM*, Vol. 34 (12), 88-90.

O'Malley, C. (1987). *Understanding explanation.* Paper presented at the third CeRCLe Workshop, Ullswater, UK.

Piaget, J. (1928). *The language and thought of the child.* New York: Harcourt.

Reusser, K., Kampfer, A., Sprenger, M., Staub, F., Stebler, R., & Stussi, R. (1990). *Tutoring mathematical word problems using solution trees.* Research Report No 8, Abteilung Pädagogishe Psychologie, Universität Bern, Switzerland.

Rogoff, B. (1990). *Apprenticeship in thinking.* New York: Oxford University Press

Rogoff, B. (1991). Social interaction as apprenticeship in thinking: guided participation in spatial planning. In L. Resnick, J. Levine & S. Teasley (Eds.), *Perspectives on Socially Shared Cognition* (349–364). Hyattsville, MD: American Psychological Association.

Roschelle, J. .(1990). *Designing for Conversations.* Paper presented at the AAAI Symposium on Knowledge-Based Environments for Learning and Teaching, March. Stanford, CA.

Roschelle, J. (1992). Learning by Collaborating: Convergent Conceptual Change. *Journal of the Learning Sciences,* 2, 235–276.

Salomon, G. (1988). AI in reverse: computer tools that turn cognitive. *Journal of educational computing research,* 4, 12–140.

Salomon, G. (1990). Cognitive effects with and of computer technology. *Communication research,* 17 (1), 26–44.

Suchman, L. A. (1987). *Plans and Situated Actions.* The problem of human-machine communication. Cambridge: Cambridge University Press.

Vygotsky, L. S. (1978). Mind in Society. *The Development of Higher Psychological Processes.* Edited by M. Cole, V. John-Steiner, S. Scribner & E. Souberman. Cambridge, Massachusetts: Harvard University Press.

Wenger, E. (1987). *Artificial Intelligence and Tutoring Systems: Computational and Cognitive Approaches to the Communication of Knowledge.* Los Altos, CA: Morgan Kaufmann

Wertsch, J. V. (1979). The regulation of human action and the given-new organization of private speech. In G. Zivin (Ed.), *The development of self-regulation through private speech,* 79–98. New York: John Wiley & Sons.

Wertsch, J. V. (1985). Adult-Child Interaction as a Source of Self-Regulation in Children. In S.R. Yussen (Ed.), *The growth of reflection in Children* (69–97). Madison, Wisconsin: Academic Press.

Wertsch, J. V. (1991). A socio-cultural approach to socially shared cognition. In L. Resnick, J. Levine & S. Teasley. *Perspectives on Socially Shared Cognition* (85–100). Hyattsville, MD: American Psychological Association.

Zivin, G. (1979). Removing common confusions about egocentric speech, private speech and self-regulation. In G. Zivin (Ed.), *The development of self-regulation through private speech,* 13–50. New York: John Wiley & Sons

10 Interactivity in Cooperative Problem Solving With Computers

Gellof Kanselaar
Gijsbert Erkens
University of Utrecht

Research within the field of intelligent computer-assisted instruction (CAI) is focused mainly on domain-specific questions of content representation, student modeling, and didactic intervention by the program acting as a tutor. However, tutoring is interactive by nature. Its effect greatly depends on the coordination and fine tuning of communication between tutor and student. This process not only concerns the conceptual aspects of information exchange, but also involves knowledge about the communicative aspects of the specific problem-solving situation. Coordination of communication between student and system becomes even more crucial when their interactional roles are less asymmetrically defined and not as well divided as that of tutor and tutee. This is the case in educational systems, which are meant to adopt a more cooperative role toward the student, acting as a partner in dealing with a problem-solving task. In a cooperative situation, more symmetry, flexibility, and mixed initiative are required in the interaction between student and program. This can only be achieved by a mutually controlled process of coordination at a communicative level.

A lack of insight still exists about the way students communicate and coordinate their information processing while cooperating in a problem-solving context. When students cooperate and communicate in natural language information is exchanged, regarding the problem itself, as well as about meta-cognitive aspects such as the plausibility of the information and beliefs about the value of the information of the other.

In this chapter, we examine how 10- to 12-year-old students cooperate in two problem-solving contexts: two students working together, and a student working with a computer program. First, we discuss the advantages of a more cooperative approach for intelligent educational systems, in which the system functions as a partner and cooperates with a student who is working on a task. Implications for the design of such educational systems are addressed. Second, we discuss the results of our research on cooperative problem-solving. In this research, we collected protocols of dialogues between 10- to 12-year-old students cooperating on a problem-solving task. These protocols have been analyzed in depth with regard to the relationship between problem-solving processes and communication.

On the basis of this study's results, a prototype of a Dialogue Monitor for an intelligent cooperative system (ICS) has been implemented. This monitor is the central part of a computer-assisted educational program that can "think along" with the student and cooperates in solving a problem task. Student and system interact in a mixed-initiative dialogue that is argumentative by nature. The program has been experimentally tested with students (10- to 12-year-olds) from two elementary schools. Some of the results are described in this article. The chapter ends with a discussion of this research's implications, and our further plans for the construction of ICSs.

INTELLIGENT COOPERATIVE SYSTEMS

Three Approaches

In research into intelligent computer-assisted learning, two main approaches can be distinguished: One approach is the development of a tutoring system which acts as a teacher and guides the student and controls his or her learning path. Emphasis lies on the development of domain expert- and diagnosis-modules, and ultimately the effectiveness of such tutoring depends on instructional and curriculum expertise in specific knowledge domains. The other approach is the development of open learning environments, in which the student is able to take over control and determine his or her own learning path. These systems can take the shape of a simulation environment, a laboratory, a microworld, and so on. The effectiveness of this approach depends on the validity of a specific learning principle- that of (guided) discovery learning.

Control over the learning path lies either with the system or the student. Who has control depends neither on the ongoing problem-solving process nor the ongoing interaction process. Presently, however, a third approach seems to emerge: Research increasingly aims at a more cooperative approach (Cumming & Self, 1989). Examples are mixed-initiative systems, systems in which the student acts as a teacher to the system, advisory systems, and intelligent help-systems (Chan & Baskin, 1990; Winkels, 1992). We propose to call these systems that are meant to cooperate with the student intelligent cooperative systems (ICSs; Kanselaar, Andriessen, Barnard, & Erkens, 1990). In this approach, neither the student nor the system has complete control of the learning path. They work together as intellectual partners on a learning task (Salomon, 1988; Self, 1990).

Cooperative Learning in Education Research

Research on cooperative learning in education has a long-standing tradition. The main interest in this field was triggered by the observation that, in some circumstances, students seem to learn more from their peers than from their teachers. Besides advantages in cognitive learning, cooperative learning seems to foster social development and interpersonal (or interethnic) attitudes in the class (Johnson & Johnson, 1975; Sharan & Sharan, 1976; Slavin, 1983). The main research questions concerned the organization and effectiveness of cooperative learning in the classroom as a teaching method. Most of this research on the effectiveness of cooperative learning was directed toward the prerequisites (e.g., heterogeneous vs. homogeneous groups), the comparison with individual learning or whole-class instruction, and the final products of cooperation (Cooper & Cooper, 1984; Webb, 1982). Few researchers focused on the questions of why and how cooperative learning could facilitate learning (Doise & Mugny, 1984), or on what actually happens in the process of cooperation between students.

However, in recent educational research, cooperative learning is reemphasized (Brown & Palincsar, 1989). This emphasis follows a reformulation of learning as a social process of enculturation in recent constructivistic or situated learning views on cognition and instruction (Duffy & Jonassen, 1991; Cognition and Technology Group at Vanderbilt, 1990). Aspects of cooperation play a central role in the constructivistic approach of learning. Peer cooperation is seen, in a Vygotskian way, as an intermediate stage in the developmental process of internalization of social activities. Furthermore, notions like *cognitive apprenticeship, anchored instruction* and *scaffolding* seem to be partly based on a cooperative paradigm. The (social) learning environment should help and support the learner to construct his or her own knowledge and skills. Brown, Collins, and Duguid (1989) saw learning-both inside and outside school-advancing through collaborative social interaction and through the social construction of knowledge. They mentioned the following salient features for group learning:

1. Collective problem solving: Groups may give rise to insights and solutions that would not come about in individual situations.

2. Displaying multiple roles: Groups permit different roles needed to carry out an authentic cognitive task to be displayed by and distributed among different members in the group.

3. Confronting ineffective strategies and misconceptions: Groups may be effective in confronting and discussing faulty or non-optimal ideas of individual members.

4. Providing collaborative working skills: Group work may give the opportunity to situate experiences for future cooperative working situations.

As for the role that computers play with regard to education, the focus is on
the construction of computer-based, multimedia environments: open learning
environments that may give rise to multiple, authentic learning experiences
(Vanderbilt Cognition and Technology Group, 1990). The cooperative aspect is
mainly realized by offering computerized (intelligent) tools that can help solve
the task at hand. Cooperating systems-offering tools and distributing tasks, and
working together with the student-could be the next step. What should we expect
of a computer-based intelligent partner in a learning context? Which criteria
should a cooperative system meet?

Which Criteria Should an ICS Meet?

In natural educational settings, we can define a *cooperative learning situation* as
one in which two or more students work together to fulfill an assigned task within
a particular domain of learning to achieve a joint product. From this definition,
the following criteria for an ICS can be inferred:

1. Complementary abilities or information: Only when the participants have
abilities or information that are complementary can cooperation be fruitful. To be successfully completed, an ICS requires tasks that call for
cooperation. This could also imply that an ICS does not have complete
knowledge about a domain, and thus is not able to solve all the problems
encountered.

2. Mixed control: In a cooperative learning situation, none of the participants
is able to determine the process one sided. The participants are dependent
on mutual cooperation. System and student in an ICS should have the
opportunity to take control of the exchange, as well as the processing of
information.

3. Mixed initiative: Both system and student have to be able to take the
initiative in interaction. They must be able to take initiative in asking
questions, making remarks, transferring information, suggesting solutions, and so on.

4. Common interest and common goal: In cooperation, system and student
must have a common interest in solving the problem at hand. They have to
reach common goals and subgoals that determine the flow of the problem-
solving process.

Implications for Research and Design

Cooperation concerns a complex interaction between task strategies and communication processes. Cooperation requires that the cooperating subjects acquire a

common frame of reference to negotiate and communicate about their individual viewpoints and inferences. The problem with cooperation is that the processes of representation formation and communication often take place implicitly. Natural language communication is implicit by nature-viewpoints are not always advanced, task strategies are not always open to discussion, and so forth. Although implicitness may be ineffective because it masks differences in knowledge, viewpoints, and attitudes, it also results in efficient and non redundant transfer of information. Coordination in information transfer is accomplished by multifunctional dialogue acts. With respect to an ICS, this puts a heavy burden on the interpretive power of a program. Most notably, it should deal with the functions of utterances in the situated context.

To acquire more knowledge about the coordination between communicative and problem-solving processes, it is necessary to investigate, step by step, the interaction between these processes with cooperating students. However, such an approach has been followed only scarcely within the field of cooperative learning, although the necessity of process-directed research has been expressed quite frequently (Cooper & Cooper, 1984; Webb, 1982).

Research is needed regarding how coordination between information exchange and information processing operates for students in natural learning situations. This is true for both student–student interaction and student–computer interaction. The dialogue structure analysis (DSA) project of interactive problem-solving aims to gain more insight into the relationship between processing and exchange of information in cooperative problem solving. Our central research questions are these: is the communicative process (with students in an interactive problem solving situation) determined by the problem-solving process? Conversely, how does the communicative process affect problem solving? To answer these questions, dialogues between students were analyzed within a limited, but semantically rich, domain. The goal of our research project is the development of a prototype "cooperative" computer-assisted educational program.

COOPERATION IN A PROBLEM-SOLVING ASSIGNMENT

The "Camp Puzzle"

The task that is used to study the relation between information exchange and information processing during cooperative problem solving is called the "Camp Puzzle." It is meant for students in the highest grades of elementary school (10- to 12-year-olds). The Camp Puzzle is similar to so-called "Smith, Jones, and Robinson" problems (Wickelgren, 1974). In this kind of logical problem, one has to combine different statements of information to derive some characteristics of a specified group of individuals. However, in the Camp Puzzle this task information has been split and distributed among the two cooperating partners.

By splitting this information, cooperation becomes necessary to complete the task. The cooperation partners have to exchange the relevant information, explain their reasoning, and negotiate about their inferences and task strategies.

In the instruction of the Camp Puzzle, the following situation is described: A group of six children has gone for a week-long camping holiday. Two of the children separately wrote a letter about the children in their group. The two students who work on the task are each given one of these letters. The information in each letter is insufficient to answer all the questions. For example, one letter contains the information, "The friend of Jill comes from Haarlem." In the other letter, the sentence "Ann comes from Haarlem" can be found. The students may infer that Ann is the friend of Jill, thereby ignoring the possibility that more children may come from the same city.

The students have to infer four characteristics of the six children. The collectively found solutions for the 24 subproblems can be written down in a (4 × 6) solution matrix. In both versions (the student–student and student–system situations), the students are allowed to work on the task for 45 minutes. The number of correctly solved subproblems can be taken as an indication of overall task performance. Although the task is perceived as difficult, the motivation and task orientation of the students (on both versions) were remarkably high.

Verbal Observation System

Protocols of the task dialogues were obtained with the aid of a semiautomatic transcription system on the basis of video recordings. This system is the verbal observation system (VOS). The VOS is a comprehensive and finely grained coding system, containing some 300 communicative and semantic coding categories. It was developed to transcribe propositional content, as well as pragmatic and communicative characteristics of utterances.

The VOS uses literal clue words in the utterances to encode the communicative function and content. The system is semiautomatic: the encoding of an utterance is being asked for by the program step by step for different variables, and the codes entered are being checked on consistency with the sets of categories defined for those variables. By the use of clue words and (limited) automatic checking, a sufficient degree of reliability in coding with this complex system could be achieved. In a reliability study with two raters coding 350 utterances, interrater-agreement percentages were found ranging from 67% to 97% for the different variables. In only 4.5% of the cases, the full encodings of an utterance were discrepant at such a degree that the communicative or semantic meaning differed in an important aspect between the raters. In the VOS, utterances are transcribed along three main characteristics: propositional content, dialogue act, and illocution.

The *propositional content* is encoded in a predicate form in which the arguments can be embedded. For example, "The friend of Jan comes from Haarlem," is represented in a form like: (city, (friend, Jan, X), Haarlem). The following types of propositions are distinguished: direct assignments, indirect references, equalities, set distributions, and axioms. The *dialogue act* represents the communicative action of an utterance. Utterances like "Does the friend of Jan come from Haarlem?", "But from Haarlem comes Jan's friend," or "No, the friend of Jan comes from Haarlem!" all have the same propositional content, but differ in dialogue act (question, counter, and denial, respectively). In the VOS 65 dialogue acts are distinguished in 19 main categories representing five communicative functions. In Fig. 10.1, the 19 main categories are given, together with their communicative function. The *illocution* represents explicitly stated illocutionary force, as described by Searle (1969). The illocutionary part of an utterance provides the listener with extra information on how to interpret the information transferred. The category system only considers explicitly stated illocution. In the Camp Puzzle, the illocution refers, in most cases, to the certainty of the information (e.g., "I am not sure that . . . ," etc.).

Protocol Analysis of Cooperative Problem Solving

The Camp Puzzle was solved by 72 pairs of students from several elementary schools. A set of 30 videotaped sessions was selected at random for analysis. The main results of protocol and statistical analyses of the cooperative task dialogues are summarized as follows.

First, on the task-content level, several logical inference procedures and task

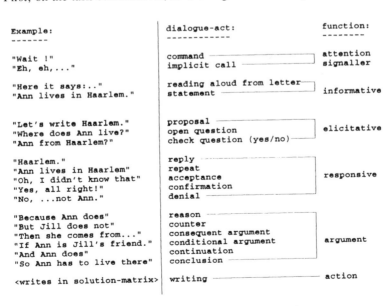

FIG. 10.1. Main dialogue acts and examples.

strategies have been distinguished. The task is rather complex for the students. Unlike normal "Smith, Jones, and Robinson" puzzles, not all the solutions in the Camp Puzzle are unique. That is, more than one child can come from a certain city, engage in a certain sport, and so on. Essentially, the Camp Puzzle can be represented as a constraint-satisfaction problem, in which forward reasoning (finding positive instantiations) and elimination by constraints (finding negative instantiations) can be used to solve the problem.

Second, regarding the task dialogues, the topical structure in the dialogues coincides with the subproblem structure of the task (see Grosz, 1978). The sequence of subproblems is not rigid, and a solution path has to be found. For this purpose, topics have to be initiated, tried, and evaluated in the ongoing dialogue. Remarkably, topics are seldom explicitly proposed ("Let's search for the friend of Jan"), but are initiated implicitly by exchanging relevant information concerning a topic.

Third, most of the dialogue acts in the Camp Puzzle are informative, responsive, or argumentative (see Table 10.1). Contrary to what one would expect, the dialogues contain few open questions (e.g., "In which city does Jan live?"). The students seem to hold onto another cooperative principle (cf. Grice, 1975): "If my partner has found something interesting, he will tell me, I don't have to ask for it." Check questions (i.e., yes–no questions), are found more frequently (e.g., "Does Jan live in Haarlem?"). These questions mostly function to check information exchanged by the partner. Furthermore, the students are concerned with the plausibility or certainty of the propositions transferred or inferred by themselves or their partners (25% of the utterances have an explicit illocution part). Several plausibility levels (five in our model) can be distinguished, depending on the source of information and the depth and complexity of the inference procedure.

Fourth, on the basis of statistical sequential analyses, different topic structures and different argumentation or reasoning sequences have been identified in the protocols (Barnard, Erkens, & Sandberg, 1990). By way of illustrating the

TABLE 10.1
Difference in Percentages of Dialogue Acts Between Two Conditions

Dialogue Acts	Student-Student (%)	Student-System (%)
Statements	34	31
Supports	28	29
Questions	9	28
Denials	5	6
Arguments	20	3
Proposals	2	3
Pre-signaler	2	-

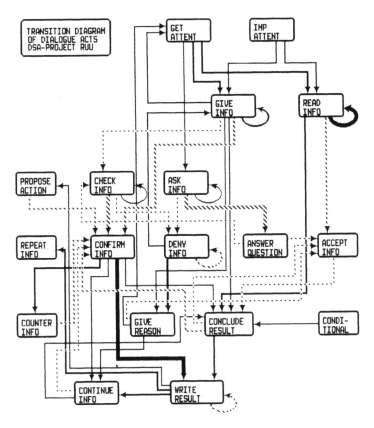

FIG. 10.2.   Transition diagram of dialogue acts in student–student dialogues. The thickness of the lines indicates number of transitions, the dashed lines indicate turn taking, and the solid lines refer to auto relations.

complexity of the dialogues, a transition diagram of the student–student dialogues is represented in Fig. 10.2.

In this figure, the main transitions of dialogue acts in the students' protocols are shown. The most common pattern for the topic structure is as follows:

1. Attention signaling to the partner,
2. Or: exchange of information,
   Or: elicit information exchange,
3. Or: conclusion (of a solution),
   Or: support of information by the partner,
   Or: check of information by the partner, followed by:
      Or: confirmation,

Or: discussion with counterarguments, denials,
    explanation, and reasons,
4. Or: responding to the question for information, followed by:
    Or: support of the reply,
    Or: checking of the reply,
5. Or: writing a solution in the matrix and continuing,
    Or: continuing with new information transfer.

The prototype of the dialogue monitor has been developed based on these and other findings in the dialogue protocols.

COOPERATION WITH THE COMPUTER

Model of Cooperative Problem Solving and Dialogue Processing

The kind of task being discussed here, in which information exchange is central, contains a complex relationship between the problem-solving and dialogue processes. The DSA model of cooperative problem solving and information exchange is based on our analyses of dialogue protocols and similar approaches in the literature (in particular, Carberry, 1985; Fortescue, 1980; Grosz, 1978; Reichman, 1985). The model contains a number of cognitive information-processing subsystems, and specifies the predicted relations between these subsystems as part of the individual student in his or her interaction with the outside world, including the task partner (see also Barnard & Erkens, 1989).

The DSA model is reflected in the modular architecture of the prototype Dialogue Monitor for an ICS. In principle, the Dialogue Monitor is meant to be used for cooperative problem solving in different domains of declarative knowledge and logic. A first version of the Dialogue Monitor has been implemented for cooperation with the Camp Puzzle. Following a description of the Dialogue Monitors architecture, we discuss some of the first results of experimenting with the program.

Architecture of the Dialogue Monitor Program

The Dialogue Monitor computer program contains five different modules, each with a specified function. The program's architecture is presented in Fig. 10.3, and represents our model of problem-solving and information exchange for a single student in a cooperative-task situation.The program is programmed in Prolog and runs on 80286 or higher IBM/MS-DOS machines.

In this model, the *external world* represents the external sources of information with which the monitor communicates: the cooperation partner and the task

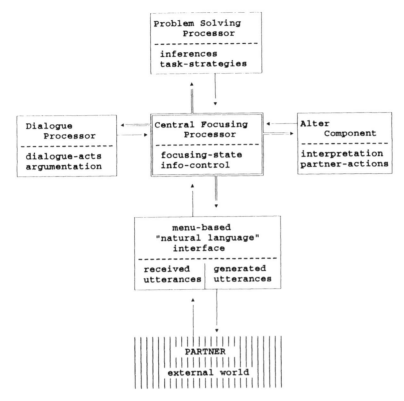

FIG. 10.3. Architecture of the dialogue monitor.

material (letter and solution matrix). The *interface* is the channel through which communication with the outside world (i.e., the cooperation partner) takes place. Internally, four components are assumed to process incoming and outgoing information. The arrows indicate the internal-information exchange between the various components. The double arrows from the central-focusing processor indicate a control function.

The *problem-solving processor* contains knowledge of problem-solving procedures (i.e., rules indicating which [sub]problems are to be tackled). About 40 different logical-inference procedures and subprocedures are implemented in this module. Two faulty inferences are also implemented, and these can be optionally addressed. All intermediate steps are being saved as frames in a limited working memory, with an estimation of the certainty level of the inference itself. These frames can be used later for explanation or question answering. In this module, task strategies (which subproblem next?) and information evaluation (what kind of information is interesting?) are also performed.

The *dialogue processor* contains knowledge about dialogue acts, (i.e., about the forms of the utterances by which information is exchanged and reactions from the partner can be elicited). The dialogue processor also can interpret the communicative function of the dialogue acts coming from the partner. Furthermore, the dialogue processor contains argumentative and explanatory scenarios.

The *alter component* contains some inference rules from which a picture of the partner's current cognitive and communicative activities might be derived. For example, a partner's silence could lead to the conclusion that he or she is busy looking for information in his or her own letter.

These three components operate on information stored in frame-based working memories, which contain the currently relevant information about problem solving, dialogue process and partner.

The *central-focusing processor* is the central part of this model: It has a monitoring function for the internal coordination and working of the program as a whole. This component determines the flow of information between the various components, as well as from and toward the outside world. The focusing processor combines the results of the various components. The general task of the central-focusing processor is to interpret and check incoming utterances of the partner, and to generate utterances in a reacting or initiating way. An important task in this context is determining the focus and topic of the current dialogue context.

The importance of checking the information put forward by the partner is reflected in our simulation model by a checking procedure that operates on every incoming utterance of the partner. By this checking procedure, the information transferred is compared with the knowledge base, and the plausibility of this new information (i.e., the credibility) is estimated before the information is accepted and used for further inferencing. Besides checking questions, this procedure accounts for most of the confirmations, acceptances, repeats, denials, and counters observed in the protocols.

For the actual interaction with the system a menu-based "natural language" interface has been constructed (see Miller, 1988; Tennant, Ross, Saenz, Thompson, & Miller, 1983). By means of interconnected menus, the student can select different constituents of the utterance he or she wants to make. Connective, type of sentence, subject, predicate (i.e., verb), object, and illocution can be picked separately and repeatedly. After each selection, the utterance made so far is being updated in a grammatically correct, "natural language" form and shown in a window. In this way, the interface is flexible and easy to use. With the interface, many different sentences can be made (about 3.2 million). In working with the interface, the student makes, in reality, a proposition in the internally used VOS representation of the program. A separate module translates these propositions, as well as the propositions generated by the monitor, in "natural" (Dutch) sentences. The advantages of this kind of interface should be obvious: No ambivalent semantic parsing and no typing skills are required. In Fig. 10.4, an untrans-

Maar Piet en Jan slapen naast.

FIG. 10.4.   Screen dump of the menu-based language interface.

lated screen display of the interface is shown. The sentence, "But Piet and Jan sleep next to (each other)" is being made.

Procedure

After a short instruction by the experimenter, the student receives a letter (in an envelope) and is asked to type his or her first name. The rest of the interaction with the system takes place by means of menus. The program asks which letter the student received so that he or she can take the other one. Subsequently, use of the interface is trained by an instruction module. After this instruction, the cooperation session starts. The screen is divided into three parts, from top to bottom: solution matrix, dialogue window, and sentence window of the interface. In the dialogue window, the current dialogue scrolls up. The menu-based, "natural language" interface can be activated at any time by any key. On activation of the interface, interaction and initialization of dialogue acts by the program stop until the student has finished his or her sentence. Task dialogues are logged and stored by the program.

SOME RESULTS ON STUDENT-SYSTEM INTERACTION

The program has been experimentally tested on 40 students in the highest grade of two elementary schools (10- to 12-year-olds). The students cooperated with the program under four different conditions, representing optional levels of task content and communicative expertise. On the task-content level, low expertise was simulated by also allowing the system to make faulty (bi-implicational) inferences. Different levels of communicative expertise concern the tendency of the monitor to check or accept the information exchanged by the partner. We discuss the main preliminary results and our first experiences with the program in this section. We concentrate on the comparison between student–student and student–system interactions. A full report of the experiment's results is given in Erkens (in press).

First, and most important of all, the program was able to maintain a cooperative dialogue with a student for 45 minutes (adjusted session period) without too many bugs or inconsistencies. Figure 10.5 represents a dialogue fragment of the monitor's interaction with a 12-year-old student. The fragment is literally translated from Dutch. Utterances made by the student are prefixed with alter. The sign "[]" at the end of a line indicates a pause of more than 2 seconds.

```
alter    =  12 year-old male student      [] = pause >
monitor  =  Dialogue Monitor                   2.0 sec.
─────────────────────────────────────────────────────────
 1 alter   : "Chris does gymnastics;
              that is in my letter."                     []
 2 monitor: "Does Chris do gymnastics ?"                 []
 3 alter   : "Yes."                                      []
 4 monitor: "So Chris does gymnastics."
 5 alter   : "Yes."                                      []
 6 monitor: "Oh..."                                      []
 7 monitor: "We can write that : Chris on gymnastics."
 8 monitor: "Well, I have written it."
              [ie. filled in the solution-matrix]
 9 monitor: "All right !"                                []
10 alter   : "Let's search : the partner of Jan."        []
11 monitor: "Yes..."
12 monitor: "With whom does Jan work together ?"
              [i.e. cooperate with]                      []
13 alter   : "And the partner of Jan is a girl;
              that is in my letter."                     []
14 monitor: "Oh..., the partner of Jan is a girl"        []
15 alter   : "Yes; that is correct."                     []
16 monitor: "Oh..."                                      []
17 alter   : "From which city does Jan come from ?".     []
18 monitor: "The city of Jan I don't know;
              it is not in my letter."                   []
19 alter   : "Jan does the same sports as Jill;
              I am sure of that."                         []
20 monitor: "So, Jan does the same sports as Jill."      []
21 monitor: "Jan does the same sports as Jill;
              you said that."
22 monitor: "Jill does swimming; that is in my letter."
23 monitor: "Then Jan does swimming."
24 monitor: "We can write that: Jan on swimming."
25 monitor: "It is written !"
              [ie. filled in the solution-matrix]
26 monitor: "What else do you know ?"                    []
27 alter   : "Wait a minute...
```

FIG. 10.5.   Fragment of a dialogue protocol of a student and the dialogue monitor.

As can be seen in the fragment, the dialogue has a rather "natural" flavor with a lot of implicit proposals, ellipsis ("Yes," "Oh"), nonspecific replies (13), plausibility checking (2), and unexpected topic shifts (17, 19). In fact, most dialogues, look, at first sight, rather similar to student-student dialogues which is promising for the aims of our research. Although in this fragment the student takes most of the initiative, this is not a characteristic feature of all dialogue protocols (in fact, this student was too quick for the monitor to be able to initiate).

The analyses also revealed some problems in using the program, which may complicate the comparison of the student–student version with the student–computer version of the task. One important drawback is the slowness of written interaction. The student–system dialogue needed much more time than the verbal speech dialogues between students. In the student–student version, the Camp Puzzle was solved in about 25 minutes. In addition, the average score of correctly solved subproblems in a student–student version was 20.5, whereas in the student–system version the average score was only 13.2. The lower score is not caused by an abundance of mistakes and faulty solutions, but simply by the fact that the students are not able to complete the task in the 45 minutes.

Another problem was that the students do not seem to make full use of the interface. They tend to stick to the same sort of sentences; they do not vary much, especially in the first half of the session. The time allowed for instruction and exercises with the menu-based interface is probably too short. Most students only seem at ease with the interface in the last 10–15 minutes of the session. Only then do they start to experiment with the sentences they construct, use various connectives and illocutions, and seem more comfortable with the program as a whole. This problem could be solved by a separate instruction session to get familiar with the program and its interface.

There may be another factor involved, which is perhaps more fundamental and disturbing to our research. Quite a few students seem to be impressed by the program—they seem to comply with the actions of the monitor and take little initiative themselves. In short, they do not seem to cooperate with an equal partner, but with an authority (see Table 10.1). Although the program can make mistakes as well, most mistakes made in the low-expertise condition are accepted or believed by the students. As can be seen in Table 10.1, the percentage of questions in the student–system condition are rather high compared with student–student dialogues on the same task. On the whole, the number of denials, arguments, and proposals in the student–system condition is very low. In contrast to this, there are more argumentative utterances in the student–student interaction.

Another complicating factor may be an artifact of the program. The constraint put on the dialogue for the students is that only one utterance at the time is accepted. Accordingly, the length of each student's turn in the dialogue is set to one utterance. Although the student is able to relate an argument to another argument in his or her next turn, he or she is not allowed to build an "argumentation" in a sequence of directly connected arguments. We did not observe students to have problems or frustrations concerning this constraint. Still, the constraint causes asymmetry in the dialogues because the monitor bypasses this constraint. The constraint was implemented in the program out of fear of combinatorial explosion when interpreting multiple utterances.

FINAL REMARKS

Presently we have not fully analyzed he student–system dialogues collected with the Dialogue Monitor. A more elaborate comparison with the student–student dialogue protocols also need to be made. These results will further improve the program. The main improvements were referred to in the results section. They encompass a longer period of instruction and more exercises with the menu-based, natural language interface. By these means, the students will be better prepared for cooperation with the program. Furthermore, we plan to solve the direct interpretation of student utterances on the part of the Dialogue Monitor, also giving the student the opportunity to make multiple utterances in one turn.

Further developments could be implementing the Dialogue Monitor on another domain of learning (biological taxonomy), and experimenting with speech synthesis to get spoken utterances by the Dialogue Monitor. To be sure, the Camp Puzzle knowledge domain of the Dialogue Monitor is restricted and, furthermore, rather artificial in the school curriculum. In the construction of the Dialogue Monitor, we have tried to separate the domain-dependent knowledge and inference procedures to enable the use of the program in other domains. We already developed a similar cooperation task on biological taxonomies. An implementation of the program on this domain would test our expectation of the potential generalizability of dialogue processes in cooperative problem solving.

Although the students did not argue very much with the program, the argumentation of the program is not optimal either. As yet, we are not satisfied with the rigid, rather standardized way the program acts in situations of contra-argumentation. This is a difficult problem to solve because it has to do with belief revision. In contra-argumentation, in the case of disagreement on a line of reasoning, one of the cooperation partners should be convinced in the end (Van Eemeren & Grootendorst, 1984). The problem is how to specify the conditions under which the program will have to lose its faith in its own line of reasoning. It is hard to specify when and how the program will have to revise its knowledge— not only some factual knowledge, but a complete inference procedure. More research on natural argumentation and conviction will be needed to simulate these processes in a cooperative system. In general, we think this may be one of the main problems in future development of ISCs. Dynamic adaptation of reasoning procedures is of the utmost importance because it has to do with the core of current views on learning and interactivity: the negotiability of knowledge (Winograd & Flores, 1986). In conclusion, the program and session procedure will have to be improved in several respects. However, the nature of the task dialogues between students and systems already obtained gives rise to optimism about the possibility to construct ICSs.

ACKNOWLEDGMENT

This research was funded by the Institute for Educational Research (SVO-project 203.7003).

REFERENCES

Barnard, Y. F., & Erkens, G. (1990). Simulation and analysis of problem solving and dialogue processing within cooperative learning. In H. Mandl, E. De Corte, N. Bennett, & H. F. Friedrich (Eds.), *Learning and instruction. European research in an international context* (pp. 181–196). Oxford: England: Pergamon Press.

Barnard, Y. F., Erkens, G., & Sandberg, J. A. C. (1990). Interaction in intelligent tutoring systems. *Journal for Structural Learning, 10,* 197–213.

Brown, A. L., & Palincsar, A. S. (1989). Guided, cooperative learning and individual knowledge acquisition. In L. B. Resnick (Ed.), *Knowing, learning and instruction* (pp. 393–451). Hillsdale, NJ: Lawrence Erlbaum Associates.

Brown, J., Collins, A., & Duguid, P. (1989). Situated cognition and the culture of learning, *Educational Researcher, 18,* 32–41.

Carberry, M. S. (1985). *Pragmatic modelling in information system interfaces.* Unpublished doctoral dissertation, University of Delaware, Newark, DE.

Chan, T. W., & Baskin, A. B. (1990). Learning compagnion sytems. In C. Frasson & G. Gaulthier (Eds.), *Intelligent tutoring systems: At the crossroad of artificial intelligence and education* (pp. 6–34). Norwood, NJ: Ablex.

Cognition and Technology Group at Vanderbilt (1990). Anchored instruction and its relationship to situated cognition. *Educational Researcher, 19*(6), 2–10.

Cooper, C. R., & Cooper, Jr. R. G. (1984). Skill in peer learning discourse: What develops? In S. A. Kuczaj II (Ed.), *Discourse development. Progress in cognitive development research* (pp. 77–97). New York: Springer.

Cumming, G., & Self, J. (1989). Collaborative intelligent educational systems. In D. Bierman, J. Breuker, & J. Sandberg (Eds.), *Artificial intelligence and education: Proceedings of the 4th International Conference on AI and Education* (pp. 24–26) Amsterdam: Netherlands, IOS.

Derry, S. J. (1992). Metacognitive models of learning and instructional systems design. In M. Jones & P. H. Winne (Eds.), *Adaptive learning environments: Foundations and frontiers* (pp. 257–287). Berlin/Heidelberg: Springer-Verlag.

Doise, W., & Mugny, G. (1984). *The social development of the intellect.* New York: Pergamon.

Duffy, T. M., & Jonassen, D. H. (1991, May). Constructivism: New implications for instructional technology? *Educational Technology* (pp. 7–12).

Van Eemeren, F. H. & Grootendorst, R. (1984). *Speech acts in argumentative discussions: A theoretical model for the analysis of discussions directed towards solving conflicts of opinion.* Dordrecht, Holland: Foris.

Fortescue, M. D. (1980). *A discourse production model for "Twenty Questions."* Amsterdam: John Benjamins.

Grice, H. P. (1975). Logic and conversation. In P. Cole & J. Morgan (Eds.), *Syntax and semantics* (pp. 41–58). New York: Academic Press.

Grosz, B. J. (1978). Discourse knowledge. In D. E. Walker (Ed.), Understanding spoken language (pp. 229–344). New York: Elsevier-North-Holland.

Johnson, D. W., & Johnson, R. T. (1975). *Learning together and alone.* Englewood Cliffs, NJ: Prentice-Hall.

Kanselaar, G., Andriessen, J. E. B., Barnard, Y. F., & Erkens, G. (1990). Some issues on interaction in intelligent cooperative systems. In J. Pieters (Ed.), *Intelligent tutorial systems and instruction* (pp. 45–65). Enschede, The Netherlands: Twente University.

Miller, J. M. (1988). The role of human-computer interaction in intelligent tutoring systems. In M. C. Polson & J. J. Richardson (Eds.), Foundations of intelligent tutoring systems (pp. 143–184). Hillsdale, NJ: Lawrence Erlbaum Associates.

Reichman, R. (1985). *Getting computers to talk like you and me; discourse context, focus and semantics (an ATN model).* Cambridge, MA: MIT Press.

Salomon, G. (1988). *Technology of the mind: Partner and nourisher.* Paper presented at the Educational Research Conference, Leuven, Belgium.

Searle, J. R. (1969). *Speech acts, an essay in the philosophy of language.* London: Cambridge University Press.

Self, J. A. (1990). Bypassing the intractable problem of student modeling. In C. Frasson & G. Gaulthier (Eds.), *Intelligent tutoring systems: At the crossroad of artificial intelligence and education* (pp. 107–124). Norwood, NJ: Ablex.

Sharan, S., & Sharan, Y. (1976). *Small-group teaching.* Englewood Cliffs, NJ: Educational Technology Publications.

Slavin, R. E. (1983). *Cooperative learning.* New York: Longman.

Tennant, H. R., Ross, K. M., Saenz, R. M., Thompson, C. W., & Miller, J. R. (1983). Menu-based natural language understanding. In *Proceedings of the 21st Annual Meeting of the Association for Computational Linguistics* (pp. 151–158). New York: Association of Computing Machinery.

Webb, N. M. (1982). Student interaction and learning in small groups. *Review of Educational Research, 52*(3), 421–445.

Wickelgren, W. A. (1974). *How to solve problems: Elements of a theory of problems and problem solving.* San Francisco: Freeman.

Winkels, R. (1992). *Explorations in intelligent tutoring and help.* Amsterdam: IOS Press.

Winograd, T., & Flores, F. (1986). *Understanding computers and cognition: A new foundation for design.* Norwood, NJ: Ablex.

11

Conceptual Change Among Adolescents Using Computer Networks and Peer Collaboration in Studying International Political Issues

Judith Torney-Purta
University of Maryland

The purpose of this chapter is to describe a learning environment that employs networked computers (with software similar to a sophisticated electronic mail system), and the nature of peer-group collaboration in this environment. The purpose of the technology is to facilitate communication about political, economic, and social issues among secondary and university students. The aspects of the learning environment and prototypes of the networking software, which are the basis of the International Communications and Negotiations Project (ICONS), were developed by a political scientist in the late 1970s, when such uses of computer technology were rare. The original purpose was to enhance the experience of advanced undergraduate students specializing in international relations at the University of Maryland. In the intervening years, the project has expanded and been adapted for three settings: first, in two- to six-week summer centers for adolescents from both gifted and less highly achieving populations; second, in semester-long academic courses in secondary schools in the United States, Canada, and several other countries; and third, in a semester-long course focused on political science and international negotiation for first- and second-year non-specialist university students, including communication over the computer system with teams in Finland, Russia, Hungary, and Poland. The networking software in each setting is the same; the elements that structure the learning environment are parallel; the resulting interactions between students are also very similar. This chapter focuses on the Maryland Summer Center for International Studies, where the most intensive research has taken place.

ICONS was originally designed without any particular educational or developmental theory in mind. Rather, it was intended to meet a pragmatic goal of involving students in simulated international negotiation about political issues.

Subsequently, during the 1980s and early 1990s, the notion that students construct knowledge—and that active involvement in dialogue with peers enhances the process—has been the subject of a great deal of research. Understanding of conceptual change in students has also been elaborated (Vosniadou, 1991). Extensions of the Vygotskian approach have been articulated, in which peers and teachers are seen as adaptive experts who can scaffold experience (Hatano, 1993).

Even in the mid-1990s, however, research on conceptual restructuring, modes of problem solving, movement toward expertise, scaffolding, and intersubjectivity is primarily available in the subject areas of science and mathematics (Cobb, 1992; Ericsson & Smith, 1991; Forman & McPhail, 1993; Vosniadou, 1991). Research on the computer as a vehicle for conceptual change has also been largely confined to science (Carlsen & Andre, 1992; Lin & Songer, 1990). Harel (1991) extensively observed fourth graders for a semester as they wrote Logo software to teach other children about fractions, but no such field study is available in social studies or history classrooms.

The way in which learning is situated within a classroom as a discourse community has been studied in elementary-school mathematics (Lampert, 1990); Cobb, Wood, & Yackel (1993) studied how norms about how to do mathematics (communal mathematics practices) are negotiated through joint activity in school. Research on socially shared cognition and the co-construction of knowledge has primarily illumined our understanding of children's scientific concepts (Resnick, Levine, & Teasley, 1991).

There are several reasons why studies of cognitive restructuring, technology-rich environments, and peer collaboration in learning have concentrated on the subject areas of science and mathematics. One is the high value placed on these subject areas by the economy; another is that the sociopolitical knowledge domain, and problems within it, are ill-structured and more difficult to study; further, social institutions and associated social representations play an important role in defining socially and politically relevant problems and concepts (e.g., national interest and legitimate government power).

Networking has been implemented as an aspect of technology-based learning environments in some social studies classrooms. However, research on networking has been largely confined to adults in work groups and patterns of message flow or group accomplishment of work tasks; it has not considered cognitive processing or conceptual change of group members (see McGrath & Hollingshead, 1994). The ICONS program is a relatively rare example of a technology-based environment that uses networking to enhance individual students' learning in the social sciences, on which research is available.

The chapter's first purpose is to examine the extent to which research in the domain of science and mathematics—in which the classroom has been viewed as a discourse community prompting individuals to elaborate concepts and in which technology's potential for enhancing conceptual development has been explored—can help us to understand the sociopolitical domain.

The chapter's second purpose is to identify the particular features of networked communication, in a program emphasizing peer-group co-construction of knowledge, that seem most effective in promoting conceptual change.

The chapter's third purpose is to lay out research issues in light of an emerging set of perspectives on cognition and contrasting views of peer collaboration, especially based in the Vygotskian tradition.

THE INTERNATIONAL COMMUNICATIONS AND NEGOTIATIONS PROJECT

ICONS, housed at the University of Maryland in College Park, is the site of the research. Figure 11.1 describes, in graphic terms, the Maryland Summer Center for International Studies, in which about 40 adolescents from Maryland participate. As noted, during the school year a variation of this project design is used; it includes teams from schools in other areas of the United States as well as other countries. The research reported here has been conducted at the Maryland Summer Center because there it is possible to collect observational data from all teams, as well as data about sociopolitical schemata from individual participants. The within-team interchange is similar in the other settings.

This project uses a sophisticated computer-network software (POLIS, developed by Jonathan Wilkenfeld, a professor of political science) to link students who are role-playing or pretending to be diplomats from different countries. Figure 11.1 indicates the ways in which the experience is structured for participants. Students receive, in advance, a lengthy scenario set in the near future that lays out the world situation with respect to international political and economic issues; the scenario also includes a brief outline of the countries' positions on these issues (Fig. 11.1, Cell 1B). When students arrive at the Summer Center, they are assigned to teams of 5–7 (e.g., Brazil, France) and they meet their team leader (usually a graduate student). During the first 5 days, there are introductory lectures, and each team writes a position paper on foreign policy in the assigned country (Fig. 11.1, Cell 2B). Then students begin negotiations in conferences centered around scenario issues such as human rights, international debt, and the global environment (see Fig. 11.1, Cells 1B, 1A, and 2A, respectively).

The function of the computer and software is to provide a sophisticated communication network. All communication within the team, about the message to be sent, takes place face to face within a designated team room (Cell 2A); all communication between teams takes place using the network provided by one computer per team linked by modem to the system (Cell 2B). A role-play coordinator provides structure for these conferences, collecting proposals to place on agendas, making suggestions when a team's messages are off topic, and calling a vote on issues (Cell 1B). Sometimes student teams send electronic mail to other teams, but most messages are sent during scheduled online conferences, in which

A. In the role-play exercise, what are the units and levels of communication?

| Between-team interaction among U.S. peers representing different countries and sending messages via computer network (1A) | Within-team interaction and co-construction of messages in oral discourse resulting in message entry (2A) | Individual processing, cognitive representations/schemata, restructuring (3A) |

B. What are the sources of structure that set the context?

| POLIS communication software (online conferencing; printout); World political reality reflected in scenario; Role-Play Coordinator (SIMCON); U.S. team (graduate students) (1B) | Team leaders (more competent); Peer leaders (equally competent and shifting); Team's position paper; Record of past messages generated by team; Socially constructed schemata (2B) | Individuals' entry schemata; Socially constructed schemata from team discourse; Researcher's probes (3B) |

C. What are the sources of data?

| Archives and messages sent (1C) | Observations (narrative notes and videotapes); Participant self-ratings of participation (2C) | Think-aloud problem solving protocols and schema maps; Student generated materials (3C) |

D. What are the characteristics of the program and the technology that motivate participation and push restructuring?

| Importance of team's reputation among other teams of peers based on messages sent over the system; Authenticity of experience in relation to real world; Screen as attention focus (1D) | Messages sent in written form; Typist enters message that becomes available onscreen; Speed of message-generation demanded by system; Peer interchange within shifting team leadership; Ownership of content through identification with role of diplomat and country (2D) | Continuity in individual structures; Preferences for type of participation and goals (3D) |

FIG. 11.1. Elements of International Communications and Negotiations Project: Orienting table.

students communicate simultaneously with teams representing other countries and see messages both on screen and in a printed record (Cell 1A). Heated face-to-face debate takes place about the wording of what the team will send over the network. This is a collaborative and contextualized experience in the co-construction of sociopolitical knowledge.

The major differences between the Summer Center setting and the semester programs are that electronic mail is utilized more during the school year because of time differences between sites; there is less time pressure, especially for the preparation of position papers; the team is likely to be somewhat larger; and the teacher, rather than a graduate student leader, organizes the interaction and may grade some assignments. These differences between program settings are far less substantial than the similarities in the role of technology, the type of interchange, and the way networking enhances interaction. Both the Summer Center and the semester programs contrast in many ways with more traditional study of global issues. There is little use of a textbook; problems are presented in an open-ended fashion, without a single or specific solution; students are constantly reminded that they are to get inside the role of a real diplomat and make decisions about international problems; and most writing is produced primarily for the critique of peers, rather than the teacher's approval.

RESEARCH ON PEER INTERCHANGE WITHIN THIS DISCOURSE COMMUNITY OF INTERNATIONAL RELATIONS SPECIALISTS

The first aim of the research was to capture salient aspects of peer interaction and the collaborative construction of knowledge within the teams (through the analysis of narrative observations based on field notes and video tapes; Cell 2C). Participants in this project were acquiring experience as participants in a discourse community of international relations specialists, much as the students Lampert (1990) studied were learning to be participants in a discourse community of mathematicians. They were moving from peripheral to more central participation in a discourse community by making explicit their assumptions and explanations. They were also establishing, modifying, reflecting on, and refining their goals so as to collaborate with their peers, much as the dyads of students studied by Forman and McPhail (1993).

The particular character of these discourse communities can be illustrated by two excerpts from narrative observations conducted in 1990 during the process of message construction. Those quoted here took place in the face-to-face team meetings during hour-long online conferences on the debt and economic problems of developing countries—a topic that is always central in the conferences. These observations document the participation structure of these groups, and the way in which the processes of thinking, revising, explaining, and mutual construction took place in this discourse community. These narrative observations illustrate collaborative construction and socially shared public cognition within the teams (corresponding to Cells 1C and 2C on Fig. 11.1).

For example, the following interchange took place among the French team during an online conference on the debt problems in southern-hemisphere nations, and the economic difficulties faced by the Soviet Union (in 1990). A, B, C, and D are student participants.

A: Do we have to pass this through and get the opinion of the South?
B: We wrote that we would in our position paper.
C: How much does USSR want?
B: 100 billion, that's about right. We have to make sure the others know. But I think instead of a percent we should say how much. We have to make the G7 countries pay more, correct?
D: I thought future exports were to reduce the debt.
B: Like a proportion of them, they were.
Leader: What about collateralization?
D: I thought that was one of our options. Is this money going to the IMF (International Monetary Fund)?
Leader: What is Japan's position? And why are you changing your mind about percentages?
B: It should still work.

Note the several places in which the students serve as resources to each other in articulating and examining assumptions about messages they have received and those they are planning to send—the assumption that a country cannot make unilateral policies without "passing it through" other countries, that to make up the required amount "G7 countries must pay more," and that loans or grants are meant to be repaid with "future exports." A student refers to the position paper as providing scaffolding for negotiation. The leader uses questions to focus attention on options not yet discussed (collateralization), on the position of other countries (Japan), and on the justifications for what she perceives as "changing your mind." One of the students also gives metacognitive direction to the team's process, suggesting that they "make sure the others know" what has been decided, while another comments on how a policy may have changed but still relates to overall goals ("it should still work").

This transcript was picked up a little later in the same conference:

A: I don't like what the U.S. is putting out.
B: How much should be collateralized for each nation, like how much should each nation pay to make up the total?
Leader: We proposed a total amount not a percent.
B: I think that was because we thought we would grow a lot.
Leader: Remember there is inflation in there too. . . .
E: We should think about the Arab countries and the Swiss (as sources).

A: They have all that oil, and the Swiss have it because they don't have to buy arms. . . .
Leader: Are you all clear?
D: (Reading the screen) The U.S. is agreeing with us.
A: Is the USSR going to donate money?
Leader: They are not members.
D: We did that.
B: We want a little less.
A: What exactly has the U.S. voted yes to?
D: To 10%.
Leader: 10% of debt and .3% of GNP.
E to A: Did you get your question answered?

Again there are assumptions being made public and examined (e.g., how economic growth might influence assessment for the fund). There are a number of metacognitive questions by both leader and participants, including, "Are you clear?" and "Did you get your question answered?" There are several identity-asserting statements (e.g., taking credit for the fact that the USSR was not a member, and expressing pleasure that the "U.S. is agreeing with us [meaning France]").

Analysis of another session in the Brazilian team shows challenges by students to other countries' positions and assumptions (Nigeria's interests and those of Japan), and the proposing of analogies ("like the Marshall Plan"). The leader's interventions there are primarily pressing for clarification of who is to invest, and whether the team understands the difference between loans and grants. One student also asserts his identity with Brazil and focuses on safeguarding its interests.

Similar interchanges can be found in many other teams' transcripts and in discussions of other topics (such as the global environment). The discourse communities and participation structures within these team groups parallel many of the elements in mathematics classrooms viewed as discourse communities. The participants make public and examine their own assumptions and those implied in the messages received from other teams; they co-construct and challenge each other's opinions and strategies of negotiation; they assert their identity as representatives of a country and participants in the discourse of diplomacy, and develop norms and share understanding about how one "does diplomacy"; and they guide the team's participation structure by metacognitive monitoring of discourse, or by making linkages between the structures of current and past or future team positions. Many of the things that team members say to each other resemble the ways in which teachers scaffold student engagement during reciprocal teaching (e.g., restoring direction to the discussion when it has been lost, linking previous statements to new issues, and reworking other's comments so they carry the discussion forward; Palincsar, Brown, & Campione, 1993).

The communication technology has brought messages expressing the positions of other teams into the discourse, and has also served to stimulate students to clarify their own positions and take on new identities. These are definitely U.S. adolescents, however, and the socially shared schemata associated with their background and citizenship still influence their interpretation. For example, when negotiating about human rights, they assume that ensuring civil and political rights is the goal of every government.

There are several important characteristics of the discourse communities created within these teams:

1. These discourse communities are more authentic than most classes in history and social studies because the students see consequences to their actions within the context created by ICONS.

2. These discourse communities foster socially shared cognition and the co-construction or interactive construction of knowledge between peers in a spirit of mutuality and equality. For example, participants interrupt each other constantly when deciding what message is to be sent.

3. These discourse communities develop leadership that is lodged in a designated, "more competent" leader—who provides scaffolding by asking generative questions of the adolescents—and also in emerging peer leadership that shifts among equal participants and includes substance (suggesting how to word a message), social guidance (making sure all team members' views are heard), and metacognitive monitoring (suggesting what the team needs to consider next or how much progress has been made toward a goal).

4. These discourse communities' educational aim is to promote individual change in cognitive structures in the domain of political thinking. That change seems similar to the deepening of the problem space described in mathematics classrooms by Lampert (1990) and others.

5. These discourse communities map onto real-life political communities of discourse. The scenario for negotiation and the role-play coordinator who keeps the dialogue between teams anchored in reality structure this. The mapping of the simulation onto real political life is encouraged by urging participants to "think like diplomats" and to substitute technical terminology (interest moratorium) for everyday terms (get the bank to wait).

The analysis of these within-team interactions confirms the extent to which the motivation for participating and the goal structure in these teams has a dual center, simultaneously within the peer group and within the individual. This closely resembles the type of participation that has been found to be effective in prompting individual cognitive restructuring in science and mathematics, and cognitive change generally.

RESEARCH ON INDIVIDUAL RESTRUCTURING
OF POLITICAL SCHEMATA

A second aim of the research was to assess salient aspects of individuals' cognitive representations of the international system before and after the ICONS sessions. This part of the research was designed under a model that Forman and others recently criticized for being overly individualistic, emphasizing the internalization of knowledge, and failing to adequately address the way in which individual and sociocultural practices and goals are mutually constitutive and a product of constant renegotiation within the group setting. This issue is reexamined in the concluding section.

Basic to this part of the research is the concept of an individual's schema or cognitive representation of the international system. Data from think-aloud problem solving, in response to scenarios of international relations, were collected from participants before and after the sessions. These data were analyzed by drawing graphic schema maps for individual participants. The intent was to use think-aloud problem-solving tasks administered before and after participation in the project to assess cognitive structures relating to the international system and their change in the direction of greater complexity during participation in the discourse communities described earlier.

Interviews were conducted with 30 adolescents, ages 14–17 in 1987 and 1989. They were predominantly White students from a range of socioeconomic backgrounds who had applied for the Maryland Summer Center for International Studies described previously. The following hypothetical problem was used:

> Imagine you are the finance minister of a developing country. The interest payment on your debt to banks in the developed countries is due, but there is not enough money in your treasury to pay it. What actions would you take to solve this problem? What would you do? What would you ask others to do? Just think aloud and tell me whatever comes to your mind about what you would do to solve this problem if you were the finance minister.

Trained interviewers presented this problem (and another concerning Apartheid) to participants in this program on the second day of the 2-week session, and again 10 days later as the simulation was concluding. After the interviewee stopped volunteering solutions, the interviewer would ask whether there were any problems with the solutions given—whether there were any reasons they would not work—to probe for constraints. Respondents were also asked about their attitude toward the debt of developing countries, and whether there were any solutions they had considered but not mentioned because they thought the actions were unethical.

Research on logical problem solving provided a prototype for the mode of analysis adopted for these think-aloud responses. There are similarities between discussions of actors, actions, and constraints upon actions in solving logical problems (e.g., in the Tower of Hanoi problem), and the way specialists in international relations discuss political actors (e.g., leaders or international organizations) and actions in which they can engage (e.g., negotiating or declaring war). Hence, an actors–actions–constraints model was used.

Each interview transcript was read, and a graphic model of the schema models of the international system implied in the student's answer was drawn. The elements of these sociopolitical schemata included: (a) actors who might be approached by the finance minister or diplomat (e.g., banks or other countries), (b) actions that these actors might be asked to undertake (e.g., refinancing the loan or joining an embargo on trade), and (c) constraints on actions (e.g., banks or countries might not agree).

As an example, a graphic schema map is presented in Figures 11.2 (presession)

Presession

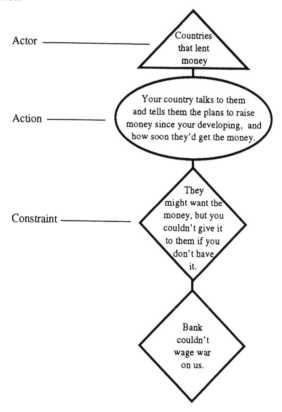

FIG. 11.2. Schema map of respondent's presession answer to the finance minister problem; student in French diplomat role.

Postsession

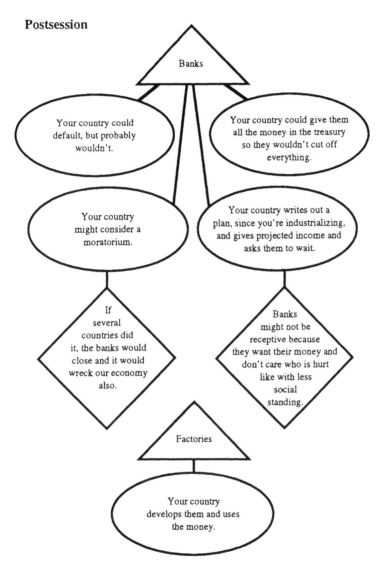

FIG. 11.3. Schema map of respondent's postsession answer to the finance minister problem; student in French diplomat role.

and 11.3 (postsession). The basic elements of the models, represented by triangles, are the actors mentioned who might be approached by the finance minister to solve the problem. In the figures, the ovals represent particular actions that these actors might perform. Below that, represented by diamonds, are constraints on these actions, elicited by a probe question: Are there any problems with the solutions you have suggested, any reasons they might not work?

On the average, the networks of actors and actions mentioned by individual students were more dense and complex after the ICONS experience. In responding to the finance minister problem, the students were more likely after the simulation to propose getting together with other southern or debtor nations to form an interest cartel, or in some way put pressure as a group on the developed countries to moderate the debt load. They were also more likely after the simulation to refer to actions within their own economies, such as austerity measures, and to mention organizations such as the World Bank or the International Monetary Fund (IMF). In responding to the Apartheid problem, approaches that involved cooperation with other countries to institute economic sanctions were more likely after the simulation. For most individuals, there was some similarity between the pre- and postsession interviews regarding the actors in the economic or political systems who were mentioned and their actions. However, the schemata had clearly been restructured in the direction of more complexity after the simulation experience for the majority of participants.

One can view the responses along a continuum of expertise. In most previous studies of expertise, the procedure has been to compare two groups: one relatively more expert than the other. In contrast, this research has defined a continuum of expertise. There are prenovices, who lack knowledge of the most basic political structures and beliefs. They mention talking to the banks in the finance minister problem, but have almost no sense of the existence of other potential actors in the international system. At the second and third levels are novices and postnovices, who have accessible and increasingly knowledge-rich cognitive representations of politics that are partially differentiated and include some connections. At the fourth and fifth levels are preexperts and experts, who have a wide range of representations of political actors and actions and see them with more connections and complexities than do novices. They also have well-defined strategies for representing and solving political problems. Most adolescents are at the prenovice and novice levels, with some of the students after ICONS found at the postnovice position (Torney-Purta, 1992).

In summary, the experience within the team groups of peers as they debated messages to be entered into the system, and some evidence of cognitive restructuring, have been described. The next section contains speculations about characteristics of the program, as well as the technology that appear to be related to both the character of the discourse and the existence of conceptual change.

CHARACTERISTICS OF THE PROGRAM
AND TECHNOLOGY

The majority of what we know about technology-rich environments comes from the reflections of skilled observers framing what they have seen in field settings through the lens of a theoretical framework. Further understanding comes from a few more carefully controlled studies of peer interaction, many of them conducted within the framework of Vygotskian theory (Forman & McPhail, 1993; Tudge & Winterhoof, 1993). Among the variables identified by these studies are: (a) attention to the screen and task (Trowbridge, 1987), (b) *intersubjectivity* defined as shared meaning evidenced by a dyad member adapting a new explanation (Tudge & Winterhoff, 1993), (c) justifications for statements (Forman & McPhail, 1993), (d) different types of collaboration (Granott, 1993), and (e) different types of transactive interchange (Leadbeater, 1988). With this background in mind, the rich dataset from ICONS was examined to identify the characteristics of this program, along with its technology and associated structure, which seemed successful in promoting change in cognitive structures and producing the high level of involvement observed (Fig. 11.1, Cells 1D, 2D, 3D).

First, an important feature of the technology used in the program is that one student, acting as the typist, enters a proposed message that then becomes visible to all team members. Group members then suggest revisions to that message as it is displayed before them. Co-construction and group revision of the message on the screen seem to provide a potent stimulus for elaborating an individual's representations as other individuals agree with some aspects of the message, disagree with others, clarify goals, and suggest revisions. Many participants discover that what seems obvious to one about a situation is not obvious to another. The computer screen is an object of highly focused student attention because it is constantly changing, providing valued information in a way the blackboard or textbook does not, and representing concretely the product of the co-construction of knowledge in the form of a message. The displays on the computer screen create an interpsychological or intersubjective reality shared by the group members watching. It is not merely that each individual sees others' point of view in a discrete fashion, but that there is a concrete manifestation of a group product that several (or all) members have participated in constructing. A more individualistic interpretation is that the computer screen provides information corresponding to an example in a science text that pushes individuals to process at a deep level.

Second, the program design moves participants from referencing to adults to referencing to the opinions of peer team members. Like situations involving collaborative problem solving in science, participants are pressed to arrive at an agreed on solution (message). Unlike much collaborative problem solving, there is no way to designate correct solutions; this seems to lead students to search for their own judgment criteria to satisfy themselves and their peers. Often teams express concern that a message they sent allowed other country teams to take advantage of them. These perceived "errors" are the source of after-conference discussions, in which leaders help identify repair processes for the next conference. As Rogoff (1993) discovered, the members of groups such as these take more and more responsibility for themselves and appropriate new forms of activity, forming a community of practice in which they move from being apprentices to full participants. These observations suggest the vital importance of peer groups as a context situating discourse about social issues, especially for adolescents (Torney-Purta, 1994).

Third, the existence of the messages in a printed form, as well as on screen, and repeated pressure to state their opinions as diplomats representing a country lead to ownership of ideas among team members. The existence of concrete artifacts—in the form of piles of printouts representing all messages sent—gives a powerful sense of authenticity, and focuses the students on the words they are using and their precise meanings (a point raised by Crook, 1992). ICONS participants realize the importance of writing clearly what they mean. This contrasts with programs like the Model UN held face to face, where between-team communication takes place orally and there is one person making statements for the country, which allows the team to disavow responsibility for a position. Hatano (1993) noted that multiple sources of information and representations add value to a discourse. Here information comes from discussion with peers during coconstruction, on screen over the system from other teams as well as one's own, and from the printer in written form. In addition, messages are often read aloud to the team as they are printed. The printouts also allow participants to refer back to a previous message, making cognitive connections between past, present, and future positions.

Fourth, because many interchanges take place in real time (not through electronic mail), there is a sense of urgency to make points in a message clearly and quickly. If a team gets stuck revising a message, there will be 20 new messages once it returns to the receiving mode. The intersubjectivity and sense of shared meaning referred to earlier seem to be stimulated by this pace, at least for most students.

Fifth, continually being pressed to state positions as "Nigeria believes" or "France concludes," and (in some exercises) actually communicating with other teams in Siberia or Japan, increases identification with one's own team members in a community, to which prestige is attached, and also with a recognizable national perspective. In one survey, 90% of the participants reported high or moderate levels of identification with the country they represented. On the last day, a participant said sadly, "It's really too bad; next week there won't be any messages for us as Nigerian diplomats. We'll have to go back to just being students." There are few opportunities for young people in the regular school experience to identify with a community to which prestige is attached.

Sixth, the team can designate that a given message be sent to all other country teams or only to selected countries (e.g., allies or countries from whom one is trying to get concessions). This develops students' awareness of the difference in representations of world problems, especially between developed and developing nations, and it gives them important ways to test hypotheses about their more and less successful negotiating strategies.

CONCLUSIONS

In many respects, the developmental and educational models applied in the domains of mathematics and science appear to be appropriate for this program in the domain of international politics. Involvement in discourse communities, cognitive restructuring, intersubjectivity, and co-construction of knowledge were observed extensively among the participants in these networked negotiations on international issues.

The technological dimension of the project served to enhance the quality of participants' experience in several ways. It created a press for mutuality and intersubjectivity in groups, and it pushed the cognitive restructuring of political concepts in individual students. However, this positive result creates a problem of interpretation. Is this best viewed as an intraindividual process of conceptual restructuring or as an interindividual process of knowledge construction? Forman and Larreamendy-Joerns (in press) contrasted these approaches and pointed out that one needs to go beyond change within individuals to examine a group's changes, functioning, and expertise over time.

Studying these models and this technology in ICONS has pointed to inter-penetrating and interlocking aspects of this learning environment, which are difficult to study with standard psychological research models. The technology and other structuring aspects of the program, although easily separated in descriptions of the program and in Figure 11.1, tended to merge in the actual program and the observations. Further, aspects that a research design would separate from each other and view in a linear fashion as cause and effect could not easily be isolated. Pre- and posttests of individuals' cognition, even with the open-ended think-aloud methodology, did not fully capture the complexity of students' thinking. It seemed quite inappropriate to view the experience with the computer and the groups as a "treatment," and an individual's conceptual change as the results of that treatment (see also Crook, 1992; Forman & McPhail, 1993). In a technology-rich setting such as this, which also included extensive peer-group interaction, it was difficult to decide on the appropriate unit of analysis (see also Granott, 1993).

More specifically, there was an interpeneteration of individual and group cognition. This appeared to be intensified by the technology—in particular, the visibility of the group's product on the computer screen, the pace, and the authenticity of the situation, as well as by the feedback from peers in the process of co-constructing messages. Many individuals in this setting, as in those described by Forman and Larreamendy-Joerns (in press), approached the task in a different way and renegotiated the goals of the exercise with peers. The group "situated" the sociopolitical cognition. The strengths of the program led to difficulties in assessing its effects.

It is possible that the subject matter of politics, and social science, an ill-structured domain characterized by problems lacking easily agreed on solutions, intensified the feature of interpenetration of group and individual cognition. However, others studying mathematics classrooms have also noted these effects (Harel, 1991).

Future study of these technology-rich learning environments should take account of the technology as well as these factors: (a) the way the technology is situated and modified by the structure of interchange among students, (b) the control exercised by those with power over the technology, (c) the scenario or curriculum that sets goals for interaction with the technology, and (d) the relation of the simulated world to the real-world situation. In addition, programs incorporating group interaction need to be built around more complex models of cognition, including ways to track these complex co-constructions and interpenetrations of the individual and the group. Developing the cognitive and social models and methods for doing this is a priority.

REFERENCES

Carlsen, D., & Andre, T. (1992). Use of a microcomputer simulation and conceptual change text to overcome student preconceptions about electric circuits. *Journal of Computer Based Instruction, 19*, 105–109.

Cobb, P. (1992). Interaction and learning in mathematics classroom situations. *Educational Studies in Mathematics, 23*, 99–122.

Cobb, P., Wood, T., & Yackel, E. (1993). Discourse, mathematical thinking, and classroom practice. In E. Forman, N. Minick, & C. Stone (Eds.), *Contexts for learning: Sociocultural dynamics in children's development* (pp. 91–119). New York: Oxford University Press.

Crook, C. (1992). Cultural artifacts in social development: The case of computers. In H. McGurk (Ed.), *Issues in childhood social development* (pp. 207–231). Hove, England: Lawrence Erlbaum Associates.

Ericsson, K. A., & Smith, J. (Eds.). (1991). *Toward a general theory of expertise.* Cambridge, England: Cambridge University Press.

Forman, E., & Larreamendy-Joerns, J. (in press). Learning in the context of peer collaboration. *Cognition and Instruction.*

Forman, E., & McPhail, J. (1993). Vygotskian perspective on children's collaborative problem-solving activities. In E. Forman, N. Minick, & C. Stone (Eds.), *Contexts for learning: Sociocultural dynamics in children's development* (pp. 213–229). New York: Oxford University Press.

Granott, N. (1993). Patterns of interaction in the co-construction of knowledge: Separate minds, joint effort, and weird creatures. In R. Wozniak & K. Fischer (Eds.), *Development in context: Acting and thinking in specific environments* (pp. 183–207). Hillsdale, NJ: Lawrence Erlbaum Associates.

Harel, I. (1991). *Children designers.* Norwood, NJ: Ablex.

Hatano, G. (1993). Time to merge Vygotskian and constructivist conceptions of knowledge acquisition. In E. Forman, N. Minick, & C. Stone (Eds.), *Contexts for learning: Sociocultural dynamics in children's development* (pp. 153–167). New York: Oxford University Press.

Lampert, M. (1990). When the problem is not the question and the solution is not the answer. *American Educational Research Journal, 27*, 29–63.

Leadbeater, B. (1988). Relational processes in adolescent and adult dialogue: Assessing the intersubjective context of conversation. *Human Development, 31*, 313–326.

Linn, M., & Songer, N. (1990). Cognitive and conceptual change in adolescence. *American Journal of Education, 99*, 379–417.

McGrath, J., & Hollingshead, A. (1994). *Groups interacting with technology: Ideas, evidence, issues, and an agenda.* Newbury Park, CA: Sage.

Palincsar, A., Brown, A., & Campione, J. (1993). First grade dialogues for knowledge acquisition and use. In E. Forman, N. Minick, & C. Stone (Eds.), *Contexts for learning: Sociocultural dynamics in children's development* (pp. 43–56). New York: Oxford University Press.

Resnick, L., Levine, J., & Teasley, S. (Eds.). (1991). *Perspectives on socially shared cognition.* Washington, DC: American Psychological Association.

Rogoff, B. (1993). Children's guided participation and participatory appropriation in sociocultural activity. In R. Wozniak & K. Fischer (Eds.), *Development in context: Acting and thinking in specific environments* (pp. 121–153). Hillsdale, NJ: Lawrence Erlbaum Associates.

Torney-Purta, J. (1992). Cognitive representations of the political system in adolescents: The continuum from pre-novice to expert. In H. Haste & J. Torney-Purta (Eds.), *The development of political understanding: A new perspective* (pp. 11–25). San Francisco: Jossey-Bass.

Torney-Purta, J. (1994). Dimensions of adolescents' reasoning about political and historical issues: Ontological switches, developmental processes, and situated learning. In M. Carretero & J. F. Voss (Eds.), *Cognitive and instructional processes in history and the social sciences* (pp. 103–122). Hillsdale, NJ: Lawrence Erlbaum Associates.

Trowbridge, D. (1987). An investigation of groups working at the computer. In D. Berger & W. Banks (Eds.), *Applications of cognitive psychology* (pp. 47–58). Hillsdale, NJ: Lawrence Erlbaum Associates.

Tudge, J., & Winterhoff, P. (1993, March). *The cognitive consequences of collaboration.* Paper presented at the Society for Research in Child Development, New Orleans, LA.

Vosniadou, S. (1991). Designing curricula for conceptual restructuring: Lessons from the study of knowledge acquisition in astronomy. *Journal of Curriculum Studies, 91*, 219–237.

III MEANINGFUL CONTEXTS AND MULTIPLE PERSPECTIVES

12 MOST Environments for Accelerating Literacy Development

John D. Bransford
Diana Miller Sharp
Nancy J. Vye
Susan R. Goldman
Ted S. Hasselbring
Laura Goin
Learning Technology Center, Vanderbilt University

Keisha O'Banion
Jean Livernois
Elizabeth Saul
The Cognition and Technology
  Group at Vanderbilt

Our goal in this chapter is to describe a relatively new project underway in our Learning Technology Center. The program is designed to accelerate the development of literacy in young children, where *literacy* is defined as the ability to read, write, speak, listen, compute, think critically, and learn on one's own. Our work involves the design of what we call MOST environments, where MOST stands for "Multimedia environments that Organize and Support Text." MOST environments build on our center's work in the areas of mathematics (e.g., Cognition and Technology Group at Vanderbilt, 1990, 1991, 1992a, in press-a, chap. 14, this volume), science (e.g., Cognition and Technology Group at Vanderbilt, 1992a; Goldman et al., chap. 13, this volume), and language arts and social studies (e.g., Bransford, Kinzer, Risko, & Vye, 1990; Cognition and Technology Group at Vanderbilt, 1990). A major goal of MOST environments is to accelerate children's learning by organizing instruction around visually rich, meaningful "macrocontexts" that students and teachers can mutually share and explore. An important feature of MOST environments is that they are designed to support a wide variety of individual differences in linguistic and conceptual development. We want to make it possible for children who are at risk of school failure to interact with, teach, and learn from other students who may be developmentally more advanced. In this way, students learn from one another, as well as from teachers and the formal curriculum in school.

This chapter is organized into four sections:

1. A discussion of the growing need to help students who are at risk of school failure, and of problems with traditional approaches to working with such children.
2. An examination of the argument that MOST environments that include dynamic visual support for comprehension can be much better for accelerating linguistic and conceptual development than typical school environments, which are primarily language based.
3. An examination of our plans to create MOST environments that are more effective than traditional environments for helping students learn to read.
4. An overview of some additional design features of our MOST environments that seem crucial for success.

Most of our discussion focuses on the first two areas because that is where we have completed the most research. Nevertheless, we briefly discuss plans for the third and fourth areas to encourage discussion about problems we might avoid and directions we might take.

THE IMPORTANCE OF FOCUSING ON YOUNG CHILDREN WHO ARE AT RISK OF SCHOOL FAILURE

The need to focus on literacy, and especially early literacy, is clear from the research literature. Literacy skills are foundational for lifelong learning. Difficulties in learning to read, along with difficulties in acquiring the cognitive and metacognitive skills for using reading to learn, are major reasons for referral to special education services (Means & Knapp, 1991; Vellutino, 1979; Wong, 1985). Success is particularly important at the beginning stages of reading because strategies, behaviors, and beliefs established early are difficult to change (DeFord, 1990; Palincsar & Klenk, 1991).

Students for whom literacy development is particularly problematic are often disadvantaged in several ways: in their social and economic status, in the support for school-based literacy that they receive at home, and in their experiences with everyday events and language (e.g., Heath, 1982; Pallas, Natriello, & McDill, 1989). Such students overwhelmingly come from minority groups whose literacy rates are lower than those of the mainstream culture (Kirsch & Jungblut, 1986). For example, studies by the National Commission on Excellence in Education (1983) indicate that whereas 13% of 17-year-olds can be considered functionally illiterate, illiteracy among minority youth may run as high as 40%. In addition, studies by the National Assessment of Educational Progress indicate that, historically, at-risk populations continue to perform poorly relative to the national population at each grade level, and the performance gap between better and poorer readers widens as they progress through school (see also Juel, 1992).

The need to tackle problems of literacy development becomes especially striking when one looks at demographic data. These predict a rapid increase in the number of children from minority groups, who disproportionately suffer from cultural discontinuity with traditional school values (Pallas et al., 1989). Such children often suffer from poverty, which is increasing in this country. In addition, about 4.6 million children who are not native English speakers currently attend American schools, and this figure is expected to increase by 10%–15% by the turn of the century (Scarcella, 1990). Many children in rural communities have only a limited range of experiences to draw on and hence find it difficult to compete in the workplace (Elder & Hobbs, 1990; note that about one fourth of the nation's students are served by school districts in rural America). Overall, demographic data indicate that, without dramatic changes in our success rates for literacy development among those who are at risk of school failure, our nation's special education services will experience even greater demands in the years ahead.

Problems With Traditional Approaches to Literacy Instruction

Clearly, problems of literacy development, and especially early literacy development, have long been recognized as important. Nearly all schools have programs for dealing with children who are having difficulty learning to read (e.g., Means & Knapp, 1991). Unfortunately, many of these programs are based on assumptions that are directly at odds with current theory and data on ways to facilitate learning (e.g., Bransford, Goldman, & Vye, 1991; Means & Knapp, 1991; Resnick & Klopfer, 1989). It is useful to consider these assumptions to contrast them with the ones we propose later.

General Problems.   A key assumption that has strongly influenced the development of educational curricula is that there is a strict hierarchy of skills development that must proceed from the "basics" to "higher order thinking" (for more discussion, see Bransford, 1979; Means & Knapp, 1991; Resnick & Klopfer, 1989). In the area of reading, this assumption has often led to an emphasis on decontextualized drills of sounding and blending; "read-aloud" exercises that concentrate almost exclusively on sounding out words rather than making inferences and predictions to construct meaning from texts, and isolated drills on new vocabulary items. It is assumed that activities involving "higher order thinking" cannot occur until these basics have been acquired.

NAEP data indicate that there are severe problems with many " basics first" approaches to reading instruction. For example, these approaches may lead children to develop misconceptions about the goals of reading. Poplin (1988) noted that many elementary children view books as "something you look at and say the words." Other data indicate that many students have learned to decode, but have not learned to read, in order to learn and defend their evaluations and interpretations of what they have read (National Assessment of Educational Progress, 1988). Especially problematic for many students is the ability to learn from expository texts rather than simple narrative texts. Even the ability to decode can be made difficult for some students because it is often taught in isolation as "sound exercises," rather than explored in the context of reading and writing (see e.g., Calfee, 1991).

Basics-first programs that attempt to place more emphasis on discussions of extended texts can often fail to help students acquire the comprehension skills necessary for effective lifelong learning. Durkin's (1978, 1979) study of 24 classrooms indicated a strong lack of instruction in reading comprehension strategies; more recent studies have indicated that this is still a problem, and one that is not easily overcome (C. Collins, 1992; Duffy, 1992; Pressley, El-Dinary, & Marks, 1992; Wong, 1985). One reason for this is that when students have questions about content, teachers have a natural tendency to explain the content rather than help students develop the skills necessary to clarify the content on their own (e.g., Bransford, 1992; Langer & Applebee, 1987).

Special Problems With Programs for At-Risk Students.   Programs designed for students who are having difficulty are likely to provide a diet of decontextualized practice on "the basics." The emphasis in these programs is on what students lack, rather than on what they know, and instruction is targeted at remediating these deficits (e.g., Means & Knapp, 1991). Therefore, at-risk students often receive instruction in phonics, vocabulary, and decoding, where each is taught as an isolated skill that is, unintegrated with other aspects of thinking and learning (Allington, 1983). Because many at-risk students must struggle with a pronunciation system that is different from their spoken language or dialect, they receive less instruction in higher order skills than their peers who are in regular classrooms (Allington & McGill-Frazen, 1989; Oakes, 1986).

Overall, at-risk students receive repetitive instruction on things they do not know—instruction that does not allow them to utilize the rich sources of everyday knowledge that they bring to the classroom (e.g., Palincsar & Klenk, 1991). Knapp and Turnbull (1990) argued that typical instruction for at-risk students tends to:

- underestimate what disadvantaged students are capable of doing;
- postpone more challenging and interesting work for too long—in some cases, forever; and
- deprive students of a meaningful or motivating context for learning or using skills that are taught.

Good, Slavings, and Mason (1988) emphasized that decontextualized, repetitive instruction in "the basics" can be especially damaging to those children who are the most vulnerable because it contributes to dependence and passivity, which often results in confusion and withdrawal. The students are continually working on tasks they do not know how to do, and they have little idea of why they are doing them. There is almost no emphasis on building on knowledge or intuitions that the students have already acquired (e.g., Bransford & Vye, 1989; Palincsar & Klenk, 1991).

Alternative Assumptions About Instruction and At-Risk Students

Problems with the assumptions that underlie traditional instruction for at-risk students can be highlighted more clearly by contrasting them with an alternative set of assumptions. Means and Knapp (1991) discussed the following characteristics of new approaches to instruction (see also Collins, Hawkins, & Carver, 1991):

1. Taking a New Attitude Toward At-Risk Learners

   - Appreciate the intellectual accomplishments that all learners bring to school
   - Emphasize building on strengths rather than focusing solely on the remediation of deficits
   - Learn about childrens' cultures to avoid mistaking differences for deficits

2. Reshaping the Curriculum

   - Focus on authentic, meaningful problems
   - Embed instruction on basic skills in the context of more global tasks
   - Make connections with students' out-of-school experience and culture

3. Applying New Instructional Strategies

   - Model powerful thinking strategies
   - Encourage multiple approaches to tasks
   - Provide scaffolding to enable students to accomplish complex tasks
   - Make dialogue a central medium for teaching and learning (p. 8)

Programs such as Palincsar and Klenk's (1991) adaptation of reciprocal teaching to the early grades are consistent with these new approaches. So are the MOST environments described in the next section. In addition, MOST environments move beyond the traditional text-based curricula found in most elementary schools, and make use of multimedia technologies that allow the interaction of print and oral language with video and audio media.

Why Multimedia?

Before proceeding with our discussion, it is important to acknowledge that many people question our assumptions about the benefits of using multimedia to accelerate the development of literacy, and others consider them ludicrous. They point to television and movies as prime examples of visually based presentations, and argue that these formats are generally the enemy of print. Thus, they argue that television viewing often discourages children from reading books, and it is primarily a passive activity that is harmful for developing the habits of mind necessary to become an active reader. For example, Healy (1990) estimated that fifth graders now read an average of only four minutes a day outside of school.

We agree that television viewing can sidetrack students from learning to read, and that it does not necessarily help students develop the skills necessary to actively comprehend information. Nevertheless, these are not necessary evils of the visual medium. As Salomon (1983, 1984) noted, for example, it is possible to help students become active, rather than passive, viewers of television. In addition, Kozma (1991) and others emphasized that new technologies, such as videodisc and CD ROM technologies, make it possible to review scenes just as one can reread sentences in a book. So the possibility exists for actively exploring information, rather than being restricted to superficial soundbites and cliches that are so characteristic of television. In the following discussion, we present two major reasons for moving from classrooms that focus primarily on oral and written language to ones that emphasize multimedia: (a) They provide alternate pathways to knowledge that facilitate conceptual and language development, and (b) they facilitate the process of learning to read. Discussion in the next section first focuses on listening comprehension, and then on multimedia and learning to read.

MOST ENVIRONMENTS AND LISTENING COMPREHENSION

A longitudinal study conducted by Juel (1988, 1992) illustrates the plight of many at-risk students and, in our view, provides a strong rationale for moving beyond traditional print-based curricula. Juel began her longitudinal study by collecting data on a number of first-grade children enrolled in a low-income neighborhood school. At the beginning of first grade, all of these children tested below the 39th percentile on a test of listening comprehension. These children were also tested at the end of first grade and, on average, were found to be below grade level on the listening comprehension subtest of the Iowa Test of Basic

Skills. In addition to tests of listening comprehension, Juel assessed the development of children's word recognition and decoding skills.

Juel followed as many of her children as she could through fourth grade, and continued to assess both word recognition and decoding and listening comprehension. Some of the children caught on to decoding and became good readers; others remained very poor at decoding and word recognition, and were considered to be poor readers. A striking finding was the relationship between students' skills at decoding and word recognition and their scores on listening-comprehension tests at the end of fourth grade. Children who became good readers overcame their below-grade-level scores on listening comprehension that had been apparent in the first grade, and by the end of fourth grade were scoring above grade level—at an average grade level of 5.2. In contrast, students who had poor decoding and word recognition skills scored at a grade level of 2.6 at the end of fourth grade. Overall, there was more than a two-year difference between the two groups on the listening-comprehension tests.

It is possible that there is something about the children who did not become fluent readers that also hampered the development of their skills in listening comprehension. An alternate hypothesis, and the one favored by Juel, is that the poor readers lagged in listening comprehension because, being unable to read and uninterested in it, they failed to acquire the relevant concepts and vocabulary necessary to adequately comprehend orally presented information. Juel cited the argument of Nagy and Anderson (1984)—that "beginning in about third grade, the major determinant of vocabulary growth is amount of free reading" (p. 327). She also cited Stanovich's (1986) description of this problem:

> The effect of reading volume on vocabulary growth, combined with the large skill difference in reading volume, could mean "a rich get richer" or cumulative advantage phenomenon is almost inextricably embedded within the developmental course of reading progress. The very children who are reading well and who have good vocabularies will read more, learn more word meanings, and hence read even better. Children with inadequate vocabularies—who read slowly and without enjoyment—read less, and as a result have slower development of vocabulary knowledge, which inhibits further growth in reading ability. (p. 381)

Imagine that Juel's poor readers had been in an elementary-school environment, where important information was presented visually as well as through print. It seems quite plausible that as the poor readers continued to work on decoding skills, they could have been helped to achieve at grade level on listening comprehension because new concepts and vocabulary could have been communicated with strong visual support (e.g., Bransford, Kinzer, Risko, Rowe, & Vye, 1989). Please note that MOST environments are designed to do more than enhance oral comprehension; they are also designed to facilitate decoding, word recognition, and strategic reading. Our goal in this section is to explore, in more detail, the idea of providing visual support for acquiring the concepts and skills that can enhance listening comprehension.

Studies of Language Acquisition

One of our major reasons for believing in the potential of multimedia environments for accelerating literacy development is the fact that natural language acquisition is strongly "multimedia" (Bransford & Heldmeyer, 1983). In 1972, MacNamara argued that children comprehend extralinguistic events and use these to crack the linguistic code and figure out new vocabulary. Chapman's (1978) article provided some excellent illustrations of this point of view. She begins her article by noting that mothers of young children often believe erroneously that their children are quite advanced linguistically. As an illustration, Chapman cited a study by Lewis and Freedle (1973) that involved a child and his mother and the interaction between the two. When the child was sitting in his crib, the mother handed the child an apple and said, "Eat the apple." The child made biting movements, suggesting that he understood. Later, when the child was in his playpen, the mother handed him an apple and said, "Throw the apple," and the child threw it. The mother was convinced that the child knew the meaning of *apple*, as well as *eat* and *throw*.

You can imagine what happened when the experimental psychologists Lewis and Freedle entered the scene. When the child was in his high chair, they said, "Throw the apple" and he began to eat it. When the child was in his crib, they said, "Eat the apple" and the child threw it. The child was using his knowledge of the extralinguistic setting to attempt to interpret the linguistic remarks of others. Because there is usually a match between extralinguistic situations and linguistic statements when adults talk to children, children can eventually crack the linguistic code and determine what others mean by what they say.

The benefits of using extralinguistic information to interpret linguistic information are not restricted to young children. Several years ago, several members of our Learning Technology Center at Vanderbilt conducted some demonstration experiments to illustrate the advantages of extralinguistic information on subsequent learning (e.g., Sherwood, Kinzer, Hasselbring, & Bransford, 1987). In several studies, we first asked college students to watch the initial 25 minutes of the movie *Swiss Family Robinson*. We asked them to "keep this context in mind" as they participated in the rest of the experiment. We then presented them with linguistic information that would be difficult to process without the *Swiss Family Robinson* context. For example, some students were presented with passages that contained new vocabulary items that they did not know. These items were actually nonsense words, but they allowed us to simulate the experience of confronting unfamiliar vocabulary words and attempting to infer their meaning. For example, students heard: "The Lel was in trouble so they needed to reach the Geck. They sawed some bics to make a vac." Students who had seen *Swiss*

Family Robinson, and who were told to interpret the passages from that perspective, were much better able to infer the meaning of the nonsense words than were students in the control group, who did not share the *Swiss Family Robinson* perspective.

Of course, one can argue that the college students did not really need *visual* information to make appropriate inferences about new vocabulary items; *Swiss Family Robinson* could have been communicated to them verbally, and they could have performed just as well. We agree with this argument. Nevertheless, it seems clear that there are many areas of knowledge that are relatively unfamiliar to most college students, and that these could be made more comprehensible by the appropriate use of dynamic visual information (e.g., information about the dynamics of plate tectonics or the orbital path of a rocket taking off from earth). Similarly, the availability of appropriate visual information should be extremely useful to young children, especially those who are at risk of school failure. Because they are less likely than their developmentally average or advanced peers to understand all the vocabulary used by their teachers and story authors, they are less likely to benefit from purely verbal descriptions of background information, which could help their subsequent comprehension. This hypothesis is explored in the studies described next.

Studies Conducted by Rich Johnson

The beginnings of our opportunities to explore multimedia environments' benefits for at-risk children arose in the context of research conducted by Richard Johnson, who graduated from Peabody with a degree in early childhood education. Johnson conducted his research at an inner-city school in Nashville, Tennessee, with children from low-income families. Over 75% of the children in the school came from single-parent homes. He reported that when these children entered school, most could not speak in complete sentences, identify colors, or recognize letters from the alphabet. One third of these children scored below the third stanine of a national test for prereading and math skills, 6% did not even test well enough to score.

Johnson also gave his children the Peabody Picture Vocabulary Test (PPVT) as another measure of their verbal ability. This test focuses on vocabulary comprehension, and does not require a verbal response. In administering the test, the experimenter tells the child a word (e.g., *tambourine*) and shows the child a card with four pictures. The child then points to the picture that best matches the word. The PPVT has been extensively normed so that the average score for children of a particular age is the 50th percentile. The average score of Johnson's at-risk students was the 35th percentile. As we see shortly, the average score of at-risk students with whom we have been working has been around the 10th percentile.

Given their low PPVT scores, it is not surprising that Johnson found that his at-risk students were less able than the ones who were not at risk (and who had higher PPVT scores) to retell and answer comprehension questions about a story that was read to them. However, the main purpose of Johnson's work was to explore the possibility that multimedia resources might enhance the comprehension abilities of young, at-risk children.

In one of his studies, Johnson (1987) prepared two versions of a substory in *Swiss Family Robinson*—the part where they are shipwrecked, build a raft and stock it with supplies, and finally get to shore. One version of the story was in a verbal format; the other was a movie version that was shown on videodisc. Individual 4- and 5-year-old children whom teachers considered at risk of school failure were randomly assigned to either the verbal or video condition. The children were then asked to retell the story and answer comprehension questions posed by the experimenter. The differences in the performances of children in the verbal versus video group were clear: There was a definite advantage for children in the video group in the retelling and comprehension tasks. When the retellings were scored only for central idea units, rather than memory for peripheral detail, the advantage for the video group remained in place.

Johnson's studies were not designed to permit in-depth analyses of the reasons underlying the differences in performance. For example, it is difficult to know whether the verbal and video versions of Johnson's stories were of equivalent difficulty. Furthermore, the fact that the video group in Johnson's study recalled more statements about the story and answered more inference questions does not guarantee that the visual support actually facilitated the students' language comprehension. An alternate hypothesis is that the students in the video group simply remembered visual information and used it to generate verbal descriptions at time of testing. We consider this possibility in more detail later.

Johnson recognized that his findings had potentially important practical implications. The most striking was that the children in the video contexts were much more verbal. They talked more, answered more questions, and, when given opportunities to explore the video, asked many questions. From the perspective of stimulating language production and inquiry, the video environments had many positive effects on the children. We believe they had effects on teachers as well. As adults work with children of various ages, it is natural for the former to form both implicit and explicit expectations about what the latter are capable of doing. At an intuitive level, the expectations formed by watching these children perform, given purely verbal information, are quite different from expectations generated when these children are supplied with visual, dynamic information to support their comprehension, production, and inquiry. Data from a number of investigations suggest that teacher and parent expectations about children play an important role in affecting the quality of children's development (see e.g., Bransford, Delclos, Vye, Burns, & Hasselbring, 1987; Feuerstein, Rand, & Hoffman, 1979; Lidz, 1987).

Johnson also explored the issue of assessing and repairing students' understanding of events in a story. He argued that it was much easier to assess students' understanding, and repair it when necessary, when he could return to a video scene shown earlier and ask "What was going on here?" and then talk about the children's interpretations. He was able to elicit more ideas from the students than when he merely repeated a verbal statement from a story and asked about that. We return to this issue in the following section.

Experiments on Support for Mental Model Building

Thanks to a grant funded by the National Institute of Health, we extended the work begun by Johnson. We concentrated on 5- and 6-year-old kindergartners whose language and conceptual skills seemed underdeveloped. For example, in one of our studies, we worked with a group of students whose average score on the PPVT was the 10th percentile.

Our experiences with administering the PPVT provide an indication of how many at-risk students can be found in a single school or setting. For example, we visited two inner-city schools and gave the PPVT to 41 children, from whom we had received permission letters. Only two of these children (less than 5%) scored at or above the 50th percentile (i.e., at or above grade level). The mean percentile for all 41 children was 16%. In contrast, we gave the PPVT to 50 children with permission letters at a suburban school. Thirty-three of them (66%) scored at or above the 50th percentile; only 17 (34%) scored below the 50th percentile. The mean percentile for these children on the PPVT was 58%. If you believe, as we do, that a great deal of language and concept learning goes on as children interact with one another, data such as those we collected in our inner-city schools represent considerable cause for alarm.

We noted earlier that students who participated in Johnson's video-based condition engaged in more language production and showed better evidence of comprehension than did those in his verbal condition. However, we also noted that Johnson's data did not allow us to analyze the reasons for the increased retelling and comprehension scores. It is possible that the video condition did not really help students better understand the language used to convey the story. Instead, those in the video condition may simply have remembered images from the movie and generated statements about them at time of test. Our new study was designed to allow more precise inferences about the degree to which visual support actually enhances language comprehension.

At the beginning of our study, we read at-risk kindergartners a short nine-sentence story without any pictures to aid comprehension. Despite being seemingly motivated to do well, the children generally had great difficulty remembering and retelling what they had just heard to a puppet who was "asleep" during the story. We then conducted a within-subjects study, where these children listened to three types of stories: (a) no-video stories, (b) stories with only minimal video clips, or (c) stories with video clips that were designed to help them build a mental model of the story. In stories with a helpful-video framework, each sentence was read and followed by a video clip that illustrated the dynamic relationships between characters, actions, and objects in a story scene. Stories with minimal video included only close-ups of characters or nondetailed views of scenes, without the dynamic spatial relationships that are important for a mental model (see Johnson-Laird, 1983; McNamara, Miller, & Bransford, 1991). *All of the stories concluded with sentences that were not accompanied by video, and children had to comprehend these ending story statements and integrate them with the previous sentences in the story.* Video was shown at the beginning of the story, rather than at the end, because research suggests that the most difficult part of building a mental model is the building of a framework at the beginning of a story (for a review, see Gernsbacher, 1990).

An example of one of the stories we used is the Donald Duck story, partially outlined in Figure 12.1. For students in the helpful-video group, the story began with video clips accompanying each sentence, (i.e., the reading of each sentence was followed by a dynamic video clip that illustrated the sentence). The final sentence in the story that was accompanied by video was: "One of the nephews raced downstairs to try to catch the bank before it hit Donald in the head." The video clip that was displayed after children heard this sentence showed the nephew running downstairs, and ended with a picture of Donald Duck asleep on his couch, with the bank in mid-air, a foot from his head. The nephew was standing next to the couch, with his arm outstretched to catch the bank. At this point, children were asked to imagine the rest of the story sentences, which were

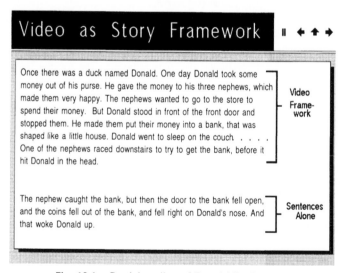

Fig. 12.1.   Partial outline of Donald Duck story.

TABLE 12.1
Overall Mean Scores per Story (Maximum = 6) for the Final Imagination Sentences

Story Condition	Mean Score
Helpful video	2.66
Minimal video	1.63
No video	.85

then read without any accompanying video: "The nephew caught the bank, but then the door to the bank fell open, and the coins fell out of the bank and right on Donald's nose. And that woke Donald up."

We wanted to test whether video at the beginning of a story would help children build a mental model and successfully imagine the story's ending sentences. For our experiment, we worked with 18 inner-city kindergartners who scored below age level on the Peabody Picture Vocabulary Test-R (PPVT-R; mean percentile = 9.9). We told them 12 stories across four sessions. The children had to retell the stories to a puppet, including the ending sentences. Each child listened to some of the 12 stories accompanied by a video framework, other stories with no video at all, and still other stories with a minimal-video framework. Stories were counterbalanced so that each occurred equally often in the helpful-, minimal- and no-video conditions.

For present purposes, we focus on children's abilities to remember the last sentences in the stories—the sentences that received no visual illustrations even for the helpful-video conditions. These data are illustrated in Table 12.1. They indicate a clear advantage for the helpful video condition over both the minimal- and no-video conditions. This suggests that the helpful-video condition enabled the children to create an initial, well-developed mental model of the situation, which they were then able to modify on their own by comprehending linguistic information that was read to them.

Several points about these data are noteworthy. First, we have conducted control experiments where college students hear and see the helpful-video versions of each story and then attempt to guess the ending sentences. Except in a few instances, the college students were not able to guess the endings. When we reanalyzed our data for only those stories where there was no room for guessing, we still found the same marked advantage for our at-risk students in the helpful-video condition. This suggests that they are not simply remembering visual images and generating responses at time of test. Instead, the visual information seems to provide a context that enables them to better understand the significance of the story endings as they are read to them in purely verbal form (see e.g., Bransford & Johnson, 1972, 1973).

A second point about our data for the at-risk children is that they complement and extend work with children that has explored the effects of static pictures on comprehension. Levin, Pressley, and their colleagues conducted a series of important studies on the role of pictures in facilitating language comprehension and memory (e.g., Levin, Anglin, & Carney, 1987; Pressley, Cariglia-Bull, Deane, & Schneider, 1987). They found that only some pictures help (i.e., those that provide important information about settings and relationships among characters). They also found that pictures that only partially illustrate a statement can facilitate comprehension and memory for information in the statement that is not visually illustrated. However, they noted that, for young students in kindergarten, there appears to be a definite limit on the amount of new verbal information that the students can process without visual support—the use of partial pictures only helped when the to-be-learned verbal information was only a single, short sentence. Our data indicate that partial visual support can facilitate kindergartners' comprehension and memory for a greater amount of verbal information than has previously been reported. One reason for this is that dynamic visual images provide more support for initial mental model building than do static pictures, such as those usually found in texts.

The Need for Meaningful Content

One of the shortcomings of the work just mentioned is that we were restricted to sources of video that were readily available to us. Thus, we used scenes from a Disney videodisc to illustrate sentences from the *Donald Duck* story noted earlier. Unfortunately, the content of the videos that were available to us was far from ideal for helping our children acquire concepts that would build a strong foundation for lifelong learning. For example, the videos rarely illustrated any advantages of literacy in the everyday world, and they provided few opportunities to engage in scientific and mathematical inquiry.

In the fall of 1991, we had the opportunity to work with a highly talented group of community members and video producers to create a video-based story that would allow us to extend our research in a number of directions. The story was written in conjunction with teenagers who lived in the projects in inner-city Nashville, and hence knew the settings that were familiar to most of our at-risk students. However, we also decided to focus on themes that were universal, and hence would be relevant for children irrespective of the environments in which they lived. One interesting feature of the story we developed is that its themes and setting should be much more familiar to at-risk students than *Swiss Family Robinson,* used in Johnson's studies. As we explain shortly, however, we nevertheless expected that, for many events, comprehension would be enhanced by dynamic visual support.

The video we produced is *One Hundred Million Billion Eyes.* A summary of the story is provided in Figure 12.2. The video's format contains an outer story

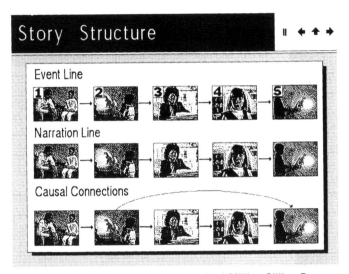

Fig. 12.2. Summary of *One Hundred Million Billion Eyes.*

and an inner story. In the outer story, we meet Angel and learn that it is her sixth birthday. Tony, one of the older boys in the neighborhood, is making a videotape of Angel as his birthday present to her. He asks her to speak into the camera, and she suddenly becomes frightened and runs away. Angel goes to the home of Ms. Emma, a friend who lives in the area. Ms. Emma senses Angel's fear and tries to intervene by asking her to help water some plants. Then she gives Angel her birthday present—a book that Ms. Emma has written. Ms. Emma and Angel join Derrick under a tree, and Angel remarks that the book has no pictures. Ms. Emma explains that the pictures will be in their heads, and she helps Angel and Derrick imagine scenes for themselves. Then she begins to read the book.

The book is about a boy named Jerome, and it constitutes the inner story in our video. Jerome is afraid to go to school because he has to participate in show and tell. He has some interesting shadow puppets to show the class, but he is afraid that he will not do well. His father helps him practice and gain the courage to give it a try. Jerome's presentation goes well; then he faces the challenge of reacting to questions from his classmates. For example, one asks him to make the shadow bigger. He almost freezes, but then remembers how he practiced doing that at home.

As the video ends, we return to the outer story. Tony is walking by with his camera and Ms. Emma points him out to Angel. She jumps up, runs to Tony, and explains that she needs to face her fear. The story ends with her triumphantly saying her name as the video camera rolls.

We are using *One Hundred Million Billion Eyes* (we call it *Ms. Emma* for short) in a number of studies. In one, we are comparing groups of kindergartners at risk of school failure with peers whose average score on the PPVT is the 75th percentile. One of our goals is to compare how these two groups perform given the video version of *Ms. Emma* versus a verbal version that has been recorded by a professional storyteller on videotape.

We used a number of procedures to ensure some degree of informational equivalence between the verbal and visual versions of *Ms. Emma*. For example, we asked college students to view *Ms. Emma* without sound. We divided the video into scenes; after each scene, we asked the students to describe what they thought had happened in the scene. We used their retellings as an indication of key, salient visual information in the scene—information that we wanted to ensure was also available for our verbal version. For example, almost all of the college students reported in one scene that Ms. Emma picked up a blanket before going outside. This action was not described in the original audio soundtrack, so we added it to the verbal version. That way, both the video and verbal groups could potentially include this information in their retellings. However, none of the college students reported the color of the blanket, so we did not add this information to the verbal version. If, in our study with the children, a child in the video group reports the color of the blanket, we do not score it as a correct piece of recalled information, because it is not available from the verbal version.

After determining the descriptions of visual information to be added to our verbal version of *Ms. Emma*, we asked a professional writer of children's stories to help us add it to the original video soundtrack in a manner that would be entertaining and comprehensible to children. A professional narrator then recorded the story on audiotape. The video version of our story is 11 minutes long; the oral version is 13 minutes and 15 seconds long.

The experiment we are conducting involves a 2 × 2 design with at-risk and non-at-risk students receiving either the video or verbal versions of *Ms. Emma*. Students who hear the verbal version get to see stills of the faces of the main characters as they are mentioned in the story, but they do not see visual information about settings or dynamic events.

After they view either the video or verbal version of the story, we ask each child to retell the story, and then follow with a number of specific probes. One month later, we ask more questions about the story to assess long-term effects.

Much of our data are currently being analyzed, so therefore we cannot report our overall findings. However, we were able to analyze students' answers to some specific questions that we felt would be particularly sensitive to the degree to which they could build mental models with and without visual support. One question was, What did Jerome do to make the shadow bigger? To answer this question, students needed to understand the part of the story that described Jerome working with his shadow puppets in his room. The narration for the video version of the story is supplied by Ms. Emma and as follows: "Jerome had a red dinosaur stick puppet. He held the puppet in one hand and shone the flashlight toward it with the other hand. This made the puppet's shadow on the wall. When he moved the puppet closer to the flashlight, the shadow got bigger. Big shadows. Little shadows. Oh no! It's time to go to school." The video in this version shows these actions as they are read by Ms. Emma.

Later in the story, we return to the theme of changing the size of the shadow puppets when a girl in Jerome's class asks him to make the shadow bigger. The narration for the video is as follows: "Jerome froze. He got real scared again. He thought to himself, how am I going to make the shadow bigger? Then he remembered practicing in front of George. He moved his puppet and the shadow got bigger and bigger and bigger! Chris said, 'Awesome!'"

Here is the way this information was conveyed in the verbal version of *Ms. Emma*. Additions to the soundtrack, which were added based on our control experiments with the college students described earlier, are indicated in italics: "Jerome had a red dinosaur stick puppet. He held the puppet in one hand and shone the flashlight toward it with the other hand. This made the puppet's shadow on the wall. When he moved the puppet closer to the flashlight, the shadow got bigger. *But when he held the puppet far away from the light, the shadow got smaller.* Big shadows. Little shadows. *Suddenly, Jerome noticed the time.* Oh no! It's time to go to school." The scene that occurred later in the story is as follows: "Jerome froze. He got real scared again. He thought to himself, how am I going to make the shadow bigger? Then he remembered practicing in front of George. He moved his puppet *closer to the flashlight* and the shadow got bigger and bigger and bigger! *A little boy named* Chris said, 'Awesome!'"

In the verbal version, the idea of moving the puppet closer to the flashlight to make a bigger shadow is actually explicitly mentioned twice, whereas it is only explicitly mentioned once in the video version. Nevertheless, as indicated in Table 12.2, the video version clearly helped the at-risk students answer the question, What did Jerome do to make the shadow bigger? In contrast, the non-at-risk students were almost as good at answering this question from the verbal version as they were from the video version. These data suggest that visual support for difficult-to-model situations can have an especially beneficial effect on students who are at risk of doing poorly in school.

Our initial analysis of the data also indicate that the video version of *Ms. Emma* helped both at-risk and non-at-risk students make inferences about the

TABLE 12.2
What Did Jerome Do to Make the Shadow Bigger?

Students	Verbal (%)	Video (%)
At risk	25	56
Non-at-risk	75	88

Note. Percentages indicate percent of students who correctly answered this comprehension question.

story. For example, the answer to the question, Why was Angel ready to talk to the camera?, was not provided in either the video or verbal version of the story. The information provided by the video soundtrack and verbal version was as follows: From the video soundtrack—Narrator: Angel was ready to try. She knew she could do it. She took a deep breath. She looked into the camera and remembered *One Hundred Million Billion Eyes*. She turned to Ms. Emma. Ms. Emma was smiling real big. When she looked at the camera, she could imagine Ms. Emma's smile. From the verbal version—"Angel was ready to try. She knew she could do it. She took a deep breath and held the microphone up to her mouth. She looked into the camera and remembered *One Hundred Million Billion Eyes*. She turned to Ms. Emma. Ms. Emma was smiling real big. When she looked at the camera, she could imagine Ms. Emma's smile." As indicated in Table 12.3, the video version helped students infer that Angel got the idea of facing her fear from reading the story about Jerome.

Additional Findings With *Ms. Emma*

All of our studies indicate that both at-risk and non- at-risk children liked *Ms. Emma* and asked to watch it numerous times. This is important because we want to create environments that are interesting to a wide range of children. However, despite liking the video, the majority of the students seemed to dislike extended sessions, where they were asked questions about what they had seen or heard. Our impression is that these sessions became boring for the non-at-risk students, but that something else was going on with the at-risk students. They seemed uncomfortable in the situation, perhaps because they were unable to answer many questions and perceived this as a failure experience. These experiences challenged us to find ways to motivate the students further and increase their probabilities for success.

Puppets to Teach.   One approach that we began using early in our work was to have a puppet that would interact with the children. Initially, the puppet was someone to whom the children retold stories: The children and experimenters pretended that the puppet could understand children but not adults. Children

TABLE 12.3
Why Was Angel Ready to Talk to the Camera?

Students	Verbal (%)	Video (%)
At risk	19	44
Non-at-risk	50	75

Note. Percentages indicate percent of students who correctly answered this comprehension question.

liked the puppet very much because it put them in the role of teacher, rather than someone being tested.

Visual Cues.   Despite being motivated to retell information to a puppet, children frequently had trouble remembering. Much of their difficulties seemed to involve retrieving information. To increase the probability that they could retrieve adequately, we let children review relevant visual scenes with the sound deleted. These silent visual cues had a marked effect on improving students' abilities to retell relevant parts of a story. They also increased students' experiences of success.

Discrepancy Detection.   We found that we could prompt retrieval even more precisely by asking children to correct the puppet's rendition of the story. The errors the puppet made could vary from ones that were obvious to ones that were quite subtle. For example, the puppet might "remember" that it was Angel's special day because it was Christmas. The children would then correct the puppet and tell it that it was her birthday. When children had difficulties with discrepancies, we let them resee silent visual cues to prompt their recall. For example, in one instance, a puppet erroneously remembered that Jerome did not want to go to the park to play. A child realized that this was wrong, but could not remember where it was that Jerome did not want to go until she saw a silent visual scene of Jerome and his father sitting on the bed. This was sufficient to remind the child that Jerome did not want to go to school because of his fear of show and tell. (In the movie, the father and son had discussed these issues in this particular scene.)

Making Multimedia and Traditional Books.   The children's favorite activity seemed to be helping the puppet understand the story by reshowing silent scenes and then using MacRecorder to describe what was happening in each scene. When children used the computer to play back the segments, the puppet was treated to an illustrated retelling of the story from the children's point of view. Ultimately, these multimedia products are transformed into print-based books with pictures from the video that children can take home and share with their parents and family members.

Exploring Other Aspects of the Story.   As noted earlier, *Ms. Emma* was designed to be explored from a variety of perspectives. One approach that we are beginning to explore is the task of teaching a computer-based tutee to ask relevant questions about the story—especially questions about what needs to be clarified to understand more deeply. Research on reciprocal teaching (e.g., Palincsar & Brown, 1984) and intentional learning (e.g., Bereiter & Scardamalia, 1991) provides important guidelines for this work.

We also want to help children engage in"what-if" thinking about stories; for example, what if Ms. Emma had given Angel a doll for her birthday rather than a book? Children can use "what-if" thinking to generate their own versions of the story, or they can teach this information to a tutee.

Ms. Emma also includes information relevant to the study of science and mathematics. One of its science themes is light and shadows; the light sources shown in the movie include Jerome's flashlight and the sun. There is also information about changes in shadows during the day as a function of changes in the sun's position relative to earth, and information about the importance of sunlight for other things such as plants.

In one of our new experimental settings for science exploration, a computer-based tutee asks children to help it learn about shadows. It begins by showing selected scenes from the movie, and asks the children to help it identify the scenes that do and do not contain shadows. Then it asks for help learning about the direction and size of shadows as a function of the light source's position. Teachers help the children by clicking on the responses necessary to interact with the tutee and help it learn properly. As the lesson progresses, the children help the tutee make a book that captures the essence of the science lessons it has learned.

Transfer and "Representational Literacy"

We emphasize that the ultimate goal of our MOST environments is not simply to help students learn new information by providing them with visual support when needed. Instead, the goal is to help students learn to create their own mental models from purely linguistic information and vice versa. We refer to the ability to translate from language to mental models and vice versa as representational literacy (e.g., Sharp, Bransford, Vye, Goldman, Kinzer, & Soraci, 1992).

The next step in our listening comprehension research with at-risk students is to begin to explore the processes involved in helping them transfer to verbally-conveyed stories and other sources of information that vary in their similarity to the Ms. Emma story and its science and mathematics extensions. As an example of an analogous story, imagine an inner story and outer story involving two new characters—Sally and Bill. In the outer story, Bill is afraid of the water and doesn't want to go to swimming lessons; in the inner story Sally conquers her fear of heights and is eventually able to climb a rope ladder to her friends' treehouse. Bill then uses the information from the book to solve his own problem. The story could also include analogous science information that can be explored by students—for example, information about the properties of sound rather than light. Other stories that we create will be less analogous to the Ms. Emma story but will include some type of problem to be solved.

A major goal of our research is to explore ways to facilitate transfer from *Ms. Emma* to purely verbal stories. Research on analogical transfer in young children, conducted by Brown and colleagues (e.g., Brown & Kane, 1988; Chen &

Daehler, 1989), provides useful guidelines. Part of our assessments will be to see how students teach a tutee about the similarity between the two stories. We also want to assess transfer from the scientific inquiry part of *Ms. Emma* to new instances of inquiry. Again, our ultimate goal is to help children learn to learn from linguistic information alone.

The major issue we explore involves how helping students develop particular types of mental representations of information and goals for learning affects transfer. For example, imagine asking students to teach a tutee who wants to learn how to summarize *Ms. Emma*. Our children are helped to do this by picking out events that are most important to the causal chain comprising the plot line. Causal linkages among events are an important component of mental models for stories (e.g., Trabasso & Sperry, 1985; Trabasso & van den Broek, 1985), and these linkages can be illustrated with the capabilities of the software. For example, children can explore an "event line," similar to a number line, that shows pictures from various scenes of the disc. By pressing on these pictures, children can review the entire scene or a portion of the scene. In addition to being linked temporally, event scenes are also linked causally, with events early in the story often being linked to events later in the story. Again, the flexibility of the software plays an important role in these activities, allowing children to either provide many of the linkages themselves or to discern the linkages.

In addition to exploring the effects of different types of external representations of experiences on subsequent transfer, we plan to study the effects of different goal orientations on subsequent learning. For example, Scardamalia and Bereiter (1991) noted that effective learners try to identify what they do *not* understand, rather than merely attempt to engage in "knowledge telling." We plan to give our at-risk students the task of working with verbal sources of information to create dynamic books that will help younger children understand successfully. This means that our students will have to monitor their own comprehension and decide when they need dynamic visual support for various ideas, when they need additional verbal support, and so forth. These experiences should have a positive effect on transfer by affecting the kinds of questions that children ask when new information is presented to them.

MOST ENVIRONMENTS AND READING

We noted in the beginning of this chapter that MOST environments are designed to help students learn to *read,* as well as learn to become effective at listening comprehension. Our work in this area is just beginning, but we want to provide an overview of our plans in the hope of generating discussion about problems we might avoid and paths we might pursue.

The Overall Approach

Overall, reading instruction in MOST environments takes place in the context of the Peabody Multimedia Literacy Program that is currently being used in adult literacy contexts. The program is based on the idea of using video-based macrocontexts which were discussed earlier. However, the program supports reading, rather than simply listening, comprehension. For example, one component of the program involves the use of written, rather than spoken, discrepancy passages. Students have to choose which of a set of written passages best describes information presented by the video-based macrocontext that they saw earlier. The need to choose among these passages helps ensure that students read for meaning rather than simply engage in "word calling." In addition, because the discrepancy passages are similar to one another, students get the advantages of repeated reading on fluency of decoding and word recognition. The discrepancy passages are written at different levels of readability, and hence are adapted to the children's particular skills.

The Peabody Multimedia Literacy Program also provides support for pronouncing words, including sounding them out, and for learning about unfamiliar vocabulary words that are used in the written passages. A voice-recognition device helps students become fluent at word recognition and helps them develop phonemic awareness which is explained in more detail later.

Consistent with our previous discussion of listening comprehension, MOST environments emphasize the value of books as especially efficient vehicles for communicating and transporting information. Because the computer in our MOST environments allows us to keep track of each child's reading vocabulary, it is relatively easy to help students create books that contain familiar (for them) vocabulary. They can then read these books to parents, peers, and other community members.

Decoding Skills

MOST environments emphasize phonics skills because research has shown that phonics skills are critically important tools used by good readers (Adams, 1990; McCutchen, Bell, France, & Perfetti, 1991; Perfetti, 1985, 1986; Perfetti & Bell, 1991; Perfetti, Beck, Bell, & Hughes, 1987; Perfetti & Hogaboam, 1975; Wagner, 1986). Unfortunately, the traditional curriculum has major flaws in the way it tries to teach these skills to at-risk students. First, it often teaches these skills with decontextualized "drill-and-kill" worksheets that fail to convey the usefulness of these skills. This practice can lead to low motivation for acquiring literacy, and to a dangerous deemphasis of comprehension skills.

A second flaw has also recently come to light in educational research. Traditional phonics approaches were structured with the assumption that children already possessed conscious, analytical awareness of the phonetic structure of oral language. Children were expected to transfer this knowledge to the decoding of written words. For example, children were required to extend sound-blending skills to letter sound blending. However, research highlights that children vary greatly in the degree to which they have developed phonemic awareness (Wagner & Torgesen, 1987; Yopp, 1988). Many children are unable to blend isolated sounds together or recognize similar sounds in different words. As a result, they find that trying to read in a traditional phonics program is a mysterious and frustrating task.

Recent research underscores the importance of understanding phonemic-awareness skills and developing training programs when children lack these skills (Wagner, Torgesen, & Rashotte, 1992). Although many phonemic-awareness skills probably have a reciprocal relationship with reading to some degree (Wagner, 1988), researchers have distinguished those phonemic skills that appear to be causally related to good reading from those that appear to result from reading practice. For example, coding sounds in working memory and blending sounds together are skills that seem to lead to good reading, whereas segmenting and deleting phonemes in words appears to follow from reading practice (Wagner, Balthazor, Hurley, Morgan, Rashotte, Shaner, Simmons, & Stage, 1987; Perfetti et al., 1987; Wagner & Torgesen, 1987; Yopp, 1992). This kind of research supports the potential for highly effective phonemic awareness instruction when the instruction concentrates on phonemic awareness skills that lead to good reading.

An important feature of MOST environments is that they embed decoding instruction in meaningful contexts and authentic tasks. Technology is used to provide instruction in letter sound correspondences through graphics and sound, as well as to scaffold phonemic-awareness instruction. As a result, children who have not yet learned letter sound correspondences can effectively practice phonemic-awareness skills, like blending and storing phonemic codes that are important for reading in memory. Previous research has emphasized that training in phonemic-awareness skills is not effective if children work only with sounds. However, it is effective when these skills are made visually concrete through the conjunction of letters and sounds (Bradley & Bryant, 1985). Similarly, recent cognitive views of phonemic awareness stress that phonemic-processing systems and orthographic-processing systems are mutually strengthening (Dreyer, 1992). The visual and sound capabilities of computers make them particularly well suited for coordinating oral and visual representation, and for supporting training in phonemic-awareness skills, like blending, without requiring children to have already learned individual letter sounds. Our concept of *representational literacy* in these tasks relates to the use of graphics and sound support in such a way that children learn the phonemic structure of spoken language using both sound and visually concrete representations (Bradley & Bryant, 1985). At the same time, children learn the correspondence between written letters and phonemic sounds. As a result, children should become highly flexible in translating between visual and oral codes for words in meaningful texts.

ADDITIONAL ASPECTS OF MOST ENVIRONMENTS

MOST environments are also designed with an eye toward two additional components of instructional programs that greatly affect their efficacy: professional development and links to the home and community. Our plans for both of these aspects of MOST design are discussed next.

Professional Development

Professional development has been identified as the "missing link" in successful educational reform (e.g., DeFord, Lyons, & Pinnell, 1991). Many teachers are not prepared to work with diverse groups of students—especially those students who are least ready for school. Without adequate preparation for and attention to effective professional development, implementation projects tend to remain one-shot ventures that are not replicated on a wide scale.

MOST environments employ the same technology used in the classroom with students for professional development. For example, professional development begins by asking the teachers to engage in the same types of activities that the students will engage in (see Cognition and Technology Group at Vanderbilt, in press-c). It is supplemented by the use of video case examples that allow teachers to directly see a wide range of approaches to activities that different children may engage in, plus a range of ways that teachers have worked within the context of MOST environments to interact with other teachers. In addition, video-based cases are used to highlight children's changes in literacy development that take place over time. A number of our colleagues at Vanderbilt are using video-based cases for professional development (e.g., Goldman, Barron, & Witherspoon, 1991; Michael, Klee, Bransford, & Warren, 1993; Randolph & Evertson, 1992; Risko & Kinzer, 1993), and data indicate that these programs can be highly effective. Data also suggest that the opportunity to see video-based evidence of students' changes over time is much more powerful for influencing teachers' beliefs about students' potential than are data presented in an oral or written form (e.g., Vye, Burns, Delclos, & Bransford, 1987).

Continuing support for working in MOST environments could be provided through two-way video-conferencing, where experts can "see" problems that teachers experience with the technology or instruction, and teachers can receive immediate feedback on the best solutions. This technology is cost-effective and includes adding a "board" to the computer which is already used in MOST environments.

Effective Connections to Homes and Other Aspects of the Community

Recent research underscores that students' capabilities and motivation to learn are shaped by many influences. These include their families, teachers, school climates, community organizations, community values, and community expectations—each of which provides incentives and opportunities for further education and employment (e.g., Comer, 1980; Heath, 1983; Nettles, 1991; Shields, 1991). Children's home environments are particularly important. Although schools can compensate for some deficiencies in children's home environments, home influences still exert a significant impact on children's literacy development (Snow, Barnes, Chandler, Goodman, & Hemphill, 1991). Kaiser (personal communication, January 15, 1992) noted that a particularly important aspect of the degree to which parents learn to interact with their children—in ways that promote literacy—is the parents' mental models of what their children are capable of learning, and the importance of literacy for success in the everyday world.

Our MOST environments use technology to help students make connections among school, home, and community. First, our macrocontexts model the importance of literacy in many environments that children encounter outside the classroom (recall the earlier description of *Ms. Emma*). Data indicate that experiences such as these increase the probability that students spontaneously access information about school-related experiences when they are outside of school (e.g., Bransford, Sherwood, Vye, & Rieser 1986; Cognition and Technology Group at Vanderbilt, 1992b).

The availability of video-based macrocontexts also provides a structure that allows parents and children to share ideas that are taking place in the classroom. Because MOST environments are video-based, videotape versions can be shared with parents at home. Several studies have found that the provision of shared video-based contexts greatly increases the quality of the conversations between parents and children about important issues, especially when some instruction is provided to parents about how the macrocontexts can be used (e.g., Cognition and Technology Group at Vanderbilt, 1992b; Pichert & Kinzer, 1992).

The emphasis in MOST environments on student-produced books provides an additional means for seeding connections among home, family, and community. With technology, we can help children create interesting books composed of vocabulary that they already know; hence, they can read these books to parents, peers, siblings, and other community members. Because these books can also be linked to our macrocontexts, a context is provided that supports extended conversation about a number of events.

SUMMARY, CONCLUSIONS, AND NEXT STEPS

This chapter's goal was to discuss the idea of creating MOST environments that are useful for all children, but especially for those who are at risk of school failure. Our chapter was organized into four sections:

1. A discussion of the growing need to help students who are at risk of school failure, and of problems with traditional approaches to working with such children.

2. An examination of the argument that MOST environments that include dynamic visual support for comprehension can be much better for accelerating linguistic and conceptual development than are typical school environments, which are primarily language based.

3. An examination of our plans to create MOST environments that are more effective than traditional environments for helping students learn to read.

4. An overview of some additional design features of our MOST environments that seem crucial for success.

Most of our discussion focused on the first two areas because that is where we have completed the most research. We discussed plans for the other areas in the hopes of encouraging discussion about problems we might avoid and directions we might take. Our hope is that MOST environments will help all children—especially those who are at risk of school failure—to develop fundamental decoding skills while practicing high-level skills that are definitive of literate persons. With technology as a scaffolding tool, MOST environments provide the following features:

1. Flexible technology: Software that can be tailored to provide support for children with a wide range of abilities, and to elicit unique contributions from each student;

2. Authentic tasks: Children use literacy to teach, learn, and create products for effective communication;

3. Representational literacy: Through the use of videos and computers, children learn to flexibly communicate ideas using the multiple representations of spoken words, pictures, and print;

4. Mental model building: With support from technology, children practice deep comprehension and high-level verbal production;

5. Contextualized development of phonemic awareness: Children learn to blend sounds and letters in meaningful contexts;

6. Content-based narrative and expository texts: Children practice literacy skills while building a base of useful, general world knowledge;

7. Professional development programs that include training with video cases and ongoing support through video conferencing; and

8. Technology-based connections to homes and communities: Children's homes, families, and communities are linked with the children's learning through shared video macrocontexts, student-produced books, presenta-

tions to parents and community members, telephone connections, and two-way video conferencing.

REFERENCES

Adams, M. J. (1990). *Beginning to read: Thinking and learning about print.* Cambridge, MA: MIT Press.

Allington, R. L. (1983). The reading instruction provided readers of differing reading abilities. *The Elementary School Journal, 83,* 548–559.

Allington, R. L., & McGill-Frazen, A. (1989). School response to reading failure. *The Elementary School Journal, 89,* 529–542.

Anderson, R. C., Hiebert, E. H., Scott, J. A., & Wilkinson, I. A. G., with contributions from members of the Commission on Reading, the National Academy of Education, The National Institute of Education, & The Center for the Study of Reading. (1985). *Becoming a nation of readers: The report of the Commission on Reading.* Washington, DC: The National Institute of Education.

Anderson, R. C., Osborn, J., & Tierney, R. (Eds.). (1984). *Learning to read in American schools: Basal readers and content texts.* Hillsdale, NJ: Lawrence Erlbaum Associates.

Bauch, P. A. (1992, April). *Toward an ecological perspective on school choice.* Paper presented at the annual meeting of the American Educational Research Association, San Francisco, CA.

Bereiter, C., & Scardamalia, M. (1991). Higher levels of agency for children in knowledge building: A challenge for the design of new knowledge media. *Journal of the Learning Sciences, 1,* 37–68.

Berlin, D. F. (1991). A bibliography of integrated science and mathematics teaching and learning literature. *School Science and Mathematics Association Topics for Teachers Series Number 6.* Columbus, OH.

Bradley, L., & Bryant, P. (1985). *Rhyme and reason in reading and spelling.* Ann Arbor: University of Michigan Press.

Bransford, J. D. (1979). *Human cognition: Learning, understanding, and remembering.* Belmont, CA: Wadsworth.

Bransford, J. D. (1984). Schema activation versus schema acquisition. In R. C. Anderson, J. Osborn, & R. Tierney (Eds.), *Learning to read in American schools: Basal readers and content texts* (pp. 259–272). Hillsdale, NJ: Lawrence Erlbaum Associates.

Bransford, J. D. (1992). *Improving cognitive strategy instruction: Pitfalls and promises.* Discussion for the American Educational Research Association annual meeting, San Francisco, CA.

Bransford, J. D., Delclos, V. R., Vye, N. J., Burns, M. S., & Hasselbring, T. S. (1987). State of the art and future directions. In C. S. Lidz (Ed.), *Dynamic assessment: An interactional approach to evaluating learning potential* (pp. 479–496). New York: The Guilford Press.

Bransford, J. D., Goin, L. I., Hasselbring, T. S., Kinzer, C. K., Sherwood, R. D., & Williams, S. M. (1988). Learning with technology: Theoretical and empirical perspectives. *Peabody Journal of Education, 64*(1), 5–26.

Bransford, J. D., Goldman, S. R., & Vye, N. J. (1991). Making a difference in people's abilities to think: Reflections on a decade of work and some hopes for the future. In L. Okagaki & R. J. Sternberg (Eds.), *Directors of development: Influences on children* (pp. 147–180). Hillsdale, NJ: Lawrence Erlbaum Associates.

Bransford, J. D., & Heldmeyer, K. (1983). Learning from children learning. In J. Bisanz, G. Bisanz, & R. Kail (Eds.), *Learning in children: Progress in cognitive development research* (pp. 171–190). New York: Springer-Verlag.

Bransford, J. D., & Johnson, M. K. (1972). Contextual prerequisites for understanding: Some investigations of comprehension and recall. *Journal of Verbal Learning and Verbal Behavior, 11,* 717–726.

Bransford, J. D., & Johnson, M. K. (1973). Considerations of some problems comprehension. In W. Chase (Ed.), *Visual information processing* (pp. 383–438). New York: Academic Press.

Bransford, J., Kinzer C., Risko, V., Rowe, D., & Vye, N. (1989). Designing invitations to thinking: Some initial thoughts. Cognitive and social perspectives for literacy research and instruction. In S. McCormick, J. Zutrell, P. Scharer, & P. O'Keefe (Eds.), *Cognitive and social perspectives for literacy research and instruction* (pp. 35–54). Chicago, IL: National Reading Conference.

Bransford, J. D., Kinzer, C., & Sherwood, R. (1986). Computers and education. In J. D. Bransford, C. Kinzer, & R. Sherwood (Eds.), *Computer strategies for education* (pp. 3–13). Columbus, OH: Merrill.

Bransford, J. D., Sherwood, R. S., Vye, N. J., & Rieser, J. (1986). Teaching thinking and problem solving: Research foundations. *American Psychologist, 41,* 1078–1089.

Bransford, J. D., & Stein, B. S. (1984). *The IDEAL problem solver.* New York: Freeman.

Bransford, J. D., & Vye, N. J. (1989). A perspective on cognitive research and its implications for instruction. In L. Resnick & L. E. Klopfer (Eds.), *Toward the thinking curriculum: Current cognitive research* (pp. 173–205). Alexandria, VA: ASCD.

Bransford, J. D., Vye, N., Kinzer, C., Risko, V. (1990). Teaching thinking and content knowledge: Toward an integrated approach. In B. F. Jones & L. Idol (Eds.), *Dimensions of thinking and cognitive instruction: Implications for educational reform* (Vol. 1, pp. 381–413). Hillsdale, NJ: Lawrence Erlbaum Associates.

Brown, A. L., & Kane, M. J. (1988). Preschool children can learn to transfer: Learning to learn and learning from example. *Cognitive Psychology, 20,* 493–523.

Bryant, D., Tversky, B., & Franklin, N. (in press). Internal and external spatial frameworks for representing described scenes. *Journal of Memory and Language.*

Calfee, R. (1991). What schools can do to improve literacy instruction. In B. Means, C. Chelemer, & M. S. Knapp (Eds.), *Teaching advanced skills to at-risk students* (pp. 176–203). San Francisco: Jossey-Bass.

Case, R. (1991). *The mind's staircase: Exploring the conceptual underpinnings of children's thought and knowledge.* Hillsdale, NJ: Lawrence Erlbaum Associates.

Chapman, R. S. (1978). Comprehension strategies in children. In J. Kavanaugh & W. Strange (Eds.), *Speech and language in the laboratory, school, and clinic* (pp. 308–329). Cambridge, MA: MIT Press.

Chen, Z., & Daehler, M. W. (1989). Positive and negative transfer in analogical problem solving by 6-year-old children. *Cognitive Development, 4,* 327–344.

Cognition and Technology Group at Vanderbilt. (1990). Anchored instruction and its relationship to situated cognition. *Educational Researcher, 19*(6), 2–10.

Cognition and Technology Group at Vanderbilt. (1991). Technology and the design of generative learning environments. *Educational Technology, 31,* 34–40.

Cognition and Technology Group at Vanderbilt. (1992a). The Jasper experiment: An exploration of issues in learning and instructional design. *Educational Technology Research and Development, 40,* 65–80.

Cognition and Technology Group at Vanderbilt. (1992b). The Jasper series: A generative approach to mathematical thinking. In K. Sheingold, L. G. Roberts, & S. M. Malcolm (Eds.), *This Year in Science Series 1991: Technology for teaching and learning* (pp. 108–140). Washington, DC: American Association for the Advancement of Science.

Cognition and Technology Group at Vanderbilt. (1993). Toward integrated curricula: Possibilities from anchored instruction. In M. Rabinowitz (Ed.), *Cognitive science foundations of instruction* (pp. 33–55). Hillsdale, NJ: Lawrence Erlbaum Associates.

Cognition and Technology Group at Vanderbilt. (in press-a). Integrated media: Toward a theoretical framework for utilizing their potential. *Journal of Special Educational Technology.*

Cognition and Technology Group at Vanderbilt. (in press-b). The Jasper series as an example of anchored instruction: Theory, program description and assessment data. In R. Lehrer (Ed.), *Educational psychologist*.

Cognition and Technology Group at Vanderbilt. (in press-c). The Jasper series: A design experiment in complex, mathematical problem solving. In J. Hawkins & A. Collins (Eds.), *Design experiments: Integrating technologies into schools*. New York: Cambridge University Press.

Collins, A., Hawkins, J., & Carver, S. M. (1991). A cognitive apprenticeship for disadvantaged students. In B. Means, C. Chelemer, & M. S. Knapp (Eds.), *Teaching advanced skills to at-risk students* (pp. 216–243). San Francisco: Jossey-Bass.

Collins, C. (1992). *Facilitating teacher change: How teachers learn to teach in ways that they were not taught themselves*. Paper presented at the annual meeting of the American Educational Research Association, San Francisco, CA.

Comer, J. P. (1980). *School power: Implication of an intervention project*. New York: The Free Press.

Compu-Teach. (1991). *Once Upon a Time* (Version 1.1.3). New Haven, CT: Author.

Curtis, M. E. (1980). Development of components of reading skill. *Journal of Educational Psychology, 72*, 656–669.

DeFord, D. (1990). *Literacy learning in at-risk graders*. Paper presented at 37th Annual Conference on Literacy, University of Pittsburgh, Pittsburgh, PA.

DeFord, D. E., Lyons, C. A., & Pinnell, G. S. (Eds.). (1991). *Bridges to literacy: Learning from reading recovery*. Portsmouth, NH: Heineman.

Discis Knowledge Research. (1990). *Discis books (Vol 1)*. Toronto, Ontario: Author.

Dreyer, L. G. (1992). *Why phonological awareness is related to reading: A preliminary investigation*. Paper presented at the annual meeting of the American Educational Research Association, San Francisco, CA.

Duffy, G. G. (1992). *Learning from the study of practice: Where we must go with strategy instruction*. Paper presented at the annual meeting of the American Educational Research Association, San Francisco, CA.

Durkin, D. (1978–1979). What classroom observations reveal about reading comprehension instruction. *Reading Research Quarterly, 14*(4), 481–533.

Elder, W. D., & Hobbs (1990). From reform to restructuring: New opportunities for rural schools. *Rural Sociologist, 10*, 10–12.

Feuerstein, R., Rand, Y., & Hoffman, M. (1979). *The dynamic assessment of retarded performers: The learning potential assessment device, theory, instruments, and techniques*. Baltimore, MD: University Park Press.

Gernsbacher, M. A. (1990). *Language comprehension as structure building*. Hillsdale, NJ: Lawrence Erlbaum Associates.

Gibbons, J., Anderson, D. R., Smith, R., Field, D. E., & Fischer, C. (1986). Young children's recall and reconstruction of audio and audiovisual narratives. *Child Development, 57*, 1014–1023.

Glenberg, A. M., & Langston, W. E. (in press). Comprehension of illustrated text: Pictures help to build mental models. *Journal of Memory & Language*.

Glenberg, A. M., Meyer, M., & Lindem, K. (1987). Mental models contribute to foregrounding during text comprehension. *Journal of Memory and Language, 26*, 69–83.

Goldman, E., Barron, L., & Witherspoon, M. L. (1991). Hypermedia cases in teacher education: A context for understanding research on the teaching and learning of mathematics. *Action in Teacher Education, 13*(1), 28–36.

Goldman, E. S., Barron, L. C., & Witherspoon, M. L. (1992). *Integrated media activities for mathematics teacher education: Design and implementation issues*. Paper presented at the annual meeting of the American Educational Research Association, San Francisco, CA.

Goldman, S. R., & Pellegrino, J. W. (1986). Microcomputer: Effective drill and practice. *Academic Therapy, 22*(2), 133–140.

Goldman, S. R. , & Pellegrino, J. W. (1987). Information processing and educational microcomputer technology: Where do we go from here? *Journal of Learning Disabilities, 20*(3), 144–154.

Goldman, S. R., & Saul, E. U. (1990). Flexibility in text processing: A strategy competition model. *Learning and Individual Differences, 2,* 181–219.

Good, T. L., Slavings, R. L., & Mason, D. A. (1988). Learning to ask questions: Grade and school effects. *Teaching and Teacher Education, 4,* 363–378.

Griffin, S., Case, R., & Capodilupo, A. (in press). Rightstart: A program designed to improve children's performance in early mathematics by developing the central conceptual structure on which this performance depends. In S. Struass (Ed.), *Development and learning environments.* Norwood, NJ: Ablex.

Hayes, D. S., Kelly, S. B., & Mandel, M. (1986). Media differences in children's story synopses: Radio and television contrasted. *Journal of Educational Psychology, 78,* 341–346.

Healy, J. M. (1990). *Endangered minds: Why our children don't think.* New York: Simon and Schuster.

Heath, S. B., (1982). What no bedtime story means: Narrative skills at home and school. *Language in Society, 11,* 49–76.

Heath, S. B. (1983). *Ways with words.* Cambridge, England: Cambridge University Press.

Hull, G. A. (1989). Research on writing: Building a cognitive and social understanding of composing. In L. B. Resnick & L. E. Klopfer (Eds.), *Toward the thinking curriculum: Current cognitive research* (pp. 104–128). Alexandria, VA: ASCD.

Johnson, R. (1987). *The ability to retell a story: Effects of adult mediation in a videodisc context on children's story recall and comprehension.* Unpublished doctoral dissertation, Vanderbilt University, Nashville, TN.

Johnson-Laird, P. N. (1983). *Mental models.* Cambridge, MA: Harvard University Press.

Juel C. (1988). Learning to read and write: A longitudinal study of fifty-four children from first through fourth grades. *Journal of Educational Psychology, 80,* 437–447.

Juel, C. (1991, March). *Longitudinal research on learning to read and write with regular and atrisk students.* Paper presented at the Maryland Conference on Literacy for the 90's: Perspectives on Theory, Research and Practice, College Park, MD.

Juel, C. (1992). Longitudinal research on learning to read and write with at-risk students. In M.J. Dreher and W. H. Slater (Eds.), *Elementary school literacy: Critical issues* (pp. 73–99). Norwood, MA: Christopher-Gordon Publishers.

Kamil, M. (1991). *A proposal for the national reading research center.* Manuscript submitted for Publication.

Karweit, N. (1989) Effective kindergarten programs and practices for students at risk. In R. E. Slavin, N. L. Karweit, & N. A. Madden, (Eds.), *Effective programs for students at risk* (pp. 103–141) Boston: Allyn and Bacon.

Kirsch, I., & Jungblut, A. (1986). *Literacy: Profiles of America's young adults* (ETS Rep. No. 16-Pl-02). National Assessment of Educational Progress.

Knapp, M. S., & Turnbull, B. J. (1990). *Better schooling for the children of poverty: Alternatives to conventional wisdom.* (Vol. 1.). Washington, DC: U. S. Department of Education, Office of Planning, Budget and Evaluation.

Kozma, R. B. (1991). Learning with media. *Review of Educational Research, 61,* 179–211.

Langer, J., & Applebee, A. (1987). *How writing shapes thinking: A study of teaching and learning* (Research Rep. No. 22). Urbana, IL: National Council of Teachers of English.

Levin, J. R., Anglin, G. J., & Carney, R. N. (1987). On empirically validating functions of pictures in prose. In D. M. Willows & H. A. Houghton (Eds.), *The psychology of illustration: Vol. 1. Basic Research* (pp. 51–85). New York: Springer-Verlag.

Lidz, C. S. (1987). *Dynamic assessment: An interactional approach to evaluating learning potential.* New York: Guilford Press.

MacNamara, J. (1972). Cognitive basis of language learning in infants. *Psychological Review, 79,* 1–13.

Malone, T. W., & Lepper, M. R. (1985). Making learning fun: A taxonomy of intrinsic motivations for learning. In R. Snow & M. Farr (Eds.), *Aptitude, learning, and instruction: Cognitive and affective process analyses* (Vol. 3, pp. 223–253). Hillsdale, NJ: Lawrence Erlbaum Associates.

McCutchen, D., Bell, L. C., France, I. M., & Perfetti, C. A. (1991). Phoneme-specific interference in reading: The tongue-twister effect revisited. *Reading Research Quarterly, 26*(1), 87–103.

McGee, L. M., & Richgels, D. J. (1990). *Literacy's beginnings: Supporting young readers and writers.* Boston: Allyn and Bacon.

McGinley, W., & Kamberelis, G. (1992). *Personal, social, and political functions of children's reading and writing.* Paper presented at the annual meeting of the American Educational Research Association, San Francisco, CA.

McKeough, A. (1991a). A neo-structural analysis of children's narrative and its development. In R. Case (Ed.), *The mind's staircase: Exploring the conceptual underpinnings of children's thought and knowledge.* Hillsdale, NJ: Lawrence Erlbaum Associates.

McKeough, A. (1991b). Testing for the presence of a central social structure: Use of the transfer paradigm. In R. Case (Ed.), *The mind's staircase: Exploring the conceptual underpinnings of children's thought and knowledge* (pp. 207–255). Hillsdale, NJ: Lawrence Erlbaum Associates.

McNamara, T. P., Miller, D. L., & Bransford, J. D. (1991). Mental models and reading comprehension. In R. Barr, M. L. Kamil, P. B. Mosenthal, & P. D. Pearson (Eds.), *Handbook of reading research* (Vol. 2, pp. 490–511). New York: Longman.

Means, B., Chelemer, C., & Knapp, M. S. (Eds.). (1991). *Teaching advanced skills to at-risk students.* San Francisco: Jossey-Bass.

Means, B., & Knapp, M. S. (1991). Introduction: Rethinking teaching for disadvantaged students. In B. Means, C. Chelemer, & M. S. Knapp (Eds.), *Teaching advanced skills to at-risk students* (pp. 1–26). San Francisco: Jossey-Bass.

Meringoff, L. K. (1980). Influence of the medium on children's story apprehension. *Journal of Educational Psychology, 72,* 240–249.

Michael, A. L., Klee, T., Bransford, J. D., & Warren, S. (1993). The transition from theory to therapy: Test of two instructional methods. *Applied Cognitive Psychology, 7,* 139–154.

National Assessment of Educational Progress. (1988). *Who reads best?* Princeton, NJ: Educational Testing Service.

National Commission on Excellence in Education. (1983). *A nation at risk: The imperative for educational reform.* Washington, DC: U.S. Government Printing Office.

Nettles, S. M. (1991). Community involvement and disadvantaged students: A review. *Review of Education Research, 61*(3), 379–406.

Nix, D., & Spiro, R. (Eds.). (1990). *Cognition, education, and multi-media: Exploring ideas in high technology.* Hillsdale, NJ: Lawrence Erlbaum Associates.

Oakes, J. (1986). Tracking, inequality, and the rhetoric of school reform: Why schools don't change. *Journal of Education, 168,* 61–80.

Palincsar, A. S., & Brown, A. L. (1984). Reciprocal teaching of comprehension-fostering and comprehension monitoring activities. *Cognition and Instruction, 1,* 117–175.

Palincsar, A. S., & Brown, A. L. (1989). Instruction for self-regulated reading. In L. B. Resnick & L. E. Klopfer (Eds.), *Toward the thinking curriculum: Current cognitive research* (pp. 19–39). Alexandria, VA: ASCD.

Palincsar, A. S. & Klenk, L. J. (1991). Dialogues promoting reading comprehension. In B. Means, C. Chelemer & M. S. Knapp (Eds.), *Teaching advanced skills to at-risk students* (pp. 112–131). San Francisco: Jossey-Bass.

Pallas, A., Natriello, G., & McDill, E. L. (1989). The changing nature of the disadvantaged population: Current dimensions and future trends. *Educational Researcher, 18,* 16–22.

Perfetti, C. A. (1985). *Reading ability.* New York: Oxford University Press.

Perfetti, C. A. (1986). Continuities in reading acquisition, reading skill, and reading disability. *Remedial and Special Education, 7,* 11–21.

Perfetti, C. A., Beck, I., Bell, L. C., & Hughes, C. (1987). Phonemic knowledge and learning to read are reciprocal: A longitudinal study of first grade children. Special Issue. Children's reading and the development of phonological awareness. *Merrill Palmer Quarterly, 33*, 283–319.

Perfetti, C. A., & Bell, L. (1991). Phonemic activation during the first 40 ms of word identification: Evidence from backward masking and priming. *Journal of Memory and Language, 30*, 473–485.

Perfetti, C. A., & Hogaboam, T. W. (1975). The relationship between single word decoding and reading comprehension skill. *Journal of Educational Psychology, 67*, 461–469.

Phelps, L. W. (1988). *Composition as a human science*. London: Oxford University Press.

Pichert, J. W., & Kinzer, C. K. (1992, April). *Embedded data in diabetes patient education*. Paper presented at the annual meeting of the American Educational Research Association, San Francisco, CA.

Poplin, M. S. (1988). The reductionist fallacy in learning disabilities: Replicating the past by reducing the present. *Journal of Learning Disabilities, 21*(7), 389–400.

Pressley, M., Cariglia-Bull, T., Deane, S., & Schneider, W. (1987). Short-term memory, verbal competence, and age as predictors of imagery instructional effectiveness. *Journal of Experimental Child Psychology, 43*, 194–211.

Pressley, M., El-Dinary, P. B., & Marks, M. (1992). *Rites of passage: The perils of becoming a strategies instruction teacher*. Paper presented at the annual meeting of the American Educational Research Association, San Francisco, CA.

Randolph, C. H., & Evertson, C. M. (1992). *Enhancing problem solving in preservice teachers' approaches to classroom management using video technology*. Paper presented at the annual meeting of the American Educational Research Association, San Francisco, CA.

Resnick, L. (1987). *Education and learning to think*. Washington, DC: National Academy Press.

Resnick, L. B., Bill, V. L., Lesgold, S. B., & Leer, M. N. (1991). Thinking in arithmetic class. In B. Means, C. Chelemer, & M. S. Knapp (Eds.), *Teaching advanced skills to at-risk students* (pp. 27–53). San Francisco: Jossey-Bass Publishers.

Resnick, L. B., & Klopfer, L. E. (Eds.). (1989). *Toward the thinking curriculum: Current cognitive research*. Alexandria, VA: ASCD.

Risko, V. J. (1992). *Creating videodisc problem-solving environments to manage the complexity of literary instruction*. Paper presented at the annual meeting of the American Educational Research Association, San Francisco, CA.

Risko, V. J., & Kinzer, C. K. (1993, October). *Using video cases*. Invited paper presentation for Using Cases to Prepare Teachers and Administrators: A Working Conference on Case-based Teaching. Lake Tahoe, NV.

Salomon, G. (1979). *Interaction of media, cognition, and learning*. San Francisco: Jossey-Bass.

Salomon, G. (1983). The differential investment of mental effort in learning from different sources. *Educational Psychologist, 18*, 42–50.

Salomon, G. (1984). Television is "easy" and print is "tough": The differential investment of mental effort in learning as a function of perceptions and attributions. *Journal of Educational Psychology, 76*, 658–674.

Samuels, S. J. (1987). Factors that influence listening and reading comprehension. In R. Horowitz & S. J. Samuels (Eds.), *Comprehending oral and written language* (pp. 295–325). New York: Academic Press.

Sanford, A. J., & Garrod, S. C. (1981). *Understanding written language*. New York: Wiley.

Scarcella, R. (1990). *Teaching language minority students in the multicultural classroom*. Englewood Cliffs, NJ: Prentice-Hall.

Scardamalia, M., & Bereiter, C. (1991). Higher levels of agency for children in knowledge building: A challenge for the design of new knowledge media. *Journal of the Learning Sciences, 1*, 37–68.

Sharp, D., Bransford, J. D., Vye, N. J., Goldman, S. R., Kinzer, C., & Soraci, S., Jr. (1992). Literacy in an age of integrated media. In M. J. Dreher and W. Slater (Eds.), *Elementary school literacy: Critical issues* (pp. 183–210). Norwood, MA: Christopher-Gordon Publishers.

Sherwood, R., Kinzer, C., Hasselbring, T., & Bransford, J. (1987). Macro-Contexts for learning: Initial findings and issues. *Journal of Applied Cognition, 1,* 93–108.

Shields, P. M. (1991). School and community influences on effective academic instruction. In M. S. Knapp & P. M. Shields (Eds.), *Better schooling for the children of poverty: Alternatives to conventional wisdom* (pp. 313–328). Berkeley, CA: McCutchan Publication.

Slavin, R. E. (1991). Reading effects of IBM's "Writing to read" program: A review of evaluations. *Educational Evaluation and Policy Analysis, 13*(1), 1–11.

Snow, C. E., Barnes, W. S., Chandler, J., Goodman, I. F., & Hemphill, L. (1991). *Unfulfilled expectations: Home and school influences on literacy.* Cambridge, MA: Harvard University Press.

Tierney, R. J. (1986). Functionality of written literacy experiences. In M. R. Sampson (Ed.), *The pursuit of literacy: Early reading and writing* (pp. 108–115). Dubuque, IA: Kendall/Hunt.

Trabasso, T., & Sperry, L. L. (1985). Causal relatedness and importance of story events. *Journal of Memory and Language, 24,* 595–611.

Trabasso, T., & van den Broek, P. (1985). Causal thinking and the representation of narrative events. *Journal of Memory and Language, 24,* 612–630.

United States Department of Education. (1988–1989). Cited in *The Columbus Dispatch,* September 29, 1991.

van Dijk, T. A., & Kintsch, W. (1983). *Strategies of discourse comprehension.* New York: Academic Press.

Vellutino, F. R. (1979). *Dyslexia: Theory and research.* Cambridge, MA: MIT Press.

Vye, N.J., Burns, M.S., Delclos, V.R., & Bransford, J.D. (1987). Dynamic assessment of intellectually handicapped children. In C.S. Lidz (Ed.), *Dynamic assessment: An interactional approach to evaluating learning potential* (pp. 327–359). New York: Guilford.

Wagner, R. K. (1986). Phonological processing abilities and reading: Implications for disabled readers. *Journal of Learning Disabilities, 19,* 623–630.

Wagner, R. K. (1988). Causal relations between the development of phonological processing abilities and the acquisition of reading skills: A meta-analysis. *Merrill Palmer Quarterly, 34,* 261–279.

Wagner, R. K., Balthazor, M., Hurley, S., Morgan, S., Rashotte, C., Shaner, R., Simmons, K., & Stage, S. (1987). The nature of prereaders' phonological processing abilities. *Cognitive Development, 2,* 355–373.

Wagner, R. K., & Torgesen, J. K. (1987). The nature of phonological processing and its causal role in the acquisition of reading skills. *Psychological Bulletin, 101,* 192–212.

Wagner, R. K., Torgesen, J. K., & Rashotte, C. A. (1992). *Individual and developmental differences in reading-related phonological processing abilities.* Paper presented at the annual meeting of the American Educational Research Association, San Francisco, CA.

Wong, B. Y. L. (1985). Metacognition and learning disabilities. In D. L. Forrest-Pressley, G. E. MacKinnon, & T. G. Waller (Eds.), *Metacognition, cognition and human performance* (Vol. 2, pp. 137–180). New York: Academic Press.

Yopp, H. K. (1988). The validity and reliability of phonemic awareness tests. *Reading Research Quarterly, 23,* 159–176.

Yopp, H. K. (1992, April). *A longitudinal study of the relationship between phonemic awareness and achievement in reading and spelling.* Paper presented at the annual meeting of the American Educational Research Association, San Francisco, CA.

13 Anchoring Science Instruction in Multimedia Learning Environments

Susan R. Goldman
Anthony J. Petrosino
Robert D. Sherwood
Steve Garrison
Daniel Hickey
John D. Bransford
James W. Pellegrino
Learning Technology Center, Vanderbilt University

Our group has been working within a framework that we call *Anchored Instruction* (Cognition and Technology Group at Vanderbilt, 1990). The anchored-instruction approach represents an attempt to help students become actively engaged in learning by situating or anchoring instruction in interesting and realistic problem-solving environments. These environments are designed to (a) invite the kinds of thinking that help students develop general skills and attitudes that contribute to effective problem solving, and (b) acquire specific concepts and principles that allow them to think effectively about particular domains (e.g., Bransford, Vye, Kinzer & Risko, 1990; Bransford, Sherwood, Vye & Rieser, 1986; Cognition and Technology Group at Vanderbilt, 1990). In this chapter, we specifically address the issue of what an anchored approach to science instruction might mean, and discuss an example project: our series *Scientists-in-Action*. The overall goal of the project is to use videodisc and computer technology to re-create the kinds of experiences that would be available to students if they apprenticed themselves to real scientists working on problems important to us all (Cognition and Technology Group at Vanderbilt, 1992a).

Much of our rationale for the *Scientists-in-Action* series rests on the assumption that students need to have experiences that enable them to appreciate what it is like to be a "real" scientist. Students need to experience the actual "doing" of science, not just the finished, polished product of that process. One way to accomplish this is to have students conduct experiments in science classes. Such activities address only a small aspect of being a real scientist, in that students do not see how science affects people, or the societal and health needs that are related to the scientific activity. Furthermore, they see neither the genesis of the problems that scientists investigate, nor the fact that scientists frequently collaborate to achieve their goals.

An alternative method for facilitating students' access to scientific inquiry would be to have them work with actual scientists who are working on real issues. But these types of opportunities are difficult to provide to large numbers of students, especially those in middle school or high school. The *Scientists-in-Action* series is part of our plan to use video technology to simulate a series of opportunities to work with professional scientists on a variety of issues. For example, the pilot episode that is discussed later, *The Overturned Tanker,* features a hydrologist and a chemist working with others to form a problem-solving team.

We hope to achieve several important student outcomes with the series. These outcomes are coincident with those published by the American Association for the Advancement of Science in *Science for All Americans* (Rutherford & Ahlgren, 1990). First, we want to help students see science (and mathematics) as important, vital, and integral to their everyday lives, and to have them pay attention to "scientists in action" in their own communities. We want to alter students' stereotypical conceptions of the "mad scientist," typically male, who works in total isolation from others. We also want to increase students' skills at solving problems that require an understanding of the relationships between data and theory—problems like those presented in our videos. Finally, we are particularly interested in increasing students' interest in science and engineering careers—especially for women and minorities. We believe that interest in science and engineering will be increased due to our choice of problems to be explored (ones of obvious importance) and our portrayal of methods of exploration (highly collaborative and collegial). In addition, we include powerful role models of both genders and from a variety of ethnic groups.

In this chapter, we first review the theoretical and empirical backgrounds of the anchored-instruction approach. We then discuss a set of design principles for creating environments that can be used to enhance thinking in many different domains, including science, mathematics, literacy, and social studies. We illustrate these principles by describing *The Overturned Tanker,* a prototype for our *Scientists-in-Action* series. We report two preliminary studies that explore the efficacy of our approach for altering students' conceptions of science, and for facilitating their acquisition of scientific concepts and thinking skills.

ANCHORING INSTRUCTION
IN MEANINGFUL CONTEXTS

In an article appearing in the *Educational Psychologist* (Cognition and Technology Group at Vanderbilt, 1992c), we proposed that a major goal of anchored instruction is to allow students and teachers to experience the kinds of problems and opportunities that experts in various areas encounter (Cognition and Technology Group at Vanderbilt, 1990, 1992b). Experts in an area have been immersed in phenomena and are familiar with how they have been thinking about these phenomena. When introduced to new theories, concepts, and principles that are relevant to their areas of interest, the experts can experience the changes in their own thinking that these ideas afford (e.g., Dewey, 1933; Hanson, 1970; Schwab, 1960). For novices, however, the introduction of concepts and theories often seems like the mere introduction of new facts or mechanical procedures to be memorized. Because the novices have not been immersed in the phenomena being investigated, they are unable to experience the effects of the new information on their own noticing and understanding.

The general idea of anchored instruction has a long history. Dewey discussed the advantages of theme-based learning. In the 1940s, Gragg (1940) argued for the advantages of case-based approaches to instruction (see Williams, 1992). One variation of case-based instruction is to use a variety of minicases that serve as microcontexts. Our contexts are usually complex and revisited from many perspectives over periods of weeks and months, hence we refer to them as *macrocontexts*. The purpose of these contexts is to serve as environments for cooperative learning and teacher-directed mediation (e.g., Feuerstein, Rand, Hoffman, & Miller, 1980; Vygotsky, 1978). Our contexts are meant to be explored and discussed, rather than simply read or watched.

Anchored-instruction environments also share some of the characteristics of inquiry environments, which have been suggested as a model, especially for science instruction, since Schwab (1960). They are similar in that anchored-instruction environments, as well as inquiry environments, do not propose to "directly" instruct students, but provide a situation where learning can take place, often including many types of inquiry activities.

EMPIRICAL WORK THAT ANCHORED SCIENCE INSTRUCTION IN THE CONTEXT OF INDIANA JONES' QUEST FOR THE GOLDEN IDOL

The empirical roots of this project lie in earlier research done with a variety of science concepts, including density (Sherwood, Kinzer, Bransford, & Franks, 1987). This earlier work involved the use of commercially available movies to create problem-solving environments that helped students understand the importance of science information. Students who learned the information in a problem-solving context (Indiana Jones' trip to the South American jungle in the film *Raiders of the Lost Ark*) were better able to remember and spontaneously use the information in new situations than were students who had learned the information with the intent to remember it. For example, in a transfer task, students were asked to imagine planning a journey to a desert area to search for relics in Pueblo caves. Students who had simply read facts to remember them tended to be quite general in their responses. In contrast, students who had acquired the information in the problem-solving condition were much more specific, and gave greater evidence of being aware of various sets of constraints that they would need to consider. For example, when discussing food, most of them focused on the importance of its nutritional contents. When discussing water, they emphasized the importance of calculating its weight.

Overall, students who received information in a problem-solving context were much more likely to remember what they read and to spontaneously use it as a basis for creating new sets of plans. Similar effects were found with seventh- and eighth-grade students on knowledge of why it might be useful to know these concepts and, to a lesser degree, on recall of science information (Sherwood, Kinzer, Hasselbring, & Bransford, 1987). These results suggest that an important goal for science materials would be to involve students in actual problem solving. These data, along with other data on the acquisition of science concepts from video-based materials (for discussion, see Cognition and Technology Group at Vanderbilt, 1992a), convince us of the potential for using video to create inquiry environments that can increase students' interest in science and facilitate their understanding of science concepts.

DESIGN PRINCIPLES FOR ANCHORED INSTRUCTION IN SCIENCE

We have developed a set of design principles for anchored instruction. We have used these, with slight modifications, in a variety of domains, including science, mathematics, and literacy. Descriptions of the general set of design principles appear in several previously published articles (Cognition and Technology Group at Vanderbilt, 1991, 1992b, 1993b,1994b; McLarty et al., 1990). In the present context, we provide a brief summary of them. They are instantiated in the architecture of the *Scientists-in-Action* series, described in the next section.

There are seven design principles that guide our work in a variety of domains including mathematics and literacy (see Cognition and Technology Group at Vanderbilt, chap. 14, this volume; Bransford et al, chap. 12, this volume). These design principles mutually influence one another and operate as a Gestalt, rather than a set of independent features of the materials. For example, the *narrative format,* the *generative design of the stories,* and the fact that the adventures include *embedded data* make it possible for students to learn to generate problem-solving goals, find relevant information, and engage in reasoned decision making. The *complexity of the problems* helps students deal with this important aspect of problem solving, and the *use of video* helps make the complexity manageable. The video format also makes it easier to embed the kinds of information that provide opportunities for *links across the curricula*. It is important for *pairs of episodes* to be developed to afford discussions about transfer of problem-solving skills.

Design of the *Scientists-in-Action* Series

The instantiation of the design principles in the *Scientists-in-Action* series reflected three modifications of those that guided our work in mathematics and literacy. These modifications were necessitated by differences in the kinds of problems that we deal with in our work in mathematics and literacy, as compared with our work in science.

First, challenges are posed several times during the course of the story, rather than at the end, as in the math and literacy anchors (Cognition and Technology Group at Vanderbilt, 1991, 1992a, 1992b, 1993, 1994b). These interruptions to deal with a problem enable students to be part of the problem solving, and to have multiple opportunities to work on the same problems that the scientists are working on in the video. When the video resumes, students can compare and contrast their solutions to what the scientists actually did. There is a trade-off in this design as contrasted with the design of the mathematics anchors: The modification made in the *Scientists-in-Action* series provides fewer opportunities for students to gain experience formulating solutions to complex, ill-defined problems. However, having multiple problem-solving opportunities within the same context affords the possibility for meaningful process learning during the course of solution.

A second modification in design principles is that much of the data needed to solve the problem occur in ancillary materials, rather than all of the data being embedded in the video—the design used in the mathematics problem-solving series. These ancillary materials are authentic, and teachers are encouraged to help students conduct all or some of the laboratory tests in the classroom. We incorporated ancillary materials because we wanted students to work with the kinds of source documents that scientists would routinely use in their activities. We also felt it was important for students to have the hands-on experiences associated with conducting their own tests. Providing the laboratory tests on video enables teachers and students to see how such tests are conducted, and to see the results of tests that would be too dangerous or expensive to conduct in individual classrooms. However, for tests that are feasible for teachers and students, the video provides a dynamic model of how to conduct them correctly and safely.

A third feature is that the video is seen from a first-person point of view. The first-person voice and the direct appeal to the students make them feel more a part of a team solving a problem than they might have if the story had been told in a third-person, narrative voice. Note that the third-person narrative voice has never been a problem in our mathematics and literacy anchors. Students seem to have little trouble identifying with the characters and their situations, perhaps because the adventures are based on people, places, and events generally familiar to most students. We were concerned that the situations in the video would be less familiar, and that students might feel estranged from the characters and situations. Hence, our use of first-person voice is a way to invite inclusion and participation.

We were guided by the foregoing design principles when we developed the prototype of the *Scientists-in-Action* series, the episode *The Overturned Tanker*. The basic format of the video is a "day-in-the-life" format: As the video opens, the viewer is welcomed to the office of Gina Davis (played by a White female), a hydrologist for the county. She begins to explain what a hydrologist does when a student intern (played by a 22-year-old White male) enters her office with some questions. A few moments later, they are interrupted by the hurried entry of Gina's secretary, who is quite agitated. It seems that a tanker truck has overturned on the highway and is spilling an unidentified chemical all over the highway. There is the danger that the liquid will spill into the river at the base of the highway; if it does, it will be the hydrologist's responsibility to deal with the emergency. The tanker has a "dangerous chemical" sign on it, but the driver is unconscious and the identity of the chemical is unknown. More information is provided about the properties of the liquid, and they find out that it is running off into the river. At this point, the video goes to black; students are asked to figure out (a) what the chemical might be, (b) possible reactions with water, and (c) whether it will flow toward the lake or the city (it flows downstream toward the city).

Students are provided with authentic materials—the same ones that real emergency teams use and that the student intern is given in the video—as they work on these problems. Once the students have finished, the video resumes and the students see how the hydrologist, the intern, and an additional member of her team—a fire chief—have answered the same questions. The team discusses the properties of the liquid, the likely chemicals the liquid could be, and that it is flowing toward the city and right past the town's water-treatment plant. They enlist the help of a chemist (played by an African-American female) to determine the exact nature of the chemical. She is shown in her laboratory conducting a series of tests that identify the chemical as a highly toxic compound—phosphorus trichloride. Additional information about methods for preventing contamination of the town's water supply is provided, and the video goes to black as students are asked to help the team determine the best method of dealing with the spill. Again, after working on this problem, students return to the video to find out what the "experts" have figured out. There is a final problem posed that deals with determining the flow rate and the time the chemical will reach the water-treatment plant.

In the remainder of this chapter, we report the results of two initial studies, in which we examined the effects of using *The Overturned Tanker* as a macrocontext for scientific problem solving. We were interested in examining: (a) students' learning of the specific content, (b) students' attitudes toward science and the experience of using the video, and (c) the degree of application to the situations in students' own communities. In both experiments, we included comparison groups that did not see or solve *The Overturned Tanker*. In Experiment One, we included two conditions that provided an initial test of the value-added of the "fictional" video over learning experiences based solely on "actual" events of a similar nature that had been broadcast on TV news. Students who viewed *The Overturned Tanker* had the opportunity to actively solve the problems on which the scientists were working; the TV news group's experience was much more passive. In Experiment Two, we included the same groups as in Experiment One, plus a group that saw but did not solve *The Overturned Tanker*; we compared the impact of active involvement in the problem solving on cognitive and affective outcomes. Assessment instruments were designed to allow us to examine changes in content knowledge and attitudes toward science and scientists. We expected specific rather than general effects, so we included types of sciences and scientists that were not featured in the videos, as well as those that were.

EXPERIMENT ONE

Method

Subjects. Forty-four fifth graders (age range 10–11 years) in a suburban Nashville-area school served as subjects for this pilot study. Most of the students were average to above average in achievement compared with their peers in Tennessee.

Materials. Two types of instructional materials were used for this study. The basic science information to be learned was presented in the embedded format of a video entitled *Scientists-in-Action: The Overturned Tanker*. As we described previously, the story centers around a truck that has gotten into an accident and is spilling an unknown chemical into a river. The problem is complicated by the fact that a nearby town draws its drinking water from the same river. In addition to the video, there are supplemental materials for the students to interpret: topographical maps, an official 1990 Emergency Response Guidebook (DOT P 5800.5), and an acid-base, "hands-on" chemistry experiment.

The second type of instructional material used for this experiment was a 7-minute video of network news coverage following a train derailment near Lake Shasta, California, in July 1991. The train was carrying a strong pesticide that spilled into the Sacramento River and had a disastrous effect on the local ecosystem. The river feeds into the Lake Shasta Reservoir, one of the largest in the country. How the spill spread out over the area, and the immediate and long-term effects on the fish, vegetation, and recreational life of the river system were depicted. At one point in the footage, a biologist was shown examining the damage done to fish in the river. The effects of the spill on the area's residents and were prominently featured. Footage was obtained on educational loan from the Vanderbilt University Video Achives.

Procedure.   Two classes of fifth-grade students (10- to 11-year-olds) were used in this study. The classes were randomly assigned to either the network news group (Network) or *The Overturned Tanker* group (Tanker). Both groups were given pretests in three areas: content knowledge, attitudes toward science, and interest in wanting to learn more about particular scientific professions.

Students in the Network group saw the 7-minute segment of network news covering the Lake Shasta, California train derailment and chemical spill. A laser-disc recorder and large monitor were used to present the segments. Students were then posttested on the same instruments used for the pretest.

Students in the Tanker group also saw the news segment on the Lake Shasta spill. They then viewed *The Overturned Tanker* and solved the problems at each stopping point, as described previously. In addition, they participated in a demonstration of an acid-base chemical reaction. As in the Network group, students were posttested at the conclusion of these activities.

Assessment Instruments and Scoring.   Students were administered three kinds of test items at pretest and posttest. First, there was a set of "free-response" content questions constructed to assess the amount of content learned. These asked students: (a) who would be involved in dealing with a chemical spill into a local river, (b) to list four or five steps that would need to be taken in the event of a spill, (c) what chemical could be used to make an acid spill less dangerous, (d) what hydrologists do, and (e) what fire chiefs do. Quantitative scores were assigned to responses in the following manner: For Questions (a) and (b), we recorded the number of unique responses; for Questions (c), (d), and (e), students received two points for a complete answer, one for a partially correct answer, and zero for incorrect or extremely ill-specified answers. Responses to the first question were analyzed and scored with respect to the type of person(s) mentioned (i.e., scientists, police, etc.), and to the second for type of action(s) mentioned (i.e., identify the chemical, assess the chances of fire).

Second, we administered a set of attitude questions. Students were asked to respond, on a 3-point scale (*disagree, not sure, agree*), to questions about where and how scientists work (e.g., in laboratories, alone, etc.), and whether they thought they (personally) could be a scientist. A final set of interest questions asked students to rate, on a 4-point scale (*not at all, a little, some, a lot*), how much they wanted to learn more about what a variety of scientists do. Hydrologists, chemists, biologists, and physicists were included in the list of scientists rated.

Results

Scores on each of the content questions were submitted to repeated-measures analysis of variance (ANOVA), in which *group* (Network vs. Tanker) and *time of test* (pre- and posttest) were variables. The content questions assessed the degree of mastery of the concepts and information presented in the videos. Note that the network news segment about the Lake Shasta spill contained information that was relevant to answering the content questions. For the first content question (*What kinds of people do you think would be involved in trying to solve the spill problem?*), there was a significant group x time of test interaction, $[F(1, 42) = 9.81, MS_e = 4.54, p < .01]$. As Fig. 13.1a shows, there was greater improvement in the Tanker group (*M* change = 1.46) compared with the Network group (*M* change = .54).

Responses at pre- and posttest show interesting shifts indicating that the treatment group provided more responses specific to people involved in dealing with chemical spills. The categories of scientists that were named at pre- and posttest are shown in Figure 13.1b. The Tanker group gave more hydrologist and chemist responses at posttest than at pretest and more than the Network group as well.

Students also reported a number of nonscientists who would be involved in cleaning up a spill. The distributions of these responses in the Tanker and Network groups were similar at pretest and again at posttest. The one exception to this similarity in the responses was that the Tanker group more frequently gave the response *fireperson,* consistent with the characters featured in *The Overturned Tanker.* The quantitative and categorical results indicate that the students in the Tanker group had a more articulated view of scientific occupations, commensurate with having been exposed to a greater variety of scientists, after viewing both the news segment and *The Overturned Tanker.*

For the second content question: (List four or five steps that you think people would need to take to solve the problem of the spill.), again there was a significant group x time of test interaction, $[F(1,42) = 13.80, MS_e = 8.28, p < .001]$. At pretest, there was no difference in the means for the Tanker group (*M* = 1.77) and Network group (*M* = 2.0). At posttest, the Tanker group reported more specific actions and received higher scores (*M* = 2.91) than did the Network group (*M* = 1.91). We separated students' responses into protective actions and actions taken on the chemical, and the latter are shown in Figure 13.2. The Tanker group reported specific actions appropriate to chemical spills more frequently than did the Network group (i.e., identify the chemical and neutralize it, as compared with dilute it, clean it up, or contain it). *Clean up* and *contain* were the two verbs stressed in the network news segment, hence it is somewhat surprising that the Network group did not show any increases over their pretest scores in the number of children naming these words. This result may indicate that typical news broadcasts by themselves are not sufficient for children's acquisition of new content. On protective actions that should be taken, the only

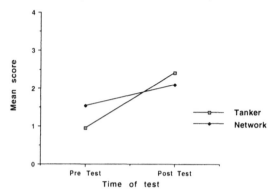

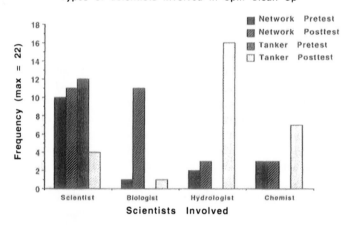

FIG. 13.1. Experiment One results: (a) Mean number of different kinds of responses to this question: What kind of people would be involved in solving a spill problem: (b) Types of scientists mentioned by Network and Tanker groups at pre- and posttest.

difference between the groups was in assessing the likelihood of fire—a more frequent response on posttest for the Tanker group.

Students in the Tanker group also acquired specific information related to chemical reactions. In response to the question about what chemical would make an acid spill less dangerous, performance at pretest was exceedingly low (Tanker $M = .23$, Network $M = .09$). At posttest, the Tanker group's score ($M = 1.59$) was significantly greater than the Network group's score ($M = .05$), for the group x time interaction [$F(1, 42) = 65.31$, $MS_e = .167$, $p < .01$].

The final two content questions examined what students had learned about the job responsibilities of hydrologists and fire chiefs. As expected, on the hydrologist question, there was a significant interaction of group x time, $[F(1, 42) = 9.41, MS_e = .204, p < .01]$. The Tanker group ($M$ change $= .71$) learned more about hydrologists' work than did the Network group (M change $= .23$). Knowledge of a fire chief's work activities was the same across groups, and did not change from pre- to posttest.

The results of the content questions indicate that the network news segment alone was not sufficient for students to acquire specific information about how scientists would deal with chemical spills. As expected, students who viewed and solved the problems embedded in *The Overturned Tanker* had a more differentiated understanding of spills, and the responsibilities of different kinds of scientists in an emergency situation such as a chemical spill.

Of the three attitude questions that students answered, two were designed to determine the degree to which students believed in the traditional stereotype of the lone scientist working away in a laboratory, isolated from the rest of humanity. We wanted to determine if our brief intervention altered students' initial views. Students were asked whether they *agreed* (3), *disagreed* (1) or were *not sure* (2) that scientists usually work alone. Students in both groups and at pre- and posttest overwhelmingly agreed with this statement. The mean rating in each group was 2.73 at pretest and 2.75 at posttest. The lack of change is perhaps not so surprising, given that *The Overturned Tanker* actually showed two scientists working by themselves. For example, the hydrologist in *The Overturned Tanker* had her own, single-person office, and the chemist worked by herself in a

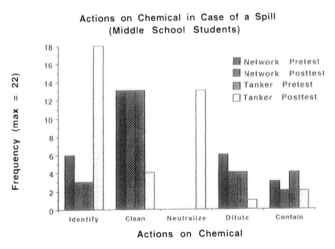

FIG. 13.2. Experiment One results: Types of actions reported by Network and Tanker groups at pre- and posttest in response to this question: What would people need to do to solve the problem of a spill?

laboratory, although she was hooked up with the team via the telephone. This example provides a good lesson for future projects.

There was more change in the responses to this statement: Most scientists spend their time in laboratories. There was a main effect of time [$F(1, 42) = 32.44, MS_e = .38, p < .001$], but no group main effect or interaction. The mean rating data are shown in Figure 13.3a, where it can be seen that at posttest both groups were less likely to think that scientists spend their time in laboratories. At pretest, 45% of the students in the Tanker group and 50% in the Network group agreed with the statement; at posttest, the numbers dropped to 9% in the Tanker

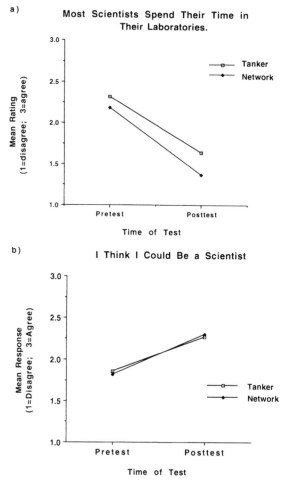

FIG. 13.3.   Experiment One ratings on attitude items: (a) Most scientists spend their time in their laboratories. (b) I think I could be a scientist.

group and 23% in the Network group. In this context, the change in the Network group was probably due to the fact that the Lake Shasta news segment showed a biologist working in the field rather than a laboratory.

For the final attitude question (I think I could be a scientist), which was directed at students' concept of themselves as scientists, responses showed a significant effect of time $[F(1, 42) = 18.36, MS_e = .223, p < .01]$. The means are shown in Figure 13.3b. At pretest, the majority of students in the Tanker group were unsure (50%) or disagreed (32%) with the statement. Comparable means for the Network group were 36% and 41%, respectively. At posttest, 45% of the students in the Tanker group agreed with the statement, whereas only 14% disagreed. There were comparable shifts in the Network group, where at posttest 41% of the students agreed and only 14% disagreed. These data are encouraging because students seem to feel more positively disposed toward the possibility of actually becoming scientists, despite the short intervention that we conducted.

The effects on interest in learning more about the scientists depicted in the videos were mixed. Students' interest in learning more about hydrologists increased somewhat from pretest to posttest for the Tanker group, but not for the Network group, although the interaction shown in Figure 13.4a was not significant (nor were the main effects). There were also no effects on interest in learning about chemists or physicists. We expected not to affect interest in physics, but we did expect to increase students' interest in learning about chemists. As indicated, the chemist was shown in her lab working by herself. Although we are not sure this is the reason there was no change in interest in learning about chemists, it is a possibility. This interpretation is strengthened when we look at the results for interest in biologists: A significant effect of time of test $[F(1, 42) = 5.32, MS_e = .419, p = .03]$ indicated that both groups were more interested in learning about biologists (see Fig. 13.4b). Biologists were prominently featured in the network news segment, and were shown scuba diving in the river to examine the pesticide spill's effects on the fish. Thus, although there may be other differences between biologists and chemists, we keep these results strongly in mind as we move beyond our prototype.

Students were enthusiastic about their experience in the *Scientists-in-Action* context. They reported enjoying the video, the problem solving, and the hands-on activities. Representative comments included the following:

- I loved the video. I learned more than I thought I would. As first I had know (sic) knowledge of any of that stuff. Thank you.
- I liked the lady who was the chemist (I liked watching her mix the chemicals together).
- I learned a lot of new interesting things. I wasn't sure what a hydrologist did. Now I know it's hard and exciting.

a)

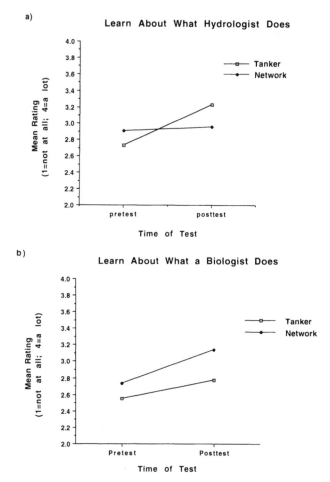

FIG. 13.4. Experiment One ratings on interest items: (a) Learn about a hydrologist. (b) Learn about a biologist.

In terms of our goals for the initial study, we clearly obtained positive evidence about the *Scientists-in-Action* concept. There are obviously many deeper questions that might be asked about the instruction. For example, our measures were heavily focused on the content in the video and problem solving, and did not look at transfer. We conducted a second, replication experiment with older students and included a transfer task. Students had to use information they had learned about topographical maps to answer several questions about a new map. In addition to the map transfer task, we wanted to compare a group of students that only watched the video to one that actually solved it. Finally, we wanted to determine if the intervention had the same impact on students' attitudes toward science and their interest in different kinds of scientists.

EXPERIMENT TWO

Method

Subjects. Forty-nine adolescents enrolled in the ninth grade (approximate age range 14–16 years of age) of a predominately Hispanic, inner-city, urban-high school served as subjects for this study. The school tracks students into three levels based on performance on the California Test of Basic Skills. Students from this study were chosen from the middle track (slightly below average compared with national norms, average school wide). The majority of students in this study were determined "at risk" of academic failure and/or dropping out by the guidelines set forth by the state of New Jersey.

Materials. Most materials used in Experiment One were duplicated for this study. A slightly modified version of the questions described previously were used in this experiment. Transfer materials consisting of a topographic map (see Appendix) and a set of questions about that map were constructed.

Design. The study was run in three intact classrooms. Three experimental conditions were implemented, with the first two representing a replication of Experiment One: (a) *The Overturned Tanker* preceded by network news, and (b) network news. The third group saw the network news segment and then *The Overturned Tanker,* but did not solve the problems; instead, this group watched the video straight through. All students completed each of the assessment instruments at pre- and posttest, with the exception of the transfer test, which was administered only at posttest.

The number of students in each group varied. There were 19 in the Tanker plus Network group that solved the video (Tanker Solve), 16 in the Network group (Network), and 14 in the group that did not work through the problems (Tanker Watch). Note that the difference between the Tanker Solve and Tanker Watch groups also included the fact that the former received some practice in how to use the topographical map.

Procedure. The three classes used in this study were randomly assigned to either the Network group, the Tanker Solve group, or the Tanker Watch group. The groups were given pretests in the area of content knowledge, attitudes, and interest in wanting to learn more about particular kinds of scientists. These were similar to the pretests given to the fifth graders in Experiment One, except that we changed the wording on a couple of questions for clarity. Two random orders of the questions were used to avoid serial-order effects. A laser-disc player, video-cassette recorder, and large monitor were used to present the segments. Students were then posttested. The transfer test was the final assessment instrument.

Students in the Tanker Solve group experienced the same treatment as the

Tanker group in Experiment One: They saw the news segment and then viewed *The Overturned Tanker,* solving the problems at each stopping point. The students were given a demonstration on acid-base reactions; they worked a flow-rate problem, and had experience using the chemical guidebook and topographic map at the appropriate stopping points in the video. The Tanker Watch group saw the news segment and then was shown *The Overturned Tanker.* At the stopping points, the students were given 1 minute to "think about" the problems presented by the video and then proceeded to the next segment. All three groups were then posttested.

Assessments and Scoring. The content, attitude, and interest questions were scored as described in Experiment One. Students were also administered a transfer task on topographic map reading after their respective treatments and posttesting were completed. Students were asked to identify features such as steep slopes, low elevations, and slopes on a previously unseen topographic map. In addition, the students were asked where they would build "a well-protected castle."

RESULTS

We replicated the basic results of Experiment One for the content questions about people involved in a spill, and the actions that would be taken in case of a spill. In terms of scores on the people question, the main effect of group was significant, $[F(2, 46) = 5.39, MS_e = .2.24, p < .01]$, as was the main effect of time $[F(1, 46) = 68.12, MS_e = .64, p < .001]$, and the interaction, $[F(2, 46) = 4.59, p = .02]$. The interaction, shown in Figure 13.5, indicates that the Tanker Watch and Tanker Solve groups showed significant increases in the number of people named, but the Network group showed no change in performance. Most important for our purposes, increased specificity in responding is evident in the response-frequency distributions, shown in Figure 13.6. The percentage of students in the Tanker Solve and Tanker Watch groups that named hydrologists and chemists increased substantially from pre- to posttest, but did not change in the Network group. However, the percentage of students responding with the generic term *scientists* remained at approximately 30% in all groups at both testing times.

On the question that asked students to list actions that would be taken in the event of a spill, the main effects of group $[F(2, 46) = 7.92, MS_e = 1.61, p < .01]$, and time $[F (1, 46) = 36.86, MS_e = .875, p < .01]$, were significant, but the interaction was as well $[F(2, 46) = 10.28, p < .01]$. The means for the interaction are shown in Figure 13.7, and indicate that the degree of change was greatest in the Tanker Solve group, followed by the Tanker Watch group. There was effectively no change in the Network group. The Tanker Solve group had a better sense of the specific actions one would take on the chemical, when com-

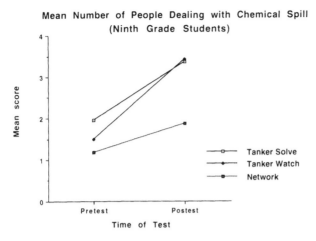

FIG. 13.5. Experiment Two results: Mean number of different kinds of responses to this question: What kind of people would be involved in solving a spill problem?

pared with either the Tanker Watch group or the Network group, as can be seen in Figure 13.8. As was the case with the fifth graders in Experiment One, there were no changes in the frequency of reporting *contain* or *clean up*, the two action verbs mentioned in the news segments.

The advantage of the Tanker groups over the Network group continued when students answered this question: What chemical would help make an acid spill less dangerous? Mean performance on this question is shown in Figure 13.9a. The main effects of group and time were significant, as was the interaction [$F(2, 46) = 12.6, MS_e = .17, p < .01$]. The two groups that watched *The Overturned Tanker* clearly learned how to deal with acidic chemicals, whereas the Network group did not. A similar pattern of effects was obtained for the question about a hydrologist's responsibilities, as shown in Figure 13.9b. The Tanker groups scored significantly higher than the Network group at posttest, but not at pretest. (The main effects and the interaction were all significant.) In contrast, we expected no advantage of *The Overturned Tanker* on the question about what a fire chief does. There was none. Performance in each group was equivalent at pre- and posttest, and there were no differences among the groups at either testing time.

The responses to the content questions indicated that *The Overturned Tanker* did impact the content knowledge of the students who saw it over those students who just saw the network footage about an oil spill. The Tanker groups became more specific in their responses, as if they were differentiating in important ways between different kinds of environmental disasters. As expected, there were only minor effects on the content questions of having engaged in the problem solving,

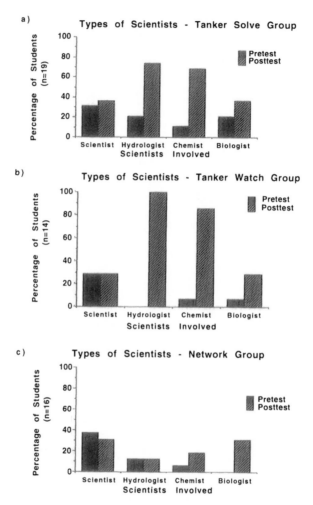

FIG. 13.6. Experiment Two results: Types of scientists mentioned by the three treatment groups at pre- and posttest.

as compared with having watched the video. The effect of solving versus watching was strongest for questions that dealt with treating a specific chemical spill. This finding is noteworthy because the Tanker Solve group had a hands-on demonstration that directly dealt with neutralizing acidic chemicals.

On the content knowledge questions, the results for these adolescent, inner-city, minority students are quite similar to those observed in the fifth-grade students who participated in Experiment One. Changes in attitudes toward science tended to be weaker, but we were not expecting to dramatically alter them. We recognize that, even in fifth-grade students, it is quite remarkable to find

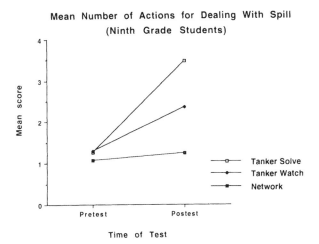

FIG. 13.7. Experiment Two results: Mean number of actions reported for dealing with a spill.

evidence of attitude change as a result of just one experience. Older students' attitudes have had a longer time to develop, and thus may be more entrenched. This seemed to be the case with respect to the ratings on this statement: Scientists spend their time in laboratories. Students generally agreed with this statement at pretest; at posttest, the percentage decreased by only one or two students in each group, with shifts into the *not sure* or *disagree* category. As we noted in discussing the attitude question results for Experiment One, the video itself may be responsible for this lack of change, in that there were actually multiple messages in *The Overturned Tanker:* In addition to the team assembled in a conference room to deal with the emergency, the chemist was shown in her laboratory.

There was no change in responses to the question of whether scientists work alone, but we were pleasantly surprised to discover that these ninth graders generally disagreed with this statement at pretest ($M = 1.7$ over all groups, where 1 was *disagree* and 3 was *agree*). Indeed, 55% of the students in the Tanker Solve group, 70% of those in the Tanker Watch group, and 63% of those in the Network group disagreed. At posttest, the overall mean was 1.3, indicating a slight increase in level of disagreement with the statement—the direction of change that we expected. The percentages of disagreement had increased to 58% and 93% in the Tanker Solve and Tanker Watch groups respectively, but had actually decreased to 50% in the Network group. In contrast to the fifth graders, a substantial number of the ninth graders already held the attitude we had hoped to induce. Expecting additional change in the desired direction was probably unrealistic.

A potential danger in any intervention is that it will have undesired effects. In our case, our goal was to encourage students to think of themselves as scientists.

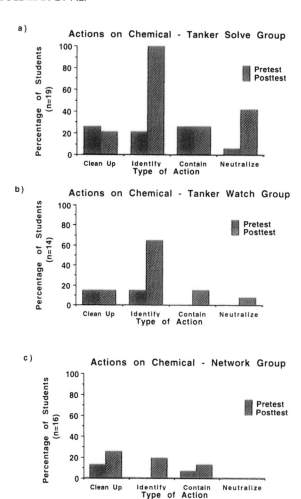

FIG. 13.8. Experiment Two results: Types of actions reported by the three treatment groups at pre- and posttest in response to this question: What would people need to do to solve the problem of a spill?

It would have been possible for *The Overturned Tanker* to have negatively affected students' attitudes toward science and their concepts of themselves in the role of scientist. For example, had the video left students with the impression that doing science was boring or ridiculously hard, the video's result might have been less positive views of science as a career option. Happily, the intervention did not have this undesirable effect. The results for one question—I think I could be a scientist—showed a small increase from pre- to posttest in the percentage of students who agreed with this statement, although there were no statistically significant main effects of time, group, nor interactions. In the Tanker Solve

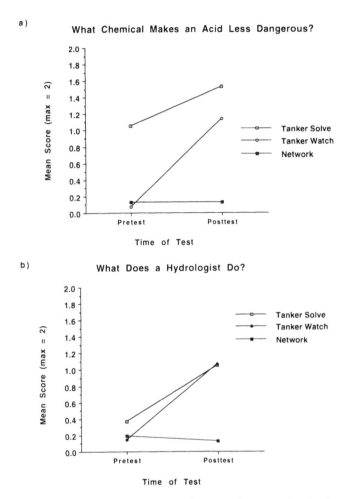

FIG. 13.9. Experiment Two results: Mean performance by the three treatment groups at pre- and posttest in response to the questions: (a) What chemical makes an acid less dangerous? (b) What does a hydrologist do?

group, 42% agreed with this statement at pretest, and 52.6% at posttest; in the Tanker Watch group, the increase was from 28.6% to 35.7%; and in the Network group, it was from 12.5% to 18.8%. Furthermore, of all the students who agreed with this statement at pretest, only one made a different response at posttest. These shifts were more modest than those observed in the younger students; however, the percentage of agreement at posttest was similar for the Tanker groups in the two grades. In contrast, the Network ninth graders were less likely to agree than the Network fifth graders.

We observed trends on the interest questions that were similar to those observed for the fifth graders. At posttest, all three groups were significantly more interested in learning about hydrologists $[F(1, 46) = 5.65, MS_e = .46, p = .02]$, but the degree of change was small. A similar pattern, although nonsignificant, was found for changes in interest in learning about chemists and physicists, replicating the findings with the fifth graders. Unlike the fifth graders, there was not an increase in any of the groups in interest in learning about biologists. However interest (at pre- and posttest) was at about the same level as the posttest ratings of the fifth graders (i.e., approximately 3 on the 4-point scale).

The attitudes toward science and interest data suggest that the video intervention had relatively minor effects on students' attitudes and interest. However, we wish to stress that students tended to stay positive if they were positive and interested at the outset. To our surprise, these students expressed more positive attitudes prior to the intervention than we had expected.

Transfer Map Task

One of the specific skills in solving *The Overturned Tanker* problems is reading and interpreting a topographical map. In solving the problems, students had to determine the slope of the terrain near the spill site to figure out which way the spill would flow. The Tanker Solve group received practice in doing this, but the other two groups did not. The Tanker Watch group saw the use of the topographical map and the explanation in the video, but the Network group never even saw a topographical map. Students were given the map shown in the Appendix and were asked a series of questions about it. (Note that two of the questions turned out to be ambiguous and were dropped.) One of the questions, What points are located at elevations greater than 600 feet?, was extremely easy for all groups: Performance in the two Tanker groups $(M = 2.0)$ reflected perfect scores, and mean performance in the Network group was close to perfect, $(M = 1.87)$.

On two of the questions, the performance of the two Tanker groups was equivalent and better than that of the Network group. This was true on this question: Where is the best place to build a castle? $[F(2, 46) = 4.6, MS_e = .81, p = .02]$, which required students to find a high spot at the top of a steeply pitched mountain. This pattern also held for the question that asked students to identify locations on the map where the slope of the hill was gradual $[F(2, 46) = 9.8, MS_e = .75, p < .01]$. The data are shown in Figure 13.10a. On both of these questions only one student in the Network group correctly responded, as contrasted with correct responses from half to two thirds of the students in the two Tanker groups.

On the remaining two questions, the group that had been actively involved in solving the problems posed in the video outperformed both the Tanker Watch group and the Network group. These questions (Which points have low elevation? What is the elevation of the shoreline?) required students to have specific

a)   **Topographical Map Transfer Questions**

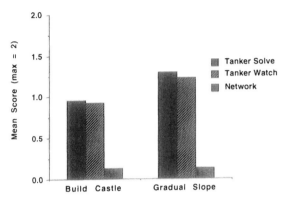

b)

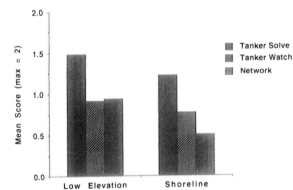

FIG. 13.10. Mean performance on transfer items for the three treatment groups.

topographical map-reading skills; they had to interpret the numbers on the elevation lines on the map to answer the question. The means for these questions for each group are shown in Figure 13.10b. Thus, the group that had actively used the topographical maps had some advantage over the groups that had not. However, watching someone else use the map did lead to some understanding of how to deal with it. Only the most obvious question could be answered by students who had not been exposed to the topographical map earlier.

The results of the intervention with the inner-city adolescents indicated that seeing *The Overturned Tanker* was associated with significant increases in knowledge specific to chemical spills. There was also transfer of one set of skills that were used in solving the problems posed by the video. The attitude and interest questions indicated that the intervention had had modest effects on these beliefs—an outcome that came as no great surprise to us. We also asked students to jot down some of their reactions to the experience. These were quite positive, as indicated by the following student comments:

- I know what a chemist does, so I wanted to learn more. A chemist looks like fun, with testing liquids, finding densities and mixing other liquids to see a reaction. I like that and would like to learn more.
- I'd like to learn more about a hydrologist because I'm into saving the environment.
- I had fun watching the video. I don't like all this textbook stuff.
- It (hydrologist) seems very exciting and suspenseful. I don't want a boring "behind the desk all day" kind of job.

We were also quite encouraged by the teachers' responses to the intervention: All of them asked for copies of the video along with the related materials, and they did this without our soliciting these requests.

NEXT STEPS AND CONCLUSIONS

Our initial tests of a multimedia environment for science problem solving have been encouraging. From a content perspective, both fifth- and ninth-grade students showed significant increases in their understanding of how to deal with the specific emergency situation in *The Overturned Tanker* (chemical spills). On the content questions, there was no advantage to having solved the problems as compared to having watched the video without solving, except in the case of the specific question about how to neutralize an acid. On the transfer task administered to the ninth graders, there was evidence of specific effects of solving the problem, as well as evidence that watching someone else solve the problem impacted student understanding of how to use a topographical map. The more specific the topographical map skill, the greater the advantage for having actually worked through the problem. We expected this, and one line of research that we intend to pursue is to do more tests of "watching" versus "doing."

Generally speaking, attitudes toward science were not dramatically affected, but then we would not expect to find dramatic effects after only one intervention. In general, the ninth graders' pretest responses left less room for change in the direction we had predicted than did the responses of the fifth graders. However, in both the fifth and ninth graders, when change occurred it tended to be in the direction we had predicted: toward more positive attitudes about being scientists and away from stereotyped images of a solitary scientist working in a laboratory.

We think the network footage may have authenticated the problem of chemical spills in the real environment, and students did learn some things from it. It would be nice if we could just use network footage to accomplish our goals of enhancing scientific thinking and problem solving. The problem with network footage, and the reason for producing our own, involves the need to build in the information needed for students to actually work as scientists on these problems. News footage does not provide such information. Rather, it provides a context for inquiry. A second line of research that we intend to explore compares inquiry contexts for science. For example, in one study, we plan to examine the differences in learning that result from doing experiments that are evolved by a team in a problem-solving context, and doing isolated experiments that are essentially decontextualized.

In additional episodes in this series, we look toward providing inquiry contexts that deal with issues and situations that are similar to the ones depicted in *The Overturned Tanker*—issues that affect people's everyday lives, (e.g., lead poisoning, fetal alcohol syndrome). We are hopeful that as students are exposed to a series of these episodes, we will see evidence of more significant attitude changes.

From the data we have collected thus far, it seems that multimedia environments can be effective in increasing specific content knowledge. But we also want to assess their effects on transfer to scientific inquiry in new domains. We will examine the impact of generative activity on transfer, as well as learning, by continuing to pursue contrasts between watching a solution versus doing the solution. This endeavor is tricky because it relies on being extremely precise in one's understanding of what skills, knowledge, and expertise might be developed via watching as compared with doing. Simplistic notions of transfer, and accompanying simple tests of the same, will be inadequate to reflect what are sometimes subtle, but we think important, differences in the two situations' outcomes. One type of task with which we have been working in the mathematics domain (Cognition and Technology Group at Vanderbilt, chap. 14, this volume, 1992b, 1994a) employs "what-if" thinking to deepen students' understanding of problem domains and how variables are related to one another.

"What-if" tasks will also play a large role in our work in science. Indeed, we are conducting a related project on an authentic "what-if" scenario, space travel to Mars (Hickey, Pellegrino, Petrosino, & Cognition and Technology Group at Vanderbilt, 1991). In that work, we are using a contemporary video format to stimulate students' generative problem solving for a mission to Mars. Work on the Mars mission, as well as the work with the *Scientists-in-Action* materials, indicate that students are enthusiastic about being instrumentally involved in planning a mission and do become actively engaged in problem solving. However, for productive learning to occur, students often need careful guidance through quite complex information, events, and situations that they generate and encounter as they navigate solutions. The nature of the support and guidance needed to facilitate students' thinking is one of the things we are examining and will continue to pursue in our efforts to enhance scientific reasoning and problem solving.

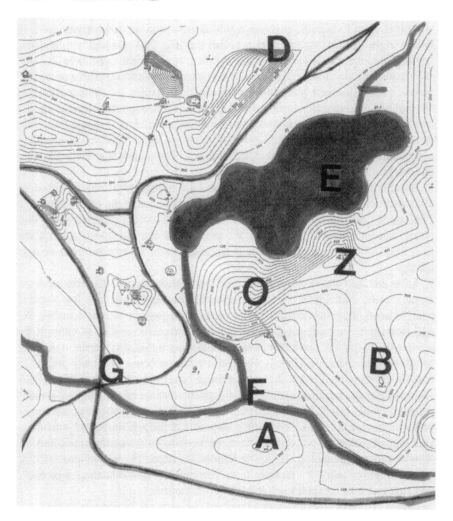

LincolnTown

ACKNOWLEDGMENTS

The research reported in this chapter was supported, in part, by a grant from the James S. McDonnell Cognitive Studies in Education Program. D. Hickey and A. Petrosino were supported by Fellowships from the Tennesse Space Grant Consortium. We thank the staff and students in Nashville, Tennessee, and Hoboken,

New Jersey, who graciously participated in the research. We acknowledge the tireless efforts of Beth Leopold as production assistant on *The Overturned Tanker.*

REFERENCES

Bransford, J. D., Sherwood, R. S., Vye, N. J., & Rieser, J. (1986). Teaching thinking and problem solving: Research foundations. *American Psychologist, 41,* 1078–1089.

Bransford, J. D., Vye, N., Kinzer, C., & Risko, V. (1990). Teaching thinking and content knowledge: Toward an integrated approach. In B. F. Jones & L. Idol (Eds.), *Dimensions of thinking and cognitive instruction: Implications for educational reform* (Vol. 1, pp. 381–413). Hillsdale, NJ: Lawrence Erlbaum Associates.

Cognition and Technology Group at Vanderbilt. (1990). Anchored instruction and its relationship to situated cognition. *Educational Researcher, 19*(6), 2–10.

Cognition and Technology Group at Vanderbilt. (1991). Technology and the design of generative learning environments, *Educational Technology, 31,* 34–40.

Cognition and Technology Group at Vanderbilt. (1992a). Anchored instruction in science and mathematics: Theoretical basis, developmental projects, and initial research findings. In R. A. Duschl & R. J. Hamilton (Eds.), *Philosophy of science, cognitive psychology, and educational theory and practice* (pp. 245–273). New York: State University of New York Press.

Cognition and Technology Group at Vanderbilt. (1992b). The Jasper series as an example of anchored instruction: Theory, program description and assessment data. *Educational Psychologist, 27,* 291–315.

Cognition and Technology Group at Vanderbilt. (1992c). The Jasper experiment: An exploration of issues in learning and instructional design. *Educational Technology Research and Development, 40*(1), 65–80.

Cognition and Technology Group at Vanderbilt. (1993). Toward integrated curricula: Possibilities from anchored instruction. In M. Rabinowitz (Ed.), *Cognitive science foundations of instruction* (pp. 33–55). Hillsdale, NJ: Lawrence Erlbaum Associates.

Cognition and Technology Group at Vanderbilt. (1994a). From visual word problems to learning communities: Changing conceptions of cognitive research. In K. McGilly (Ed.), *Classroom lessons: Integrating cognitive theory and classroom practice* (pp. 157–200). Cambridge, MA: MIT Press/Bradford Books.

Cognition and Technology Group at Vanderbilt. (1994b). Multimedia environments for developing literacy in at-risk students. In B. Means (Ed.), *Technology and educational reform: The reality behind the promise* (pp. 23–56). San Francisco: Jossey-Bass, Inc.

Dewey, S. (1933). *How we think: Restatement of the relation of reflective thinking to the educative process.* Lexington, MA: Heath.

Feuerstein, R., Rand, Y., Hoffman, M. B., & Miller, R. (1980). *Instrumental enrichment.* Baltimore, MD: University Park Press.

Gragg, C. I. (1940, October 19). Because wisdom can't be told. *Harvard Alumni Bulletin,* pp. 78–84.

Hanson, N. R. (1970). A picture theory of theory meaning. In R. G. Colodny (Ed.), *The nature and function of scientific theories* (pp. 233–274). Pittsburgh: University of Pittsburgh Press.

Hickey, D. T., Pellegrino, J. W., Petrosino, A., & Cognition and Technology Group at Vanderbilt. (1991, October). *Reconceptualizing space science education: A generative, problem solving approach.* Paper presented at the Florida Space Education conference, Cocoa Beach, FL.

McLarty, K., Goodman, J., Risko, V., Kinzer, C. K., Vye, N., Rowe, D., & Carson, J. (1990). Implementing anchored instruction: Guiding principles for curriculum development. In J. Zutell & S. McCormick (Eds.), *Literacy theory and research: Analyses from multiple paradigms* (pp. 109–120). Chicago, IL: National Reading Conference.

Rutherford, F. J., & Ahlgren, A. (1990). *Science for all Americans.* New York: Oxford University Press.

Schwab, J. J. (1960). What do scientists do? *Behavioral Science, 5,* 1–27.

Sherwood, R. D., Kinzer, C. K., Bransford, J. D., & Franks, J. J. (1987). Some benefits of creating macro-contexts for science instruction: Initial findings. *Journal of Research in Science Teaching, 24*(5), 417–435.

Sherwood, R., Kinzer, C., Hasselbring, T., & Bransford, J. (1987). Macro-contexts for learning: Initial findings and issues. *Journal of Applied Cognition, 1,* 93–108.

Vygotsky, L. S. (1978). *Mind in society.* Cambridge, MA: Harvard University Press.

Williams, S. M. (1992). Putting case-based instruction into context: Examples from legal and medical education. *The Journal of the Learning Sciences, 2*(4), 367–427.

14 Multimedia Environments for Enhancing Learning in Mathematics

Cognition and Technology Group at Vanderbilt
Peabody College of Vanderbilt University

Criticism abounds regarding the mathematical and scientific literacy and general problem solving-skills of students when they leave the secondary-school system. This criticism and commentary comes in many different forms, and it appears in both the research and policy literatures. For example, in 1988, Nickerson summarized the results of national tests administered in the United States. He stated that, in the aggregate, the findings from such studies conclude that it is possible to finish 12 or 13 years of public education in the United States without developing much competence as a thinker. Students' poor test scores seem to correlate with the perceptions of many business leaders about the characteristics of today's graduates (see e.g., Resnick, 1987).

These general comments about thinking and problem solving can be juxtaposed with a set of salient facts about mathematical problem solving. The literature on mathematics instruction and problem solving indicates that the primary vehicle by which problem solving is taught and assessed is through the use of word or story problems. Students typically demonstrate poor performance on tests of word-problem solving. Furthermore, teachers abhor this element of the curriculum. The universal dislike of word problems is captured well in a cartoon created by Gary Larson, a contemporary American cartoonist. Imagine, if you will, your own personal Hell's Library. Larson's personal Hell's Library is one filled with book after book of math story problems. If you ask many students, as well as teachers, they share this conceptualization. Educators are therefore faced with an interesting and significant dilemma. Word problems constitute the primary vehicle for teaching, learning, and assessing problem-solving skills. However, students do extremely poorly at solving these problems, teachers abhor this part of the curriculum, and current efforts to improve these skills are typically not very effective.

What has educational and psychological research contributed? We now have more than two decades of psychological and instructional research on word-problem solving, and the conclusions are hardly scintillating. The research has progressed from simple, descriptive performance data to extremely elaborate analyses, including computer simulations and cognitive models of the knowledge and processes that underlie the solution of simple and complex word problems. Unfortunately, little of this work has contributed directly to improved instructional programs or assessment strategies. Thus, our scientific understanding of the nature of the problem is significantly improved, but our pedagogical understanding or practice is not.

We can combine the findings on mathematical problem solving with a related literature focusing on analogical transfer and learning from examples. There is a relatively well-developed, albeit equally distressing, research literature illustrating this general conclusion: When students learn from worked-out examples, they frequently fail to demonstrate understanding and analogical transfer to new problems. This is particularly true if the new problems represent only minor variations from the example problems that were worked on originally.

These negative results and conclusions can be contrasted with those from another emergent literature. This literature focuses on everyday mathematical reasoning and problem solving—what is sometimes referred to as *practical intelligence.* A different set of conclusions and issues emerge from work of individuals such as Rogoff, Lave, and Saxe (e.g., Lave & Wenger, 1991; Rogoff, 1990; Rogoff & Lave, 1984; Saxe, 1991). This body of work indicates that individuals can often demonstrate sophisticated forms of reasoning and problem solving. However, such problem solving and reasoning are situated in specific contexts that have practical significance for the individuals involved. Examples include children who are functioning as candy sellers in Brazil, individuals who are operating in the context of their own kitchen, or individuals operating in the contexts of stores or factories.

This work has led a number of individuals to talk about the gap between what occurs in schools and what occurs in natural settings that seem to foster learning and transfer (e.g., J. Brown, Collins, & Duguid, 1988; Cognition and Technology Group at Vanderbilt, 1993a; Resnick, 1987; Resnick & Klopfer, 1989). Much of this work has taken on the labels of *situated cognition* and *cognitive apprenticeship.* It is well beyond the scope of this chapter to review the work and its relative strengths and weaknesses. Our point here is to indicate that there is an increasing awareness that learning takes place in social contexts and social settings, and that much of schooling seems to be divorced from the type of learning that naturally occurs in apprenticeship settings. As noted by Resnick (1987), there appear to be large gaps between school tasks and tasks found in the everyday world. These gaps lead students to naturally question why they are asked to learn the material being presented, particularly in a domain like mathematics. Connections between textbook algebra, geometry, and calculus and applications in the real world remain absent from many classrooms. Perhaps this is also the reason that many students find word problems difficult and perform so poorly on them. In many cases, the content of word problems seems relatively arbitrary and abstract.

Studies of the learning that occurs in informal, everyday environments and in organized apprenticeships are also providing ideas for models of instruction. Such models are quite different from the decontextualized practices that tend to characterize formal schooling. In informal and apprenticeship learning, knowledge is learned in the context of meaningful goals. Hence, the uses for action are clear, rather than obscured. Collins, Brown, and Newman (1989) and others (e.g., A. Brown et al., 1993; Cognition and Technology Group at Vanderbilt, 1994) have begun to discuss how schools might be restructured to create cognitive apprenticeships that let students engage in authentic and productive mental work. Their focus is on the creation of meaningful tasks and work environments, rather than specific facts, concepts, and skills that students practice in isolation.

However, it is a long way from circumscribed examples to environments that can be imported for use in schools. As we and others have discussed elsewhere, an apprenticeship model has both strengths and limitations (Cognition and Technology Group at Vanderbilt, 1991). In this chapter, we focus on how we have attempted to circumvent some of these problems. Our goal has been to apply the concepts of *apprenticeship* and *situated cognition,* as well as more general cognitive theory, to develop meaningful and workable environments for the teaching and learning of complex mathematical problem solving. In this chapter we provide an overview of one of our programs (*The Adventures of Jasper Woodbury*), the theoretical framework that guides its ongoing development, and some of the research issues and results associated with this work. This chapter is one of a series of works by the Cognition and Technology Group at Vanderbilt that provide information about our development activities and the associated cognitive and instructional research.

The chapter is divided into four sections: (a) a brief discussion of the larger theoretical framework that motivates our work, (b) a brief description of the Jasper Woodbury mathematical problem-solving series as a particular example of our theoretical framework, (c) discussion and illustration of cognitive research on children's learning in these environments, and (d) a discussion of new approaches to assessment that can enhance learning and mesh well with these new environments. The discussions in the first two sections borrow heavily from previous discussions (Cognition and Technology Group at Vanderbilt, 1992a, 1992b). A full description of our theoretical framework, program components, and research findings is beyond the scope of this chapter. We indicate omissions as we come to them, and refer readers to relevant articles for further information.

THEORETICAL FRAMEWORK

The theoretical framework that guides our work is consistent with a class of theories called *constructivist theories* (e.g., Bransford & Vye, 1989; Clement,

1982; Duffy & Bednar, 1991; Minstrell, 1989; Perkins, Farady, & Bushey, 1991; Resnick & Klopfer, 1989; Scardamalia & Bereiter, 1991; Schoenfeld, 1989; Spiro, Feltovich, Jacobson, & Coulson, 1991). Theorists who emphasize the constructive nature of learning argue for the need to change the nature of the teaching-learning process that occurs much of the time in many classrooms. Instead of having teachers "transmit" information that students "receive," these theorists emphasize the importance of having students become actively involved in the construction of knowledge. For example, constructivist theorists want to help students learn to construct and coordinate effective problem representations through the use of symbolic and physical models, through reasoning and argumentation, and through deliberate application of problem-solving strategies (e.g., Brown, Collins, & Duguid, 1989; Clement, 1982; Minstrell, 1989; Palincsar & Brown, 1989; Resnick & Klopfer, 1989; Schoenfeld, 1989; Scardamalia & Bereiter, 1991). A basic assumption of the constructivist position is that students cannot learn to engage in effective knowledge-construction activities simply by being told new information (e.g., Bransford, Franks, Vye, & Sherwood, 1989). Instead, students need repeated opportunities to engage in in-depth exploration, assessment, and revision of their ideas over extended periods of time.

The approach to instruction that we have been testing within such a constructivist framework is called *anchored instruction* (e.g., Cognition and Technology Group at Vanderbilt, 1990, 1991). The essence of the approach is to anchor or situate instruction in the context of meaningful problem-solving environments that allow teachers to simulate in the classroom some of the advantages of "in-context" apprenticeship training (Brown et al., 1989). Our anchored-instruction approach shares a strong family resemblance to many instructional programs that are case and problem based (e.g., Barrows, 1985; Gragg, 1940; Spiro et al., 1991; Williams, 1992). The primary goal that guides our selection and development of anchors is to allow students who are relative novices in an area to experience some of the advantages available to experts when the latter are trying to learn new information about their area (e.g., Bransford, Sherwood, Hasselbring, Kinzer, & Williams, 1990; Cognition and Technology Group at Vanderbilt, 1990).

THE JASPER SERIES: AN EXAMPLE
OF ANCHORED INSTRUCTION

The Cognition and Technology Group at Vanderbilt is experimenting with a variety of anchored instruction programs that focus on specific content areas, and is also providing opportunities for cross-curricular extensions (e.g., Cognition and Technology Group at Vanderbilt, 1993b). We have created anchors, plus instructional activities to accompany them, that focus on the areas of mathematics (e.g., Cognition and Technology Group at Vanderbilt, 1991, 1992b); science (Cognition and Technology Group at Vanderbilt, 1992a; Hickey, Pellegrino,

Petrosino & Cognition and Technology Group at Vanderbilt, 1991); and literacy (e.g., Cognition and Technology Group at Vanderbilt, 1990; McLarty et al., 1990; Sharp et al.,1992).

The Adventures of Jasper Woodbury is a video-based series designed to promote problem posing, problem solving, reasoning, and effective communication. Each adventure is a 15- to 20-minute story. At the end of each story, the major character (or group of characters) is faced with a challenge that the students in the classroom must solve before they are allowed to see how the movie characters solve the challenge. The adventures are designed in pairs, with each pair sharing a common problem schema. The first pair of adventures deals with issues of trip planning, the second pair involves generating a business plan using statistics, and the third pair involves meaningful uses of geometry. We have also created analog and extension problems, with videos to accompany each adventure.

One link between our theoretical framework and our materials development is Gibson's (1977) concept of *affordances*. Gibson argued that different features of the environment afford classes of activities for particular organisms, such as "walk-onable," "climbable," "swimable," and so forth. Our notion is that instructional materials can be viewed from a similar perspective. Different types of materials are differentially effective for helping students engage in particular kinds of learning activities (Jenkins, 1979).

We noted earlier that the primary method of teaching problem solving in mathematics involves word problems, and that these have limitations. Traditional word problems often provide the goal and only those numbers needed to solve the problem, hence they afford only computational selection. In other cases, even the type of computation is made clear to the students (because the chapter focuses on a particular operation, such as addition), so the word problems actually provide only computational practice (Porter, 1989). Our Jasper adventures afford activities such as generating subgoals, identifying relevant information, cooperating with others to plan and solve complex problems, discussing the advantages and disadvantages of possible solutions, and comparing perspectives by pointing out and explaining interesting events. Of course, the mere existence of these affordances does not guarantee that "afforded" activities will occur. The degree to which these affordances are realized depends on the teaching model that one adopts in the context of Jasper. Space does not permit a description of the teaching and learning activities that accompany Jasper in the classroom; discussions of different teaching models appear in Cognition and Technology Group at Vanderbilt, (1992b).

The types of learning activities that we want our materials to support are consistent with recommendations suggested by the National Council of Teachers of Mathematics' 1989 Commission on Standards for School Mathematics. The NCTM's suggestions for changes in classroom activities include: (a) more emphasis on complex, open-ended problem solving, communication, and reasoning; (b) more connections from mathematics to other subjects, and to the world outside the classroom; and (c) more use of calculators and powerful computer-based tools, such as spreadsheets and graphing programs, for exploring relation-ships (as opposed to having students spend an inordinate amount of time calculat-ing by hand). In proposing a more generative approach to mathematics learning, the NCTM stated:

> (the) mathematics curriculum should engage students in some problems that de-mand extended effort to solve. Some might be group projects that require students to use available technology and to engage in cooperative problem solving and discussion. For grades 5–8 an important criterion of problems is that they be interesting to students. (p. 75)

Design Principles and an Example From the Jasper Series

Our attempt to create instructional materials that afford generative learning activ-ities has been guided by the following seven basic design principles: video-based format, narrative with realistic problems (rather than a lecture on video), genera-tive format (i.e., students must generate the subproblems to be solved at the end of each story), embedded data design (i.e., all the data needed to solve the problems are in the video), problem complexity (i.e., each adventure involves a problem of at least 14 steps), pairs of related adventures (to discuss issues of transfer), and links across the curriculum. These design principles are discussed in more detail elsewhere (Cognition and Technology Group at Vanderbilt, 1991, 1992b; Hickey et al., 1991; McLarty et al., 1990). For present purposes, it is sufficient to note that the design principles mutually influence one another and operate as a Gestalt, rather than as a set of independent features of the materials.

A description of one of the adventures should help clarify the design of the Jasper series. We describe the adventure *The Big Splash* which is a 15-minute (approximately) video about a young teen named Chris who wants to set up a dunking booth at his school fair (for brief descriptions of the two trip-planning adventures, see Cognition and Technology Group at Vanderbilt, 1991, 1992b). Briefly, the story begins with Chris' visit to the local fire station to obtain information for a report he is writing. While there, he notices a strange device that turns out to be a dunking machine that the fire station rents out for fairs and carnivals. Subsequently, back at school Chris learns about the upcoming fun fair. The school principal announces that they are still looking for good ideas for booths and activities to help raise money. Chris is reminded of the dunk tank he saw at the fire station and comes up with the idea of selling tickets for the opportunity to dunk teachers in a pool of water. The money earned from the booth would go toward the purchase of a video camera for the school's TV studio. The principal of Chris' school, Ms. Stieger, offers to loan money to students who wish to have booths at the fair. Chris meets with Ms. Stieger and learns that the maximum amount of each loan is $150, and to qualify the estimated income from the booth must be double the estimated expenses. To be eligible for the loan, he must prepare a business plan detailing his estimated income and expenses, as well as his compliance with these rules. All of this must be done in a relatively short period of time.

In the video, Chris, with the help of his neighbor, Jasper, gathers the information he needs to develop his plan. He conducts a survey of students at his school to determine if they would be interested in buying a ticket to dunk a teacher, and, if so, how much they would be willing to pay. Chris also explores where to get the dunking machine and pool, and various options for filling and emptying the pool. Chris gathers information relevant to several means of filling the pool, including using the school hose, having the fire department deliver the water, and buying water from the pool store. Similarly, there is information in the video relevant to several methods of emptying the pool (e.g., the pool store can remove it, the city's public works truck can be used, or the water can be siphoned or drained out).

The problem posed at the end of the video is to prepare the business plan that Chris should present to Ms. Stieger. As we show later, the problem is rather complex; it requires evaluating multiple elements and options to construct an acceptable alternative that meets Ms. Stieger's constraints. Even college students have difficulty generating a solution that meets all of the constraints and makes effective and appropriate use of the sampling data.

After solving the major problem for each Jasper adventure, we encourage teachers to have groups of students work on analog and extension problems. The purpose of these materials is to help students: (a) develop flexible knowledge representations, (b) better understand key mathematical principles embedded in the Jasper adventures, and (c) make connections between the adventures and the thinking and planning that took place in many historical and contemporary events. Analog problems are formed by altering one or more of the parameters of the original Jasper problem. Additional kinds of analog problems are designed to help students explore important concepts in mathematics. For example, a particularly critical one for *The Big Splash* is the idea of representative sampling. The students can be presented with a range of possible sampling scenarios and asked to determine whether it is reasonable to extrapolate from them to the larger population of all students at the school. Extension problems are designed to help students integrate their knowledge across the curriculum. In the ideal implementation of Jasper, students continue their exploration of each Jasper adventure by researching particular aspects of the adventures that interest them (e.g., the history of fairs and carnivals, water conservation) and teaching that information to others. In some cases, this phase of Jasper may take place in classes other than the mathematics class (e.g., in science, English, or social studies).

RESEARCH ISSUES AND OUTCOMES

We find it helpful to frame our overall research and development work in the general context of three classes of interacting activities: theory-based materials development, field-based implementation, and cognitive and instructional research. Within this context, it is possible to carry out a program of serious theoretical and empirical research that focuses on several major topics in cognition and instruction. We also need to point out that our goal in conducting research has not been to prove that the Jasper adventures work, or to study them per se. Evidence with regard to such questions is a by-product of the types of studies we conduct and the broader issues they address. We see the Jasper adventures and other anchored-instruction materials and designs as vehicles for studying a number of important theoretical and empirical issues relating to children's thinking and learning. They also provide a vehicle for studying key issues relating to instructional theory and assessment.

The Gibsonian concept of *affordances* mentioned earlier applies not only to the instructional activities, but the research agenda as well. We argue that materials and learning environments such as these afford certain types of research that are otherwise difficult to conceptualize, let alone conduct. It is our contention that materials situated in meaningful contexts afford a whole new class of research. Furthermore, such research is absolutely essential if we are to have any significant impact on the problems noted earlier in this chapter. We illustrate our argument by overviewing one area of research that we are currently conducting in parallel with the materials development activity. We focus on children's learning in the Jasper context, including: (a) representation and assessment of the knowledge for solving Jasper adventures and (b) issues of analogical transfer.

Knowledge Representation and Transfer

Planning Net Analyses. A critical research focus involves detailed cognitive analyses of what children learn when they work with these kinds of materials. Complex mathematical problem solving involves several processes: (a) formulating the subproblems needed to solve the overall problem; (b) formulating a plan or organization of the subproblems to solve the overall problem, in some cases formulating multiple, alternative plans; (c) testing the feasibility of alternative plans; (d) distinguishing data that are relevant from data that are not; (e) coordinating relevant data with appropriate subproblems; and (f) using computational procedures to solve subproblems and, ultimately, the overall problem. The Jasper adventures are designed to require all these elements for solution. However, the complexity of the Jasper adventures also tests our current capacity to understand and represent the kinds of general and specific knowledge that middle-school and college students acquire in the course of solving these individual problems.

Earlier we provided a brief verbal description of *The Big Splash*, and explained some of the elements of the overall solution. Verbal descriptions are not sufficient if one wishes to study knowledge representation and acquisition. A more formal analysis is needed of the problem itself, and what students need to consider to solve it. This formal representation can then provide a basis for detailed analyses of performance and transfer. We captured the elements of the plan and the kinds of processes needed to solve *The Big Splash* by using a planning-net representation, as shown in Figure 14.1. These types of representations have also been used to represent the structure of other Jasper adventures, and to analyze student performance (see Goldman et al., 1991; Goldman, Vye, Williams, & Rewey, 1992).

In Figure 14.1, the order of execution is conveyed in the vertical arrangement of elements, not in the horizontal arrangement. The solution involves developing a business plan by estimating revenue and expenses, and testing expenses against the two constraints set forth in the story: Expenses cannot exceed $150, and they must be twice the estimated revenue. Estimating revenue involves determining the ticket price that will produce the greatest estimated income based on the sample, and then extrapolating to the population to estimate total income. In estimating expenses, there are two complications: The challenge is to find the combination of variables that produces the lowest overall cost. Some expenses, like the dunking machine, are fixed. Others vary because different pool filling and emptying options have implications for the number of days the pool must be rented. As a result, the total expenses for the pool are conjointly determined, and the optimal solution involves selecting the pool plan that minimizes total expenses.

An important aspect of the solution space is that there are multiple plans for filling and emptying the pool. Each plan needs to be tested against time and risk or conservation constraints. If a particular plan meets these constraints, costs for the filling or emptying plan need to be determined. Optimizing the solution implies looking for as many filling or emptying plans as meet the constraints, so that the overall expense for the pool can be found. Minimizing only the filling or emptying expense may not produce the lowest expense for the overall pool plan because of the interdependencies among solution space elements. An interesting aspect of *The Big Splash* solution space is that some of the filling options have no costs, but either take a long time (using the school hose) or are risky (having the fire department bring the water). There are also trade-offs for the emptying options (e.g., if the water is drained or siphoned out, it will take time and be ecologically irresponsible).

In previous work on complex problem solving using planning-net representations for the first two Jasper adventures, we observed that uninstructed college students and high-achieving sixth-grade mathematics students encounter two primary sources of difficulty: (a) generating embedded plans in response to the discovery of an obstacle (i.e., subproblems that were not evident at the intial phase of problem formulation were rarely considered in the solution), and (b)

The Big Splash Solution Space

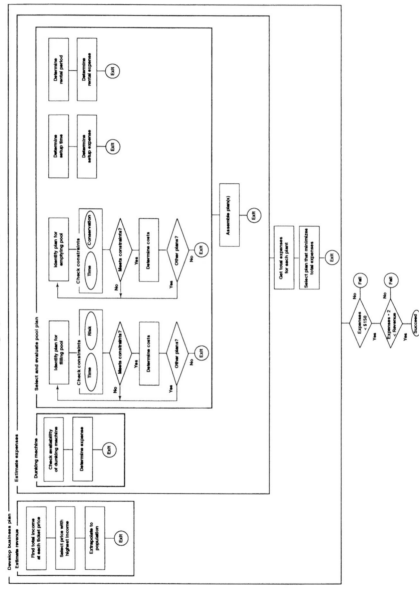

optimizing solutions by considering the feasibility of alternative plans and selecting the optimal one. In addition, the students experience difficulty coordinating relevant data with appropriate subproblems and accurately executing certain computational procedures. We have also observed that these difficulties diminish for middle-school students following instruction in the Jasper problem-solving environments. In fact, their level of performance approximates that of "uninstructed" college students (see Goldman et al., 1991, 1992).

Most recently, we were interested in pursuing these same issues in the context of *The Big Splash*. College and sixth-grade students first viewed *The Big Splash*. They were advised to pay close attention to the video because they would be asked questions afterward about the problem posed therein. After viewing the video, students were interviewed individually in a single session (the maximum session duration was 1.5 hours). They were asked to prepare a business plan for Chris, solving all of the necessary problems. To ensure that students understood what a business plan entails, the experimenter reshowed the scene from the video where the principal explained the meaning of the terms "income" and "expenses", and detailed her criteria for making a loan.

Students were asked to talk aloud as they solved the problem. Paper and pencils were provided for doing calculations, and the interviewer volunteered to perform calculations on a calculator if requested by a student. To eliminate memory demands during problem solving, students were provided with a written summary of the story. The summary contained all of the data (solution relevant and irrelevant) and the major story events from the video. College students' and children's think-aloud interview protocols were analyzed from three perspectives on problem solving: statement types, error types, and the business-plan elements, reflected in Figure 14.1. The data and analyses are described in detail in Goldman et al. (1992). The data and analyses lead to five primary conclusions:

1. Solution to *The Big Splash* requires the use of statistical inference as originally intended, and students—even those who were enrolled in college—were not very good at this. When they were inaccurate, they were mislead by high raw frequencies, and they failed to construct the cumulative distribution called for by the problem.

2. Plan feasibility was not carefully tested with respect to time constraints, and instead students focused on expenses. They need to consider that time is actually embedded in costs for the pool. The low frequency of attending to this subgoal may be due to its embedded status, consistent with our previous findings on embedded goals in the other Jasper adventures.

3. Although the business-plan domain provides explicit constraints against which to test their solutions, the majority of students failed to do so. Despite the focus on costs at the pool-plan level, most students did not test whether their business plans in fact met the principal, Ms. Stieger's, overall constraints.

4. In the business-plan domain, compared with trip planning, students were somewhat better able to coordinate different pieces of information with the appropriate plan element, perhaps because of the salient differences among the plan options.

5. Major sources of differences between college students and sixth graders were in the number of attempts and correct solutions, in the tendency to consider multiple plans, and in the breadth of exploration of the solution space. There were no particular differences in their skill at generating the subproblems that needed to be solved.

Analogical Transfer.   The Jasper materials and learning environments also allow us to look at issues of transfer and generalization of complex problem solving in ways that were not previously possible or manageable. Of particular interest is the issue of fostering analogical transfer. At the beginning of this chapter, we noted that the problem-solving and transfer literature indicates that students frequently demonstrate difficulty in transfering a solution from one worked-out problem or example to another related problem. This is a significant obstacle to producing the types of generalizable knowledge and skill that we would like to see in students. This is one reason that we have included analog and extension problems as part of the materials and activities for each Jasper adventure. Our goal is to create problem-solving environments and activities that foster the development of flexible knowledge and problem-solving skill that will support analogical transfer. Obviously, this is a critical objective, as shown by the following results from our own research.

Data collected in previous studies indicate that, without instruction in the context of the Jasper problem, high-achieving sixth-grade students have a difficult time solving a complex problem analogous to the Jasper problem. In contrast, fifth graders who have received a week of instruction in the Jasper context do much better on the same problem. In fact, they perform as well as college students who have not received instruction in the Jasper context (Goldman et al., 1991; Van Haneghan et al., 1992;). Although these data are encouraging, there are also indications that there is room for improvement in several areas.

First, there is a need for improvement in problem solving. Although students learn much from their instruction in the Jasper context, their performance is far from optimal. Even with prompting, most students are unable to formulate and solve all the steps of the analogous problem without errors. Further practice with similar problems is needed to develop expertise in solving this type of problem.

Second, students need to learn to solve complex problems individually. Because Jasper problems are complex, students often solve them as a whole class or in small groups with the guidance of the teacher. Although this type of instruction can improve the average performance in planning and solving complex problems, it does not give individual students the opportunity to develop expertise as independent problem solvers. To solve complex problems by themselves, students need extended, individualized practice with similar problems.

To provide opportunities for practice, a series of "what-if" analog problems were created by reusing the setting, characters, and objects of the videos and perturbing the values of one or more of the variables (e.g., in the adventure *Journey to Cedar Creek,* What if Jasper's boat had traveled at a rate of 9 miles per hour, rather than 8?). Students who have solved the original Jasper problem should have a number of advantages when they attempt to solve a "what-if" problem, rather than a problem that is structurally analogous but has totally different variables. With "what-if" problems, aspects of the previous solution remain invariant. Students can take shortcuts by simply recalling, rather than recalculating, some parts of the problem. In short, declarative knowledge from previous experiences can facilitate problem solving for "what-if" problems, but not for analogous problems with all new values, such as the ones used in previous analogical reasoning research in mathematics (e.g., Novick, 1988).

In a baseline study, two groups of sixth-grade students were asked to solve a "what-if" problem (Williams, Bransford, Vye, Goldman, & Carlson, 1992). One group had received Jasper instruction, the other had not. The results of this experiment indicate both positive and negative effects of prior experience. Students who had instruction in solving the Jasper problem were less likely to have misconceptions about the story or the task they were being asked to perform than those who were unfamiliar with the Jasper problem. Students with prior experience were also more likely to attempt a mathematical solution to the problem.

The results of this study also indicate that inappropriate use of specific declarative knowledge acquired while solving the Jasper problem often led to errors when solving the "what-if" problem. In these cases, students retrieved old outcomes even when changes in the variables should have led them to calculate new ones. One explanation for these errors is that the students did not understand the mathematical relationship between the variables of the problem and its outcomes. Another explanation is that they did not know how to calculate new outcomes, and therefore resorted to the retrieval of previous outcomes as an alternative strategy.

As part of research currently underway, a computer-based analog tutor is being designed to provide students instruction in solving "what-if" problems. This tutor will focus on the relationship between the problem presented in *Journey to Cedar Creek* and "what-if" problems that are formed by perturbing the variables in this problem. The analog tutor will encourage students to predict who will win a race—Jasper's boat or another boat that is just like Jasper's except for one important variable. Students are then asked to explain their predictions. Explanations must include identifying which outcome is affected by the change in variable (i.e., difference between the two boats). They also must include calculations that show the difference in outcomes (trip time, fuel burned, or money required) between the two boats. Students who are unable to explain their predictions will be helped to recall their solution to the original Jasper problem, and to adapt this solution to solve the race problem. Various boats will be paired with Jasper's boat in a series of races to give practice in solving the problem, and to target aspects of the problem that the student has difficulty in solving. Feedback will be provided via animation and sound effects.

Although students show negative transfer when solving "what-if" problems, there are many reasons to believe that their use as practice problems can be valuable. As mentioned previously, students who had prior experience with the Jasper problem were less likely to have misconceptions about the problem, and were more likely to attempt a mathematical solution. In addition, the ability to focus on particular aspects of a complex problem space by systematically changing the variables may help students (a) learn the relationship between variables and outcomes and (b) generalize their knowledge of these relationships. The current research hopes that instruction can overcome negative transfer to reap these benefits.

ALTERNATIVE APPROACHES TO ASSESSMENT

Instructional materials and programs such as *The Adventures of Jasper Woodbury* exemplify a constructivist approach to teaching and learning. Their design creates a different context for what can happen between and among students and teachers in the course of learning mathematics, science, and so on. By their very nature such programs also raise major issues about the appropriateness of current approaches to assessment. This point was made especially clear to us in the context of conducting a field-based implementation project during the 1990–1991 academic year (see Cognition and Technology Group at Vanderbilt, 1992c; Goldman, Pellegrino, & Bransford, 1994; Pellegrino et al., 1991).

The results from the Jasper implementation project were extremely positive on a number of dimensions. These included teacher, student, and parent reaction, as well as quantitative assessment data. Details are presented and summarized in other articles, and thus are not repeated here (see Cognition and Technology Group at Vanderbilt, 1992c; Pellegrino et al., 1991). Interestingly, as part of this project, we engaged in an extensive assessment of student performance using paper-and-pencil instruments of various types. The one negative comment about the Jasper implementation project was universally expressed by every one of our Jasper teachers. They were unanimous in their opinions of our assessment instruments, and noted that they and their students grew to hate them intensely. Here are some representative quotes:

Teacher No. 4: "My kids, as much as they liked Jasper, as much as they begged for Jasper, they finally told me: 'If I have to take another test on Jasper I don't want to see another Jasper'."

Teacher No. 3: "The reaction of our students when they saw anything come in from Vanderbilt that was in a brown envelope or box was 'another test!' . . . You could see them when they started out—most of them were pretty good, they'd think and then they would get tired. You could see them just filling pages or leaving a lot of it blank."

Teacher No. 9: "It seems to me that we're really asking kids to do something strange when we've introduced this wonderful technology and we've gotten them involved in the video experience . . . Then you give them this test that's on paper."

Teacher No. 7: "For children who can't read very well . . . they feel like giving up before they even try."

These quotes represent only a sample of negative reactions by our teachers, and their statements are much more forceful when one can hear the emotion behind them, rather than merely read them in print. It also seemed clear to us that, although students had done reasonably well on a variety of tests and tasks, there was considerable potential to do even better. For example, students did well on instruments designed to assess their mastery of each Jasper adventure, but many were still less than perfect. Some of the data already mentioned from instructional studies conducted in local schools lend additional support to this conclusion. Therefore, we asked ourselves what we could do to ensure better learning by all children at each site, and what the proper role was for assessment in that process.

One way to increase learning seemed to be to create more opportunities for formative assessments—assessments that help teachers make better decisions about instructional practice. If assessments help teachers see the need for further work on a Jasper adventure, for example, they could extend and tailor their instruction to ensure that more students learned more completely. We devised assessment instruments for the Jasper implementation project that assessed mastery of each Jasper adventure, but these instruments were not used to help teachers make instructional decisions about further work on each adventure. Instead, they were used as summative assessments of what students had learned at the end of the instructional sequence for each adventure.

It occurred to us that an excellent experiment might be to compare the effects of an implementation of Jasper, such as the one reported earlier, with a second type of implementation—one that made more use of formative assessments and included instruction about ways to use them to tailor teaching. However, there was a problem with this plan. As noted earlier, our Jasper teachers and students hated our paper-and-pencil assessment instruments. To ask them to do the same thing again, and especially to do even more assessment, seemed unthinkable. Our attempts to grapple with this problem suggested a new use of technology— in this case teleconferencing technology—that could provide a basis for formative assessments by teachers and students. We refer to this approach as our *Challenge Series,* and we discuss initial pilot tests of this model next.

Our pilot tests have involved the production of an experimental teleconference that included a game show featuring three college students as contestants, each of whom claimed to be an expert on flight and on the Jasper adventure *Rescue at Boone's Meadow*. Approximately 1 week prior to the show, students were told about the upcoming teleconference; they were informed that their task would be to listen to the answers that these "experts" (contestants) gave to various questions, and to judge for themselves who was the true expert. A representative from each class would call in their votes during the live teleconference.

The answers given by our "expert" contestants were scripted. All contestants were correct on the first round of questioning. By the fourth round, everyone except the true expert had made some erroneous arguments. It was at this point in the teleconference that the students were to call in their votes.

To prepare for the teleconference, the students were presented with video versions of Jasper "what-if" analog problems similar to the ones discussed earlier (e.g., What if Emily faced a 4-mile-per-hour headwind?). They worked on the solutions to these problems prior to the teleconference. The answers given by the game-show contestants could be evaluated provided that students had worked through these analog problems and understood the solutions. In contrast to reactions to our paper-and-pencil assessment instruments, teachers reported that the students enjoyed working through the analog problems. The students felt that they were learning something new (about headwinds and tailwinds), rather than simply going through the motion of practicing a specific set of "old" skills.

The teleconference turned out to be an extremely popular event for our Jasper sites. Videotaped and oral reports from teachers revealed groups of students actively discussing the strengths and weaknesses of each contestant's answers. At voting time, 85% of the students picked the real expert. To do so required them to understand that a trip of 65 miles with a headwind, followed by a return trip of 65 miles with a tailwind, did not mean that the headwind and tailwind canceled each other out.

We followed up this initial pilot test with a similar Challenge format and teleconference linked to the pair of adventures that cover statistics and business plans. Students were again given a set of analog problems with which to work. These problems were designed to extend the knowledge and understanding that students had gained from solving *The Big Splash*. The analogs involved concepts such as *representative sampling, variability in data,* and *feasibility of plans.* In addition, they were shown two plans by businesspersons who presented their ideas about schemes that would be more effective at making money than Chris' original dunking booth plan. These plans included relevant data to back up their claims, and it was the students' job to determine whether each plan was sound. This experience in evaluating plans and looking for flaws or unsubstantiated claims laid the foundation for what was to happen during the teleconference. On that day, students saw a show called *Rate That Plan* with a panel of college students as judges. For each of three business plans, students were asked to rate the quality of the plan as it was presented. This rating was done twice; once right after the presentation by each businessperson, and a second time following a series of questions directed to each businessperson by the college-student panelists. The questions were designed to focus on key issues, such as choice of the sample, estimates of other costs, and so on. At the end of the show, students were asked to pick the plan they thought was best. Students voted in each class and then phoned in their responses, which were then tallied and telecast. The children varied in their choices, although the majority of them chose one of the plans as the best. It turned out that the middle-school students' primary choice differed from the selection of the college-student panelists. Each of the plans had things to recommend it, and we are now examining in greater detail the reasons that students provided for the choices they made and the evaluations of each plan. As with the first teleconference, the students and teachers again found the work in preparation for the challenge and teleconference to be interesting and exciting. They also felt they had learned something in the course of doing these activities, which is one of our primary goals for any assessment format.

Our work to date with this Challenge model is part of a larger project experimenting with ways to develop teleconference ideas for each of the Jasper adventures, and to use video-based "what-if" analogs (like the ones used to prepare for the teleconference) to help teachers engage in formative evaluations of student learning following each Jasper adventure. In addition, we plan to experiment with the Challenge format in a variety of different content areas in addition to Jasper. The essence of the approach we are developing is to: (a) give students experience with a project-based curriculum (e.g., Jasper, Voyage of the Mimi, Kidsnet's Acid Rain projects, etc.); (b) provide them with an opportunity to prepare for specific challenges by working with analog and extension problems that are related to their curriculum; and (c) let them think "on-line" during the challenge and receive immediate feedback about their thinking in comparision with others from around the country. Ideally, students and teachers also get the opportunity to (a) analyze the strengths and weaknesses of their initial performance during the challenge, and (b) show improvement through their participation in a similar type of challenge the following week (for more discussion, see Goldman et al., 1994). We see this approach to instruction and assessment as being more consistent with project-based curricula, as well as current thinking that advocates systemic and dynamic assessment models vis-á-vis curriculum and instruction (e.g., Frederiksen & Collins, 1989; Lidz, 1987).

SUMMARY AND CONCLUSIONS

At the beginning of this chapter, we pointed out some of the critical issues facing cognitive and instructional theorists and educational practicioners, with regard to understanding the nature of problem solving and converting that understanding into effective instructional practice. Our goal in this chapter was to illustrate how our group is attempting to address some of these issues by drawing on cognitive theory and research to design alternative instructional environments. We then provided a theoretical overview of our center's approach to instruction, which we call *anchored instruction*. This approach is consistent with constructivist theories of knowledge acquisition, as well as contemporary views about the importance of situating or grounding learning in realistic and meaningful contexts. Such contexts provide ways to re-create some of the advantages of apprenticeship learning. We then described an example of our anchored-instruction approach— *The Adventures of Jasper Woodbury* mathematical problem-solving series. This series has an explicit set of design principles that govern the creation of each individual adventure. Each adventure is a video-based story that requires students to solve a complex, but realistic, problem. To do so, students must generate the necessary goals and subgoals of the overall problem space, find the relevant information embedded in the story, and construct the overall quantitative solution. This typically requires multiple class periods; once the solution has been achieved, there are additional materials and learning activities designed to extend and enhance the understanding of the solution and promote transfer. Students are typically highly motivated to work with these materials and achieve reasonable levels of success.

Another major goal of this chapter was to illustrate cognitive research on the nature of the knowledge representations that result from learning environments of this type. Specifically, we focused on the use of planning-net representations to capture the underlying structure of these complex problem-solving contexts. Such representations provide a powerful framework for examining the performance of children and adults, and for studying the issue of analogical transfer. Finally, we briefly considered the implications of such learning environments and the associated cognitive research for new approaches to assessment.

There is a large research-and-development agenda that obviously needs to be pursued with and about multimedia learning environments, such as the one described in this chapter. This agenda includes issues of learning, transfer, knowledge representation, assessment, teacher training, materials development, and instructional design. We hope that we have shown two things: (a) how we have begun to make inroads in pursuing some of the many issues, and (b) that our efforts to date are promising, especially in light of the acknowledged need for improved methods for the teaching and learning of problem solving.

ACKNOWLEDGEMENTS

Preparation of this chapter and its research were supported, in part, by a National Science Foundation Instructional Materials Development Grant MDR 9050191, and by the James S. McDonnell Foundation. However, neither should be held responsible for the contents of this chapter. Members of the Cognition and

Technology Group at Vanderbilt contributing to this chapter are Linda Barron, John Bransford, Laura Goin, Elizabeth Goldman, Susan Goldman, Ted Hasselbring, Daniel Hickey, Ron Kantor, Charles Kinzer, Allison Moore, James Pellegrino, Tony Petrosino, Dan Schwartz, Diana Sharp, Robert Sherwood, Sashank Varma, Nancy Vye, Susan Warren, and Susan Williams.

REFERENCES

Barrows, H. S. (1985). *How to design a problem-based curriculum for the preclinical years.* New York: Springer.

Bransford, J. D., Franks, J. J., Vye, N. J., & Sherwood, R. D. (1989). New approaches to instruction: Because wisdom can't be told. In S. Vosniadou & A. Ortony (Eds.), *Similarity and analogical reasoning* (pp. 470–497). New York: Cambridge University Press.

Bransford, J. D., Sherwood, R. S., Hasselbring, T. S., Kinzer, C. K., & Williams, S. M. (1990). Anchored Instruction: Why we need it and how technology can help. In D. Nix & R. Spiro (Eds.), *Cognition, education, and multi-media: Exploring ideas in high technology* (pp. 115–141). Hillsdale, NJ: Lawrence Erlbaum Associates.

Bransford, J. D., & Vye, N. J. (1989). A perspective on cognitive research and its implications for instruction. In L. Resnick & L. E. Klopfer (Eds.), *Toward the thinking curriculum: Current cognitive research* (pp. 173–205). Alexandria, VA: American Counseling Association.

Brown, A. L., Ash, D., Rutherford, M., Nakagawa, K., Gordon, A., & Campione, J. C. (1993). Distributed expertise in the classroom. In G. Salomon (Ed.), *Distributed cognitions: Psychological and educational considerations* (pp. 188–228). Cambridge, England: Cambridge University Press.

Brown, J. S., Collins, A., & Duguid, P. (1989). Situated cognition and the culture of learning. *Educational Researcher, 18*(1), 32–41.

Clement, J. (1982). Algebra word problem solutions: Thought processes underlying a common misconception. *Journal of Research in Mathematics Education, 13,* 16–30.

Cognition and Technology Group at Vanderbilt. (1990). Anchored instruction and its relationship to situated cognition. *Educational Researcher, 19*(6), 2–10.

Cognition and Technology Group at Vanderbilt. (1991). Technology and the design of generative learning environments, *Educational Technology, 31,* 34–40.

Cognition and Technology Group at Vanderbilt. (1992a). Anchored instruction in science and mathematics: Theoretical basis, developmental projects, and initial research findings. In R. A. Duschl & R. J. Hamilton (Eds.), *Philosophy of science, cognitive psychology, and educational theory and practice* (pp. 245–273). New York: State University of New York Press.

Cognition and Technology Group at Vanderbilt. (1992b). The Jasper experiment: An exploration of issues in learning and instructional design. *Educational Technology Research and Development, 40,* 65–80.

Cognition and Technology Group at Vanderbilt. (1992c). The Jasper series as an example of anchored instruction: Theory, program description, and assessment data. *Educational Psychologist, 27,* 291–315.

Cognition and Technology Group at Vanderbilt. (1993a). Integrated media: Toward a theoretical framework for utilizing their potential. *Journal of Special Education Technology, 12,* 71–85.

Cognition and Technology Group at Vanderbilt. (1993b). Toward integrated curricula: Possibilities from anchored instruction. In M. Rabinowitz (Ed.), *Cognitive science foundations of instruction* (pp. 33–55). Hillsdale, NJ: Lawrence Erlbaum Associates.

Cognition and Technology Group at Vanderbilt. (1994). From visual word problems to learning communities: Changing conceptions of cognitive research. In K. McGilly (Ed.), *Classroom lessons: Integrating cognitive theory and classroom practice* (pp. 157–200). Cambridge, MA: MIT Press/Bradford Books.

Cognition and Technology Group at Vanderbilt. (in press). The Jasper series: A design experiment in complex, mathematical problem-solving. In J. Hawkins & A. Collins (Eds.), *Design experiments: Integrating technologies into schools.* New York: Cambridge University Press.

Collins, A., Brown, J. S., & Newman, S. E. (1989). Cognitive apprenticeship: Teaching the crafts of reading, writing and mathematics. In L. B. Resnick (Ed.), *Knowing, learning and instruction: Essays in honor of Robert Glaser.* Hillsdale, NJ: Lawrence Erlbaum Associates.

Duffy, T. M., & Bednar, A. K. (1991). Attempting to come to grips with alternative perspectives. *Educational Technology, 31*(9), 12–15.

Frederiksen, J. R., & Collins, A. (1989). A systems approach to educational testing. *Educational Researcher, 18*(9), 27–32.

Gibson, J. J. (1977). The theory of affordance. In R. Shaw & J. Bransford (Eds.), *Perceiving, acting, and knowing* (pp. 67–82). Hillsdale, NJ: Lawrence Erlbaum Associates.

Goldman, S. R., Pellegrino, J. W., & Bransford, J. D. (1994). Assessing programs that invite thinking. In E. Baker & H. F. O'Neil, Jr., (Eds.), *Technology assessment in education and training* (pp. 199–230). Hillsdale, NJ: Lawrence Erlbaum Associates.

Goldman, S. R., Vye, N. J., Williams, S. M., & Rewey, K. (1992, April). *Planning net representations and analyses of complex problem solving.* Paper presented at the annual meeting of the American Educational Research Association, San Francisco, CA.

Goldman, S. R., Vye, N. J., Williams, S. M., Rewey, K., Pellegrino, J. W., & The Cognition and Technology Group at Vanderbilt. (1991, April). *Solution space analyses of the Jasper problems and students' attempts to solve them.* Paper presented at the American Educational Research Association, Chicago, IL.

Gragg, C. I. (1940, October 19). Because wisdom can't be told. *Harvard Alumni Bulletin*, pp. 78–84.

Hickey, D. T., Pellegrino, J. W., Petrosino, A., & Cognition and Technology Group at Vanderbilt. (1991, October). *Reconceptualizing space science education: A generative, problem solving approach.* Paper presented at the Florida Space Education conference, Cocoa Beach, FL.

Jenkins, J. J. (1979). Four points to remember: A tetrahedral model and memory experiments. In L. S. Cermak & F. I. M. Craik (Eds.), *Levels and processing in human memory* (pp. 429–446). Hillsdale, NJ: Lawrence Erlbaum Associates.

Lave, J., & Wegner, E. (1991). *Situated learning: Legitimate peripheral participation.* Cambridge, England: Cambridge University Press.

Lidz, C. S. (1987). *Dynamic assessment: An interactional approach to evaluating learning potential.* New York: Guilford.

McLarty, K., Goodman, J., Risko, V., Kinzer, C. K., Vye, N., Rowe, D., & Carson, J. (1990). Implementing anchored instruction: Guiding principles for curriculum development. In J. Zutell & S. McCormick (Eds.), *Literacy theory and research: Analyses from multiple paradigms* (pp. 109–120). Chicago, IL: National Reading Conference.

Minstrell, J. A. (1989). Teaching science for understanding. In L. B. Resnick & L. E. Klopfer (Eds.), *Toward the thinking curriculum: Current cognitive research* (pp. 129–149). Alexandria, VA: American Counseling Association.

National Council of Teachers of Mathematics. (1989). *Curriculum and evaluation standards for school mathematics.* Reston, VA: Author.

Nickerson, R. S. (1988). On improving thinking through instruction. *Review of Research in Education, 15*, 3–57.

Novick, L. R. (1988). Analogical transfer, problem similarity, and expertise. *Journal of Experimental Psychology: Learning, Memory, & Cognition, 14*, 510–520.

Palincsar, A. S., & Brown, A. L. (1989). Instruction for self-regulated reading. In L. B. Resnick & L. E. Klopfer (Eds.), *Toward the thinking curriculum: Current cognitive research* (pp. 19–39). Alexandria, VA: American Counseling Association.

Pellegrino, J. W., Hickey, D., Heath, A., Rewey, K., Vye, N. J., & The Cognition and Technology Group at Vanderbilt. (1991). *Assessing the outcomes of an innovative instructional program: The 1990–1991 implementation of the "Adventures of Jasper Woodbury"* (Tech. Rep. No. 91–1). Nashville, TN: Vanderbilt University, Learning Technology Center.

Perkins, D. N., Farady, M., & Bushey, B. (1991). Everyday reasoning and the roots of intelligence. In J. F. Voss, D. N. Perkins, & J. W. Segal (Eds.), *Informal reasoning and education* (pp. 83–106). Hillsdale, NJ: Lawrence Erlbaum Associates.

Porter, A. (1989). A curriculum out of balance: The case of elementary school mathematics. *Educational Researcher, 18,* 9–15.

Resnick, L. (1987). *Education and learning to think.* Washington, DC: National Academy Press.

Resnick, L. B., & Klopfer, L. E. (Eds.). (1989). *Toward the thinking curriculum: Current cognitive research.* Alexandria, VA: American Counseling Association.

Rogoff, B. (1990). *Apprenticeship in thinking.* New York: Oxford University Press.

Rogoff, B., & Lave, J. (Eds.). (1984). *Everyday cognition: Its development in social context.* Cambridge, MA: Harvard University Press.

Saxe, G. B. (1991). *Culture and cognitive development.* Hillsdale, NJ: Lawrence Erlbaum Associates.

Scardamalia, M., & Bereiter, C. (1991). Higher levels of agency for children in knowledge building: A challenge for the design of new knowledge media. *Journal of the Learning Sciences, 1,* 37–68.

Schoenfeld, A. H. (1989). Teaching mathematical thinking and problem solving. In L. B. Resnick & L. E. Klopfer (Eds.), *Toward the thinking curriculum: Current cognitive research* (pp. 83–103). Alexandria, VA: American Counseling Association.

Sharp, D. L. M., Bransford, J. D., Vye, N., Goldman, S. R., Kinzer, C., & Soraci, S., Jr. (1992). Literacy in an age of integrated-media. In M. J. Dreher & W. H. Slater (Eds.), *Elementary school literacy: Critical Issues* (pp. 183–210). Norwood, MA: Christopher-Gorden.

Spiro, R. J., Feltovich, P. L., Jacobson, M. J., & Coulson, R. L. (1991). Cognitive flexibility, constructivism, and hypertext: Random access instruction for advanced knowledge acquisition in ill-structured domains. *Educational Technology, 31*(5), 24–33.

Van Haneghan, J. P., Barron, L., Young, M. F., Williams, S. M., Vye, N. J., & Bransford, J. D. (1992). The Jasper series: An experiment with new ways to enhance mathematical thinking. In D. F. Halpern (Ed.), *Enhancing thinking skills in the sciences and mathematics* (pp. 15–38). Hillsdale, NJ: Lawrence Erlbaum Associates.

Williams, S. M. (1992). Putting case-based instruction into context: Examples from legal and medical education. *The Journal of the Learning Sciences, 2*(4), 367–427.

Williams, S. M., Bransford, J. D., Vye, N. J., Goldman, S. R., & Carlson, K. (1992, April). *Positive and negative effects of specific knowledge on mathematical problem solving.* Paper presented at the American Educational Research Association, San Francisco, CA.

15

Learning to Apply: From "School Garden Instruction" to Technology-Based Learning Environments

Heinz Mandl
Hans Gruber
Alexander Renkl
University of Munich, Germany

FUNCTIONS OF SCHOOLING

Do schools do what they are supposed to? According to sociological structure-functionalistic theories, schools as well as universities have to fulfil several functions for the society and for the individual. Within this framework, two functions of the school are qualification and integration-enculturation (cf. Fend, 1980; Parsons, 1959). These functions are related to learning that takes place in school. School instruction should teach students important facts and skills that are necessary for later working life. Ideally, the proverb *Non scholae sed vitae discimus* ("We do not learn for school, but for life") should be true in order to adequately qualify students.

The school life and the role expectations that students are confronted with are supposed to be the media by which ethical norms, values, and belief systems are acquired. Some authors conceive of the function of integration-enculturation in a more negative way: They argue that this function of school is purposed to maintain the existing system of rules. However, the acquisition of social norms in school may provide the basis for being a responsible member of society, thus fulfilling an important function of institutionalized education in school.

In recent years doubts have been expressed whether knowledge and skills acquired in school are useful for later life. Some critics describe learning in school by varying the previously mentioned proverb, which should then be written as follows: *Non vitae sed scholae discimus* ("We do not learn for life, but for school"). Particularly, it has been criticized, most urgently in the United States, that an abstract form of instruction leads to knowledge that is very often inert (Bransford, Goldman, & Vye, 1991; Rumpf, 1987; Wagenschein, 1968).

307

Inert means that this knowledge cannot be used in solving problems of real-world complexity. Furthermore, basic qualifications such as "skill and will" (Paris, 1988) for cooperation and the flexible use of tools are neglected in school learning (Resnick, 1987). Hence, in view of the present situation, it is highly questionable whether schools can fulfil their qualification function. However, this type of criticism against the school system is not new. At the end of the 19th and at the beginning of the 20th centuries, the German *Reformpädagogik* (reform pedagogy) postulated similar arguments and realized alternative instructional models. One new idea was the *Schulgartenunterricht* (school garden instruction; Kerschensteiner, 1907), which is discussed later in this chapter, together with the basic *Reformpädagogik* ideas.

Recently, alternative instructional models have also been proposed, such as the *cognitive-apprenticeship* model, or the *anchored-instruction* approach. Within these approaches, learning is conceived in a broad sense. Besides knowledge of specific facts and skills, a learner has to acquire the ways of thinking that exist within the "communities of practice" of the respective domains. The acquisitions of belief systems and of tricks of the trade are important learning objectives as well. Learning is conceived as enculturation. Hence, at least implicitly, the criticism of present school instruction concerns the integration-enculturation function as well.

The criticism of traditional instructional models is primarily related to elementary and secondary education. Comparatively, fewer arguments have been postulated against university education and vocational training. Recently, however, the conventional models of instruction adopted in contemporary German universities have also been increasingly criticized. At first glance, there seem to be several parallels. For example, the adoption of abstract instruction and the neglect of cooperation and of tool use are as prevalent in university and vocational education as they are in school. However, it might be possible that university students and vocational school students have already acquired more prerequisites for learning (knowledge, study skills, etc.) as compared with elementary-school or secondary-school students. For this reason they might be able to profit even more from traditional forms of instruction. In the next section we present some empirical studies of the knowledge-application capabilities of students of vocational and university students in the domains of economics and medicine. The empirical evidence reveals that the problems of vocational and university education resemble those that are prominent in school.

KNOWLEDGE APPLICATION PROBLEMS OF STUDENTS OF VOCATIONAL SCHOOL AND UNIVERSITY

Studies in Business Management

In an investigation by Mandl, Gruber, and Renkl (1992), vocational school students participated in a computer-based simulation game in the domain of economics (JEANSFABRIK [jeans manufacturing]; Preiß, 1992). Cooperative dyads were given the task of maximizing the profit of a computer-simulated jeans factory. During the problem-solving phase, a hypercard system was made available as external knowledge base, in which economic terms and relations relevant to the task were illustrated. The subjects were permitted to use this knowledge base at any time. The communicative exchange within the cooperative dyads, with regard to hypothesis generation and decision making, was analyzed using verbal protocols. In addition, individually assessed knowledge structures were taken into account using several elicitation techniques (e.g., structure-formation technique). We found deficits in knowledge application and problem-solving with regard to three aspects.

Use of One's Own Declarative Knowledge.   Subjects showed considerable deficits in using their own declarative knowledge. For example, one subject wrote in an unstandardized test of prior knowledge: "The lower the selling price, the more sales, and vice versa." He obviously did not draw on this knowledge when he told his partner as they were handling the computer-simulation task: "If our selling price is too low, nobody would buy the jeans." The subjects were certainly able to write about the relation between selling price and sales. However, this knowledge remained inert. The subjects were, at least in part, not able to use that knowledge as a tool in their business decision making. Their knowledge was not sufficiently conditionalized to the relevant application conditions.

Use of External Tools.   Throughout the simulation, the subjects were permitted access to the external knowledge base in the form of a hypercard system covering the main terms and relations. In the observed dyads, information access was never attempted. The subjects did not use the available tool. This deficit is not surprising, because "declarative performance" is paramount in schooling. The flexible use of external tools is even forbidden in most classrooms. At least three positive consequences were lacking which would have resulted from the use of the external knowledge base. First, knowledge that the subjects lacked could have been obtained. Second, existing but unexploited knowledge could have been activated. Third, erroneous concepts and assumptions could have been corrected.

Characteristics of the Interaction.   In many instances, no real problem-related debate took place within the cooperative dyads. The partner's point of view was often adopted in an uncritical and passive way. This substantially reduced the probability of erroneous concepts being corrected through debate. Furthermore, sociocognitive conflicts, which are supposed to foster learning, and constructive processes had little chance to evolve.

These deficits in knowledge application had been observed in vocational school students who were at the beginning of expertise development. There is some evidence that similar deficits can be found in university students. Dahlgren and Marton (1978) showed that the misconceptions about economic terms held by university students are sometimes resistant to change. Several university instruction courses on business management, observed by Dahlgren and Marton, only provided additional knowledge: that correct and incorrect concepts stood side by side. Such knowledge compartmentalization is problematic: In situations where knowledge has to be applied, the problem solver often relies on the old, deficient misconceptions, instead of resorting to the newly acquired concepts, which might be more adequate.

Mandl, Gruber, and Renkl (1994) investigated the knowledge-application processes of more expert subjects (viz, graduate students of economics). Even these subjects had enormous difficulties in knowledge utilization; novices (students of psychology and education) outperformed them in the computer-simulated business management task described earlier, despite that the subjects had been given ample opportunity to explore the simulation before working with it. The graduates, who can be considered as intermediate experts, were obviously hindered by their extensive knowledge base. One factor that might contribute to these knowledge-application problems is the largely abstract nature of university instruction. The following reasons were identified to explain the poor problem-solving performance of the intermediate experts compared with novices: (a) Intermediate experts put forward hypotheses that were too complicated. They had complex and correct mental models of the system that lacked adequate hierarchical organization. Thus they took into account more aspects than they could integrate into a sound decision. (b) Intermediate experts held assumptions that were theoretically true and consistent with economics theory, but were not relevant to the present problem-solving task. (c) Intermediate experts had difficulties deducing appropriate operators from their declarative knowledge of domain rules. (d) Intermediate experts were too cautious in manipulating the variables (selling price, production quantity) in the simulation. On the whole, even quite advanced economic students showed serious deficits in knowledge application.

Studies in Medicine

In a completely different domain, analyses of medical students' knowledge application provided analogous evidence that university instruction often does not adequately prepare students to solve domain-relevant problems.

One important goal in medical education is the acquisition of diagnostic competencies because a wrong diagnosis might entail serious consequences for a patient's health. The knowledge relevant to solve diagnostic problems cannot easily be acquired because medicine is an ill-structured complex domain, with multiple relations between symptoms and diagnoses (Feltovich, Spiro, & Coulson, 1989).

Our research project on medical instruction (Gräsel, Mandl, & Prenzel, 1992;

Mandl et al., 1991) dealt with the analysis of clinical reasoning of students working with a case-based computer program (PlanAlyzer; Trustees of Dartmouth College, 1989) on the diagnosis of anemia. When working with the PlanAlyzer, students take the role of the physician and must diagnose different types of anemia in simulated patients. The structure of the cases simulates the examination of a patient in a clinical setting. Before making the final differential diagnosis, the student must analyze information about the patient's history, physical examinations, and blood smear to construct preliminary diagnostic hypotheses.

In studies with 4th-year medical students, think-aloud protocols were analyzed with regard to three indicators for the quality of knowledge construction and application processes; in each of these indicators deficits were found even with advanced medical students.

Attention to Salient Data.   Gräsel, Prenzel, and Mandl (1993) provided evidence that medical students often selected the data presented in a manner which was too strict and premature for the diagnostic process, instead of trying to use all findings and symptoms presented to them. Six out of 14 advanced medical students took less than 10% of the patient's symptoms into account; 5 more subjects took between 10% and 20% of the information into account. Thus, most subjects were extremely selective in their initial information seeking. They mistook that only a limited portion of the patients' data were useful for making correct diagnoses. The high degree of selectivity also appeared when considering the most salient symptoms (results of the blood examination), which had been presented to the learners from the very beginning of the case-based reasoning. About half of the students did not pay any attention to the blood scores. This means that even the most salient symptoms in many cases were not adequately considered during diagnosis, although the subjects could verbally acknowledge the importance of these symptoms.

Organization of Concepts.   It has often been shown that the degree of structure and organization of concepts (e.g., symptoms and diagnoses) play an important role in expertlike problem solving. The ability to sort symptoms and diagnoses according to their redundancy or according to causal relations is therefore crucial for being able to apply one's knowledge to problem situations. Expert ratings of the case representations extracted from the verbal protocols revealed that only 4 out of 14 representations could be classified as *well organized,* the other 10 protocols showing severe deficiencies in organization and structure. Obviously only few medical students were able to adequately organize their ample knowledge of symptoms and diagnoses. Badly organized knowledge, however, cannot be applied.

Relations Between Symptoms and Diagnoses.   A central aspect in knowledge application in medical reasoning is the degree of relations established between symptoms and possible diagnoses. Subjects showed considerable deficits in constructing causal explanations. Several subjects did not draw any relations between symptoms and diagnoses, or only established relations that narrowly connected one single symptom with one single diagnosis ("parallel relations"). Subjects using such parallel relations constructed new diagnostic hypotheses whenever new findings were presented to them. As a result, these subjects formulated many different hypotheses—each being connected with a single symptom. Such problem solving of course always proves to be unsuccessful. A systematic combination of hypotheses and newly presented findings about the patient was constructed by only two subjects.

In summary, the studies showed severe deficits in medical students' diagnostic skills. This is in accord with studies of other research groups (e.g., Schmidt, Norman, & Boshuizen, 1990). A major reason for this deplorable state of affairs can be traced back to medical education. One problem with medical education especially in Germany, is the dominance of a basic-science curriculum during the first years of study. In comparison with U.S. medical schools, German students are exposed to real patients relatively late. Even then, university clinics provide only a restricted number of opportunities for practice because of the limited number of available patients.

Taken together, a bulk of evidence from school, vocational school, and several domains of university reveals that the traditional instructional system has severe problems in teaching applicable knowledge. Therefore, there seems to be a need for a fundamental reform of instruction. Ideas for alternative instructional models that utilize the potentials of new technology-based media, have been developed in recent years (e.g., Cognition and Technology Group at Vanderbilt, 1992; Collins, 1991). The basic ideas of these approaches can be traced back to the historical root in the German *Reformpädagogik,* which is discussed in the next section.

INSTRUCTIONAL ALTERNATIVES: FROM *REFORMPÄDAGOGIK* TO *SITUATED LEARNING*

As a consequence of the problems encountered with knowledge application, current forms of instruction have recently been severely criticized by the situated-learning movement. New instructional approaches have been proposed. For German researchers in education, a strong dejá-vu feeling is elicited in this context, remembering the German *Reformpädagogik* movement, which began at the end of the 19th century. However, due to their democratic potential, most of its organizations were violently dissolved at the beginning of the Third Reich in 1933.

The representatives of *Reformpädagogik* criticized the *Buchschule* (book school; Kerschensteiner, 1912) in much the same way as it was criticized in the situated-learning literature. The central idea in the German *Reformpädagogik* was the *Arbeitsschule* (work school). Among the most prominent proponents were Georg Kerschensteiner (1854–1932) and Hugo Gaudig (1860–1923). Their approaches are presented in short in the next two sections. *Reformpädagogik* did not deal with university education. However, many parallelisms are to be found, thus the basic message of *Reformpädagogik* seems to be relevant to university education as well. A comparison between these "ancient" German models, and more recent instructional models, concludes the chapter.

Kerschensteiner's Work-School Approach

In addition to his theoretical work, Kerschensteiner was the senior school inspector in Munich (1895–1918). This position allowed him to broadly realize many of his ideas on instruction. He completely reorganized the elementary-school system and the vocational-school system, and their respective curricula in Munich. He was a practitioner until later life, when he became a university professor.

Kerschensteiner criticized the intellectualism and abstractness of the then-existing schools. He called the schools *book schools* with all the negative implications this term may have. In contrast to book schools, he proposed the concept of *work schools*. Especially in early outlines of his instructional ideas, Kerschensteiner emphasized the importance of manual work that should be connected with mental work as much as possible (much later, Resnick (1987) wrote: "Symbol manipulation in school versus contextualized reasoning outside schools," p. 14). In addition, Kerschensteiner (1907) created activity settings by which he tried to avoid the problem of fragmentation of different subject matters. These settings served somehow as a *macrocontext* (a term used by the Cognition and Technology Group at Vanderbilt, 1992). One of Kerschensteiner's first innovations in the Munich schools was the introduction of the *Schulgartenunterricht* (school garden instruction; Kerschensteiner, 1907). Based on authentic activities in the school garden, eighth graders learned biology, zoology, and botany, thus avoiding an artificial distinction between schoolwork and real-world activity (more than 80 years later Brown, Collins, and Duguid, 1989, expressed a similar idea: "When authentic activities are transferred to the classroom, their context is inevitably transmuted; they become classroom tasks and part of the school culture," p. 34). As part of the school garden instruction, aquaria and terraria were introduced as learning media, and the students had to grow flowers and plants in the school garden. A basic principle of Kerschensteiner's conception was the claim that instructional questions should not be posed by the teacher, but rather through a relevant problem presented at the beginning of an instructional sequence. This problem should be rather complex so that it could not easily be solved by already available routines. In that way, questions should be raised that motivate the students to search for answers.

Although Kerschensteiner strictly opposed transfigured educational conceptions like "let the child grow out of itself," he emphasized the importance of the learner's *Selbsttätigkeit* (self-regulated activity). This self-regulated activity which characterizes the learning processes in early childhood, usually gets lost at the beginning of traditional school life, as Kerschensteiner (1907) noted:

> Gone is all the activity that seized the child, gone is all the reality of the house, of the workshop, of the kitchen, of the cowshed, of the garden, and of the fields. Gone is the child's world. A new, strange world with hundreds of puzzles and curious demands and purposes imposes on the child. (p. 1, translation by the authors)[1]

When entering the traditional school the child journeys into an *Ersatzwelt* (surrogate world) in which *ersatz activities* ("surrogate activities"; the term "ersatz activities" is used by Brown et al., 1989, nicely illustrating that the German word *Ersatz* has found its way into English) are to be carried out. The *Ersatzwelt* hardly bears any relation to the outside (authentic) world. In contrast, in Kerschensteiner's work schools, the problems posed were of relevance to the children's real life outside the school context. In addition to specific skills and knowledge, the learners were expected to acquire socially conscious attitudes and a sense of responsibility as a member of society (later called "learning as entering the culture of expert practice"; Collins, Brown, & Newman, 1989). One means to achieve the latter goals is the employment of group work and cooperative learning, which has recently received renewed interest. The role of the teacher was to provide support only when necessary. Otherwise he or she had to withdraw as far as possible during the course of learning.

The modern theme of sequencing instructional units played a central role in Kerschensteiner's approach. Kerschensteiner (1914a) proposed that each instructional sequence should be composed of the following five steps. First, a complex real-world problem should be set to raise motivating questions. Thus, the learning process is driven by student questions instead of teacher questions. According to Kerschensteiner, this is one of the most important points of the instructional process (resembling modern conceptions of problem-oriented learning). Second, the student should generate hypotheses out of his or her prior knowledge and from heuristic reasoning. Third, the student should not blindly accept the first hypothesis that appears, but critically test the assumption through active exploration and reflection. Fourth, the student should verify; this means that the student should not dwell on intellectual exercises, but start to act and produce a "visible" object. Fifth, the student critically self-evaluates the product. This

---

[1] Original: Weg ist alle Beschäftigung, die das ganze Kind erfaßte, weg alle Realität des Hauses, der Werkstatt, der Küche, des Stalles, des Gartens, des Feldes. (. . .) Weg ist die ganze Welt des Kindes. Eine neue, fremde Welt mit hundert Rätseln und unfaßbaren Forderungen und Zwecken steht vor ihnen.

evaluation should include two directions: The critical *Außenschau* (outer view) concerns the visible product, the *Innenschau* (inner view) pertains to the rational self-evaluation of the internal processes (e.g., the mental processes that lead to errors). The more the inner view is emphasized, the more useful self-evaluations become. Kerschensteiner also explicitly mentioned that new ways of learning had to be evaluated by new methods of assessment.

Besides education of elementary-school and secondary-school children, Kerschensteiner was extremely concerned with how school prepares for work life. Thus, he played an important role in the educational foundation of the German vocational-training system, which has become internationally known as the *dual system* and which represents one idea of the German *Reformpädagogik* that has survived until now. The dual system is a form of training tied to the place of work, with supplementary teaching in the compulsory part-time vocational school (Deutsche Forschungsgemeinschaft, 1990). In German vocational training, each student must study in a vocational school for 3 years and about 1.5 million students per year enter a vocational school (Kutscha, 1982). There is a high degree of educational efficiency through the combination of theory and practice (e.g., the combination of working and learning). Furthermore, the dual system is characterized by its high flexibility and its permeability between practical needs and educational curricula concerning innovations in the domains considered. The coordination between factories and vocational schools in the dual system should ideally provide a powerful learning environment. In practice, however, factories and schools have drifted apart from each other so that the initial idea has lost much of its strength (Lisop, 1989). Nevertheless, in Germany, the theoretical and practical job training is defined by a combination of vocational schools and practical work in companies or workshops. The educational foundings of the Munich *Reformpädagogik* have spread throughout Germany and have survived until now, although not in their original form.

Kerschensteiner's concept of *work* changed through the course of time. After initially stressing manual work, Kerschensteiner later used the notion of work primarily to denote mental self-regulated thinking and learning processes. This shift was a consequence of Hugo Gaudig's criticism, who argued that Kerschensteiner's conception of work put too much emphasis on manual work.

Gaudig's Principle of Free Mental Activity

Gaudig was the founding father of another work-school approach that had much in common with Kerschensteiner's model. Like Kerschensteiner, Gaudig was not a pure theoretician; he was a practitioner as a teacher, as well as a director of several schools and of a teaching-training college. He turned down offers for scientific or political positions to keep in contact with the practice aspects of his field. The main goal of Gaudig's educational approach was the development of personality. In his conception, personality was comprised of both individuality and acknowledgement of society's rules. *Freie geistige Arbeit* (free mental work) was the central motto. As for many proponents of *Reformpädagogik,* a main means and goal of education was the self-regulated activity of the learner. The teacher activity in traditional schools should be replaced by student activity. The following quotation from Gaudig (1922) nicely illustrates his viewpoint:

> I demand self-regulated activity in all phases of the working process. In setting goals, in planning activities, in approaching the goal, in decisions at critical points, in control of the working process and product, learning should be free. (p. 93, translation by the authors)[2]

Students' questions played a central role in Gaudig's learning concept. Gaudig's educational goal was to teach the learner effective methods for self-regulated learning, whereas in traditional instruction the learning gains were dependent on the quality of the teaching method. Thus, the teacher's goal should be the systematic teaching of the self-regulated coping strategies for problems of increasing complexity and difficulty. The teacher should give as little guidance as possible. His or her primary function is the organization of the learning environment for self-regulated learning. As a continuation of Gaudig's work, Scheibner (1930) developed an instructional model composed of five phases. First, a goal is set. Second, materials for one's work are evaluated, selected, and arranged. Third, a plan is developed and several solution steps are defined. Fourth, individual solution steps are executed. Finally, the product is considered, evaluated, and analyzed. The work involved in all stages is performed by the student himself or by a group of students after a brief introduction by the teacher.

The ideas of the *Reformpädagogik,* which broadly entered school practice, may be summarized as follows. The most central claim Kerschensteiner and Gaudig made was that learning should be *problem-oriented.* Learning should occur within *authentic contexts,* but not in an abstract form (the idea of a work school instead a book school). Authentic contexts provide ample opportunity to view the subject matter from *different directions.* Through problem-oriented learning, the students should be encouraged to learn in an *active and self-regulated* manner, either in individual learning situations or in self-guided *cooperative learning groups.* An important step in the learning process that needs to be fostered is *reflection* on inner mental processes, compared with the "outer view" on the subject matter. Reflection and discussion about the topics to be learned are easily aroused when students are learning in groups. As a consequence of these social aspects of learning, the *Reformpädagogik* instructional

---

[2]Original: Selbständigkeit fordere ich für alle Phasen der Arbeitsvorgänge. Beim Zielsetzen, beim Ordnen des Arbeitsganges, bei der Fortbewegung zum Ziel und bei den Entscheidungen an kritischen Punkten, bei der Kontrolle des Arbeitsganges und des Ergebnisses, bei der Korrektur, bei der Beurteilung soll der Schüler freitätig sein.

conception aimed not only to teach specific facts and skills, but also to educate students to become responsible members of society. Thus, *enculturation* was considered an important function of learning.

These principles of *Reformpädagogik* appear rather modern. Many observations nowadays are still valid because the parallelisms concern not only modern school instruction, but also university education. Although the old German pedagogues did not have the possibility to use modern instructional technologies, and therefore did not directly make suggestions for the design of teaching and learning media, the instructional consequences of the *Reformpädagogik* are of broad interest today. In the final section, we demonstrate some parallels between Kerschensteiner's and Gaudig's approaches and recent technology-based situated-learning models.

Modern Instructional Approaches

The instructional approaches that have been proposed in recent years to prevent the problem of inert knowledge are based on cognitive psychology and a constructivistic view of learning. We briefly review three modern instructional theories: anchored instruction, random-access instruction, and cognitive apprenticeship. Our central focus is how far these approaches can be traced back to the concepts that have been proposed by the *Reformpädagogik*. This allows for evaluating the importance of *Reformpädagogik*, as well as the progress in instructional theory through the use of technology-based learning environments.

Anchored-Instruction Approach. The anchored-instruction approach that has been developed at Vanderbilt University (e.g., Cognition and Technology Group at Vanderbilt, 1992) emphasizes the problem of inert knowledge. Central means for avoiding inert knowledge through the acquisition of flexibly applicable knowledge are the creation of situated-learning environments that integrate knowledge and action in a problem-oriented context. In anchored instruction, the students (anchored instruction involves mainly primary-school and secondary-school children) are confronted with complex stories that are presented using video-disc technology. The stories provide many anchors for solving problems that are found during the presentation. The knowledge that is necessary for solving the problem can be retrieved within the learning environment. Because the problems presented on the video discs stem from the students' natural settings, anchored instruction provides authentic learning contexts. Thus, several *Reformpädagogik* ideas can be detected in the anchored-instruction approach: problem-oriented learning, using authentic contexts, and viewing problems from different directions. By using modern technology, these concepts come to realization in a new manner which more clearly may be the object of instructional studies.

Random-Access Instruction Approach.   Random-access instruction stresses the necessity of acquiring flexibly applicable competence in complex domains (e.g., Spiro, Feltovich, Jacobson, & Coulson, 1991). It is especially concerned with the advanced construction of knowledge within ill-structured knowledge domains like medicine. Therefore, random-access instruction is suited to address problems of university instruction. Authentic contexts in learning are used to avoid the development of oversimplified concepts that may lead to incorrect applications. Another central concept is the use of multiple perspectives during learning. The learner should view the same subject matter at different times, in different contexts, and for different purposes to systematically enlarge the range of application of knowledge. *Reformpädagogik* ideas of authentic contexts and different directions of view are most important in random-access instruction. A preferable means for realizing those concepts is the use of computer-based training. Spiro et al. (1991) use hypertext-learning environments. As non-linear media, these allow for "landscape criss-crossing," which means the traversal of complex subject matter by returning to the same place of the conceptual "landscape" on different occasions and from different directions. Other technology-based media, such as case-based computer programs (cf. the aforementioned program PlanAlyzer in the domain of medicine) or complex computer simulations (cf. JEANSFABRIK in the domain of economics), may provide ample opportunity for learners to experience multiple perspectives of complex problems. The possibility of systematically presenting problems from different directions using modern technology may be the reason that the concept of *multiple perspectives* is currently more central than in *Reformpädagogik*.

Cognitive-Apprenticeship Approach.   The third modern instructional theory is the cognitive-apprenticeship approach (e.g., Collins et al., 1989), for which experts' practice is its core of interest. In their activities, experts always apply situated strategies. To develop applicable knowledge, the cognitive-apprenticeship approach stresses the use of explicit cognitive processes (e.g., strategies, heuristics) during learning. At first, these processes are externalized by experts within authentic application situations. Learning then leads the student to acquire knowledge that is applicable to a certain situation. Further learning takes place in successively sequenced learning environments of increasing complexity and diversity. For all these learning stages of the apprenticeship approach, the expert is an important role model. However, the student increasingly takes an active role as the expert fades out gradually. Articulation and reflection are promoted by the expert (i.e., the normally internal mental problem-solving processes are externalized). Thus, a student's own strategies can be compared with strategies of experts or other students, and are then open to feedback. As a result, the student increasingly may take over the role initially taken by the expert. *Reformpädagogik* ideas of authentic contexts, and self-regulated learner, and reflection are central characteristics of the cognitive-apprenticeship approach. Collins and Brown (1988) described some computer-based programs that provide an "abstracted replay" of prior problem-solving steps and, therefore, the opportunity to reflect on them. An example is ALGE-BRALAND (Brown, 1985), where the students' steps toward the solution of algebraic expressions are reified in a treelike structure, and the students can reflect on their solution strategies.

Although the instructional prescriptions of the German *Reformpädagogik* were neither based on a well-advanced cognitive psychology, nor implemented on instructional, technological devices, and, at least not explicitly, not implemented with reference to a constructivistic epistemology, most of the central features of *Reformpädagogik* could be characterizations of the modern instructional approaches as well. Of course, both *Reformpädagogik* and the modern approaches earn their merits. *Reformpädagogik* remains a relevant theoretical approach even if many ideas are included in the recent models, which are founded on a sounder scientific knowledge base. A great advantage of the older approaches is that they are not only programmatic models with some preliminary evaluations, and they were realized on a large scale. This is especially true for Kerschensteiner's approach, which was realized in the Munich school system. Thus, it is possible to experience many of these kinds of alternative instructional methods from everyday practice. However, the modern approaches take advantage of their ideas of how to combine situated-learning concepts with new technology to produce powerful learning environments. The present chapter cannot provide an extensive discussion of either aspect, but tries to provoke some interest, especially in consulting Kerschensteiner's work. A portion of his articles were translated into English (e.g., Kerschensteiner, 1911, 1913, 1914b).

We resume the question raised at the chapter's beginning: Do schools do what they are supposed to do? With regard to the students' qualification and enculturation, present schools certainly do not function as they should. In order to overcome this problem, some promising instructional approaches employing educational technology have been developed within the situated-learning movement. It may also be very useful to consult the old German *Reformpädagogik* in which ideas similar to recent instructional approaches had already been pointed out and realized on a large scale. There are multiple experiences from everyday practice that provide useful guidelines for the design of technology-based learning media, as well as for embedding them in broader didactical concepts. The importance of embedding educational technology in other instructional activities grows out of a disadvantage of technological media: that they always "disrupt" reality to some extent (von Hentig, 1984) and put demands on symbolization capacities that younger learners might lack (Mandl & Hron, 1989). A conception of learning as enculturation especially poses the need for authentic, not *technology-filtered* experiences.

REFERENCES

Bransford, J. D., Goldman, S. R., & Vye, N. J. (1991). Making a difference in people's ability to think: Reflections on a decade of work and some hopes for the future. In R. J. Sternberg & L. Okagaki (Eds.), *Influences on children* (pp. 147–180). Hillsdale, NJ: Lawrence Erlbaum Associates.

Brown, J. S. (1985). Process versus product: A perspective on tools for communal and informal electronic learning. *Journal of Educational Computing Research, 1*, 179–201.

Brown, J. S., Collins, A., & Duguid, P. (1989). Situated cognition and the culture of learning. *Educational Researcher, 18*(1), 32–42.

Cognition and Technology Group at Vanderbilt (1992). The Jasper series as an example of anchored instruction: Theory, program, description, and assessment data. *Educational Psychologist, 27,* 291–315.

Collins, A. (1991). Cognitive apprenticeship and instructional technology. In L. Idol & B. Fly Jones (Eds.), *Educational values and cognitive instruction: Implications for reform* (pp. 121–138). Hillsdale, NJ: Lawrence Erlbaum Associates.

Collins, A., & Brown, J. S. (1988). The computer as a tool for learning through reflection. In H. Mandl & A. Lesgold (Eds.), *Learning issues for intelligent tutoring systems* (pp. 1–18). New York: Springer.

Collins, A., Brown, J. S., & Newman, S. E. (1989). Cognitive apprenticeship: Teaching the crafts of reading, writing, and mathematics. In L. B. Resnick (Ed.), *Knowing, learning, and instruction* (pp. 453–494). Hillsdale, NJ: Lawrence Erlbaum Associates.

Dahlgren, L. O., & Marton, F. (1978). Students' conceptions of subject matter: An aspect of learning and teaching in higher education. *Studies in Higher Education, 3,* 25–35.

Deutsche Forschungsgemeinschaft (1990). *Berufsbildungsforschung an den Hochschulen der Bundesrepublik Deutschland* [Research of vocational education in German universities]. Weinheim: VCH Acta humaniora.

Feltovich, P. J., Spiro, R. J., & Coulson, R. L. (1989). The nature of conceptual understanding in biomedicine: The deep structure of complex ideas and the development of misconceptions. In D. Evans & V. Patel (Eds.), *The cognitive science in medicine* (pp. 113–172). Cambridge, MA: MIT Press.

Fend, H. (1980). *Theorie der Schule* [Theory of the school]. München: Urban & Schwarzenberg.

Gaudig, H. (1922). *Die Schule im Dienste der werdenden Persönlichkeit* [School's duty to personality development] (2nd ed.). Leipzig: Teubner.

Gräsel, C., Mandl, H., & Prenzel, M. (1992). Die Förderung diagnostischen Denkens durch fallbasierte Computerlernprogramme in der Medizin [Promoting diagnostic reasoning in medicine through case-based computer learning systems]. In U. Glowalla & E. Schoop (Eds.), *Hypertext und Multimedia. Neue Wege in der computerunterstützten Aus- und Weiterbildung* (pp. 323–331). Berlin: Springer.

Gräsel, C., Prenzel, M., & Mandl, H. (1993). *Konstruktionsprozesse beim Bearbeiten eines fallbasierten Computerlernprogramms* [Processes of knowledge construction while working with a case-based computer learning system] (Research report No. 13). München: Ludwig-Maximilians-Universität, Lehrstuhl für Empirische Pädagogik und Pädagogische Psychologie.

Kerschensteiner, G. (1907). *Grundfragen der Schulorganisation* [Basic questions of school organization]. Leipzig: Teubner.

Kerschensteiner, G. (1911). The continuation schools of Munich. *The Journal of the American Society of Mechanical Engineers, 33,* 46–55.

Kerschensteiner, G. (1912). *Begriff der Arbeitsschule* [The idea of the work school]. Leipzig: Teubner.

Kerschensteiner, G. (1913). *The idea of the industrial school.* New York: Macmillan.

Kerschensteiner, G. (1914a). *Wesen und Wert des naturwissenschaftlichen Unterrichts* [On the nature and worth of instruction in the natural sciences]. Leipzig: Teubner.

Kerschensteiner, G. (1914b). *The schools and the nation.* London: Macmillan.

Kutscha, G. (1982). Das System der Berufsausbildung [The vocational education system]. In H. Blankertz, J. Derbolav, A. Kell, & G. Kutscha (Eds.), *Sekundarstufe II - Jugendbildung zwischen Schule und Beruf* (Enzyklopädie Erziehungswissenschaft, Vol. 9, Part 1, pp. 203–226). Stuttgart: Klett-Cotta.

Lisop, I. (1989). Das Duale System—Realität und zukünftige Entwicklung im Verhältnis zur Weiterbildung [The dual system—state of the art and future directions in further education]. In Deutscher Bundestag—11. Wahlperiode (Ed.), *Zwischenbericht der Enquete-Kommission "Zukünftige Bildungspolitik - Bildung 2000"* (pp. 134–141). Bonn: Deutscher Bundestag.

Mandl, H., Gräsel, C., Prenzel, M., Bruckmoser, J., Lyon, H. C., & Eitel, F. (1991). *Clinical reasoning in the context of a computer-based learning environment* (Research report No. 4). München: Ludwig-Maximilians-Universität, Lehrstuhl für Empirische Pädagogik und Pädagogische Psychologie.

Mandl, H., Gruber, H., & Renkl, A. (1992). Prozesse der Wissensanwendung beim komplexen Problemlösen in einer kooperativen Situation [Processes of knowledge application in complex problem solving within a co-operative situation]. In F. Achtenhagen & E. G. John (Eds.), *Mehrdimensionale Lehr-Lern-Arrangements—Innovationen in der kaufmännischen Aus- und Weiterbildung* (pp. 478–490). Wiesbaden: Gabler.

Mandl, H., Gruber, H., & Renkl, A. (1994). *Problems of knowledge utilization in the development of expertise.* In W. J. Nijhof & J. N. Streumer (Eds.), *Flexibility in training and vocational education* (pp. 291–305). Utrecht: Lemma.

Mandl, H., & Hron, A. (1989). Psychologische Aspekte des Lernens mit dem Computer [Psychological aspects of learning with computers]. *Zeitschrift für Pädagogik, 35,* 657–678.

Paris, S. G. (1988, April). *Fusing skill and will in children's learning and schooling.* Paper presented at the annual meeting of the American Educational Research Association, New Orleans, LA.

Parsons, T. (1959). The school class as social system. *Harvard Educational Review, 29,* 297–318.

Preiß, P. (1992). *Planspiel JEANSFABRIK* [Computer simulation game JEANS MANUFACTURING]. Göttingen: Seminar für Wirtschaftspädagogik der Georg-August-Universität.

Resnick, L. B. (1987). Learning in school and out. *Educational Researcher, 16,* 13–20.

Rumpf, H. (1987). *Belebungsversuche. Ausgrabungen gegen die Verödung der Lernkultur* [Reanimations. Excarvations against devastation of the culture of learning]. Weinheim: Juventa.

Scheibner, O. (1930). *Zwanzig Jahre Arbeitsschule in Idee und Gestaltung* [Twenty years of the work school: Its idea and design]. Leipzig: Quelle & Meyer.

Schmidt, H. G., Norman, G. R., & Boshuizen, H. P. A. (1990). A cognitive perspective on medical expertise: Theory and implications. *Academic Medicine, 65,* 611–621.

Spiro, R. J., Feltovich, P. J., Jacobson, M. J., & Coulson, R. L. (1991). Cognitive flexibility, constructivism, and hypertext: Random access instruction for advanced knowledge acquisition in ill-structured domains. *Educational Technology, 31*(5), 24–33.

Trustees of Dartmouth College (1989). *Program PlanAlyzer.* Hanover, NH: Dartmouth College.

von Hentig, H. (1984). *Das allmähliche Verschwinden der Wirklichkeit* [The gradual disappearance of reality]. Hamburg: Hanser.

Wagenschein, M. (1968). *Verstehen lehren. Genetisch–Sokratisch–Exemplarisch* [Teaching to understand. Genetically–Socratically–Exemplary]. Weinheim: Beltz.

16 Mapping Models of Cognitive Development to Design Principles of Learning Environments

Patrick Mendelsohn
Universite de Geneve

THE DESIGN OF LEARNING ENVIRONMENTS
AS A RESEARCH METHODOLOGY
FOR LEARNING INSTRUCTION

One way to further the understanding of processes and outcomes of learning from instruction is to create environments that elicit and produce them (Glaser & Bassok, 1989). Theoretically, intelligent tutoring system (ITS) design could represent a solution to this approach because tutoring systems can simultaneously serve as instructional environments and test beds for theoretical principles. More recently, De Corte (1993) stated that the existing systems question whether they correspond to actual learning processes as now well established by researchers. I also question their compatibility with the outcomes and findings established by research in the field of cognitive development.

Some computer-based instructional designers suggest building systems devoted to the promotion of metacognitive skills (like LOGO-based microworlds), whereas others propose promoting conventional cognitive skills and domain-dependent abilities (like tradition computer-assisted instruction [CAI] and some ITSs). The opposition between these two views in the design of learning environments has kept these two communities in mutual isolation for a prolonged period. This opposition mirrors the split in the field of cognitive psychology between research in learning processes and research in cognitive development. Broadly speaking, developmentalists have paid more attention to domain-independent acquisition processes, and learning scientists have paid more attention to expertise acquisition through domain-dependent mechanisms. Research on learning environments seems to bring these two communities closer together. On the one hand, researchers in the learning-from-instruction community now agree that efficient learning can no longer be described as a passive recording of knowledge: It is also constructive and self-regulated. On the other hand, cognitive developmentalists are now convinced that development is more domain dependent, goal oriented, and cumulative than they thought in past decades.

THE EMERGENCE OF THE SITUATED-COGNITION PARADIGM

Operational definitions given to some of the basic concepts previously quoted may vary from one researcher to another. Nevertheless, it is now admitted, for example, that traditional ITS have little to do with a constructivist approach to learning, and that LOGO programming is a useless expertise for real-world problems. ITS designers neglected the fact (first established by cognitive developmentalists) that efficient learning is promoted by self-regulated processes, and that it supposes an active participation of the learner in the design process of the problem-solving strategies. Some microworld designers have ignored that acquiring an expertise in some basic constructive set of schemes does not guarantee transfer and use of these schemes to real-world situations.

The emergence of the situated-cognition paradigm is an opportunity for a new step toward collaboration between the two disciplines. The situation-cognition view of learning reminds us that instructional strategies must respect some of the natural processes of knowledge acquisition to lead to effective and efficient learning. Core learning (as demonstrated by classical pre- and posttest experimental designs) guarantees neither transfer nor use of acquired knowledge in problem-solving situations. In other words, we could say that the situated-cognition paradigm proposes that instruction be designed in accordance with the natural characteristics of knowledge acquisition attested by developmental research. The only difference is that schemata acquired by instruction occur in artificial worlds, whereas schemata studied by developmentalists occur in natural settings.

COGNITIVE-DEVELOPMENT CONCEPTS TO THE RESCUE OF SITUATED-COGNITION PROBLEMS

Although the concept of *stage* has been criticized in the past, it remains a useful tool to tackle some of the difficult problems raised by the theory of expertise. Providing learning environments with knowledge of relevant developmental stages could help solve two major problems met by instructional designers. First, one of the chief consequences of the situated-cognition view is that it reminds cognitive scientists that knowledge is anchored in so-called "authentic contexts" by means of sensorimotor actions performed on physical and social realities. This is exactly what developmentalists have tried to explain for years by focusing research on transition mechanisms between sensorimotor and representational schemes. Some of the propositions they have made could be an interesting source of inspiration for instructional designers. Second, the concept of *well organized, domain-specific knowledge bases,* as stated by learning scientists, has something to do with the notion of *stage* used by developmentalists. In this particular domain, designers could rediscover some interesting views on the flexible application and organizational features of scheme functioning. In addition to these two problems, we should not neglect the fruitful approach elicited by researchers in the field of sociocognition (conflict resolutions, etc.), and their links with collaborative-learning processes advocated by the situated-cognition community.

DEVELOPMENTAL CONCEPTS REVISITED AS DESIGN PRINCIPLES

Knowledge Representation in Learning Environments

Almost all cognitive developmentalists have formalized acquisition processes in a constructivist manner. This characteristic is linked to their interest in isolating the "elementary building blocks of knowledge," from which more complex behaviors can be constructed. Searching for the optimal elementary cognitive-unit decomposition has been the Holy Grail of cognitive–developmental psychology, just as the idea of creating a universal programming language has inspired computer scientists.

ILE designers have also been concerned with the same problem. What should be the generic content of an elementary unit of knowledge presented in a learning environment? How can we make learners participate in the construction of expert knowledge? Should it be an analog of the "natural" schema as they are described by developmentalists? Many solutions have been proposed by designers, each one referring to a particular family of systems. To represent domain-independent rules for managing pedagogical interaction, CAI designers have often used the notion of *frame*. This neutral concept allows the presentation of knowledge at the interface of a computer using the "conventional" format: definitions, facts, formula, texts, and so on. This solution has the advantage of presenting knowledge as it has to be mastered, but makes it impossible for the learner to be an active participant in the construction of that knowledge. The learner is a passive viewer of a cognitive entertainment, to which he or she is asked to react from time to time. In a classical CAI environment, learners can only reproduce knowledge as it is represented by designers.

ITS designers have attempted to get closer to the constructivist point of view; for this purpose, they have often considered rules as basic cognitive units. This choice was mainly imposed by technological constraints, and we must admit that it gave some good results in a few particular domains—like the acquisition of diagnosis and troubleshooting skills. One of the main criticisms that was made to this approach, advocated by cognitive scientists and some developmentalists, was that they considered knowledge as pure mental representations encapsulated and stored in a way that allowed them to be arbitrarily chosen and activated in appropriate new situations. A totally different approach was developed by microworld designers. Inspired by developmental concepts like *schema* and *microviews*, microworld designers tried to simulate the process of schema integration and differentiation by giving the learner some primitives analogous to those of human beings. LOGO is the most popular of these attempts, and the limits of this approach have already been stated.

We have taken a different approach with MEMOLAB. We consider that the learner's challenge is to master a knowledge base given as a network of various components, including powerful transformation procedures, definitions, schemata, and formulas generated by the different devices of the system. This learner's appropriation process is progressively solicited through problem-solving situations that involve manipulating these conceptual tools in the same way as in the real world. The constructivist approach is reflected in the way learners are not given already solved solutions to their problems; in this way, they actively participate in the design processes of expert knowledge representation.

States, Substages, and Knowledge Bases

The concept of *stage* is tightly linked to the constructivist view on development. It supposes that cognitive abilities are self-organized in a cumulative and hierarchical way by various constraints (e.g., cognitive load, chunking mechanisms, semantic nets, etc.). These constraints determine the development of specific knowledge bases attached to different domains, and they also lead to well-organized and flexible structures that have some common properties (e.g., automatization of recurrent skills, elaborative encoding, schema construction, etc.). In a way, we could consider that stages emerge from cognitive functioning as properties of effective learning. This position states that stages are not generative structures, as proposed by classical constructive theories, but rather descriptive structures of knowledge when it is efficiently organized for a real use.

The classical concept of *stage* centers on small knowledge subsets. Each small piece of information is represented in a specific description language making use of a relevant grammar. This set of rules and objects can be viewed as a qualitative model. For example, learning-environment designers White and Frederiksen (1985) used the concept of *qualitative model* in the architecture of their system as a precursor of more quantitative and formal models. We all agree that expert models of a domain are often too complex to be mastered directly by a novice. They also probably would not be effective for the expert if not anchored in deep sensorimotor structures.

The notion of *substage* could be considered as a tentative solution to the problem of continuity versus discontinuity in developmental processes (the cumulative component of learning). If development is viewed as a transition between large qualitative stages ruled by specific constraints, a complete description of acquisition processes necessarily needs intermediate transition stages to link local learning processes to broader changes in knowledge acquisition. This local description can be another qualitative model, as in Piaget's (1971) theory, or a quantitative description, as in Case's (1985) model. We have chosen to implement this last characteristic in MEMOLAB by proposing the metaphor of the *language shift* described in a previous work.

Some Concrete Implications of a Constructivist Approach for the Design Principles of Learning Environments

This discussion of cognitive-development concepts leads to the improvement of several learning-environment design principles. The three mentioned here are illustrated with some of MEMOLAB's components in the last section.

Learning Environments Should Be Designed as Hierarchical Knowledge-Base Generators.   In the field of instructional design, one major difficulty is interactively representing the complexity of real-world problems. To avoid this difficulty, one temptation is to oversimplify the knowledge representation given to students, and to carefully design the solution paths that are supposed to be learned. In simplifying, designers also dramatically reduce the students' actions. I propose that a powerful learning environment must allow learners to participate in an active and collaborative way in the construction of the system's knowledge base. Effective learning is an individual and personal implication in the process of schematization and abstraction of the complexity of reality. If this abstraction process is imposed as a result of the instructional environment (even if it is so for technical reasons), learning will be less efficient and poorly related to meaningful contexts in which it is supposed to be used. To reach this goal, we have implemented a hierarchy of command languages that progressively generates the complexity of the expert knowledge by a mechanism called *language shift*.

Learning Environments Should Be Designed as Powerful, Dedicated Working Environments.   In our group, we think that learning environments should be designed as real, professional working environments favoring all sorts of mental activities, such as exploration, investigation, and problem solving. The richness and complexity of what has to be learned requires well-designed knowledge bases, workbenches, integrated hypertexts, and online help. Such environments should reflect the structural and functional properties of the real "target" working settings.

Learning Environments Should Present Knowledge as a Communication System. The difference between an ordinary professional working environment and one that supports efficient learning is the devices that allow imitation and mutual regulation processes. These processes are supported by several agents (tutors and coach). Knowledge is communicated and negotiated in what we call a *community of practice.* When a learner is stuck in his or her exploration, or when he or she is not able to find the right information, he or she needs support as in real life. Kintsch (1991) proposed the idea of *unintelligent tutoring systems*— pushing students' performance beyond their current level of activity. Indeed, Kintsch's proposition is close to Vygotsky's (1978) notion of *zone of proximal development,* and this notion is largely supported by the concept of *stages* (and *substages*), as stated by cognitive developmentalists. In MEMOLAB, domain-independent knowledge about tutoring does not refer to characteristics of abstract units of knowledge, but is concerned with the mode of interaction between the learner and tutor.

MEMOLAB

Overview

MEMOLAB is a learning environment dedicated to teaching the methodology of experimental psychology. Basically, learners' activities form a cycle: design an experiment, run it, and analyze the output data. Here is an example of an experiment that learners can design: "Present a list of 10 words to two samples of 30 subjects. For the experimental group, the words are selected within the same semantic field. For the control groups, words have no close semantic relation. Let the subjects study the list for 5 minutes, and then have them identify the first list words in another list of 30 words. Performance is measured as the number of words correctly identified."

A challenge of our research was to articulate a computational architecture with psychological theories of learning. Our cognitive architecture divides the learning cycle into stages. In previous work (Dillenbourg & Mendelsohn, 1992), we used the metaphor of a *pyramid* with several floors. Floors are discriminated by the operators provided to learners for solving the problem. In MEMOLAB, we paid attention to the relationship between successive goals, and we grounded our design choices in reference to Case's (1985) hypothesis on stage transition in child development.

Actually, in MEMOLAB, each goal does not have a completely different application frame (interface). For each goal, the problem-solving situation is the

LAB (i.e., a workbench where learners can assemble and run experiments). However, the set of commands available is not the same in each goal. The LAB is the central place of interaction. It is connected to subordinate frames, such as the data tools (where learners analyze the data collected through the experiment) and the simulation. The simulation is a set of procedures that approximates the results of the learners' experiment by comparing this experiment with the most similar experiment found in a database, in which we stored experiments described in scientific literature. The simulation method is inspired by case-based reasoning techniques.

Finally, MEMOLAB includes two hypertexts. The "handbook of methodology" includes several chapters connected to the system's various goals. It includes a theoretical introduction to the design of well-formed experiments. The "encyclopedia of memory" is another hypertext, independent from any goal (i.e., that learners can access at any time), that provides them with the knowledge about human memory they could need, for instance, for determining the relevant variables.

Figure 16.1 illustrates how the learner concretely designs an experiment in the first LAB (we see later on that MEMOLAB includes several LABs). An experiment is constructed by positioning a set of events on a workbench. The vertical axis represents the time dimension. The activities of the same group of subjects are vertically aligned: First they encode some material, then there is some delay, and then some attempt to recall what they studied before. When an experiment has been designed, the learner may ask to simulate the results.

MEMOLAB as a Structured Learning Environment

If the richness of a learning environment is a quality, its complexity deteriorates learning. The designer must structure his or her learning environment in such a way that the learner may benefit from this richness. The idea of "structuring the environment" illustrates a fundamental difference of perspective between learning environments and traditional courseware: The meaning of *teaching* is moved from asking questions and providing feedback (although this is not excluded) to structuring the environment in a way that provides optimal learning conditions.

The structure we have adopted is a sequence of increasingly complex microworlds (or problem-solving situations, or laboratories for MEMOLAB). The criterion for defining this sequence is that the last world be as similar as possible to the real context, where the learner will have to apply the acquired skills. For instance, the last LAB in MEMOLAB uses the languages that are commonly used by the community of experiments in their exchanges (papers, conferences, etc.). However, if this microworld is as complex as the real world, it probably will not be efficient for learning. It should be preceded by simpler microworlds. In the first microworld, the learner will have to solve simple problems, considering only some parameters. In the next one, he or she will receive more powerful

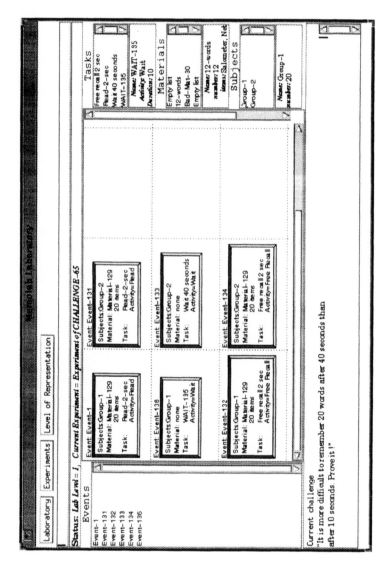

FIG. 16.1. The learner builds an experiment (at Level 1) by assembling events on the workbench. An event defines the task (read, listen, recall, wait, etc.) of a group of subjects with some material (e.g., a list of 12 words). Panes on both sides of the workbench provide libraries where the learner builds and selects the components that he or she assembles on the workbench.

operators, and will use the resources available to cope with more parameters and so forth.

The architecture of MEMOLAB includes three microworlds, referred to here-after as *levels*. Each level concerns a different set of experiments and uses a partially different interface:

1. Level 1. An experiment compares *n* groups of subjects along one dimen-sion. The interface emphasizes the concrete and chronological aspects of an experiment.
2. Level 2. The interface describes an experiment as a set of sequences. A sequence is a generic treatment that can be replicated several times with equivalent materials. The learners design experiments that test the interac-tion between two parameters.
3. Level 3. The interface reifies the logical structure of the experiment as a plan.

As soon as we have a sequence of microworlds, we face the issue of the transi-tion between microworlds. To smooth this transition, we designed the interface in such a way that these microworlds partially overlap. Each microworld uses a different set of commands to create and modify the components of an experiment (events, sequences, or plans). When an experiment has been completed at Level N, the system translates this experiment into the representation that it would have at Level N + 1. Hence, the future representation scheme is systematically associated with the scheme mastered by the learner. After some time, the learner is invited to express him or herself directly with the new language (N + 1). This principle has been called the *language shift* (Dillenbourg, 1992).

From Campbell and Bickhard's (1986) viewpoint, the language-shift mecha-nism can be viewed as a process of inducing interaction patterns. An elementary interaction associates some sequence of a user's actions and the computer's description of this sequence. Inferring the meaning of the description language can be described as the result of inducing the relationship between the actions performed and their representation. This corresponds to a view of knowledge as a mental construction that stands in the interaction between the subject and his or her environment. It creates a bridge between our model and current research on situated learning (Brown, 1990)—an important issue in artificial intelligence (AI) and education.

Our intermediate framework also introduces the designer to Vygotsky's theo-ries. The *apprenticeship* idea is reified in the pyramid model by sharing control between the coach and the learner; when the learner is able to perform at some Level L, the tutor must guide his or her activities at Level L + 1. This Level L + 1 corresponds to the concept of *zone of proximal development* (Vygotsky, 1978). At each language shift, the learner will assume more control of his or her solution process, and the coach's guidance will be reduced. Moreover, Wertsch (1985) proposed a linguistic analysis of the internalization process that relates it to the language shift. He observed (in mother–child interactions) that the move from the interindividual to the intraindividual plane was preceded by a language shift inside the interindividual level: Mothers replace a descriptive language with a strategy-oriented language (i.e., a language that refers to objects according to their role in the problem-solving strategy).

We used the metaphor of the *pyramid* to emphasize the hierarchical relationship between operators that are used in successive microworlds. This notion of *hierarchical integration* is based on the neo-Piagetian theories of Case (1985). In short, this theory states that the quantitative improvement of children's schemata is limited. To by-pass this limitation, children restructure their knowledge into higher order schemata that recombine patterns of previously existing sub-schemata.

The *pyramid* is a visual metaphor for the core structure of a learning environment. The pyramid represents the concepts and skills to be acquired by the learner, ranked bottom–up according to their level of hierarchical integration. Learning consists of moving up in the pyramid. Each level of the pyramid is defined by two languages: the command and the description. The command-language vocabulary is the set of elementary actions that the learner is allowed to do at some stage of interaction. The command-language syntax defines how the learner composes sequences of elementary actions. The description-language vocabulary is the set of symbols (strings, graphics, etc.) used by the computer to show the learner some description of his or her behavior. This description reifies some abstract features of the learner's behavior to make them explicitly available for metacognitive activities (Collins & Brown, 1988).

The command and description languages are different at each level of the pyramid. The hierarchical nature of a pyramid implies that each level integrates its lower neighbor. This integration is encompassed in the relationship between the languages used at successive levels: If a description language at Level L is used as a new command language at Level L + 1, the learner is compelled to explicitly use the concepts that have been reified at Level L. This is what we call the *language-shift mechanism* (Dillenbourg, 1992): When the learner receives a new command language, he or she must explicitly use the concepts that were implicit in his or her behavior. The meaning of the new commands has been induced at the previous level by associating the learner's behavior with some representation. This representation is now the new command. The ILE structure can then be described as a sequence of (action-language, representation-language) pairs—a sequence in which the relationship between two successive pairs is described by the language-shift mechanism.

The process by which properties that are implicit at some level of knowledge can be abstracted and explicitly reached at the higher level has been studied under the label of *reflected abstraction* (Piaget, 1971). The language-shift mechanism has two uses: It translates this psychological concept in a terminology more relevant for ILE designers, and it describes a pedagogical strategy (mainly inductive) to trigger reflected abstraction.

There is an obvious mapping between the structure defined by Case and our intermediate framework. The control structures at each level of the pyramid integrate the control structures located at the lower level. The sequence of micro-worlds within the pyramid is structured as Case's view of development: Quantitative variations define the improvement possible within some level (or micro-world or stage), whereas qualitative variations define the transition between two levels. The concept of *stage transition* is translated into the language-shift mechanism. This transition is necessary when the learner tries to solve problems that have memory-load constraints that are too high. After the language shift, the learner has at his or her disposal new control structures that enable him or her to solve the problems with a reduced cognitive load. Case's ILE-oriented reexpression allows us to ground the design of MEMOLAB in this theory.

MEMOLAB as a Rich and Complex Learning Environment

Any psychological or pedagogical theory regards learning from a specific viewpoint. For instance, some theories pay attention to the effect of practice, but neglect the importance of understanding. Some concentrate on discovery, but forget about imitation. However, when one observes an actual learning process, it is clear that learning does not result from a single activity, but from the integration of multiple activities based on multiple sources of information. A learning environment must take this complexity into account by offering a wide range of learning resources that will accommodate the variety of individual learning styles and learning needs. Therefore, MEMOLAB includes several tools.

The Make-Material Tool.   A difficult aspect in designing an experiment is to carefully select the items that the subjects will have to remember. A list of words has several features that the novice experimenter is not aware of, but that affect memory performance: the length of words (number of syllables), the frequency of words in everyday language, and the phonological or semantic homogeneity of a list of words (see Fig. 16.2).

The Hypertext "Methodology."   The idea of a learning environment is that the acquisition of procedural knowledge requires active problem solving (in contrast to questions-based courseware that focuses on declarative knowledge). MEMOLAB corrects this bias by giving access to declarative knowledge (theories, laws, facts, etc.). The hypertext structure enables the learner to find information at the level of granularity in which he or she is interested. This hypertext includes the facilities that are now common to most similar applications (i.e., trace of read nodes, webview, book view, footnotes, etc.).

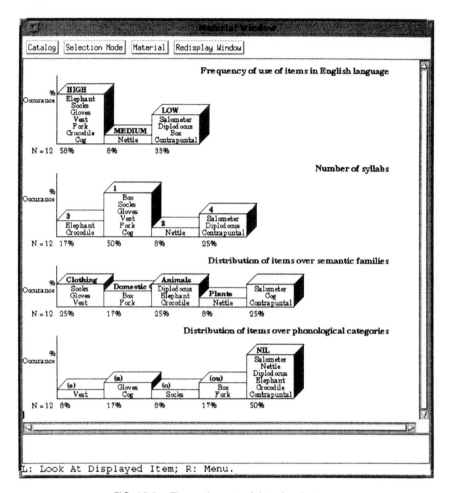

FIG. 16.2.   The make-material tools window.

The Hypertext "Encyclopedia of Memory."   Designing an experiment on human memory requires both methodological skills and some knowledge specific to the domain of memory. For instance, the learner must know what is an independent variable, but he or she must also know that *words frequency* is an interesting independent variable. MEMOLAB includes a hypertext that provides theoretical and experimental data on human memory.

The Simulation.   Research on the use of simulation in educational research has shown that the quality of this simulation is important. The simulation's role is not simply to produce the realistic results. The simulation process must be carried out in such a way that the learner or some computational agents may understand the results. The simulation built in MEMOLAB produces a commented trace of the simulation process that enables the learner to understand how these results have been computed.

The richness of a learning environment is not only the function of the number of tools, but the extent to which those tools are integrated. This integration is possible because of the homogeneity of our representation scheme—the object-oriented approach. Let us illustrate this with the simulation. The results of an experiment are computed by analogy with those of similar experiments. When MEMOLAB explains how the results have been computed, it refers to these

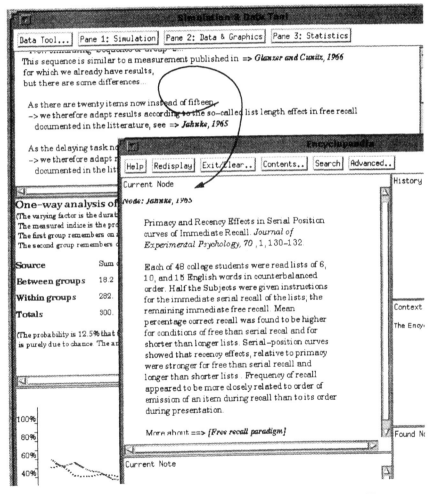

FIG. 16.3. Integration of the hypertext and the simulation: The learner clicks on an experiment.

similar experiments (simulation trace). As illustrated in Figure 16.3, the learner may double click on one of these references and jump directly into the hypertext node, where the referred experiment is described. The hypertext is also connected with the rule-based agents. Most current research on hypertext system has been concerned with the features of the hypertext. The originality of our approach is to have considered the place of the hypertext within a complex system—to situate the information search within a context that makes this information useful.

MEMOLAB as a Community of Agents

Learning results from solving problems and using tools, as well as interacting with agents about these ongoing activities. Even if the environment is rich and structured, some learners may need help while they solve the problem, whereas other learners need to be pushed forward or they will repeatedly use the same inefficient operators. An agent can be human (e.g., a tutor who monitors the learners' work, or some peer sharing the desk). Regarding computational agents, we discriminate two types.

1. Agents that conduct domain-specific interactions (i.e., helping to build an experiment). These agents can b. an expert of the domain or a computerized collaborative learner (co-learner). One can also envisage to have several experts that can solve the same problem with different viewpoints (Moyse & Elsom-Cook, 1992). The interaction with the human learner is about the domain; it is centered on how to build a problem's solution.

2. Agents that select and monitor learning activities, or help the learner to manage his or her own learning process. In MEMOLAB, we discriminated two kinds of pedagogical agents: the tutor and the coach, who is some kind of chief tutor. The various tutors have the same function, but fulfill this function differently according to their style.

This discrimination between two classes of agents has been essential to separate pedagogical knowledge from domain-specific knowledge, and hence to extract from MEMOLAB the components that constitute the toolbox. This architecture is described in the next section.

Expert–Learner Interaction

The interaction is tuned by the two slots labeled *local-interaction* mode and *global-interaction* mode. The global-interaction mode is an integer between 0 and 5 representing the learner's participation in the problem-solving process: If the global mode is 0, the learner does nothing and the expert makes a demonstration; if the global mode is 5, the learner does everything and the expert simply watches; this corresponds to a simple exercise; if the global mode is from 1 to 5, the learner increasingly participates in the solution.

The local-interaction mode describes each single step within the problem-solving process. Let us remember that the interaction between the learner and expert is performed step by step. An *expert's step* is defined by a sequence of rules firing until one rule's actions includes an interface command. A *learner's step* is defined by a sequence of commands in the problem frame, which ends when the learner uses a command that corresponds to an expert's commands.

At each step, the expert may either propose an action or observe the learner's action: If the global mode is 0, the local mode is always *propose;* if the global mode is 5, the local mode is always *observe;* when the global mode goes from 1 to 5, the number of propose steps decreases and the number of observe steps increases.

It is the tutor who decides whether the expert's next step will be a *propose* or an *observe*. This decision is the mechanism by which the tutor controls the expert. When the expert receives the control in the mode *propose,* it executes a certain number of steps without returning the control to the tutor; when the local mode is *observe,* the expert compares the command performed by the learner with the commands it would have performed.

Coaching and Tutoring

MEMOLAB aims to combine the flexibility of learning environments with the efficiency expected from advanced courseware. It achieves this goal in two complementary ways: indirect help inscribed in the system architecture (as already seen), and direct interventions by coaching and tutoring components.

This is the traditional way to design educational support, feedback, hints explanations, problem selection, goal management, and so on. Our challenge was to make this help domain independent, and to combine it with the learner's freedom to explore the environment. The answer to the issue of *domain dependency* has been tackled, creating the class of agents called *experts* described in the previous section. The other skills have been distributed between six agents: five tutors and one coach. Those agents are described in the following.

The Teaching Styles

The notion of *teaching style* refers to the consistency of sets of pedagogical decisions. A teacher or a courseware must make many decisions. We first attempted to determine these decisions by reasoning with a set of independent parameters. We progressively understood that these parameters were not independent: There are clusters of values that are more consistent. They determine what we call a *teaching style*. For instance, if a teacher likes inductive learning, he or she is probably also in favor of discovery learning, rather than expository teaching.

We arbitrarily defined five teaching styles. We refer to them by the name of a major contributor to our discipline: Piaget, Papert, Skinner, Bloom, and Vygotsky. These references mean that each style has been inspired by these famous people. It would be an exaggeration to claim that each teaching style is an implementation of the theory defended by these people.

The five styles can be roughly classified with respect to their degree of guidance, from Skinner, who inspired the CAI courseware tradition, to Papert, who launched the microworld wave: Skinner/Bloom/Vygotsky/Piaget/Papert. This classification is used by the coach (among other criteria) to select a tutor.

In the specific framework of MEMOLAB, the definition of a teaching style escapes from the philosophical discussion to determine the interaction between the learner and the expert, and a few other things listed next. Each tutor:

- decides the initial value and evolution of the global-interaction mode;
- decides the value of the local-interaction mode for the next step, given the global-interaction mode and the expert's message (which informs the tutor whether the learner did something correct or incorrect);
- determines the learner's activity, which can be doing an exercise, viewing an example (mode *demo*), or reading the theory included in the hypertext;
- chooses the problem that the learner and the expert will try to solve jointly;
- processes the learner's requests regarding the local-interaction mode, the global-interaction mode, the problem selection, and the level of difficulty;
- determines whether the learner has the right to refuse the expert's suggestion to undo the things he or she just did;
- determines whether the learner has mastered the goal, and, if so, returns the control to the coach;
- determines whether the learner has failed a goal, and, if so, returns the control to the coach; and
- determines if the learner's actual interaction still fits with its personal teaching style, and, if not (what we call a *pedagogical drift*), returns the control to the coach.

All these decisions result from a reasoning process that cannot be described by a few parameters, but can be modeled by rule bases. These rule bases are partially overlapping. We briefly describe the style of each tutor.

Skinner, or Behaviorism

Skinner is an American psychologist well known for his development of the behaviorist theory. This theory avoids the analysis of mental states, and rather bases its analysis on the association of environmental stimuli with the subject's responses. Some of these associations are biological, whereas others can be created through a process called *conditioning*. *Learning* is the creation of new associations.

Programmed learning, the ancestor of CAI, is based on these principles. Its main idea is to decompose complex skills into a sequence of elementary skills to be taught successively. Each behavior that comes closer to this skill must be immediately reinforced with a positive feedback. Inversely, negative feedback must be presented after each incorrect behavior.

Within the framework of MEMOLAB, Skinner manipulates mainly the difficulty parameter. He never chooses an interaction mode superior to 3. He is also deductive (i.e., when he teaches a new goal, he starts by presenting the theory to show any example or exercise). He does not accept any initiative from the learner (he disactivates some menus).

Bloom, or Mastery Learning

Mastery learning reuses the idea of programmed learning, without being so extreme. It keeps the idea that skills should be decomposed into a network of subskills. The links in this network describe prerequisite relations: A subskill must be mastered before trying to teach another one. Mastery learning also shares with behaviorism the role given to feedback. The main difference is in the granularity of learning and in the variety of approaches. The *granularity of learning* refers to the size of learning steps. The best size of a subskill is not necessarily the smallest one. Some subskills may be taught inductively, some by analogical method, and others deductively.

Within the framework of MEMOLAB, Bloom covers the range of interaction modes, but prefers to increase the level of difficulty to change the mode. For each goal, he starts with a rather free exploration, presents some theory, and finally proposes exercises until the learner masters the goal.

Vygotsky, or Apprenticeship

Vygotsky was a Russian psychologist who lived at the beginning of the century; he established the basis of the so-called *sociocultural approach*. His main hypothesis is that we learn by internalizing the skills that we first acquire with more able people. The main slogan of today's defenders of this approach is that participation changes understanding. This means that when we collaborate with an expert in some domain, we observe how the expert appropriates our own actions into his or her conceptual framework. We perceive how he or she uses our contribution within his or her problem-solving strategy, and thereby get familiar with this strategy. This strategy is not expressed in an abstract way, but receives its meaning from its deep connection to the context. Language is postulated to be the main vector of this internalization process. The concept of *apprenticeship* refers to this social process, by which a novice carpenter progressively acquires the skills of his or her master, rather than learning theory at school.

Within the framework of MEMOLAB, Vygotsky selects rather difficult problems. At the outset, the expert solves the problem alone (GCM = 1), and then Vygotsky progressively increases the global-interaction mode (i.e., the expert will fade out and the learner will play a more important role in the solution process) until the learner solves the problem alone (GCM = 5). In comparison with other tutors, the global-interaction mode is Vygotsky's favorite parameter. For instance, he will increase the interaction mode, rather than increase problems' level of difficulty. With respect to Papert or Piaget, Vygotsky is more interventionist: He generally allows the expert to interrupt the learner because this intervention belongs to the natural apprenticeship process.

Piaget, or Constructivism

Piaget has studied the development of intelligence in children. He claims that children pass through a rather stable sequence of stages. These stages are defined by particular structures, through which the learner acts on or reasons about his or her environment. He noticed that these structures may change when the learner perceives a conflict between his or her own structure and the environment responses. This notion of *conflict* has been reused in the pedagogical field as a tool to help the learner to change his or her structures. The main postulate is that the teacher not change the learner's structure directly; rather, the teacher may place the learner in a situation where he or she will perceive a conflict between what he or she knows and what he or she perceives, and thereby modify what he or she knows.

The notion of *conflict* has been extended to the notion of *sociocognitive conflict,* in which one learner perceives a conflict between his or her vision of the world and his or her partner's vision. This social form of conflict is present in MEMOLAB. Within the framework of MEMOLAB, Piaget works only with high-interaction modes (4 or 5). He allows the learner to explore his or her own solution, and intervenes only when he notices a conflict with the expert.

Papert, or Free Discovery

Papert is the well-known author of the microworld LOGO. The key notation is the learner's involvement in a microworld in which he or she may define his or her own project. Within the framework of MEMOLAB, Papert does not make any decisions: The learner selects the problem he or she wants, and the expert is maintained asleep and does not provide any feedback. In theory, this teaching style is only selected with successful learners (but a less successful learner may ask to shift to Papert).

The Coach

The responsibilities of the coach are to: select a goal, select a tutor, and select an expert. The goal-selection process is fairly trivial: The coach selects any goal that has no prerequisite (in the curriculum description provided by the author), and then he or she selects any goal whose prerequisites are mastered. The selection of a tutor takes several factors into account:

- the tutor level of guidance (from 1 for Papert to 5 for Skinner): If the learner masters the previous goal with Tutor X, the expert prefers a tutor with a level of guidance inferior to the level of Tutor X. If the learner fails the goal, a tutor with a higher level of guidance will be selected.
- the tutor goal history: The coach will never select for Goal X a tutor who has already failed to teach Goal X.
- the tutor history of successful and failed problems: The number of times a tutor conducted a successful activity is stored in the slot *same for the failures*. Between two tutors, the coach will prefer the one who succeeded more often, or failed less often.
- if the learner has "drifted" away from Tutor X, the coach will select a tutor whose level of guidance is inferior or superior to the level of Tutor X, depending on the direction of the drift.

Pedagogical Drift

The notion of *pedagogical drift* is related to the notion of *teaching style*. A teaching style defines a zone of the space of pedagogical decision space within which the various decisions have a high level of consistency. This implies that, between two styles, there is some discontinuity. By definition, the space between two styles suffers from being unclearly defined and inconsistent.

Given the freedom offered to the learner, the actual interaction between the learner and the tutor may not look anymore as it should look inside the particular teaching style. For instance, if Bloom is active and the learner set the global-interaction mode to 5 several times, the actual interaction will not look anymore as what Bloom would do. This learner may have left Bloom's zone of efficiency.

Each tutor has a set of rules to determine if such a drift occurs. All the utilities offered to the learner (select a problem, change the difficulty level, etc.) create an instance of the *class initiative*. This class possesses two subclasses: *want more initiative* and *want less initiative* (where we mean *want more guidance* and *want less guidance*). For instance, if the learner asks to increase the interaction mode or the level of difficulty, or if he or she asks the expert to continue the problem by him or herself, we create instances of want less initiative. If the learner asks for help or reads the theory, we create instances of want more initiative. These instances are stored in the slot *learner-initiatives-history*, and are parsed by the rules that detect the pedagogical drift. If the proportion of want more is twice superior to the proportion of want less (after some initialization period), the tutor interrupts him or herself and sends the message *drifted up* to the coach, which means "the learner would rather be in a style where he or she has more freedom."

CONCLUSION

This research has produced different types of outcomes (viz., at the design and implementation levels). We now list the outcomes of this research project, as well as some avenues for continuing research in this domain. We developed an original solution for separating domain-independent from domain-specific knowledge. Instead of searching for a domain-independent language that would describe any domain, we describe pedagogical knowledge in terms of interactions among agents. A *learning environment* is a society of agents for which we specified: (a) the role distribution over agents (coach, tutor, experts), and (b) protocols of communication among agents (global- and local-interaction mode, repair, conflicts, etc.). Some of the choices made in MEMOLAB are still arbitrary. For instance, the only domain-specific agents we implemented are *experts*, although we could integrate *peer learners*, or *semiexperts*. Another limitation is that we use the term *agent* to refer to a simple data structure, including a rulebase that drives his or her behavior. Current agents do not have the autonomy and goal-orientedness that would characterize a proper multiagent system. We are on the way to redesign MEMOLAB within a pure agent-oriented approach. The specification of well-defined protocols for communication among agents would enable us to integrate heterogeneous agents—namely, agents that are not based on rulebases and that are not written in the same programming language.

By separating pedagogical expertise from domain knowledge, we are not only able to permute the domain knowledge associated with some teaching strategy, but, conversely, we are also able to apply various teaching styles to a particular domain expertise. Instead of arguing about which teaching style is the best, we prefer to cover a large range of teaching styles. Of course, this raises the issue of selecting the teaching styles. However, if this issue is nontrivial at the theoretical viewpoint, we can apply, at a pragmatic level, a simple principle: If the learner fails, change the teaching style. We would like to develop future research on this learner's perception of teaching styles.

A third outcome of our work lies in the design metaphors that have been used for developing MEMOLAB. The *pyramid* metaphor is simple, but it enabled us to structure our sequence of microworlds on the basis of some theory of cognitive development. This metaphor is closely connected to the language-shift principle, which helps developers smooth the transition between two microworlds that use different interaction languages. We would like to collect more empirical data to check the consistency between the theory and its application to MEMOLAB, and to observe the learner-adaptation mechanisms when a language shift occurs.

Another achievement concerns the integration of multiple tools within a learning environment, especially the integration of a hypertext with rulebase agents. Currently, hypertext systems is a popular research topic. We believe that the pedagogical power of a hypertext cannot be understood without considering the context that justifies some information search in the hypertext.

A fifth lesson from this work concerns the interaction between the learner and a computerized agent. The principle we applied is simple: human–computer interaction should concern what is on the screen. This design of agents, especially the expert, has been determined by this principle: The rule conditions "read" the problem state on the screen, and the rule conclusions change the problem state display. This principle produces an opportunistic expert–learner collaboration, and makes this interaction inspectable and tunable by the tutor. The experiments helped us find problems related to this principle—namely, the difficulty of interacting about goals—but they also gave us some insight for implementing mechanisms of social grounding between a human user and a machine. Social grounding is a mechanism of joint and reciprocal modeling between two partners, based on the negotiation of shared meanings. A limitation in our current architecture is that the rule variables are instantiated by screen objects without any ambiguity. A new research avenue would be to test interactions where the computer concepts would not be directly connected to the displayed objects (the learner concepts are not either), and this relation would be negotiated with the learner through various pointing mechanisms.

REFERENCES

Bradzil, P. B. (1992). Integration of knowledge in multi-agent environments. In E. Costa (Ed.), *New directions for intelligent tutoring systems* (pp. 256–275). Berlin: Springer-Verlag.

Brown, J. S. (1990). Toward a new epistemology for learning. In C. Frasson & G. Gauthier (Eds.), *Intelligent tutoring systems at the crossroad of AI & education*. Norwood, NJ: Ablex.

Case, R. (1985). *Intellectual development from birth to adulthood*. New York: Academic Press.

Campbell, R., & Bickhard, M. H. (1986). *Knowing levels and developmental stages*. Basel: Karger.

Collins, A., & Brown, J. S. (1988). The computer as a tool for learning through reflection. In H. Mandl & A. Lesgold (Eds.), *Learning issues for intelligent tutoring systems* (pp. 1–18). New York: Springer-Verlag.

De Corte, E. (1993, November). *Learning theory and instructional science*. Paper presented at the final planning workshop of the ESF-Programme, St. Gallen, Switzerland.

Dillenbourg, P. (1992). The language shift: A mechanism for triggering metacognitive activities. In M. Jones & P. Winne (Eds.), *Adaptive learning environment* (pp. 287–316). Berlin: Springer-Verlag.

Dillenbourg, P., & Mendelsohn, P. (1992). The genetic structure of the interaction space. In E. Costa (Ed.), *New directions for intelligent tutoring systems* (pp. 15–27). Berlin: Springer-Verlag.

Glaser, R., & Bassock, M. (1989). Learning theory and the study of instruction. *Annual Review of Psychology, 40*, 631–666.

Kintsch, W. (1991). A theory of discourse comprehension: Implications for a tutor for word problems. In M. Cavelero, M. Pope, R. J. Simon, & J. I. Pozo (Eds.), *Learning and instruction. European research in an international context* (Vol. 3, pp. 235–253). Oxford, England: Pergamon.

Mendelsohn, P., & Dillenbourg, P. (1993). Le developpement de l'enseignement intelligemment assité par ordinateur. In J. F. Le Ny (Ed.), *Intelligence Naturelle et Intelligence Artificielle* (pp. 231–256). Paris: PUF.

Moyse, R., & Elsom-Cook, M. (1992). *Knowledge negotiation*. London: Academic Press.

Piaget, J. (1971). *Biology and knowledge*. Chicago: The University of Chicago Press.

Vygotsky, L. S. (1978). *The development of higher psychological processes*. Cambridge, MA: Harvard University Press.

Wertsch, J. (1985). Adult-child interaction as a source of self-regulation in children. In R. Yussen (Ed.), *The growth of reflection in children* (pp. 69–97). London: Academic Press.

White, B. Y., & Fredericksen, J. R. (1985). QUEST: Qualitative understanding of electrical system troubleshooting. *ACM Sigart Newsletter, 93,* 34–37.

IV PRINCIPLES OF SYSTEM DESIGN

17 Design Issues for Learning Environments

Allan Collins
Bolt Beranek and Newman Inc., Northwestern University

Instructional design theory comes with a belief in instructional delivery. The goal is to design an instructional system that transmits content and skills in a clear, well-structured, and efficient manner. The approach derives from the behaviorist and programmed instruction tradition of Thorndike, Skinner, and Gagne, but has assimilated aspects of cognitve research in recent years. The approach has been well summarized in two volumes edited by Reigeluth (1983, 1987).

The constructivist view of education, stemming from the work of Piaget, Dewey, and Vygotsky, argues that the goal of education is to help students construct their own understandings. In contrast to the instructional-delivery view, the constructivist view leads to an emphasis on learning rather than teaching, and on facilitative environments rather than instructional goals. A design theory for a constructivist approach to education looks very different from traditional instructional design theory. This chapter is a beginning attempt to develop such a constructivist design theory.

When designing a learning environment, computer based or not, there are a multitude of design decisions that must be made. Many of these design decisions are made unconsciously without any articulated view of the issues being addressed or the trade-offs involved. It would be better if these design decisions were consciously considered, rather than unconsciously made.

The perspective I take on design is to think of each decision in terms of its costs and benefits. From this perspective, the crucial questions are: What are the issues that must be addressed in designing learning environments? What are the cost–benefit trade-offs associated with each design issue? How should the costs and benefits be weighed? The costs and benefits relate to the effects on student learning and motivation, and to the costs in terms of time, money, and effort required to implement any aspect of a learning environment. My goal in this chapter is to raise a set of issues and some of the cost–benefit trade-offs that arise with respect to each issue. This cost–benefit approach does not lead to design prescriptions, as in instructional design theory, but rather to identifying important issues to be weighed.

The first issue to address in the design of any learning environment is what is called *authenticity* (Brown, Collins, & Duguid, 1989; Wiggins, 1989). The questions associated with authenticity are: What are the potential uses for the knowledge? How can a learning environment be created that reflects those possible uses? Too much of what we teach in school is taught because it has always been taught. We need to rethink what students should learn to live in the 21st century. For example, should we spend 12 years teaching students mathematical algorithms that computer tools can carry out for them? The goal of authenticity is to prepare students to do the kinds of complex tasks that occur in life. Much of what is learned in school is never used because it is often the wrong knowledge for the modern world; even when it is the right knowledge, people do not know how to apply it.

In previous work (Brown, Collins, & Duguid, 1989; Collins, 1991; Collins, Brown, & Newman, 1989; Collins, Hawkins, & Carver, 1991), I have proposed a "cognitive-apprenticeship" approach to designing learning environments. Before the invention of schooling, everything was taught by apprenticeship, where learning is situated in the context of work. It is the most natural way to learn. The basic method of apprenticeship involves modeling, coaching, and fading; that is, first showing apprentices what to do, next observing and helping them as they try to do it themselves, and then fading the help as they take on more responsibility. Cognitive apprenticeship attempts to apply this approach to teach thinking and problem solving. But unlike the kinds of skills taught with traditional apprenticeship, thinking is not visible. Hence, cognitive apprenticeship stresses the importance of techniques to make thinking visible, such as articulating and reflecting on cognitive processes.

This chapter attempts to extend the cognitive-apprenticeship framework to address a broad set of issues that arise in the design of learning environments. The first section on learning goals discusses central issues about what we should try to teach: Should we aim for memorization or thoughtfulness, whole tasks or component skills, breadth or depth of knowledge, and so on? The second section on learning contexts addresses cost–benefit trade-offs in the learning environments created by the designer: Does the context promote activity or passivity, incidental or direct learning, fun or seriousness, and so on? The third section discusses sequence in the learning activities: Should learning proceed from grounded to abstract, from structured to exploratory, from simple to complex, and so on? The final section on teaching methods addresses cost–benefit trade-offs associated with the cognitive-apprenticeship methods, such as modeling, coaching, articulation, and reflection.

LEARNING GOALS

The first set of trade-offs that designers need to address has to do with what students should learn. The trade-offs I address in this section are: memorization vs. thoughtfulness; whole tasks vs. component skills; breadth vs. depth of knowledge; diverse vs. uniform expertise; access vs. understanding; and cognitive vs. physical fidelity.

Memorization Versus Thoughtfulness

There is a tension throughout school between students memorizing things to do tasks fast and easily, such as memorizing the multiplication table, and learning to do things thoughtfully, such as solving complex problems. To the degree that one knows how to do something automatically (e.g., decoding), it can free the mind to be thoughtful about other things (e.g., the meaning of the text).

To illustrate the issue, in the 1930s, the superintendent in Manchester, New Hampshire, persuaded some of his teachers to give up teaching math algorithms for the first 5 years of school, and instead to focus on math discussion and estimation tasks (Benezet, 1991). When he visited schools, he would give students problems such as, "If half a stick is buried in mud, two-thirds of the rest is under water, and 1 foot is above water, how long is the stick?" Students who were taught in the traditional manner would start adding or multiplying the numbers given, whereas the students taught in the new manner would reason through the problem. He clearly had opted for thoughtfulness over memorization.

Some of the costs of memorization are evident in the examples: Memorization leads to inflexible use of the memorized knowledge and reliance on drill and practice, which is unmotivating for students. The benefits are that the memorized skills can be off-loaded to free the mind for thinking. The mastery of knowledge and skills by memorization is also empowering for students. Gaining automaticity is crucial if one is going to use a particular skill a lot. But if one will hardly ever use a skill (such as multiplying fractions), memorization is not worthwhile. When automaticity is appropriate, it is best gained by creating practice environments that reflect the uses of the skill in the real world.

Whole Tasks Versus Component Skills

There is a trade-off between having students perform whole tasks that require integration of a variety of skills vs. having students perform simplified tasks that focus on particular subskills. For example, one can have students practice sounding out different phonic patterns, or one can have them read Dr. Seuss books for enjoyment. There is a tendency in school to break everything into easy components (e.g., how to multiply fractions), but it is often difficult for students to tell what the components are good for. Much of school is like having students practice the forehand, backhand, and serve needed for tennis, without letting them know what the game is.

The costs of giving students whole tasks are that it is difficult to focus on particular weaknesses, it is difficult to manage the whole process at once, and there is always a chance of failure when the task is too complex. The benefits of whole tasks are that it is easy to see the point of the exercise, it is possible to practice the integrative skills that are necessary, and one is unlikely to develop strategies (as students do for component-skills tasks) that are counterproductive to the task as a whole.

It seems clear that focusing on subskills is sometimes very productive, but ideally this should occur when a weakness has been diagnosed. Scaffolding (Collins, Brown, & Newman, 1989; Palincsar & Brown, 1984) permits even weak students to accomplish whole tasks from the beginning. One strategy is to start by scaffolding students in whole tasks, and then going to component tasks when they seem appropriate.

Breadth Versus Depth of Knowledge

The issue is whether we want students to learn a little about a lot of things, as Hirsch (1987) argued in his plea for cultural literacy, or whether we want them to understand a few topics deeply. Our society tends to value specialists more than generalists, and yet schools are pressured to include more and more information in their curriculum.

The costs of breadth are that students do not get an authentic feel for any subject, and that a demand for breadth often gets turned into requirements that students learn particular things. The benefits of breadth include cultural literacy, which, as Hirsch argued, is critical for people to understand each other. Students are also exposed to many different ideas so that they can make knowledgeable choices about which interests to pursue. Finally, breadth allows students to make connections between many different disciplines, which can provide novel insights. A possible compromise between breadth and depth is to pursue a few topics in depth while broadly covering a wide variety of topics. Some students should become specialists and some should become generalists, and learning environments should support both goals.

Diverse Versus Uniform Expertise

Most schools attempt to ensure that all students learn the same thing. An alternative goal is for students to gain diverse expertise. This difference has profound effects on the organization of learning. For example, in a middle school in Rochester, New York, Carver (1990; Collins, Hawkins, & Carver, 1991) had eighth graders conduct research on different aspects of the city, such as the history, climate, culture, and government, in order to produce a HyperCard exhibit for the Rochester Museum and Science Center. Students specialized in different content areas and different tasks (e.g., producing text vs. graphics for the exhibit). The traditional school approach would have students read and discuss the same material on these topics.

One cost of diverse expertise is the loss of a community of shared knowledge, where students can discuss issues from similar backgrounds. Another cost is that teachers can no longer evaluate students in the same terms: whether they have learned particular content or skills. The benefits are that students can specialize in what interests them, and will feel pride of ownership in the knowledge and skills they have and that others do not have. It can also be viewed as a benefit that teachers cannot measure students on a simple metric, such as how much specific content they have gained, but rather must judge them in terms of their products and efforts (Collins, 1990). Our best examples of teaching (Lampert, 1986; Resnick, Bill, Lesgold, & Leer, 1991; Stigler & Perry, 1988) rely on uniform expertise, but the introduction of new technology and a constructivist pedagogy fosters a change to an emphasis on diverse expertise (A. Brown, 1992).

Access Versus Understanding

As we give students more powerful tools, understanding of the ideas and procedures that the tools accomplish for us is lost. For example, if we give students tools that fix the spelling and grammar in text, or that compute all the math algorithms in school, then knowledge of how to do such things will die out among students.

The cost of giving students access to powerful tools is that students will not understand how these tools work, and thus will not be able to evaluate the products derived from the tools. The benefit of giving students access to powerful tools is that they can get on with learning what they will need for the future, instead of learning spelling and algorithms. Furthermore, they will be vastly empowered by having tools that do for them what people are not so good at doing. History is replete with lost understandings. For example, how to grow crops and make clothes were once taught to practically everyone, and it seems inevitable that much of what we now teach in school will not be learned by most people in the future.

Cognitive Versus Physical Fidelity

As we create simulated environments, either on or off computers, a critical question emerges: What is the trade-off between preserving physical fidelity to the environment vs. preserving only cognitive fidelity? This trade-off is well illustrated by the difference between a simulation of the steam plant on board ships built by the navy, which preserves all the physical details—filling two large

rooms and requiring a crew of eight people to operate—and the cognitive simulation in STEAMER (Stevens & Roberts, 1983), which shows the configuration of
the entire system and its different subsystems, as well as the flow of water and
steam inside the pipes. It is much easier to understand the system from working
with the cognitive simulation, but much of the physical detail is lost.

The cost of stressing cognitive fidelity is that learners may not recognize
particular situations in the real world because they look different than in the
simulation. Another problem is that important mappings that are used for understanding a system may be lost: Any simulation that throws away a large portion
of the mapping to reality risks throwing away some critical elements on which
people rely. The benefit of stressing cognitive simulation is that it makes it
possible to focus on salient aspects of the situation, so that students do not get
lost in complexity. Moreover, cognitive simulations are much cheaper to build. It
pays to start with cognitive fidelity so that students get the big picture, and then
move to greater physical fidelity.

LEARNING CONTEXTS

There are several trade-offs that have to do with the learning contexts created for
students. These include whether the learning is highly interactive or not, incidental or direct, fun or serious, natural or efficient, and whether or not the learner is
in control.

Interactive Versus Active Versus Passive Learning

There is a difference between active learning and interactive learning that is often
overlooked. It is the difference between being in a highly responsive environment, such as playing a video game, vs. being in a fairly nonresponsive environment, such as working with a drawing program or LOGO (Harel, 1990). Both are
different from passive learning, such as listening to a lecture or watching a video,
where the learner can easily tune out what is happening.

The costs and benefits of active learning vs. passive learning are probably
well known, but the costs and benefits of interactive learning vs. active learning
are less well known. The costs of high interactivity are a lack of thoughtfulness
by the student because things move fast, and a lack of problem finding and
construction by students because everything they do is responsive to some situation. The benefits of high interactivity are that students receive immediate feedback on the success of their actions, they find such environments extremely
motivating, and they are very active trying out different skills and strategies.
Clearly, there needs to be a mix of highly interactive and less interactive environments for learning. Less interactive environments foster thoughtfulness, whereas
highly interactive environments foster automaticity.

Incidental Versus Direct Learning

When students are in a task environment, what they learn may be taught directly by the task itself or only incidentally to the task. For example, the computer game, Carmen San Diego, is designed to teach knowledge about geography incidentally to tracking down criminals, whereas a travel agent simulation program, where students find places to visit meeting different specifications (warm climate, inexpensive), would teach about the uses of geographical knowledge directly. It is possible to create very engaging tasks if one is willing to teach indirectly rather than directly.

The costs of incidental learning are subtle and have to do with authenticity. To the degree that one teaches indirectly, it is likely to promote the wrong lessons: In Carmen San Diego, the geographical facts are mostly useless (e.g., that they speak French in Cameroon) and are not integrated in any well-organized structure. Hence, the knowledge gained is not likely to be of much use when trying to do any task that requires geographical knowledge. But of course the benefit is that the task is likely to be engaging, therefore students will spend more time at it and perhaps learn more geography. My own preference is to create engaging tasks that reflect the uses of the knowledge to be learned, and let any facts and concepts be learned incidentally.

Fun Versus Serious Learning

There is a tendency to think that it is good for learning to be fun, but there is a downside. The costs are that students do not take what they are learning seriously, and so may not remember it. They also do not learn to force themselves to do difficult tasks. They come to think that all learning should be fun, but unfortunately life is not like that. The benefits are that you reach more students, and they will spend extra time and effort. Furthermore, the repetitive drill and difficult tasks in school manage to turn off many students to education generally.

My own view is that it is best to engage students by creating meaningful tasks, not by creating fun environments. An example is the project in Mississippi, where African-American students collected oral histories from adults who lived through the civil rights struggles of the 1960s, which they published as a book. This was a serious task, but it was as engaging as any fun task.

Natural Versus Efficient Learning

Most of the natural ways we learn things are inefficient, and so there is always a tendency to try to design more efficient learning environments. For example, the way we first learn language in the home is different from the more efficient ways we try to teach adults a second language. The learning children do when they invent arithmetic algorithms is different from the learning of the standard algorithms in school.

The cost of naturalness is simply its inefficiency: It takes children years to learn to speak their language. People also do not naturally learn the most effective ways to do things, as with arithmetic. The benefit of natural learning is that it is functional: Such learning enables people to achieve their goals so that the success rate is high. Learners do not learn the kinds of counterproductive strategies that Schoenfeld (1985) described for school math learning. Sacrificing naturalness is probably fine as long as we do not sacrifice functionality for the learner.

Learner Control Versus Computer or Teacher Control

There is a trade-off between putting the learner in control of his or her own learning vs. keeping control by the teacher or computer. Exploratory environments (e.g., Physics Explorer) and tool-based projects (e.g., the one in Rochester, New York) largely give control to students, whereas intelligent tutoring systems such as the LISP, geometry, and algebra tutors built by Anderson and his colleagues (e.g., Anderson, Boyle, & Reiser, 1985) keep rather tight control over what the student can do.

The cost of giving learners control is that most lack knowledge about the structure of the domain, about how to learn effectively, and about what they know vs. what they do not know. Hence, they make poor educational choices for themselves. But the benefit of giving learners control is that they can study what is most interesting and challenging to them. Furthermore, control over their own learning is motivating to many students. One strategy is to give students control over everything but pedagogical decisions; another is to give students information to help them make good pedagogical decisions (Frederiksen & White, 1990).

SEQUENCE

Because a learning environment changes as a person interacts with it, one way to treat some of the trade-offs is sequentially. I propose that the trade-offs between grounded vs. abstract learning, structured vs. exploratory learning, systematic vs. diverse learning, and simple vs. complex learning be treated in this way.

Grounded Versus Abstract Learning

Learning contexts can mimic the situations in which the knowledge is likely to be used or they can be abstracted from particular situations. For example, in order to teach arithmetic we can put students in the context of running a bank or building a clubhouse, as John Dewey did in his laboratory school in the early 1900s

(Cuban, 1984), which are grounded in particular situations. Alternatively, we can teach students abstract algorithms that can be used in any context.

The costs of grounded learning derive from the fact that students' knowledge is tied to particular situations, and so they neither learn a general framework nor learn how to apply their learning to new situations. The benefits of grounded learning are that students see the point of what they are learning, and learn at least one way to use their knowledge. Furthermore, it is difficult to remember abstractions if they are not grounded in situations that are memorable.

Currently, mathematics education starts with abstract algorithms, and then teaches students how to apply these abstractions in particular situations, through story problems. We have argued elsewhere (Brown, Collins, & Duguid, 1989) that this is backward. Students should first learn knowledge and skills in context, and by experiencing multiple contexts they should learn to generalize their knowledge.

Structured Versus Exploratory Learning

Highly structured learning environments keep students engaged in activities that can lead to learning. For example, the LISP, geometry, and algebra tutors built by Anderson et al. (Anderson, Boyle, & Reiser, 1985) provide immediate feedback and correction in response to students' mistakes, and thereby keep students from going off the correct solution path. Other systems, such as Physics Explorer and Interactive Physics allow students much more flexibility to explore and even play, although Physics Explorer does allow teachers to set up structured exercises for students.

The costs of structured learning environments are that students do not learn to find their own problems, and they do not learn to explore productively. The benefits of structured environments are that students do not end up floundering or randomly playing, and they are not as likely to get turned off by failure. Ideally, students would start out in highly structured environments and, as they master the skills of the domain, move to less and less structured environments.

Systematic Versus Diverse Learning

The problems and tasks posed to students can vary in systematic ways or in more diverse ways, as they do in life. For example, in mathematics, one can give students a whole series of distance, rate, and time problems to solve, or one can have a mixture of many different kinds of problems.

One cost of giving students problems that vary systematically is that they will learn ad hoc strategies for solving the problems, which do not apply in other settings. Another cost is that they will not learn to figure out when a particular solution method or strategy is appropriate. The benefit of systematic variation is that induction is much easier, and so learning is much more efficient. Schoenfeld's (1985) strategy in teaching problem solving is to start with systematic variation and move to more and more diverse problems.

Simple Versus Complex Learning

There has been a tendency in education to simplify problems and tasks so that all students can succeed. For example, we give students *Dick and Jane* to read, rather than books like *The Hobbit*. The cost of simplification is oversimplification for many students: The tasks often become boring and meaningless. The benefits of simplification are that more students are likely to succeed, and thus it is possible to focus on important prerequisites.

In general, one wants to proceed from the simple to complex, but ideally one should start at the optimum complexity for each student. This may mean doing some simple inquiry or assessment beforehand to determine where to start. Scaffolding (Palincsar & Brown, 1984) is designed to get students through more complex tasks with just as much support as they need, but no more.

TEACHING METHODS

There are a set of teaching methods associated with cognitive apprenticeship (Collins, Brown, & Newman, 1989; Collins, 1991; Collins & Brown, 1988) that have both advantages and disadvantages. The methods I focus on here are modeling, scaffolding, coaching, articulation, and reflection. These are discussed in more detail in the earlier papers.

Modeling

Modeling processes for students can enhance their understanding dramatically. There are two kinds of modeling that are critical to consider in the design of learning environments (Collins, 1991): (a) modeling the physical processes underlying phenomena we want students to understand, and (b) modeling the thought processes underlying expert performance. For example, in the Quest system (White & Frederiksen, 1990), the system can model how electricity flows in different circuits, and how an expert troubleshooter would locate a fault in different circuits.

The costs of modeling are that it is a passive and often boring activity for students. The benefits are that they can see normally invisible processes, and they can begin to integrate *what* happens with *why* it happens. Modeling is potentially very valuable, but it seems best to model early in the learning process and involve the learner as much as possible.

Scaffolding

Scaffolding is the support given to students as they carry out a task (Collins, Brown, & Newman, 1989; Palincsar & Brown, 1984). It can come in many different forms: the short skis that enable people to learn to ski much faster (Burton, Brown & Fisher, 1984), the cue cards that Bereiter and Scardamalia (1987) give students to prompt them as they plan to write, and the hints that Palincsar and Brown (1984) and Lesgold, Lajoie, Logan, and Eggan's (1990) Sherlock system provide students as they carry out a task.

The cost of scaffolding is that it is a crutch that students know they can fall back on, and so they may become dependent on it. The benefits of scaffolding are that it helps students accomplish difficult tasks, providing focused help at critical times and only as much as needed. In designing learning environments, it is in fact easier to provide scaffolding than to provide the kind of coaching described next. Ideally, the scaffolding would be faded as students become more expert.

Coaching

Coaching involves a whole range of activities: choosing tasks, modeling how to do them, providing hints and scaffolding, diagnosing problems and giving feedback, challenging and offering encouragement, and structuring how to do things. For example, Heath (1991) described how a little league baseball coach gets students to view mistakes as learning experiences; Lepper, Aspinwall, Mumme, and Chabay (1990) described how math tutors challenge students to get them to try difficult problems and not be afraid of failing. The most elaborate computer coach to date is the coach for the game *How the West Was Won,* built by Burton and Brown (1982). The coach diagnoses the patterns of play students are following, and then makes suggestions at opportune moments as to how the students might improve their game.

One cost of coaching has to do with the dangers of misdiagnosis, which is likely with computer coaches because of their limited bandwidth for viewing student behavior. To the degree that the diagnosis is shallow, as in the Anderson et al. (1985) tutors, the likelihood of misdiagnosis decreases. The benefits of coaching are similar to those for scaffolding: Coaching provides focused help at critical times and only as much help as needed. In the best cases, it can provide new ways to see what you are doing, which can help students out of ruts. Ideally, coaching, like scaffolding, should fade as students become more expert. But both computer and human coaching is expensive to provide, and so it must have high payoffs to be worth the cost.

Articulation

Teachers have a variety of methods for getting students to articulate their ideas and thinking processes. For example, Bereiter and Scardamalia (1987) have students describe their thinking processes while planning an essay. Schoenfeld (1985) has students work in groups to solve difficult math problems so they are forced to articulate their thinking to each other. Inquiry teachers (Collins & Stevens, 1982, 1983) pose problems and questions for students to get them to articulate and refine their theories. As Brown (1985) pointed out, programs like Robot Odyssey force students to articulate their theories to construct robot agents to carry out their plans. These kinds of articulation help students formulate their ideas in a way that makes them available on other occasions.

The cost of articulation is that students may learn to talk a good game without really understanding. Also, emphasis on articulation discriminates against the less articulate, who might be able to do tasks perfectly well without any articulation. One benefit of articulation is that it helps make people's tacit knowledge explicit, and hence it is more available. Another benefit is that articulation allows people to see how other people think about the same problem. Making knowledge more available through articulation fosters transfer of that knowledge to new situations.

Reflection

Reflection involves looking back over one's performance on a task and comparing it to other people's performances, both good and bad, on similar tasks. This exploits the method of perceptual learning (Bransford, Franks, Vye, & Sherwood, 1989). For example, one can use reflective tape to mark critical parts of an athlete's body and videotape his or her performance in swinging a racket or throwing a javelin. Then it is possible to compare how the athlete's body moves during more and less successful performances, and how he or she moves compared with other athletes. Collins and Brown (1988) called this an *abstracted replay;* it allows the student to reflect systematically on the process. Another form of reflection is possible in Algebraland (J. Brown, 1985) or the Geometry Tutor (Anderson et al., 1985), where the system keeps a record of all the student moves in solving an algebra equation or developing a geometry proof. These reifications of the problem-solving process allow similar kinds of reflection.

The costs of reflection are that students often find it tedious to have to look back at their performance, and usually do not have the patience to try to improve their performance. Most students just want to do an activity and then move on to other activities. The benefits of reflection are that students have a chance to see processes for the first time, much like their first exposure to a mirror, and to compare their ways of doing things to other people's ways. Because they can see themselves from a new angle, students begin to develop new ways of seeing and talking about what they do. I particularly recommend the kinds of abstracted replays and reifications described earlier (Collins & Brown, 1988), and the cycle of performing, reflecting, and reperforming embodied in Arts Propel (Gardner, 1991; Wolf, 1987).

CONCLUSION

These are my candidate set of issues that designers should be concerned about, omitting issues about the knowledge learned (Collins et al., 1989) and the social settings in which learning occurs (Collins, Greeno, & Resnick, 1994), which I address elsewhere. By taking a cost–benefit approach to these issues, there is a chance that designers will be able to minimize the costs and maximize the benefits of any design decisions.

ACKNOWLEDGMENTS

This work was supported by the Center for Technology in Education under Grant No. 1-135562167-A1 from the Office of Educational Research and Improvement, U.S. Department of Education to Bank Street College of Education. I thank Roy Pea for his suggestion of adding Access vs. Understanding and Depth vs. Breadth of Knowledge to the set of issues.

REFERENCES

Anderson, J. R., Boyle, C. F., & Reiser, B. J. (1985). Intelligent tutoring systems. *Science, 228*, 456–468.

Benezet, L. P. (1991, May). The teaching of arithmetic: The story of an experiment. *Humanistic Mathematics Newsletter, 6*, 2–14.

Bereiter, C., & Scardamalia, M. (1987). *The psychology of written composition*. Hillsdale NJ: Lawrence Erlbaum Associates.

Bransford, J. D., Franks, J. J., Vye, N. J., & Sherwood, R. D. (1989). New approaches to instruction: Because wisdom can't be told. In S. Vosniadou & A. Ortony (Eds.), *Similarity and analogical reasoning* (pp. 470–497). New York: Cambridge University Press.

Brown, A. L. (1992). Design experiments: Theoretical and methodological challenges in creating complex interventions. *Journal of the Learning Sciences, 2*(2), 141–178.

Brown, J. S. (1985). Idea-amplifiers: New kinds of electronic learning. *Educational Horizons, 63*, 108–112.

Brown, J. S., Collins, A., & Duguid, P. (1989). Situated cognition and the culture of learning. *Educational Researcher, 18*(1), 32–42.

Burton, R., Brown, J. S., & Fisher, G. (1984). Skiing as a model of instruction. In B. Rogoff & J. Lave (Eds.), *Everyday cognition: Its developmental and social context* (pp. 139–150). Cambridge, MA: Harvard University Press.

Burton, R. R., & Brown, J. S. (1982). An investigation of computer coaching for informal learning activities. In D. Sleeman & J. S. Brown (Eds.), *Intelligent tutoring systems* (pp. 79–98). New York: Academic Press.

Carver, S. M. (1990, April). *Integrating interactive technologies into classrooms: The Discover Rochester project.* Paper presented at the annual meeting of the American Educational Research Association, Boston.

Collins, A. (1990). Reformulating testing to measure learning and thinking. In N. Frederiksen, R. Glaser, A. Lesgold, & M. Shafto (Eds.), *Diagnostic monitoring of skills and knowledge acquisition* (pp. 325–350). Hillsdale, NJ: Lawrence Erlbaum Associates.

Collins, A. (1991). Cognitive apprenticeship and instructional technology. In L. Idol & B. F. Jones (Eds.), *Educational values and cognitive instruction: Implications for reform* (pp. 119–136). Hillsdale, NJ: Lawrence Erlbaum Associates.

Collins, A., & Brown, J. S. (1988). The computer as a tool for learning through reflection. In H. Mandl & A. Lesgold (Eds.), *Learning issues for intelligent tutoring systems* (pp. 1–18). New York: Springer-Verlag.

Collins, A., Brown, J. S., & Newman, S. E. (1989). Cognitive apprenticeship: Teaching the crafts of reading, writing, and mathematics. In L.B. Resnick (Ed.), *Knowing, learning, and instruction: Essays in honor of Robert Glaser* (pp. 453–494). Hillsdale, NJ: Lawrence Erlbaum Associates.

Collins, A., Greeno, J. G., & Resnick, L. B. (1994). Learning environments. In T. Husen & T. N. Postlethwaite (Eds.), *International encyclopedia of education* (2nd ed., pp. 3297–3302). Oxford, UK: Pergamon.

Collins, A., Hawkins, J., & Carver, S. M. (1991). A cognitive apprenticeship for disadvantaged students. In B. Means, C. Chelemer & M. S. Knapp (Eds.), *Teaching advanced skills to at-risk students* (pp. 216–243). San Francisco: Jossey-Bass.

Collins, A., & Stevens, A. L. (1982). Goals and strategies of inquiry teachers. In R. Glaser (Ed.), *Advances in instructional psychology* (Vol. 2, pp. 65–119). Hillsdale, NJ: Lawrence Erlbaum Associates.

Collins, A., & Stevens, A. L. (1983). A cognitive theory of interactive teaching. In C. M. Reigeluth (Ed.), *Instructional design theories and models: An overview* (pp. 247–278). Hillsdale, NJ: Lawrence Erlbaum Associates.

Cuban, L. (1984). *How teachers taught*. New York: Longman.

Frederiksen, J. R. & White, B. Y. (1990). Intelligent tutors as intelligent testers. In N. Frederiksen, R. Glaser, A. Lesgold, & M. Shafto (Eds.), *Diagnostic monitoring of skill and knowledge acquisition* (pp. 1–25). Hillsdale, NJ: Lawrence Erlbaum Associates.

Gardner, H. (1991). Assessment in context: The alternative to standardized testing. In B. Gifford & C. O'Connor (Eds.), *Future assessments: Changing views of aptitude, achievement, and instruction* (pp. 77–120). Boston: Kluwer.

Harel, I. (1990). Children as software designers: A constructionist approach for learning mathematics. *The Journal of Mathematical Behavior, 9*(1), 3–93.

Heath, S. B. (1991). "It's about winning!" The language of knowledge in baseball. In L. B. Resnick, J. M. Levine, & S. D. Teasley (Eds.), *Perspectives on socially shared cognition* (pp. 101–126). Washington, DC: American Psychological Association.

Hirsch, E. D., Jr. (1987). *Cultural literacy: What every American needs to know*. Boston: Houghton Mifflin.

Lampert, M. (1986). Knowing, doing, and teaching multiplication. *Cognition and Instruction, 3*, 305–342.

Lepper, M. R., Aspinwall, L., Mumme, D., & Chabay, R. W. (1990). Self-perception and social perception processes in tutoring: Subtle social control strategies of expert tutors. In J. M. Olson & M. P. Zanna (Eds.), *Self-inference and social inference: The Ontario Symposium* (Vol. 6, pp. 217–237). Hillsdale, NJ: Lawrence Erlbaum Associates.

Lesgold, A., Lajoie, S., Logan, D., & Eggan, G. (1990). Applying cognitive task analysis and research methods to assessment. In N. Frederiksen, R. Glaser, A. Lesgold, & M. Shafto (Eds.), *Diagnostic monitoring of skills and knowledge acquisition* (pp. 325–350). Hillsdale, NJ: Lawrence Erlbaum Associates.

Palincsar, A. S., & Brown, A. L. (1984). Reciprocal teaching of comprehension-fostering and monitoring activities. *Cognition and Instruction, 1*, 117–175.

Reigeluth, C. M. (Ed.). (1983). *Instructional-design theories and models: An overview of their current status*. Hillsdale, NJ: Lawrence Erlbaum Associates.

Reigeluth, C. M. (Ed.). (1987). *Instructional theories in action: Lessons illustrating selected theories and models.* Hillsdale, NJ: Lawrence Erlbaum Associates.

Resnick, L. B., Bill, V. L., Lesgold, S. B., & Leer, M. N. (1991). Thinking in arithmetic class. In B. Means, C. Chelemer, & M. S. Knapp (Eds.), *Teaching advanced skills to at-risk students* (pp. 27–53). San Francisco: Jossey-Bass.

Schoenfeld, A. J. (1985). *Mathematical problem solving.* New York: Academic Press.

Stevens, A., & Roberts, B. (1983). Quantitative and qualitative simulation in computer-based training. *Journal of Computer-Based Instruction, 10,* 16–19.

Stigler, J. W., & Perry, M. (1988). Mathematics learning in Japanese, Chinese, and American classrooms. In G. Saxe & M. Gearhart (Eds.), *Children's mathematics* (pp. 27–54). San Francisco: Jossey-Bass.

White, B. Y., & Frederiksen, J. (1990). Causal model progressions as a foundation for intelligent learning environments. *Artificial Intelligence, 24,* 99–157.

Wiggins, G. (1989, May). A true test: Toward more authentic and equitable assessment. *Phi Delta Kappan,* pp. 703–713.

Wolf, D. P. (1987, December). Opening up assessment. *Educational Leadership,* pp. 24–29.

18 Studying Novel Learning Environments as Patterns of Change

Gavriel Salomon
University of Haifa, Israel

COMPUTERS AS A TRIGGER FOR CHANGE

More imaginative and promising technology-enhanced instructional innovations —such as Newman's (1990) Earth Lab, Linn's (1991) Lab Partner, Schoenfeld's (1988) Math Project, Ann Brown's (1992) Community of Learners, or our International Science Classroom (Salomon & Associates, 1991), the Cognition and Technology Group at Vanderbilt's (1990) "anchored instruction" in science, or Pea's (1993) Optic Project—involve profound changes. Such changes typically include teamwork, authentic problems to be solved in a semiautonmous manner, teachers as guides, explorative tasks, and interdisciplinary contents. In short, such changes pertain to the whole classroom, not just to this or that practice or component.

What role does computer technology play in this kind of classroom transformation? Although technology is not the sole source of such changes, it certainly makes them possible, serving in what has been described as "a subversive tool" capacity (Sheingold, 1990). For example, it is very much due to the introduction of computers, or rather to their paucity, that teamwork was introduced into the American classroom and seriously studied (in other cultures, it is an old educational staple). Similarly, new computer-afforded activities of model building, simulation, and composition reinforced the shift in educational philosophy from instruction to construction (e.g., Resnick, 1991), and from science as a sterile, highly discipline-specific set of topics to science learning as an authentic, real-lifelike, interdisciplinary undertaking (Cole & Griffin, 1987). If we add to this the growing availability of computer-based communication and data sources to draw on, we can see how new modes of computer-facilitated learning environments gradually emerge.

Whether intended to be limited to the experimental implementation of a specific computer tool, or planned as an evaluation of a whole new approach to instruction (e.g., Brown, 1992), whole learning environments become affected. The changes brought about in innovative, technology-intensive classrooms commonly entail four major characteristics that distinguish current innovations from preceding ones: (a) they are technology intensive, employing computers for a wide range of tasks; (b) learning becomes interactive and team based; (c) learning tasks afford students the opportunity to constructively and actively deal with authentic and interdisciplinary science issues; and (d) projects are characterized by exploration and self-guidance. In all, the whole learning environment becomes transformed.

However, although the stated purpose of such changes is often no more than the facilitation of students' learning, skill mastery, and attitudes, it becomes apparent that changes of the individual greatly depend on changes distributed over a whole learning environment, in which computer use serves as the trigger. The changes in the individuals' learning are in fact a part of a larger change— that of the learning environment. Thus, although individuals' better learning is allegedly the ultimate goal, and technology the means to that goal, it is the learning environment that is the true subject of change in such cases.

Attention to the whole learning environment is not only a necessary consequence of the changes that take place in the classroom, but, as pointed out by Bronfenbrenner (1977a), it is a scholarly and practical must: Individuals' changed knowledge structures, perceptions, or attitudes cannot be well understood, let alone affected, if detached from the contexts in which these changes take place. According to Sarason (1991), failure to take into account the wider context of a learning environment and organizational structure leads to the "predictable failure of educational reform": "What I do assert is that school systems have been intractable to the reforms sought by reformers. That sad, brute fact reflects acceptance of schools systems as they are, focusing now on this part, now on that, this problem, that problem, as if the system in which they emerge is basically sound" (p. 43).

Unfortunately, researchers who design and study such innovative pedagogical projects prefer to evaluate and study the individuals' cognitions, attitudes, academic accomplishments, and such. They overlook the ways individuals' changes relate to the changes in the experienced learning environment (see e.g., Hounshell & Hill, 1989). Consequently, observed changes on the individual level are attributed to particular discrete "input" variables, although the totality of the changed learning environment accounts for the changes. Because nothing remains the same, it is impossible and invalid to attribute a "solo" change to one or another singled-out input variable. Given the package like nature of most innovative instructional projects, we cannot really attribute any change in achievement, aspiration, attitude, perceived self-efficacy in learning to any one factor, Because it is the whole learning context that changes, as well as the individual within it.

However, with the exception of general, impressionistic, qualitative descriptions of changes that a learning environment undergoes, little rigorous research is available to describe the relationship between individuals' changes and technology-triggered changes in learning environments (see e.g., Mason & Butler-Kahle, 1988). To paraphrase Lee S. Shulman of Stanford University, we measure individuals' changes by micrometer but environmental changes, to the extent that we measure them at all, by a divining rod. In short, we traditionally focus on the individual learner and poorly isolated discrete input variables, although in fact, it is the whole learning environment that is the true target of technology-enhanced (and other) innovative projects of science teaching.

Three reasons can be cited for the near-exclusive focus on the individual. First, many of the researchers involved in the design, implementation, and study of new technology-intensive instructional projects - being in fact involved in aspects of applied cognitive psychology - adopt psychology's emphasis on the individual (e.g., Goodenow, 1992). Second, despite interesting attempts to conceptually describe classrooms as learning environments (e.g., Fraser, 1989), a viable theory of such is yet to emerge to allow the simultaneous study of individual and environmental changes within the same conceptual framework. Third, even if a conceptual framework for the study of individuals and learning environments would be available, no methodology has been proposed so far to make a rigorous study empirically possible.

THE CONCEPTUAL NATURE OF LEARNING ENVIRONMENTS

Studying technology-intensive learning environments (TILE) is a difficult and challenging task. It presents two major questions: What is the generic nature of the entities we call *learning environments?* How can learning environments be studied in satisfying, rigorous, and valid ways?

A *learning environment* can be described as a composite of constituent factors: physical setting, set of agreed on behaviors, consenually held expectations and understandings, particular tasks, around prespecified contents for explicitly stated goals that are guided by a person who has been given the responsibility over that setting, its participants, and activities. In other words, a learning environment is first and foremost a system that consists of interrelated components that jointly affect learning in interaction with (but separately from) relevant individual and cultural differences (Salomon, 1991).

What would be typical, generic components of a learning environment? In every learning environment, one would find a teacher and adult who teaches or guides the students, and this teaching has different qualities (e.g., quality of explaining; Berliner, 1983; Tisher & Power, 1978). If it is a teacher who is typically in charge, there are also instrumental (e.g., fairness of grading) and personal relations with him or her (e.g., trust in teacher as personal problem-solver; e.g., Cazden, 1986). Similarly, there are relations among the students, some pertaining to the tasks to be engaged in (e.g., extent of mutual help) and others that are more socially-oriented (e.g., tensions among the genders; e.g., Goodenow, 1992). These relations "add up" to constitute the experienced climates of the learning environment: social climate and a learning climate (e.g., Moos, 1979). Aside from these, one would also find the following in a typical learning environment: a component that relates to the rules and regulations, some explicit some not, that regulate life and activities in the learning environment (Doyle, 1986); a consensually held view of the participants in the learning environment of themselves as learners (Dweck, 1986); and the mental effort they are willing to expend in learning (e.g., Bereiter & Scardamalia 1989; Salomon & Globerson, 1987). Notice that this initial list of the generic components of a learning environment pertains to the learning environment as perceived and experienced. Thus, although a learning environment is also characterized by its social class and ethnic constitution, it is experienced as having or not having tensions, competition, stratification, and such, not by its "objective" demographics.

A system's components can be characterized by the contents of each of them (e.g., more or less appreciation for science learning, greater or lesser social cohesion), and by the way they relate to each other and hang together. Whereas the examination of the content of discrete components in a learning environment is a common and traditional focus of much intervention research, the examination of how the components hang together-i.e, their pattern or configuration of relations-is not. The reason is that the latter type of focus is based on two assumptions, not commonly made when only changes in discrete variables are assumed to be carried out.

One assumption is that a factor does not operate in isolation, unrelated to the other factors. We are not dealing here with discrete componentsof which the addition or removal of does not affect the whole configuration, but rather with "clouds of correlated events" (Scarr, 1985). For example, teamwork becomes a viable factor in a learning environment when teams: engage in some shared problem solving, often around a real-lifelike issue; are guided (not taught) by a teacher; draw on the members' own resources; help and guide each other; and share a common goal. One cannot take teamwork out of this context of factors or it becomes a meaningless factor.

It follows, then, that a learning environment needs to be examined, designed, and studied as a package, not as a cluster of additive factors. It also follows that one cannot hold one factor constant and vary the other as the factors typically hang together. Thus, it would make little sense to study the impact of computer use, or any other isolated factor, independently of the other factors because one cannot assume that one factor affects outcomes independently of the others.

The second assumption is that the isolated factor has no meaning in and of itself, but in relation to other factors. The totality of a learning environment is more than the sum of its components, in terms of its perceived meanings and the way it is experienced. For example, one cannot isolate the perceived meaning of strict rules of teamwork in a classroom from the experience of being in a classroom that perceives itself as task oriented and engaged in serious problem solving. The same rules—perceived as equally strict in a classroom whose tasks are perceived to be stale and meaningless—have an entirely different meaning to the students. It is in this sense that Altman (1988) put it, using the analogy of individual actors: "There are no separate actors in an event; instead, there are 'acting relationships' such that the actions of one person can only be described and understood in relation to the actions of other persons, and in relation to the situational and temporal circumstances in which the actors are involved" (p. 268).

Taken together, these two assumptions suggest the need to study a TILE as a configuration, without ruling out the more traditional possibility of studying the way each and every factor changes over time, or as a consequence of a computer-intensive intervention in an "analytic" manner (Salomon, 1991). But studying only the way each and every factor changes—disregarding the configurational changes - is less than conceptually satisfying because it ignores the better part of the story.

Attempts have been made to develop measures of learning environment and to relate them to individuals' variables, notably achievement and attitude (e.g., Fraser, 1989). But despite a relatively rich tradition of research into classrooms as learning environments, little effort has been made to examine the extent to which the measures traditionally employed fully account for what one usually calls "learning environments" or for only a limited range of its aspects. For example, although most measures emphasize social climate, few are designed to tap students': views of science and science learning, perceived ability (better able classes are differently taught), perceived homogeneity in ability (great heterogeneity creates a different environment than homogeneity), or view of their ability to learn science (such views need not correlate with actually measured ability (Dweck, 1986). These are crucial variables that cannot be excluded from the conception and measurement of a TILE.

Even more important, given the view that a learning environment is a system, it is to be regretted that little has been done in terms of studying the way different aspects of a learning environment relate to each other, and how these relations change over time as a consequence of introducing technology and all that its introduction entails. In most cases, the learning environment is taken as a set of discrete variables. Researchers traditionally examine how each and every variable, taken alone, changes as a consequence of an intervention, but not as a system of interdependent components.

Indeed, although each of the factors that seem to constitute a learning environment has already been studied to one extent or another as an independent entity, the relations among the components—the way they configure jointly—have rarely, if at all, been studied. It is To this question that I turn next.

A WAY TO STUDY LEARNING ENVIRONMENTS

What would the source of data about a learning environment be? One possibility is to collect what might be seen as an outsider's bird's view: One could go into a classroom or a hangout and observe it as closely as possible, making inferences about its nature and "feel." Another possibility is to study learning environments as experienced and perceived by their inhabitants. Each approach has well-known strengths and weaknesses (see Roberts, Hulin, & Rousseau 1978 for detailed discussion). Having adopted an ecological point of view of the Bronfenbrenner (1977b) kind, coupled with a transactional approach of the Altman (1988) brand, I chose to take as the prefered source of information about a learning environment the way its participants perceive and experience it. This also follows directly from Weick's (1979) attempts to understand human organizations. An *organization* is the set of commonly held and negotiated agreements at which its participants have arrived. Weick described an orchestra as: "If we ask where that orchestra is, the answer is that the orchestra is in the minds of the musicians. It exists in the minds of the musicians in the form of the variables they routinely look for and the connections they routinely infer among these variables" (p. 141).

We need to distinguish here between the *analytic* approach, whereby the perceived changes in each variable, taken alone, are studied independently of changes in other variables, and the *systemic* approach, whereby the changes in the configuration are the focus of research (Salomon, 1991). In the analytic kind of study, everything is supposed to be held constant, save one or two variables of interest. This kind of study is well suited to study patterns of differences, (i.e., systematic differences among individuals, possibly partaking in some treatment groups). The clearest test for such a pattern is the researcher's ability to attribute a change or difference to a particular, and unconfounded preceding, discrete factor. Thus, one would want to accurately determine how much learning variance can be attributed to the diagnostic capabilities built into an intelligent tutoring system (ITS) that teaches light refraction, or the extent to which a certain kind of interaction with a simulator contributes to improved comprehension and motivation to learn.

The systemic study focuses on differences in patterns: the way a particular kind of learning environment is structured by the relations among its components, and the way and how this configuration changes when a new computer-intensive instructional approach is ushered in. Similar comparisons can be carried out between experimenal (TILE) learning environments and control (traditional) ones. No attempt is made to accurately attribute a change in patterns of relations among factors to one or another discrete input. First, it is the changes in the configuration that are of interest; second, such changes are attributed to the packagelike introduction of interrelated new modes of instruction, social activity, curriculum, tasks, and the like. But we are not talking here of two opposing or mutually exclusive approaches. Studying patterns of differences (the analytic approach) and differences of patterns (the systemic approach) are complementary to each other; each is based on different epistemological assumptions, and each serves to address different questions. To explain the ise differences in greater detail I take a brief methodological detour.

THE METHODOLOGY

To study patterns of differences, one needs a set of tools that is deliberately designed to represent multidimensional, systemic relations in a way that would yield rigorous, yet interpretable, descriptions and allow relatively valid comparisons between configurations. Multidimensional scaling (MDS) allows one to translate a set of correlations (or other measures of association) among scaled variables into nonmetric (ordinal) distances among points, and to locate each point relative to all others within a Euclidean space in a way that is unaffected by the orientation or metric of the dimensions (Young & Hamer, 1987). The employment of MDS is proposed here as one useful methodology that satisfies the requirements mentioned previously.

An appropriate and relevant variant of MDS is Guttman's (1968) small space analysis (SSA) which is well suited to represent the way a bunch of variables configure in two-or three-dimensional space. This methodology is not frequently employed by U.S. social scientists (see Young & Hamer, 1987 for a number of exceptions), but is becoming increasingly popular in Europe. As has been shown, SSA, like other figural MDS analyses, has a number of advantages over factor analyses and cluster analyses: in terms of the richness of the interpretable presentations that SSAs yield, and the parsimony of the mathematical assumptions they make (and the often unwarranted metric assumptions they do not need to make); (Guttman 1954; Snow, Kyllonen, & Marshelak, 1984).

SSA maps can be interpreted in two ways (or a combination of the two): according to the overall dimensions yielded by the spatial arrangement of the variables, or according to the clustering within the coordinates that they yield (Kruskal & Wish, 1990). In the case of the overall dimensional interpretation, one looks for orthogonally related dimensions, along which the different points (variables) are arranged such that the elements that are at opposite sides of a dimension are qualitatively different from each other. For example, in a study conducted by Wish (1971), subjects were asked to rate the similarity among 12 nations. MDS analysis yielded two dimensions, according to which the subjects' political perceptions were arranged: *political orientation* (pro-Western vs. pro-communist), and *degree of economic development*.

The second way to interpret SSAs (and more relevant to us) is based on clusters of neighboring variables, which, as pointed out by Guttman (1965), reveal specific patterns that a gross-dimensional interpretation would fail to yield. Variables that are more strongly related to each other—reciprocally affecting each other or providing meaning to each other—are closer together; variables that are more loosely associated are farther apart. Thus, interpretation is based on such proximities.

To illustrate, Snow, Kyllonen, and Marshelak (1984) submitted a battery of mental tests administered to 241 high school students to a two-dimensional SSA. Their analyses showed that the mental tests are arranged as: (a) "wedges" representing different content domains of ability (e.g., figural–spatial, verbal–numerical), and (b) closer to or farther away from the core, aligned according to complexity of information processing (the more complex ones are closer to the center). Human abilities that are closer to the core are more complex and share information-processing mechanisms with other abilities of equal complexity (the G factor in intelligence). Abilities farther out on the periphery of the wedges are less complex in their demands, and thus share less with one another and with the general common core of information processing. This combination of the wedge like "circumflex" and the radially expanding complex-to-simple "simplex" yields what is called a *radex*. No factor analysis or cluster analysis, as Snow, et al. showed, can yield this kind of easily interpretable and detailed presentation. Admittedly, this methodology has its limitations, and other methodologies may be employed to complement this one (e.g., Sabers, Jones, & Shiroma, 1989). The important point is not the specific methodology employed, but the new perspective it or its alternatives offer us: examination of how patterns of relations among the components that constitute a learning environment change as a result of a technology-intensive intervention.

AN ILLUSTRATION: FINDINGS FROM THE
INTERNATIONAL SCIENCE CLASSROOM

It may be useful to illustrate what is meant by the contrast between the study of "patterns of differences" and "differences in patterns" by means of a real project that was studied in a way that laid the foundations for the present chapter. For a while now, a group of high school teachers in Tucson, Arizona and University of Arizona faculty and students have been involved in the design, implementation, and study of the International Science Classroom (ISC) project (e.g., Salomon & Associates, 1991). Teams of students worked in real-lifelike, authentic, and interdisciplinary science projects related to a larger, more general topic. The larger topic was "Science and Technology in the Service of Humanity", and the specific team projects were: Physical and Social Aspects of Home Solar Systems: A Comparative Study," and "The Biological Dangers of Mixing Groundwater with Sewage and the Legislative Roadblocks to the Amelioration of the Problem in Nogales, Arizona and Tel-Aviv, Israel." For about three months, teams of students semiautonomously engaged in the definition, conception, planning, data gathering, experimentation, and solution of such open-ended questions, and in computer-mediated communication with parallel teams in Israel. All this was done in preparation for the end-of-year International Science Congress, in which students' works were presented and debated. About 400 physics, chemistry, biology, and social studies students participated during 1990–1991 in the ISC as "experimental classes," another 400 students in the same schools served as "controls," studying science the traditional way.

The combined team of university personnel and high school teachers involved in the project measured changes in students' achievements, attitudes, and perceived self efficacy in learning science, and in using advanced technologies ("patterns of differences"). Although the research team found significant and interesting increases in some of these discrete variables, relative to control classes, we could not possibly attribute these changes to any single component; in the ISC classes, everything was changed, thus creating a new "cloud of correlated events" (Scarr, 1985). Moreover, it became evident that, by focusing only on the patterns of differences (pre- vs. posttest, a comparison of one or another variable between the experimental and control classes), one was missing the better half of the story. That "better half" required examination of the "differences of patterns."

To rigorously study what went on in the ISC classrooms and how they have changed, we needed to study the changes in the learning environment as learning environments together with the changes that individuals in it underwent. To do that, it became necessary to elucidate the way the variables—those pertaining to the perceived learning environment and those pertaining to individual cognitions and attitudes—relate to each other, and how these relations change as a consequence of the project.

Pre- and posttest measures were taken of students' mastery of science problem-solving skills, proclivity to be mindful (or to avoid the expenditure of mental effort; (Salomon & Globerson, 1987), perceived self-efficacy in learning science and handling computers, and attitudes toward science and science learning. Not having yet developed the detailed factors that constitute a TILE, described in a previous section, *environment* was measured by means of a short questionnaire with only a few questions pertaining to the social-interpersonal aspects of classroom life. All measures were submitted to a SSA, separately for the experimental (ISC) and the control classes, to allow for the study of differences in developing patterns.

Examination of the preproject SSA maps of the ISC and control classes revealed little, if any, difference between them. The structure obtained was much like the one found in the control classes at the end of project's period, as shown in upper part of Figure 18.1.

The comparison between the structure of the learning environment in the

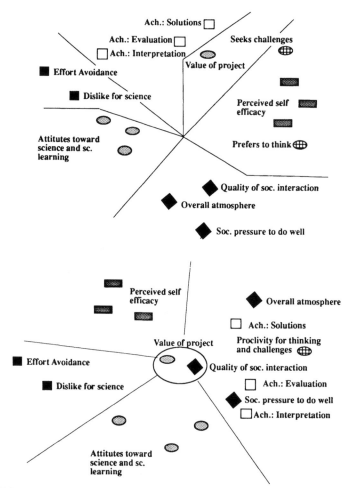

FIG. 18.1.   SSA maps of the ISC control (upper map) and experimental (lower map) classes.

control classes (upper figure) and that of the experimental classes (lower figure) is self-explanatory. In the control classes, there is no clear center, but there are about five wedgelike slices surrounding that empty center: (a) achievement and ability, (b) self-perceptions, (c) social-interactive factors, (d) attitudes toward science, and surprisingly, (e) dislike for science and effort avoidance. Achievement in science is closely related to dislike of science and effort avoidance, as if the students succeed in science as a matter of reactance. Achievement is also closely related to ability—a rather common and undesired relation. But the four variables constituting the perceived social-interactional factor appear as a separate and remote entity, unrelated to achievement.

The structure of learning environment in the experimental classes (lower part of Fig. 18.1) is different from that of the control classes. This learning environment now has a center with all variables arranged around it. The center—possibly the elements that give that learning environment its flavor—is composed of perceived value of the project and perceived quality of social interaction. These variables appear to constitute the core of the learning environment; everything else revolves around and relates to them. Whereas achievement is totally unrelated to the social-interpersonal variables in the control classes, achievement and social interaction are closely related in the experimental ones, but are relatively unrelated to effort avoidance and initial ability.

Comparison between the SSAs makes it clear that the end-of-project differences between experimental and control classes, in the configuration of individual and perceived social-interpersonal variables, tell a story that the study of the traditional patterns of differences could not. For one thing, the common and traditional separation of individuals' attitudes, achievements, and self-perceptions from social-interpersonal variables has disappeared in the experimental classes, suggesting a much closer relationship between individuals' learning and social interaction. For another, this comparison shows that the project makes science learning a matter of social interaction and mindful engagement, rather than a matter of initial ability or reactance-laden spite. Statistical comparisons between the dimensions of the two maps (Jonassen, 1987) and more traditional stepwise regression analyses upheld these findings. On this basis, it can now be said with relative confidence that the learning environment of the ISC has been radically changed in describable and comprehensible ways.

NEW RESEARCH QUESTIONS

The main argument of this chapter is that because the introduction of computer technology—in at least some of its better manifestations—affects the nature of the whole learning environment, turning these environments into the true targets of instructional innovations, one would need to study their generic structures and how changes in them relate to changes in individuals' learning achievements, cognitions, and attitudes.

The preceding discussion led me to develop a skeleton of a conceptual framework of what a TILE consists of. I distinguished between the content of such factors (e.g., how pleasant the climate) and the overall *structure of the relationships among them*. It is the latter that defines the systemic nature of a TILE. Also, I have argued that for both theoretical and methodological reasons, a TILE needs to be studied from a phenomenological perspective (i.e., through the eyes of those who participate in and experience them). Having arrived at this tentative framework, I can now present the four main clusters of questions that research on computers and learning environments would need to adress.

The first set of questions is whether the conceptualization of a TILE is valid. (a) Do the tentative factors, taken to constitute a TILE, fully account for what may be called a *learning environment?* For example, how do students' cultural and social-economic backgrounds relate to their TILEs as perceived and experienced? (b) Are the factors experienced as distinguishable from each other? (c) What kind of structures do these factors typically yield? One kind of structure, suggested by our recent studies of traditional and TILE-like classes (but not that of traditional classrooms), entails a pattern in which mindfulness, social interaction concerning learning, and attitudes toward learning constitute the center; they determine the overall tone of such learning environments. Other factors, usually at the center of life in more traditional classrooms, such as importance of grades, perceived quality of teaching, dependence on the teacher, and social tensions, are far more marginal in TILEs. But not yet having a comprehensive theoretical framework from which to deduce clear hypotheses to predict particular configurations, much is still left to be answered by open-ended questions.

The second set of questions pertains to the universality of the postulated structures of learning environments: (a) Can a particular organization of factors be consistently found to constitute a more of less uniform structure of traditional learning environments? (b) Does such a structure, if found, remain the same across cultures, socioeconomic statuse (SES), and age levels? I am not looking so much for differences among learning environments in how "high" or "low" a particular factor is, but mainly for the universality of the relationships between the factors.

The third set of questions pertains to differences among different kinds of learning environment's. (a) Does a particular and common configuration characterize and distinguish the more technology-enhanced innovative instructional projects (those that include teamwork, computer-based communication, and authentic problem-solving tasks) from the more traditional ones? For example, do the former systematically "locate" *ability* and *climate* differently than more traditional classrooms? (b) Do the two kinds of environments "locate" individual differences of achievement, attitude, or perceived self-efficacy differently from each other? Our current research suggests that this indeed is the case: More traditional learning environments "locate" perceived ability and teacher behavior at the center, together with traditional achievement measures, with social and learning climate at the outskirts. More innovative TILEs yield the opposite kind of pattern: social and learning climate, interaction, mindful engagement, and more innovative assessment of achievement at the core with ability and teacher behavior at the outskirts.

The fourth question pertains to the dynamics of how a learning environment changes as a function of the introduction of computer technology to be employed by teams of students for a variety of purposes. How do the structural attributes of a traditional learning environment change when it becomes transformed into a more innovative, technology-enhanced, team-based learning environment?

CODA

So far we have designed and implemented technology-enhanced novel modes of instruction that address the whole learning environment. But we have focused our research and evaluation attention on what happens to individual learners; we have ignored both the true target of the innovations, as well as the need to see individuals' behaviors, cognitions, motivations, and the like as interacting with the social and activity contexts in which individuals operate. We include in novel science projects the teaching of systems theory as it applies, for example, to the ecology, but fail to apply it to our own evaluation of these projects.

The arguments presented here are supposed to ameliorate this problem. First, and perhaps most important, I hope my proposal facilitats a shift in perspectives, (i.e., that it will offers a new and fresh approach to the design and study of technology-enhanced instruction, and to the evaluation of novel projects). I hope that the community of designers and researchers will start examining not only patterns of differences as well as differences in patterns. I hope that teachers, likewise, come to examine their own classrooms not as collections of individuals and individual variables, but as rule-governed and dynamic configurations of different components. Second, this shift of attentional focus is expected to contribute to the development of a theoretical framework that accounts for the nature of classrooms, the kinds of changes they undergo when computers are introduced, and, most important, the changes observed in individuals' learning. Third, I hope what I have presented here offers a viable methodology to study individuals' learning, and that projects can be evaluated in terms of individual as well as whole classroom changes.

REFERENCES

Altman, I. (1988). Process, transactional/contextual, and outcome research: An alternative to the traditional distinction between basic and applied research. *Social Behavior, 3*(4), 259–280.

Bereiter, C., & Scardamalia, M. (1989). Intentional learning as a goal of instruction. In L. B. Resnick (Ed.), *Knowing, learning, and instruction: Essays in honor of Robert Glaser* (pp. 361–392). Hillsdale, NJ: Lawrence Erlbaum Associates.

Berliner, D. C. (1983). Developing conceptions of classroom environments: Some light on the T in classroom studies in ATI. *Educational Psychologist, 18*, 1–13.

Bronfenbrenner, U. (1977a). Toward an experimental ecology of human development. *American Psychologist, 34*, 513–531.

Bronfenbrenner, U. (1977b). Lewinian space and ecological substance. *Journal of Social Issues, 33*(4), 199–212.

Brown, A. L. (1992). Design experiments: Theoretical and methodological challenges in creating complex interventions in classroom setting. *The Journal of the Learning Sciences, 2*, 141–178.

Cazden, C. (1986). Classroom discourse. In M. C. Wittrock (Ed.), *Handbook of research on teaching* (pp. 432–463). New York: Macmillan.

Cognition and Technology Group at Vanderbilt. (1990). Anchored instruction and its relationship to situated cognition. *Educational Researcher, 19*, 2–10.

Cole, M., & Griffin, P. (Eds.). (1987). *Contextual factors in education: Improving science and mathematics education for minorities and women.* Madison, WI: University of Wisconsin Press.

Doyle, W. (1986). Classroom organization and management. In M. C. Wittrock (Ed.), *Handbook of research on teaching* (pp. 392–431). New York: Macmillan.

Dweck, C. S. (1986). Motivational processes affecting learning. *American Psychologist, 41,* 1041–1048.

Fraser, B. J. (1989). Twenty years of classroom climate research: Progress and prospect. *Journal of Curriculum Studies, 11,* 19–34.

Goodenow, C. (1992). Studying interpersonal and group contacts in educational psychology. *Educational Psychologist , 27,* 177–196.

Guttman, L. (1954). A new approach to factor analysis: The radex. In P. F. Lazerfield (Ed.), *Mathematical thinking in the social sciences* (pp. 258–348). Glencoe, IL: The Free Press.

Guttman, L. (1965). The structure of interrelations among intelligence tests. In *Proceedings of the 1964 Invitational Conference on Testing Problems* (pp. 25–36). Princeton, NJ: Educational Testing Service.

Guttman, L. (1968). A general nonmetric technique for finding the smallest coordinate space for a configuration of points. *Psychometrika, 33,* 469–506.

Hounshell, P. B., & Hill, S. R., Jr. (1989). The microcomputer and achievement and attitudes in high school biology. *Journal of Research in Science Teaching, 26*(6), 543–549.

Jonassen, D. H. (1987). Assessing cognitive structure: Verifying a method using pattern notes. *Journal of Research and Development in Education, 20*(3), 1–14.

Kruskal, J. B., & Wish, M. (1990). *Multidimensional scaling.* Newbury Park, CA: Sage.

Linn, M. C. (1991). The computer as learning partner: Can computer tools teach science? In L. Roberts, K. Sheingold, & S. Malcolm (Eds.), *This year in school science 1991: Technology for teaching and learning.* Washington, DC: American Association for the Advancement of Science.

Mason, C. L., & Butler-Kahle, J. (1988). Student attitudes toward science and science related careers: A program designed to promote a stimulating gender-free learning environment. *Journal of Research in Science Teaching, 26*(1), 25–39.

Moos, R. H. (1979). *Evaluating educational environments.* San Francisco, CA: Jossey-Bass.

Newman, D. (1990). Opportunities for research on the organizational impact of School computers. *Educational Researcher, 19,* 8–13.

Pea, R. D. (1993). Practices of distributed intelligence and designs for education. In G. Salomon (Ed.), *Distributed Cognitions* (pp. 47–87). New York: Cambridge University Press.

Resnick, L. (1991). *Intelligent microworlds for scaffolding number concept development. Summary of Awards: Applications of advanced technologies, fiscal years 1987–1990* (NSF-91–97). Washington, DC: National Science Foundation.

Roberts, K. H., Hulin, C. L., & Rousseau, D. M. (1978). *Developing an interdisciplinary science of organizations.* San Francisco, CA: Jossey-Bass.

Sabers, D., Jones, P., & Shiroma, P. (1989). On methods for probing validity of intelligence tests: A commentary on the work of Zeidner and Feitelson. *Journal of Psychoeducational Assessment, 7,* 194–208.

Salomon, G. (1991). Transcending the quantitative/qualitative debate: The analytic and systemic approaches to educational research. *Educational Research, 20,* 10–18.

Salomon, G., & Associates. (1991). Learning: New conceptions, new opportunities. *Educational Technology, 31,* 41–44.

Salomon, G., & Globerson, T. (1987). Skill is not enough: The role of mindfulness in learning and transfer. *International Journal of Educational Research, 11,* 623–637.

Sarason, S. B. (1991). *The predictable failure of educational reform.* San Francisco, CA: Jossey-Bass.

Scarr, S. (1985). Constructing psychology: Making facts and fables for our times. *American Psychologist, 40,* 499–512.

Schoenfeld, A. H. (1988). Problem solving in context(s). In R. Charles & E. A. Silver (Eds.), *The teaching and assessing of mathematical problem solving* (pp. 82–92). Hillsdale, NJ: Lawrence Erlbaum Associates.

Sheingold, K. (1990, April). Using technology to develop higher order thinking. In H. Long (Chair), *Uses of technology that promote school restructuring.* Symposium conducted at the annual meeting of the American Educational Research Association, Boston, MA.

Snow, R. E., Kyllonen, P. C., & Marshelak, B. (1984). The topography of ability and learning correlations. In R. J. Stormberg (Ed.), *Advances in the psychology of human intelligences* (Vol. 2, 47–104). Hillsdale, NJ: Lawrence Erlbaum Associates.

Tisher, R. P., & Power, C. N. (1978). The learning environment associated with an Australian curriculum innovation. *Journal of Curriculum Studies, 10,* 169–184.

Weick, K. E. (1979). *The social psychology of organizing.* Reading, MA: Addison-Wesley.

Wish, M. (1971). Individual differences in perceptions and preferences among nations. In C. W. King & Dl. Tigert (Eds.), *Attitude research reaches new heights* (pp. 312–328). Chicago, IL: American Marketing Association.

Young, F. W., & Hamer, R. M. (1987). *Multidimensional scaling: History, theory, and applications.* Hillsdale, NJ: Lawrence Erlbaum Associates.

Author Index

A

Abeygunawardena, H., 159, 162
Achtenhagen, F., 109, 126
Adams, M. J., 244, 249
Aebli, H., 84, 92, 93, 100, 107, 109, 126
Ahlgren, A., 258, 284
Allington, R. L., 226, 249
Altman, I., 367, 368, 375
Amman, K., 42, 59
Anderson, C. W., 150, 153, 160, 161
Anderson, D., 31, 40
Anderson, J. A., 82, 88, 89, 92, 100
Anderson, J. R., 134, 143, 160, 161, 176, 181, 354, 355, 357, 358, 359
Anderson, L., 153, 161
Anderson, R., 50, 59
Anderson, T. H., 152, 161
Andre, T., 204, 218
Andriessen, J. E. B., 186, 202
Anglin, G. J., 236, 252
Applebee, A., 226, 252
Arcavi, A., 114, 127
Armbruster, B. B., 152, 161
Armour-Thomas, E., 111, 126
Artigue, M., 124, 126
Artzt, A. F., 111, 126
Ash, D., 109, 126, 287, 303
Aspinwall, L., 357, 360
August, D. I., 149, 161

B

Baillargeon, R., 15, 23
Baker, M., 180, 181
Bakhurst, D., 14, 23
Balthazor, M., 245, 255
Barnard, Y. F., 186, 192, 194, 201
Barnes, W. S., 247, 255
Barron, L., 246, 251, 296, 305
Barrows, H. S., 288, 303
Baskin, A. S., 186, 201
Bassok, M., 43, 59, 134, 144, 323, 343
Beck, I. L., 152, 161, 244, 253, 245, 254
Becker, H. J., 129, 143
Bednar, A. K., 288, 303
Bell, L. C., 244, 245, 253, 254
Benezet, L. P., 349, 359
Bereiter C., 89, 102, 133, 134, 136, 145, 150, 152, 154, 155, 156, 159, 160, 161, 162, 163, 172, 181, 241, 243, 249, 254, 288, 305, 357, 359, 375
Berliner, D. C., 365, 375
Berzonsky, M. D., 149, 161
Beth, E. W., 108, 126
Bickhard, M. H., 331, 343
Bill, V. L., 351, 360
Blaye, A., 165, 168, 179, 181
Bliss, J., 25, 39, 40
Bobrow, D. G., 86, 100
Borcic, B., 168, 180, 182
Bork, A., 82, 100
Boshuizen, H. P. A., 312, 321
Boyle, C. F., 82, 89, 100, 134, 143, 176, 181, 354, 355, 357, 358, 359
Bradley, L., 245 249
Bransford, J. D., 223, 225, 226, 227, 229, 230, 232, 234, 235, 237, 242, 246, 249, 250, 253, 254, 255, 257, 258, 259, 260, 283, 284, 288, 289, 297, 298, 301, 303, 304, 305, 307, 320
Brasell, H., 49, 59
Brennan, S. E., 178, 181

Brett, C., 159, 162
Brewer, W. F., 16, 17, 18, 21, 23, 150, 153, 163
Bronfenbrenner, U., 364, 368, 375
Brown, A. L., 109, 126, 149, 161, 187, 201, 209, 219, 241, 242, 250, 253, 287, 288, 303, 304, 351, 356, 357, 359, 360, 363, 364, 375
Brown, J. S., 13, 23, 28, 41, 82, 88, 100, 102, 109, 111, 126, 132, 134, 137, 143, 144, 145, 167, 172, 176, 181, 187, 201, 268, 286, 287, 288, 303, 304, 313, 314, 318, 319, 320, 331, 332, 343, 348, 350, 355, 356, 357, 358, 359, 360
Bruckmoser, J., 311, 321
Bruer, J., 1, 8
Bruner, J., 82, 93, 100
Brunner, E., 154, 162
Bryant, P., 26, 40, 245, 249
Burns, M. S., 232, 246, 249, 255
Burtis, J., 159, 162
Burtis, P. J., 159, 162
Burton, R. R., 357, 359
Bushey, B., 288, 305
Butler-Kahle, J., 365, 376

C

Calfee, R., 226, 250
Calhoun, C., 159, 162
Campbell, R., 331, 343
Campione, J. C., 209, 219, 287, 303
Carberry, M. S., 194, 201
Carey, S., 16, 23
Cariglia-Bull, T., 236, 254
Carlsen, D., 204, 218
Carlson, K., 297, 305
Carney, R. N., 236, 252
Carpenter, T., 61, 62, 79
Carson, J., 260, 283, 289, 290, 304
Carver, S. M., 227, 251, 348, 350, 359, 360
Case, R., 327, 328, 332, 343
Cazden, C., 366, 375
Chabay, R. W., 357, 360

Chan, C., 159, 162
Chan, T. W., 186, 201
Chandler, J., 247, 255
Chapman, R. S., 230, 250
Chelemer, C., 224, 225, 253
Chen, Z., 242, 243, 250
Chi, M. T. H., 15, 23, 41, 43, 59, 110, 125, 126
Clancy, W. J., 171, 181
Clark, H. H., 178, 181
Clark, R. E., 131, 144
Clement, J., 287, 288, 303
Clift, R., 149, 161
Cobb, P., 135, 137, 144, 204, 218
Cohen, A., 159, 162
Cole, M., 172, 182, 363, 376
Coleman, E. B., 159, 162
Collins, A., 13, 23, 82, 100, 109, 111, 126, 137, 142, 144, 167, 176, 181, 187, 201, 227, 251, 268, 286, 287, 288, 301, 303, 304, 312, 313, 314, 318, 319, 320, 332, 343, 348, 350, 351, 355, 356, 357, 358, 359, 360
Collins, C., 226, 251
Comenius, J. A., 81, 100
Comer, J. R., 247, 251
Cooper, C. R., 187, 189, 201
Cooper, R. G., Jr., 187, 189, 201
Corbett, A. T., 82, 100
Corkill, D. D., 173, 182
Coulson, R. L., 288, 305, 310, 318, 320, 321
Crawford-Mason, C., 151, 161
Crook, C., 216, 217, 218
Cuban, L., 130, 144, 355, 360
Cumming, G., 186, 201
Cummins, D., 62, 67, 79, 84, 86, 100

D

Daehler, M. W., 242, 243, 250
Dahlgren, L. O., 309, 310, 320
Darrow, B., 130, 144
David, Y. M., 150, 161
Davidson, N., 111, 126
Davis, R. B., 106, 107, 126

Davison, A., 152, 161
Day, J. D., 149, 161
De Corte, E., 86, 100, 131, 132, 134, 135, 136, 138, 139, 143, 144, 323, 343
de Kleer, J., 28, 31, 40
de Win, L., 86, 100
Deal, R., 31, 40
Deane, S., 236, 254
DeFord, D., 224, 251
Delclos, V. R., 232, 246, 249, 255
Derry, S. J., 82, 93, 100, 101, 176, 181
Dershimer, C., 44, 59
Dewey, S., 259, 283
Dillenbourg, P., 167, 168, 169, 175, 177, 180, 181, 182, 328, 331, 332, 343, 344
diSessa, A., 82, 87
Dobyns, L., 151, 161
Dochy, F. J. R. C., 133, 144
Doise, W., 179, 182, 187, 201
Doyle, W., 150, 161, 366, 376
Dreyer, L. G., 245, 251
Dreyfus, T., 105, 106, 107, 126
Dubinsky, E., 107, 108, 109, 110, 126
Duffy, G. G., 226, 251
Duffy, T. M., 187, 201, 288, 304
Duguid, P., 13, 23, 187, 201, 268, 286, 288, 303, 314, 319, 320, 348, 355, 359
Durfee, E. H., 173, 182
Durkin, D., 226, 251
Dweck, C. S., 366, 367, 376

E

Eggan, G., 357, 360
Eichinger, D. C., 150, 161
Eisenberg, T., 114, 126
Eitel, F., 311, 321
El-Dinary, P. B., 226, 254
Elder, W. D., 225, 251
Elsom-Cook, M., 336, 344
Engstrom, Y., 152, 153, 161
Enkenberg, J., 111, 127
Ericsson, K. A., 204, 218

Erkens, G., 186, 192, 194, 201
Ernest, P., 107, 109, 126
Evertson, C. M., 246, 254

F

Farady, M., 288, 305
Farr, M. J., 15, 23
Farrell, R., 82, 89, 100
Feeney, A., 154, 162
Feltovich, 318, 321
Feltovich, P. J., 41, 59, 288, 305, 310, 320
Fend, H., 307, 320
Feuerstein, R., 232, 251, 259, 283
Fillion, B., 153, 161
Fisher, G., 357, 359
Flavell, J. H., 149, 161
Flores, F., 201, 202
Forbus, K. D., 31, 40
Forman, E., 204, 207, 215, 217, 218
Forrester, M. A., 166, 182
Fortescue, M. D., 194, 201
Fox, B., 172, 182
France, I. M., 244, 253
Franks, J. J., 288, 303, 358, 359
Fraser, B. J., 365, 367, 376
Frederick, J. R., 354, 360
Frederiksen, J. R., 301, 304, 326, 344, 356, 360
Fussell, S. R., 178, 182

G

Gardner, H., 2, 8, 42, 59, 358, 360
Garet, M., 31, 40
Garner, R., 149, 161
Gaudig, H., 313, 316, 320
Geertz, C., 2, 8, 42, 59
Gentner, D., 17, 23, 28, 40
Gernsbacher, M. A., 234, 251
Gibson, J. J., 289, 304
Gilly, M., 179, 182
Glaser, R., 1, 8, 15, 23, 41, 59, 89, 102, 110, 126, 134, 144, 323, 343
Globerson, T., 82, 102, 366, 371, 376

Gobert-Wickham, J., 159, 162
Goldman, E. S., 246, 251
Goldman, R. S., 289, 305
Goldman, S. R., 225, 242, 249, 254, 293, 295, 296, 297, 298, 301, 304, 305, 307, 320
Good, T. L., 111, 127, 227, 252
Goodenow, C., 365, 366, 376
Goodman, I. F., 247, 255
Goodman, J., 260, 283, 289, 290, 304
Goodman, N., 45, 59
Goodyear, P., 132, 144
Gordon, A., 287, 303
Gragg, C. I., 259, 283, 288, 304
Granott, N., 215, 217, 218
Gräsel, C., 310, 311, 320
Greeno, J. G., 41, 42, 59, 67, 69, 79, 84, 93, 101, 106, 127, 359, 360
Greer, B., 131, 132, 138, 144
Grice, H. P., 192, 202
Griffin, P., 172, 182, 363, 376
Gromoll, E. W., 152, 161
Grootendorst, R., 200, 201
Grosslight, L., 78, 80, 150, 163
Grosz, B. J., 192, 194
Gruber, H., 308, 310, 321
Gurtner, J. -L., 82, 87, 101
Guttman, L., 369, 370, 376

H

Hamer, R. M., 369, 377
Hanson, N. R., 259, 283
Harel, I., 143, 144, 204, 218, 352, 360
Hasselbring, T. S., 230, 232, 249, 255, 260, 284, 288, 303
Hatano, G., 204, 216, 218
Hawkes, L. W., 93, 100
Hawkins, J., 227, 251, 348, 350, 360
Head, J., 154, 162
Healy, J. M., 228, 252
Heap, J. L., 150, 162
Heath, A., 298, 305
Heath, S. B., 224, 247, 252, 357, 360
Heldmeyer, K., 230, 249
Heller, J. I., 69, 79

Hemphill, L., 247, 255
Herrmann, D. J., 150, 163
Hickey, D. T., 281, 283, 288, 289, 290, 298, 304, 305
Hiebert, J., 107, 127
Hilario, M., 168, 180, 181, 182
Hill, S. R., Jr., 364, 376
Hirsch, E. D., Jr., 350, 360
Hobbs, 225, 251
Hoffman, M. B., 232, 251, 259, 283
Hogaboam, T. W., 244, 254
Hollingshead, A., 204, 219
Holt, J., 150, 162
Hounshell, P. B., 364, 376
Hron, A., 319, 321
Hughes, C., 244, 245, 254
Hulin, C. L., 368, 376
Hurley, S., 245, 255

I-J

Inhelder, B., 107, 127
Ioannides, C., 15, 17, 23
Jacobson, M. J., 288, 305, 318, 321
Jarvela, S., 111, 127
Jenkins, J. J., 289, 304
Johnson, D. W., 111, 127, 187, 201
Johnson, M. K., 235, 249, 250
Johnson, R. T., 111, 127, 187, 201, 231, 232, 252
Johnson-Laird, P. N., 17, 23, 234, 252
Johnston, J., 44, 59
Joiner, R., 165, 168, 181
Jonassen, D. H., 187, 201, 373, 376
Jones, P., 370, 376
Jones, R. S., 149, 161
Juel, C., 225, 228, 252
Jungblut, A., 224, 252

K

Kämpfer, A., 94, 101, 176, 182
Kane, M. J., 242, 250
Kanselaar, G., 186, 202
Kant, I., 90, 101

Kaput, J. J., 62, 79, 93, 101, 129, 130, 132, 134, 144
Karmiloff-Smith, A., 107, 127
Kasanen, E., 125, 127
Kempner, L., 17, 23
Kerschensteiner, G., 308, 312, 313, 314, 319, 320, 321
Ketola, T., 107, 127
Kinnunen, R., 112, 128
Kintsch, W., 62, 67, 68, 79, 80, 84, 86, 89, 100, 101, 134, 144, 328, 344
Kinzer, C. K., 223, 229, 230, 242, 246, 247, 250, 254, 255, 260, 283, 284, 288, 289, 290, 303, 304, 305
Kirsch, I., 224, 252
Klafki, W., 83, 101
Klee, T., 246, 253
Klenk, L. J., 224, 226, 227, 253
Klopfer, L. E., 225, 254, 286, 288, 305
Knapp, M. S., 224, 225, 226, 252, 253
Knoor-Cetina, K., 42, 59
Kohn, A. S., 66, 80
Kosulin, A., 178, 182
Kozma, R. B., 44, 53, 59, 131, 145, 178, 182, 228, 252
Krauss, R. M., 178, 182
Kruskal, J. B., 369, 376
Kuipers, B., 31, 40
Kutscha, G., 315, 321
Kyllonen, P. C., 369, 370, 376

L

Lajoie, S., 82, 101, 357, 360
Lamon, M., 155, 159, 162, 163
Lampert, M., 204, 207, 210, 218, 351, 360
Langer, J., 226, 252
Larkin, J., 41, 43, 59, 153, 162
Larreamendy-Joerns, J., 217, 218
Lave, J., 13, 23, 165, 182, 286, 304, 305
Lawler, R. W., 135, 145
Leadbeater, B., 215, 218
Lee, E., 155, 159, 162
Leer, M. N., 351, 360

Lehmensick, E., 88, 101
Lehrndorfer, A., 86, 102
Lehtinen, E., 106, 107, 111, 112, 119, 127
Lepper, M. R., 82, 87, 101, 357, 360
Leron, U., 135, 145
Lesgold, A., 88, 101, 357, 360
Lesgold, S. B., 351, 360
Lesser, V. R., 173, 182
Levenson, W., 130, 145
Levin, J. R., 236, 252
Levine, J. M., 13, 23, 204, 219
Lewis, A. M., 77, 79
Lewis, M. W., 82, 100
Lidz, C. S., 232, 250, 301, 304
Light, P., 165, 168, 181
Linn, M. C., 134, 144, 204, 219, 363, 376
Lisop, I., 315, 321
Littlefield, J., 150, 162
Logan, D., 357, 360
Luria, A. R., 178, 182
Lyon, H. C., 311, 321
Lyons, C. A., 246, 251

M

Maes, P., 178, 182
Makrakis, V., 131, 145
Mandl, H., 88, 101, 134, 144, 308, 310, 311, 319, 320, 321
Mann, L., 88, 101
Marchman, V., 87, 101
Markman, E. M., 149, 162
Marks, M., 226, 254
Marmot, M. G., 154, 162
Marshelak, B., 369, 370, 377
Marton, F., 309, 310, 320
Mason, A., 105, 106, 127, 128
Mason, C. L., 365, 376
Mason, D. A., 227, 252
Maula, E., 125, 127
Maurer, S. B., 105, 127
Mayer, R. E., 50, 59, 62, 76, 79
McArthur, D., 89, 101
McCaslin, M., 111, 127

McCutchen, D., 244, 253
McDermott, J., 41, 59, 153, 162
McDill, E. L., 224, 225, 253
McGill-Frazen, A., 226, 249
McGrath, J., 204, 219
McKeown, M. G., 152, 161
McLarty, K., 260, 283, 289, 290, 304
McLean, R. S., 89, 102, 133, 134, 136, 145
McNamara, T. P., 234, 253
McPhail, J., 204, 207, 215, 217, 218
Means, D., 226, 227, 253
Mendelsohn, D., 153, 161
Mendelsohn, P., 168, 180, 182, 328, 343, 344
Mergendoller, J., 87, 101
Michael, A. L., 246, 253
Miller, D. L., 234, 253
Miller, G. A., 1, 9
Miller, J. M., 196, 202
Miller, J. R., 196, 202
Miller, R., 259, 283
Minsky, M., 167, 182
Minstrell, J. A., 288, 304
Mitman, A., 87, 101
Miyake, N., 168, 179, 182
Mokros, J., 48, 59
Moos, R. H., 366, 376
Morgan, S., 245, 255
Moschkovich, J., 114, 127
Moser, J. M., 62, 79
Moyse, R., 336, 344
Mugny, G., 179, 182, 187, 201
Mulryan, C., 111, 127
Mumme, D., 357, 360

N

Nakagawa, K., 287, 303
Nathan, M. J., 67, 79, 89, 101
Natriello, G., 224, 225, 253
Nesher, P., 62, 79, 86, 101
Nettles, S. M., 247, 253
Newell, A., 8, 9, 41, 59
Newman, D., 167, 172, 182, 363, 376

Newman, S. E., 137, 142, 144, 167, 181, 287, 304, 314, 318, 320, 348, 350, 356, 357, 358, 359, 360
Nickerson, R. S., 285, 304
Norman, D. A., 41, 59, 166, 182
Norman, G. R., 312, 321
North, F., 154, 162
Novak, J. D., 153, 162
Novick, L. R., 287, 304
Nussbaum, J., 153, 162

O

O'Malley, C., 168, 182
Oakes, J., 226, 253
Oelkers, J., 91, 101
Ogborn, J., 25, 39, 40
Ohlsson, S., 61, 62, 79, 82, 88, 101
Olivié, H., 139, 144
Olkinoura, E., 106, 112, 127
Omanson, S. F., 62, 79

P

Packer, M., 87, 101
Padden, C., 14, 23
Paige, J. M., 86, 101
Palincsar, A. S., 150, 161, 187, 201, 209, 219, 224, 226, 227, 241, 253, 288, 304, 356, 357, 360
Pallas, A., 224, 225, 253
Papert, S., 82, 87, 101, 135, 143, 144, 145
Paris, S. G., 308, 321
Parsons, T., 307, 321
Patel, C., 154, 162
Pauli, C., 99, 102
Pea, R. D., 41, 59, 82, 92, 101, 102, 363, 376
Peled, I., 62, 79
Pelgrum, W. J., 129, 142, 145
Pellegrino, J. W., 260, 283, 288, 289, 290, 293, 295, 296, 298, 301, 304, 305
Perfetti, C. A., 244, 245, 253, 254
Perkins, D. N., 41, 59, 82, 102, 288, 305

Perry, M., 351, 360
Petrosino, A., 281, 283, 288, 289, 290, 304
Piaget, J., 28, 40, 84, 90, 102, 107, 108, 126, 127, 327, 332, 344
Pichert, J. W., 247, 254
Pinnell, G. S., 246, 251
Plomp, T., 129, 142, 145
Poplin, M. S., 225, 254
Porter, A., 289, 305
Power, C. N., 365, 377
Preiβ, P., 309, 321
Prenzel, M., 310, 311, 320, 321
Pressley, M., 226, 236, 254
Putnam, R. T., 133, 145

R

Rand, Y., 232, 251, 259, 283
Randolph, C. H., 246, 254
Rashotte, C., 245, 255
Rees, E., 15, 23, 110, 126
Reichman, R., 194, 202
Reigeluth, C. M., 347, 360, 361
Reiser, B. J., 82, 89, 100, 134, 143, 354, 355, 357, 358, 359
Rempf, H., 307, 321
Renkl, A., 308, 310, 321
Repo, S., 119, 127
Resnick, L. B., 13, 23, 41, 59, 62, 66, 79, 80, 107, 127, 204, 219, 225, 254, 286, 288, 305, 308, 313, 321, 351, 359, 360, 363, 376
Reusser, K., 62, 67, 79, 84, 85, 86, 87, 89, 91, 94, 98, 99, 100, 102, 109, 111, 127, 176, 182
Rewey, K., 293, 295, 296, 204, 298, 305
Rich, A., 113, 128
Rich, J., 113, 128
Rieser, J. J., 150, 162, 247, 250, 257, 283
Riley, M. S., 69, 79
Risko, V., 223, 229, 246, 250, 254, 257, 260, 283, 289, 290, 304
Roberts, B., 352, 360

Roberts, K. H., 368, 376
Roberts, N., 31, 40
Rogoff, B., 170, 172, 173, 182, 183, 215, 219, 305
Roschelle, J., 78, 80, 179, 183
Ross, K. M., 196, 202
Rousseau, D. M., 368, 376
Rousseau, J. J., 90, 102
Rowe, D., 260, 283, 289, 290, 304
Rowe, M. B., 152, 162
Russell, J., 44, 59
Ruthemann, U., 93, 100
Rutherford, F. J., 258, 284
Rutherford, M., 109, 126, 287, 303

S

Sabers, D., 370, 376
Sace, G. B., 286, 305
Saenz, R. M., 196, 202
Salomon, G., 82, 99, 102, 136, 145, 166, 176, 183, 187, 202, 228, 254, 363, 365, 366, 367, 368, 370, 376
Salonen, P., 112, 127
Sandberg, J. A. C., 192, 201
Sarason, S. B., 364, 376
Savimäki, A., 106, 107, 127
Saxe G. B., 13, 23
Scarcella, R., 225, 254
Scardamalia, M., 89, 102, 133, 134, 136, 145, 149, 150, 152, 154, 155, 156, 159, 160, 161, 162, 163, 172, 181, 241, 243, 249, 254, 288, 305, 357, 359, 366, 375
Scarr, S., 366, 371
Scheibner, O., 316, 321
Schmidt, H. G., 312, 321
Schneider, D., 168, 180, 182
Schneider, W., 236, 254
Schoenfeld, A. H., 105, 106, 107, 110, 114, 118, 127, 128, 150, 163, 288, 305, 354, 355, 356, 358, 360, 363, 377
Schrooten, H., 135, 138, 139, 144
Schwab, J. J., 259, 284
Schwarz, B., 66, 80
Searle, J. R., 191, 202

Selden, A., 105, 106, 127, 128
Selden, J., 105, 106, 127, 128
Self, J. A., 168, 169, 180, 182, 186,
  187, 201
Shaffer, W., 31, 40
Shaner, R., 245, 255
Sharan, S., 187, 202
Sharan, Y., 187, 202
Sharp, D. L. M., 242, 254, 289, 305
Shayer, M., 150, 163
Sheingold, K., 363, 377
Sheldon, S., 165, 168, 181
Sherwood, R. D., 230, 247, 249, 250,
  255, 257, 259, 283, 284, 287, 288,
  303, 358, 359
Shields, P. M., 247, 255
Shiroma, P., 370, 376
Shute, V., 89, 102
Simmons, K., 245, 255
Simon, D. P., 41, 59, 153, 162
Simon, H. A., 41, 59, 83, 86, 91, 92,
  101
Simon, H. S., 153, 162
Slavin, R. E., 111, 127, 128, 187, 202
Slavings, R. L., 227, 252
Sleeman, D., 82, 88, 102, 132, 145
Smith, C., 150, 163
Smith, E. L., 150, 153, 160
Smith, G. D., 154, 162
Smith, J., 204, 218
Smith, L. N., 159, 162
Smitz, C., 78, 80
Snir, J., 78, 80, 150, 163
Snow, C. E., 247, 255
Snow, R. E., 369, 370, 377
Songer, N., 204, 219
Soraci, S., Jr., 242, 254, 289, 305
Spelke, S. E., 15, 23
Sperry, L. L., 243, 255
Spiro, R. J., 288, 305, 310, 318, 320, 321
Sprenger, M., 176, 182
Stage, S., 245, 255
Stansfeld, S., 154, 162
Stasz, C., 89, 101
Staub, F. C., 84, 86, 93, 99, 100, 176,
  182

Stebler, R., 99, 102, 176, 182
Stern, E., 86, 102
Stevens, A. L., 17, 23, 28, 40, 352, 358,
  360
Stigler, J. W., 351, 360
Stoutenmyer, D., 113, 127, 128
Stüssi, R., 94, 102, 176, 182
Suchman, L. A., 167, 179, 183
Sugrue, B. M., 131, 144
Swallow, J., 89, 102, 133, 134, 136,
  145

T

Tall, D., 109, 125, 126, 128
Teasley, S. D., 13, 23, 204, 219
Tennant, H. R., 196, 201
Teubal, E., 86, 101
Thompson, C. W., 196, 202
Tinbergein, A., 16, 23
Tinker, R., 48, 59
Tisher, R. P., 365, 377
Torney-Purta, J., 214, 216, 219
Trabasso, T., 243, 255
Trowbridge, D., 215, 219
Tudge, J., 215, 219
Turnbull, B. J., 226, 252

V

van den Broek, P., 243, 255
van Dijk, T. A., 67, 80, 84, 102
Van Eemeren, F. H., 200, 201
Van Haneghan, J. P., 296, 305
VanLehn, K., 105, 109, 128, 149, 163,
  172, 181
Vansina, A., 139, 144
Vauras, M., 112, 128
Vellutino, F. R., 224, 255
Vergnaud, G., 62, 80
Verschaffel, L., 86, 100, 131, 132, 134,
  135, 138, 139, 143, 144
von Hentig, H., 319, 321
Vosniadou, S., 14, 15, 17, 23, 150, 153,
  163, 204, 219
Vuontela, U. -M., 107, 127

Vye, N. J., 223, 225, 227, 229, 232, 242,
    246, 247, 249, 250, 254, 255, 257, 260,
    283, 287, 288, 289, 290, 293, 295,
    296, 297, 298, 303, 304, 305, 307,
    320, 358, 359
Vygotsky, L. S., 2, 5, 9, 13, 14, 23, 42,
    59, 134, 145, 165, 174, 183, 331, 344

W

Wagenschein, M., 307, 321
Wagner, R. K., 245, 255
Warren, S., 246, 253
Wasson, B., 159, 162
Weaver, C. A., 68, 80
Webb, N. M., 187, 189, 202
Wegner, E., 286, 304
Weick, K. E., 368, 377
Weimer, R., 62, 67, 79, 84, 86, 100
Wenger, E., 132, 133, 145, 179, 183
Wenger, R. H., 109, 128
Weniger, E., 83, 102
Wertheimer, M., 92, 102, 105, 107, 128
Wertsch, J. V., 165, 166, 170, 176, 178,
    183, 331, 344
White, B. Y., 46, 59, 78, 80, 326, 344,
    354, 356, 360
White, I., 154, 162
Wickelgren, W. A., 189, 202
Wiggins, G., 348, 360
Williams, S. M., 259, 284, 288, 293,
    295, 296, 297, 303, 304, 305
Willmann, O., 83, 102
Winkels, R., 186, 202
Winograd, T., 201, 202
Winterhoff, P., 215, 219
Wiser, M., 16, 23
Wish, M., 369, 376, 377
Witherspoon, M. L., 246, 251
Wittmann, E. C., 83, 91, 102
Wolf, D. P., 358, 360
Wong, B. Y. L., 224, 226, 255
Wood, T., 204, 218
Woodruff, E., 89, 102, 133, 134, 136,
    145
Wylam, H., 150, 163

Y

Yackel, E., 204, 218
Yazdani, M., 135, 145
Yopp, H. K., 245, 255
Yost, G., 176, 181
Young, E., 67, 79, 89, 101
Young, F. W., 369, 377
Young, M. F., 296, 305

Z

Zivin, G., 176, 183
Zmuidzinas, M., 89, 101

Subject Index

A

Abstraction, 22, 78-79, 107-114, 121-125, 313, 327, 332, 354-355
Adaptation, 149-160
ALGEBRALAND, 176, 319, 358
Algorithms (see Thinking)
Analogies (see Transfer)
Anchored instruction, 187, 257-281, 288-291, 302, 308, 317, 324
ANIMATE, 67
Apprenticeship, 166-167, 215-216, 257, 286-288, 302, 331, 340, 348 (see also Cognitive apprenticeship)
Appropriation (see Assimilation)
Argumentation, 34, 120, 192, 196, 199-200, 288
Art, 155
Artifical intelligence, 27-28, 31, 132, 134, 180, 331
Assessment, alternative, 298-301 (see also Learner evaluation)
Assimilation, 26, 108-109, 114, 172
At-risk students (see Learners)
Attitudes (see Science, attitudes toward)
Authenticity (see Instruction)
Automaticity (see Skills)

B

Behaviorism, 81, 134, 338-339
Beliefs, 28, 31-32, 106, 153, 179, 200, 224 (see also Misconceptions; Prior knowledge)
Bildung, 83, 88

Biology, 157, 200, 264, 269-270, 371
BOXER, 87
Business management, 29, 32, 34, 289-296, 300-301

C

Chemistry, 42-59, 258, 262-270, 272-273, 280, 371
Classrooms, 107, 121, 130, 150, 155-158, 204
Coaching, 134, 137-143, 328, 331, 336-338, 341, 348, 357
Cognition/Cognitive,
    apprenticeship, 137, 167, 187, 286-287, 308, 318-319
    development, 323-343 (see also Zone of proximal development)
    distributed, 115-116, 165-180, 204-210, 215-217 (see also Expertise, distributed)
    flexibility, 14-15, 21-22, 316-317
    situated, 13-14, 257, 286-288, 319, 324-325, 331, 355 (see also Instruction, authentic; Context; Learning, meaningful)
    sociocultural approach to, 42, 165-167, 170-180, 339-340
    structures, 133, 210, 326, 332, 340
    processing system, 124, 167-168, 194
Co-learners, 166-169, 171, 175, 215-217, 336
Collaboration, 203-218, 258, 336, 339 (see also Learning)
Communication, 107, 118-121, 131, 185 189, 191, 203, 205-207, 328, 351

Communities of practice, 165, 308, 328
(*see also* Instruction, authentic)
Comprehension, 81, 99, 243
listening, 229-230
reading, 131, 226, 232-235
strategies, 84, 86
Computer-Assisted Instruction (CAI),
81, 132, 185-186, 323, 325, 338-339
(*see also* Intelligent Tutoring Systems)
Computer, (*see also* Artificial intelligence; Modeling)
animation, 45, 49, 55-56
databases, 156
electronic mail (e-mail), 156, 205, 207
hypertext, 329, 333-337, 351
Intelligent Cooperative Systems
(ICS), 186-189
Intelligent Learning Environments
(ILE), 150, 154-160, 167, 325,
333
Intelligent Tutoring Systems (ITS),
81, 88-89, 99, 132-135, 323-342
interfaces, 195-197, 325, 328-331
microworlds, 168-170, 177, 323-
324, 329-333, 340
networks, 155, 204
programming, 135-143
simulations, 22, 89, 196, 198-199,
203, 210, 214, 308-310, 329, 334-
336, 351-352
software, 50, 54-58. 130
Technology Intensive Learning
Environments (TILE), 365-375
Computer-Supported Intentional
Learning Environments (CSILE),
150, 154-160
Computer Visualization Learning
Environment (CVLE), 13-14
Conceptual change, 26, 203-218, 340
(*see also* Cognitive development;
Knowledge organization)
Constructivism (*see also* Knowledge
construction)
cognitive development and, 325-
327, 340
cooperative learning and, 187

design of learning environments
and, 109-112, 134, 327-328
instruction and, 107, 137, 287-288,
347, 351
radical, 90-91, 135
Context,
realistic, 6-7, 48, 131, 207, 226,
286-288, 348, 355, 366, 370 (*see
also* Instruction, authentic;
Situated cognition)
social, 107-108, 111-112, 188-190,
286, 366-367, 371-374
Culture,
classroom, 107
computers and, 82
learning as enculturation, 91, 307-
308, 317, 350-351
people's relationship to, 14, 91, 227,
246-247, 365, 374
shared representations, 42, 92
Curricula, 109-110, 135, 155, 260-
261, 290, 301, 350, 370

D

Decision-making, 29, 132
DERIVE, 113-126
Design of learning environments, 1-8,
19-22, 81-83, 87-93, 108-112, 131-
134, 154-160, 170-181, 188-189,
260-263, 290, 323-333, 347-359
(*see also* Didactics)
Development, cognitive, 323-343 (*see
also* Zone of proximal development)
Diagrams, 31, 41-42, 53-54 (*see also*
Representations)
Didactics, 81-84, 88, 90-91, 93, 99,
172
Discourse (*see also* Communication;
Groups)
communities, 204, 207-210, 217
cooperative principle, 192
dialogue, 189-200, 204, 227
discussion, 118-121, 309, 358
in classroom, 150, 155-158, 204
processing, 67-68, 84

Dyads (*see* Groups)

E

Economics, 203, 205, 214, 308-310, 369
Electronic mail (e-mail), 156, 205, 207
Encapsulation (*see* Assimilation)
ENVISIONING MACHINE, 179
Experimental Toolbox for Interactive
  Learning Environments (ETOILE),
  168-171
Experimentation, 26, 34, 39, 114, 257,
  261, 281, 297, 314, 328-336
Expert systems (*see* Artificial intelligence)
Expertise,
  cognitive development and, 323-
    324, 326-327
  communicative, 197-200
  decision-making and, 132
  distributed, 109-110, 350-351 (*see
    also* Cognition, distributed)
  in a domain, 92, 186, 204, 259, 262,
    326-327, 336-337, 339
  knowledge and, 15, 43-44, 186, 214
  learning and, 92, 281, 288, 314,
    336-337
  performance and, 310, 356
  problem-solving and, 15, 41-44,
    311, 340
  reasoning and, 28
  representations and, 15, 43-45, 49,
    326-327
Explanation, 33, 149, 158, 195-196,
  297, 311-312, 337

F, G

Fading, 170-171, 348, 357 (*see also*
  Scaffolding)
Feedback, 32-36, 39, 62, 88, 92, 95-
  97, 99, 112, 172, 217, 337-338, 352,
  355, 357
Generalization (*see* Transfer)
Geography, 28-29, 31, 155, 271-272,
  278-280, 282, 353

GEOMETRY TUTOR, 134, 176, 354-
  355, 358
Goals, problem-solving, 188, 210, 218,
  287, 338-339, 341
Graphs, 48-49, 51, 113 (*see also*
  Diagrams; Representations)
Groups, 111, 137, 155, 316, 366-367,
  370, 374 (*see also* Learning,
  cooperative; Social interaction)
  dyads/pairs, 39, 115-117, 309
  problem-solving in, 214-217, 258,
    296
  roles of group members, 187

H

Health and fitness, 29, 31-33
HERON, 93-99, 176
Heuristics, 136, 138
Hydrology, 258, 262, 264, 269-270,
  272-273, 280
Hypertext, 329, 333-337, 351
Hypothesis testing (*see* Experimenta-
  tion)

I, J

Inferences, 37, 50, 57-58, 98, 192,
  196, 198 (*see also* Reasoning)
Inquiry, 20, 155-156, 232, 243, 316, 358
Instruction(al) (*see also* Pedagogy)
  anchored, 187, 257-281, 288-291,
    302, 308, 317, 324
  authentic, 188, 210, 216-217, 227,
    261-262, 280-281, 312-317, 324-
    325, 348, 370
  materials, 92, 236-240, 289, 292
  models of, 133, 316-317, 329
  reciprocal, 118, 209, 227, 241-242
    (*see also* Scaffolding)
  sequence of, 18-19, 317, 354-355
  strategy/style, 121, 337-342
Intelligent Cooperative Systems (ICS),
  186-189
Intelligent Learning Environments
  (ILE), 150, 154-160, 167, 325, 333

Intelligent Tutoring Systems (ITS), 81, 88-89, 99, 132-135, 323-342 (*see also* Computer-Assisted Instruction; Coaching)
INTERACTIVE PHYSICS, 355
Interdisciplinary curricula, 260-261, 290, 370
Interest in science (*see* Science, attitudes toward)
International Communications and Negotiations Project (ICONS), 203-218
International Science Classroom (ISC), 370-373
Interpretation of information, 14, 16-17, 32, 191 (*see also* Experimentation; Learning; Reasoning)
IQON, 31, 34, 36-39
JASPER WOODBURY, THE ADVENTURES OF, 287-302
JEANSFABRIK, 308-309, 318

K

Knowledge (*see also* Learning; Mental models)
    application of, 263, 307-319, 353-355
    construction,
        process of, 15-16, 107-112, 204, 331
        social, 42, 156, 187, 204-207, 210, 215-217, 340
        vs. passive learning, 131, 133, 288, 324
    declarative, 265-267, 272-274, 277, 309-310, 333
    domain, 18-19, 43-44, 92, 132, 186, 200, 326
    everyday, 38, 226
    externalization, 111-112, 208-209, 358 (*see also* Representations)
    inert, 307-308, 317
    internalization, 174-180
    organization, 13-15, 133, 311, 325, 332
    procedural, 107, 333
    representation, 15-22, 26, 28, 37, 45, 48, 50, 88, 110, 189, 292-296, 309, 325-327

L

Language (*see also* Discourse; Communication)
    acquisition, 230-231
    processes, 66-68, 84-86
    production, 232-233
    shift, 176-177, 327, 331-333
Laserdiscs, 264, 271
Learner(s),
    at-risk, 224-243, 271
    engagement, 149-160, 209, 353
    evaluation, 314, 351 (*see also,* Assessment)
    initiative, 341-342
    self-perception, 372-373
Learning (*see also* Knowledge construction; Conceptual change)
    achievement, 372-374
    active, 133-134, 316, 324, 327, 352
    assumptions during, 26, 209, 310, 314 (*see also* Beliefs; Misconceptions; Prior knowledge)
    attention and, 56-58
    conflict and, 26, 179-180, 340 (*see also* Point of view, alternative; Co-learner)
    constraints on, 17-18, 21
    control over, 90, 92, 186-188, 218, 316, 354, 366
    cooperative, 13, 111, 134, 156, 166, 187-189, 259, 308-309, 316, 327 (*see also* Social interaction; Collaboration)
    discovery, 90-91, 186, 340
    environments,
        analysis of, 369-373
        design of, 1-8, 19-22, 81-83, 87-93 108-112, 131-134, 154-160, 170-181, 188-189, 260-263, 290, 323-333, 347-359 (*see also,* Didactics)
    exploratory, 26-39, 137, 355
    expressive, 26-39
    goals, 218, 287, 349-352, 365
    hands-on, 87, 261, 263
    impasse-driven, 149-158

meaningful, 13, 29, 226, 287, 302, 353, 356 (*see* also Instruction, authentic)
problem-oriented, 314, 316-317
strategies, 187-189, 192 (*see also* Mnemonics)
trial-and-error, 37
LISP, 354-355
Literacy, 86, 223-249 (*see also* Reading; Comprehension)
LOGO, 87, 134-142, 204, 323-324, 326, 340, 352

M

Macrocontexts, 223, 244, 259, 262-263, 313
Mathematics, 81, 129-132, 155, 157-158, 204, 209, 285-302 (*see also* Reasoning, quantitative)
equations, 42, 47-48, 86, 177
misconceptions, 106, 112
models/modeling, 28, 39, 61-79, 84-86, 93-99
problem-solving, 84-87, 93-94, 106-107
understanding, 61-79, 105-107, 116-117, 121-126
word problems, 62-79, 84-87, 93-99, 285-287, 289
Medicine, 310-312
MEMOLAB, 168-169, 172, 326-343
Memorization, 130-131, 349 (*see also* Mnemonics)
Mental models, 17-18, 28, 43, 78, 93, 116, 234-236, 242-243, 310
Metacognition, 20-21, 106, 120, 136, 208-209, 210, 224, 243, 323, 332, 354 (*see also* Reflection)
Microworlds, 168-170, 177, 323-324, 329-333, 340
Misconceptions, 16-17, 44, 106, 112, 133, 150, 187, 297-298, 310
Mnemonics, 151, 153
Modeling, 25-39, 61-79, 93-99, 137, 227, 348, 356-357

Models (*see also* Representations; Mental models)
complexity of, 32-33, 36-37
construction of, 28-29, 31, 33, 36-37, 39
instructional, 133, 316-317, 329
physical, 288, 351-352
problem, 67-68, 84-86
process, 84-86
real world vs., 22, 25, 37, 38, 48, 50, 218
qualitative, 22, 326-327
quantitative, 28, 39
situation, 67-68, 78, 84-86
Motivation, 119, 158, 171, 210, 226, 240-241, 313-314, 354
Multimedia environments,
THE ADVENTURES OF JASPER WOODBURY, 287-302
Multimedia environments that Organize and Support Text (MOST), 223-249
MultiMedia Mental Models Chemistry (4M:CHEM), 46-59
SCIENTISTS-IN-ACTION, 257-283

N, O

Naive understanding, 15-16, 28 (*see also* Prior knowledge)
Narrative (*see* Text)
Negotiation of meaning, 42, 201 (*see also* Social interaction; Groups)
Notations, 87, 93 (*see also* Representations; Models)

P

Pairs (*see* Groups)
Pedagogy, 132, 333, 351 (*see also* Instruction)
Reformpädagogik movement, 30, 312-319
tools, 81-100
PEOPLE POWER, 168, 171, 175
Physics, 15-17, 19, 21, 28, 41, 78, 179,

371
PHYSICS EXPLORER, 354-355
PLANALYZER, 310-311
PLANNER, The, 62-79
Planning, 37, 64-66, 108, 136, 138, 292-295 (*see also* Problem-solving)
Point of view, alternative, 26, 29, 31, 215, 358
first-person, 261-262
multiple, 316-317
POLIS, 205
Politics, 168, 175, 203-214, 369
Portfolios (*see* Schoolwork)
Preconceptions (*see* Prior knowledge)
Prior knowledge, 29-30, 36, 114, 133, 151, 297-298 (*see also* Beliefs; Expertise)
Problem decomposition, 84, 108-110, 136, 138
Problem-solving, 84-87, 135-136, 204, 210-215, 285-302, 308-310, 358
active, 263, 281, 333
complexity, 37, 260-261, 289-292, 308, 327, 329, 349, 356, 370
constraints on, 260, 295, 333
contexts, 131, 286-288, 339 (*see also* Situated cognition; Instruction, authentic)
cooperative, 185-201, 281, 289-290, 296, 366 (*see also* Learning, cooperative)
effects on memory, 259-260, 273-274
expert, 15, 41-44, 311, 340
goals, 97-98, 188, 210, 287, 338-339, 341
use of models in, 78, 288
realistic, 131, 210, 218, 257, 308, 329 (*see also* Instruction, authentic)
strategies, 37, 42, 288, 339, 355
Production systems, 84-86, 105, 134
Psychology, 169, 328-336

Q, R

Questioning (*see* Inquiry)

Reading, 131, 224-226, 228-229 (*see also* Literacy)
Reasoning, 151, 288 (*see also* Inferences; Experimentation; Models)
causal, 33-34, 36-37, 78, 243
contextualized, 286, 313
qualitative, 27, 36, 92
quantitative, 27-28, 30-38, 92
semiquantitative, 27-36, 86
Recall, 74-75, 151, 152-153, 232, 235-236
Reflection, 26, 108-114, 123-124, 151-152, 175-176, 316, 319, 348
Reformpädagogik (*see* Pedagogy)
Reification (*see* Reflection)
Representations, 2-5 (*see also* Models; Computer simulations)
complexity of, 57, 211, 214, 217
dynamic, 44-45, 49 (*see also* Computer animation)
external, 110-111, 115, 124, 136-138, 216
graphic or pictorial, 21, 31, 41-42, 53-58, 62, 68, 93-94, 113-115, 157, 159, 179, 229-231
mental, 16-20, 66, 84, 92, 179, 211 (*see also* Mental models)
multiple, 41-59, 110, 114-115, 119, 216
of knowledge, 15-22, 26, 28, 37, 45, 48, 50, 88, 110, 189, 292-296, 309, 325-327
qualitative, 14, 50, 84
quantitative, 50, 115 (*see also* Mathematics, equations)
symbolic, 43-45, 47-51, 54, 68, 87, 179, 288
verbal, 50, 52, 62, 67-68

S

Scaffolding, 92, 118, 137, 187, 204, 350, 356-357
by computer, 138
effect of, 111-112

in reciprocal teaching, 209-210, 227
process of, 170-171
Schema, 94, 97, 211-213, 324-326,
331 (*see also* Mental models)
Schools, 130
Arbeitsschule ("work school"),
313-316
Buchschule ("book school"), 312-
313, 316
context of, 149-151
function of, 14, 307-308 (*see also*
Culture)
Schulgartenunterricht ("school
garden instruction"), 313
vocational, 315
Schoolwork, (*see also* Instruction)
abstractness of, 313
drills, 130-131, 225, 353
memorization, 130-131
portfolios, 159
relevance of, 151, 153-154
time constraints on, 151-153
Science, 14-22, 41-59, 155, 204, 242-
243, 257-282, 363-375
attitudes toward, 258, 260-263, 267-
270, 274-278, 367, 371-373 (*see
also* Motivation)
misconceptions in, 16-17, 44, 150
naive theories of, 15-16
SCIENTISTS-IN-ACTION, 257-283
Shared cognition (*see* Socially
distributed cognition)
Situated cognition, 13-14, 257, 286-
288, 319, 324-325, 331, 355 (*see
also* Context; Instruction, authentic;
Learning, meaningful)
Situation Problem Solver (SPS), 84-87
Skills, 131, 134-138, 225, 348-349
automatization of, 109, 349, 352
component (vs. whole tasks), 349-
350
Small space analysis, 369-373
SMALLTALK, 31
Social (*see also* Cognition, distributed;
Culture; Learning, cooperative)
grounding, 177-180

interaction, 5-6, 13, 166-167, 191-
201
contexts, 107-108, 111-112, 185-
190, 286, 366-367, 371-374
process of, 115-119, 120-121, 124-
125
Social studies, 28, 155, 371
Sociocultural approach to cognition,
13, 165-168, 172-173, 339
Software, computer, 50, 54-58, 130
Solution trees, 93-94, 97-98 (*see also*
Diagrams; Representations)
Special education, 224-225
Stages of development, 324-328, 333,
340
Statistics, 291, 295, 300
STELLA, 31
Story problems (*see* Mathematics)
Strategies,
comprehension, 84, 86
instructional, 121, 333
learning, 187-189, 192
mnemonic, 151, 153
problem-solving, 37, 42
STUDENT, 86
Students (*see* Learners)
Surface features, 45, 48-49 (*see also*
Representations)
Symbolic expressions, 42-44, 48, 54-
55, 86 (*see also* Mathematics;
Representations)
Systems, 28, 31, 33, 36, 166, 336,
363-375

T

TAPS, 176
Teacher,
expectations, 232
role of, 52, 109-112, 131, 136, 138,
156, 288, 316, 354
training, 130
Teaching (*see* Instruction)
Teams (*see* Groups)
Technology Intensive Learning
Environments (TILE), 365-375

Teleconferencing, 299-301
Television, 131, 228
Text, 36-37, 39, 50, 67-68, 84-85, 151-152, 226 (*see also* Discourse; Hypertext)
Thinking, 41, 135-138, 348-349, 352
    algorithmic, 105-108, 115-117, 121-126
    abstract, 30, 112, 124-125
    externalization of, 25-39, 111-112, 348
    higher-order, 131, 225
    skills, 135, 285
TRAINWORLD, 62
Transfer,
    analogical, 242-243, 286, 296-302
    facilitation of, 135, 138, 261
    generalization of skills, 107-109, 114, 123, 355
    tasks, 159, 259-260, 270-272, 278-281
Tutoring, 132-136 (*see also* Intelligent Tutoring Systems; Coaching)

U

Understanding, 42-59, 61-79, 149-160, 335, 351

V

Video, 47, 131, 228, 257-281, 289-291, 300-301, 317, 352
Visual processes, 56-58, 228, 236, 238-241 (*see also* Representations)
    vs. auditory, 57
    vs. verbal, 52, 228, 236, 238-240

W

Word problems (*see* Mathematics)

Z

Zone of proximal development, 134, 170, 328, 331